Infinity and Continuity
in Ancient and
Medieval Thought

Infinity and Continuity in Ancient and Medieval Thought

Edited by

NORMAN KRETZMANN

Cornell University Press

ITHACA AND LONDON

First published 1982 by Cornell University Press.
Published in the United Kingdom by Cornell University Press Ltd.,
Ely House, 37 Dover Street, London W1X 4HQ.

International Standard Book Number 0-8014-1444-X
Library of Congress Catalog Card Number 81-15209
Printed in the United States of America
Librarians: Library of Congress cataloging information
appears on the last page of the book.

Contents

5

CONTENTS

Appendixes

6

Editor's Preface

In the twentieth century we have grown used to the idea that there are minimal, physically indivisible particles of matter and quantities of energy; but it still seems obvious to most of us that time and space are infinitely divisible, or continuous rather than "atomic." The various sorts of motion that take place in space and time—at least the macroscopic sorts—are likewise thought to be continuous. Even physically indivisible subatomic particles and quanta must, it seems, be theoretically (or mathematically) divisible into halves, quarters, and so on indefinitely. But despite the evident universality and unavoidability of infinite divisibility and theoretical continuity in our conceptions of time, space, and motion, or of quantity and change generally, the closely related concepts of continuity and infinity have always led to at least apparent, possibly irresoluble paradoxes. Such puzzles arose at the very beginning of philosophical or scientific thought. The earliest logical crises in intellectual history—the Pythagoreans' discovery of incommensurability and Zeno's paradoxes of motion and of quantity—are crises for the concepts of infinity and continuity in particular. And the earliest, speculative atomic theories—such as those of Leucippus and Democritus—may have been developed in part in response to problems associated with infinity and continuity as well as to other Eleatic issues.

During the two thousand years of classical antiquity and the Middle Ages, the problems of infinity and continuity were dealt with in ways that prepared the ground for the scientific revolution of the seventeenth century, but that development does not belong simply to the history of science. Ancient and medieval physical speculation was closely, sometimes indistinguishably, associated with metaphysics, with logic, even with theology; and the development of mathematics during those two thousand years was also more closely associated with philosophy than it has been since the end of the Middle Ages. Thus historians of philosophy, science, and mathematics can and must cooperate in their efforts to understand the development of these concepts, which obviously lie at the center of our understanding of nature generally. In this volume, eleven scholars from different disciplines approach different phases of the early development of the concepts of infinity and continuity in ways that reveal this neglected ancient and medieval material to be not just historically important but also fascinating in its own right.

Aristotle in his philosophy of nature is a continuist (as opposed to atomist), and his works, particularly the *Physics*, present the classical account of continuity, infinite divisibility, and the problems associated with those concepts. Several volumes the size of this one could profitably be devoted to the study of infinity and continuity in Aristotle alone, but his contribution to our topics, although incomparably important, is also entirely accessible and relatively well known. We have therefore elected to consider the career of the concepts of infinity and continuity after Aristotle. But although no chapter of our book is devoted to Aristotle in his own right, Aristotle, or Aristotelianism, emerges as its single most pervasive historical theme. (For that reason we have supplied the Aristotelian texts most important for our purposes in Appendix A.)

In Chapter I, David Furley picks up the Aristotelian line at some of its earliest stages of development, in the Greek commentators of the second, third, and sixth centuries A.D. In his discussion of difficulties that the commentators encountered in their attempts to understand and harmonize Aristotle's continuist doctrines of physical space and mathematical entities or to deal with the problems of infinite divisibility, Furley introduces the reader to several of the topics that recur at every stage of the historical development considered in this book.

As Chapter I sketches the early reception of the Aristotelian theories of space and quantity, Chapter II takes up the reaction to Aristotle's continuist theory of time. The treatise on time in *Physics*

IV begins by presenting four paradoxes regarding time. Richard Sorabji shows how those paradoxes inspired some of the most interesting theories of time in late antiquity, concentrating on the little-known treatments of time as atomic.

In Chapter III, Fred Miller returns to Aristotle himself, but in order to consider Aristotelianism in reaction to different sorts of atomism—both Aristotle's opposition to the atomists whose doctrines he knew and the capacity of Aristotelian continuism to withstand the post-Aristotelian atomists' arguments.

Chapters IV and V are devoted to problems of infinity and continuity in Greek mathematics with a view to improving our understanding of the relationship between mathematics and philosophy concerning those topics in antiquity. In Chapter IV, Wilbur Knorr, considering the mathematical side of Zeno's paradoxes and the development of such mathematical techniques as the method of exhaustion, maintains the thesis that the lines of influence in antiquity run from mathematics to philosophy rather than the other way, as has so often been supposed. In Chapter V, Ian Mueller discusses Aristotle's references to attempts to square the circle in order to clarify the roles played by infinitist methods and by conceptions of the continuous in early Greek mathematics.

With the remaining chapters we move from late antiquity to the late Middle Ages. Although the period from the end of the sixth century to the beginning of the fourteenth is by no means devoid of interesting developments in the consideration of infinity and continuity, the work of most historical importance and most intellectual interest tends to be concentrated in the fourteenth century, the center of attention in Chapters VI through XI.

Infinity and continuity, like many other topics of philosophical interest in the fourteenth century, received a very influential treatment from William Ockham. In Chapter VI, John Murdoch provides an account of the relevant fourteenth-century background, against which he considers Ockham's contributions to the development of the Aristotelian tradition regarding these topics in his commentary on the *Physics*. Eleonore Stump takes a different approach to Ockham in Chapter VII, concentrating on the perhaps unexpected importance of infinity and continuity in his treatment

9

of the Eucharist and reaching conclusions that differ in some respects from Murdoch's.

In Chapter VIII, Edith Sylla turns to theories of qualitative change as a locus for problems of infinity and continuity, particularly in Walter Burley and Richard Kilvington, the one an older, the other a younger contemporary of Ockham's. Her interest in Burley is shared by Calvin Normore, who in Chapter IX raises questions regarding Burley's concept of a continuum by relating it to recent developments in the theory of the continuum—for example, in Dedekind.

Chapters X and XI deal with fourteenth-century theories of change. I compare two such theories in Chapter X—one shared by several philosophers I label "Quasi-Aristotelians," the other Richard Kilvington's orthodox Aristotelianism—emphasizing the connections of both with Aristotelian logic. Paul Spade returns to the Quasi-Aristotelians in Chapter XI, providing evidence that their position is perhaps more valuable than its treatment in the preceding chapter suggests.

I am grateful to David Furley for arranging Appendix A. Appendixes B–F present otherwise unavailable medieval texts essential to the understanding of the discussions in Chapters VIII and X. Unless otherwise noted, English translations are the work of the authors of the chapters in which they appear. We use the classical spelling of Latin even in passages from medieval authors—e.g., *lineae* rather than *linee*. I am grateful to Mary Tedeschi for her many hours of work on the Bibliography.

The chapters of this book originated as papers presented at a conference held at Cornell University on April 20 and 21, 1979: "Infinity, Continuity, and Indivisibility in Antiquity and the Middle Ages." In being transformed into chapters, all the papers have been modified, several of them radically; none of them has been published before.

The editor and the other contributors to the volume are grateful to the Society for the Humanities and the Sage School of Philosophy at Cornell University for sponsoring the original conference, and especially to Michael Kammen, Newton C. Farr Professor of American History and Culture at Cornell and from 1977 to 1980 the director of the Society for the Humanities. Without his imagination and encouragement, neither the conference nor this volume would ever have come to be.

NORMAN KRETZMANN

Ithaca, New York

Contributors

DAVID J. FURLEY

Professor of Classics, Princeton University. Author of *Two Studies in the Greek Atomists* (1967) and of "Aristotle and the Atomists on Infinity" (1969) and many other articles on ancient philosophy and science. An editor of *Phronesis* from 1968 to 1979.

WILBUR R. KNORR

Assistant Professor of Classics and Philosophy, Stanford University. Author of *The Evolution of the Euclidean Elements* (1975) and of several articles on pre-Euclidean mathematics and the work of Archimedes.

NORMAN KRETZMANN

Susan Linn Sage Professor of Philosophy, Cornell University. Author of several books and articles having to do with ancient and medieval philosophy, logic, and natural philosophy. Co-editor of *The Cambridge History of Later Medieval Philosophy*.

FRED D. MILLER, JR.

Associate Professor of Philosophy, Bowling Green State University. Author of several articles on ancient philosophy, including "Aristotle on the Reality of Time" (1974) and "Aristotle's Use of Matter" (1978).

IAN MUELLER

Professor of Philosophy and the Conceptual Foundations of Science, The University of Chicago. Author of *Philosophy of*

13

Mathematics and Deductive Structure in Euclid's Elements (1981) and of several articles on ancient philosophy and mathematics.

JOHN E. MURDOCH

Professor of the History of Science, Harvard University. Co-editor of *The Cultural Context of Medieval Learning* (1975) and author of many articles on medieval science and philosophy. Contributor to *The Cambridge History of Later Medieval Philosophy*.

CALVIN G. NORMORE

Assistant Professor of Philosophy, Princeton University. Author of articles on medieval philosophy, including "Future Contingents in the Middle Ages," forthcoming in *The Cambridge History of Later Medieval Philosophy*.

RICHARD SORABJI

Professor of Philosophy, King's College, University of London. Author of *Necessity, Cause, and Blame* (1979) and of many other books and articles having to do with ancient philosophy, including "Aristotle on the Instant of Change" (1976).

PAUL VINCENT SPADE

Professor of Philosophy, Indiana University. Author of *The Mediaeval Liar* (1975), *Peter of Ailly: Concepts and Insolubles* (1980), and of many articles on medieval philosophy and logic. Contributor to *The Cambridge History of Later Medieval Philosophy*.

ELEONORE STUMP

Associate Professor of Philosophy, Virginia Polytechnic Institute and State University. Author of *Boethius's "De topicis differentiis"* (1978) and of many articles on medieval philosophy and logic. Associate editor of *The Cambridge History of Later Medieval Philosophy*.

EDITH DUDLEY SYLLA

Professor of History, North Carolina State University. Coeditor of *The Cultural Context of Medieval Learning* (1975) and author of many articles on medieval science and philosophy. Contributor to *The Cambridge History of Later Medieval Philosophy*.

14

Infinity and Continuity
in Ancient and
Medieval Thought

CHAPTER I

The Greek Commentators' Treatment of Aristotle's Theory of the Continuous

DAVID J. FURLEY

1. Introduction

I begin with a brief historical note, in order to explain the range of this chapter.

There were two rivals for the position of successor to Aristotle as head of the Peripatetic school: Eudemus and Theophrastus. Theophrastus was chosen, on a hint given by Aristotle himself, according to an ancient account.[1] He was succeeded, after about thirty-four years, by Strato of Lampsacus. All three men were evidently keen students of Aristotle's physical works, which will concern us in this chapter, and in addition to explicating the text, they made some criticisms and modifications. But in the second half of the third century and through the second and first centuries B.C., there was silence, or very nearly so, about Aristotle's treatises, including the *Physics*. Effectively the silence was broken toward the end of the second century A.D., when commentaries on Aristotle's treatises were written, in Greek, in various philosophical centers including the revived Peripatos in Athens. The earliest name is Aspasius, but those who are important for our present purpose are, in chronological order, Alexander of Aphrodisias, Porphyry, Themistius, Olympiodorus, and two contemporaries in the sixth century, Simplicius and John Philoponus, called the Grammarian.

---

1. Eudemus, fr. 5 Wehrli, from Aulus Gellius.

Of the earliest comments on Aristotle's treatises, most have been lost. A few minor physical works by Theophrastus survive, but they are not relevant to the continuum problem. Nothing survives, except in quotation by others, of Eudemus and Strato. Alexander's commentary on the *Physics* is lost. The relevant surviving works are these: several commentaries on the *Categories*; a paraphrase of the *Physics* by Themistius; a commentary on *De generatione et corruptione* by Philoponus, and one by the same author on the first four books of the *Physics*, together with excerpts from his commentary on the later books; and Simplicius's commentary on the whole of the *Physics*. Simplicius quotes from the works of Theophrastus, Eudemus, Strato, Alexander, and Themistius, all of which he seems to know at first hand.

The aim of this chapter is to examine the contributions made by these commentators to the elucidation of Aristotle's theory of the continuous.[2] I shall concentrate particularly on what they found problematic in that account and the attempts they made to clarify the problems. It is disappointing that the important modifications in Aristotle's doctrine made by his immediate successors survive only in a fragmentary record, whereas the views of the later commentators, who aimed more strictly at clarification, and particularly at the explanation of apparent inconsistencies in the writings of Aristotle, have reached us in fuller form.

2. The *Categories* Account of Continuity

The basis of the distinction between discrete and continuous quantities in the *Categories* is that the latter have, and the former lack, a "common boundary at which their parts join together."[3] This raises some difficulty at once because of Aristotle's notion of the manner in which parts are contained in a continuous whole. A continuous line, for example, may be divided into parts. There is a point wherever it may be divided, and there is nowhere in a line where a division may *not* be made; but it may not be divided

2. I have previously published some comments on Aristotle's theory itself, especially in its historical aspect as a rebuttal of atomism: see Furley 1967, pp. 79–103, 111–21.
3. Aristotle, *Categories*, 4b25–26.

at all possible points *simultaneously*.[4] This leads Aristotle to say that the parts of a continuum have no actual existence until the division into those parts is made in some sense or other:[5] at best, the parts, and the "common boundary" between them, have only potential existence until the division is made. Olympiodorus, in his commentary on this passage of the *Categories*, raises an objection on these grounds:

> The philosopher wishes to offer here a definition of "continuous" and "discrete," and says that the continuous is what has a common boundary, and the discrete is what has no common boundary. So we inquire here whether he has produced good definitions of these.
>
> Some raise a difficulty. They say that if a definition is well-formed, it must not do away with its definiend; for if the definition seizes the nature of the thing, it is the same as the definiend: the one defines, the other is defined. So how, in this case, has he produced a definition of the continuous, if it does away with the continuous? That it *does* do away with the continuous, to have a common boundary, we show as follows: if the continuous is what has a common boundary, and what has a boundary is discrete, and what is discrete is not continuous, then the continuous, in that it has a boundary, is not continuous.
>
> . . . . .
>
> We reply to this that we must take "common boundary" potentially here, not actually, so as not to find the discrete continuous and the continuous discrete.[6]

As we shall see again later in this chapter, there is a certain ambiguity in Aristotle's language about the continuous. He treats the continuous as if it were a special case of the contiguous: we say that two things are contiguous if they each have a boundary at which they touch and that they are continuous if these boundaries are not merely touching but unified. But in the latter case, the common boundary is not a boundary at all: the two parts are no longer two, but one. The familiar distinction between potentiality and actuality is adequate to deal with this ambiguity.

Before leaving the *Categories* passage, we should say something about its treatment of *place*. The reason given for supposing place

4. Aristotle, *De generatione et corruptione* I 2, 317a4–13.
5. Aristotle, *Physics* VIII 8, 262a22–27; see section 3 below.
6. Olympiodorus, *in Cat.*, 85.33–86.13.

to be a continuous quantity is inconsistent with the account of place given in *Physics* IV. In the *Categories,* Aristotle infers the continuity of place from the continuity of the parts of a body occupying the place. He supposes that each part of a body occupies a place, and as the neighboring parts of the body join together at a common boundary, so their places must join together at the same boundary. But in the *Physics,* he will not allow that the parts of a body have a place of their own. Simplicius is alert to this difficulty, but he does not quite solve it: "It is worth noting that here he means that the continuous parts of a body are in place not in their own right (*ou kath' heauta*). They occupy place, indeed, but not in their own right, since they are not even in place in their own right, nor contained in their own right."[7] But the point of saying that the parts of a body have no place in their own right is that if they are to be assigned a place at all, it must be by mentioning the place of the whole body. According to *Physics* IV, place is the inner surface of the container, not the interval within the inner surface of the container. So a thing can be said to be in a place only if it is contained by something that can be distinguished from itself; and that is not the case with the parts of a homogeneous body. Hence, place is continuous in the sense in which any *surface* is continuous, but it is not continuous through the whole volume contained by the surface. Clearly, in the *Categories* Aristotle is using a different (and more workable) notion of place, as compared with that in his account in the *Physics.* Simplicius's attempt to make everything consistent fails because the expression "not in their own right" must refer precisely to the discordant doctrine.

3. Contact, Contiguity, and Continuity in Commentaries on *Physics* V 3

There is a problem about Aristotle's definition of *in contact,* and since this enters into the definitions of *contiguous* and *continuous,* they are infected by the same trouble. *A* and *B* are in contact if each has an extremity that is *together* with the extremity of the

7. Simplicius, *in Cat.,* 125.29–32.

other; that is to say, substituting for "together" its definiens, if the extremities in question, one of each, are in one primary place. But is it possible to give any account of the place of an *extremity*, with Aristotle's definition of place as "the limit of the surrounding body"?[8]

This is a question on which we may expect the views of the Greek commentators to have some interest, since they were generally dissatisfied with Aristotle's definition of place and indeed expressed their criticisms at some length.[9] The dissatisfaction on this subject within the Peripatetic school can be traced back to Strato of Lampsacus and even to Theophrastus, according to Simplicius's account.[10] But let us first look at Aristotle's own words again.

Early in his discussion of place, before he settles on his own definition, Aristotle raises a number of problems, including the following:

> If indeed body has a place and a space (*chōra*) evidently [it might be said] surface and other limits have a place too, since the same argument will fit: where there were formerly the plane surfaces of water, at another time there will be plane surfaces of air. But we have no distinction between a point and the place of a point; and so, if the place is not different in this case, neither will it be different in any other; and the place is not then an item over and above its occupant.[11]

To understand how Aristotle proposed to escape from this aporia, we have to take a look at what he says in general about the place or places of parts or properties of a body whose place is under discussion. The theme can be traced all the way back to the first step of his theory, which was connected with motion. We would never have inquired into place at all, he says, if it were not for motion.[12] But among moving things, we must distinguish that which moves in its own right from that which moves incidentally.

8. See Aristotle, *Phys.* IV 4, 212a6.
9. See esp. the "corollaries on place" by Simplicius, *in Phys.*, 601–45, and by Philoponus, *in Phys.*, 557–85.
10. Simplicius, *in Phys.*, 604.5–11, 639.13–22.
11. Aristotle, *Phys.* IV 1, 209a7 ff.
12. *Phys.* IV 4, 211a12.

"What moves incidentally is on the one hand what *can* move in its own right, like the parts of a body or the rivets in a ship, and on the other hand what *cannot* move in its own right but *always* moves incidentally, like whiteness or knowledge—these change their places just because what they belong to changes its place."[13] Since the concept of place is brought in by Aristotle only to enable him to talk about change of place, this observation enables him to hold that the parts or properties of a body are not to be assigned places of their own unless or until they get away on their own. Anything that is an undistinguished part of a continuous body has no place except the place of the body as a whole:

When what surrounds something is not distinguished from it but continuous [with it], the thing is not said to be in it as in a place, but as a part in a whole. When the thing is distinguished and in contact, then it is primarily in the extremity of the surrounding [body], which is not a part of what is in it nor larger than the displacement [*diastē-ma*—interval] of what is in it, but equal to it; for the extremities of things in contact are in the same [place].[14] Being continuous [with its surrounding body] it does not move *in* it but *with* it; but when it is distinct, *in* it, and it makes no difference whether the surrounding body moves itself or not.[15]

The motivation for this doctrine can be found in Aristotle's following discussion, and rejection, of the notion that the place of a body is the three-dimensional interval occupied by the body. If he had to consider the place of each of the parts of the body, it would be hard to avoid saying that the place of a part is a part of the place of the whole; and in that case he feared place would have to be seen as a sort of ghostly duplicate of the body itself. But we need not follow up that line of thought here.

Plainly now, the extremity of a body—whether its limiting surface, or a part of the surface, or a point at the apex of an angle of the surface—must count as something that moves incidentally, in the sense given in the quotation above. Since the extremity cannot be separated from its parent body, it must count in the

13. *Phys.* IV 4, 211a19–23.
14. "Place" is presumably what is intended here, but the Greek idiom allows Aristotle to do without a noun.
15. *Phys.* IV 4, 211a29–36.

second class, as something that always moves incidentally if at all. And accordingly it has no place; and so the aporia of 209a7 is no longer worrying.

But as we have observed, the solution of that aporia seems to undermine the definition of *in contact* and hence the definitions of *contiguous* and *continuous*. Aristotle is caught in a dilemma of his own making: he must deny that the extremity of a body has a place if he is to avoid the conclusion that nothing can be distinguished from its own place; but he must affirm it if he is to hold on to his definitions of *together, in contact,* and *continuous*.

Simplicius is aware of this problem. When Aristotle says the extremities of things in contact are "in the same,"[16] Simplicius observes that if he means "in the same place," he must mean *incidentally* in the same place, since surfaces are not in place in their own right. He cannot, however, mean "in the same substratum," because each of the extremities of two touching bodies is in its own substratum; and he cannot mean "in the same" in any other sense of "in." Simplicius gives the impression of being dissatisfied with this explanation, but he offers no more on his own account at this stage. Instead he quotes a different line of comment, from Alexander.

Alexander tried to find a way out by seeking a different sense of "in" not counted in Aristotle's list of senses:[17]

> Things are said to be *in the same,* if there is nothing between them. . . . Things that fit on to each other (*epharmozonta*) and make no volume (*onkos*) and have nothing between them are "in the same." For the limit of both becomes *one* in the case of things that touch, since they coincide, on account of there being no interval in that region. Whereas in the case of things that are continuous, even the *one* is destroyed; for things are continuous when in actuality there is *no* boundary (*peras*) in between.[18]

Aristotle wanted to distinguish things *in contact* from *continuous* things by claiming that the former have extremities "in the same" and the latter have extremities that are "one." At first sight, Alex-

16. *Phys.* IV 4, 211a34.
17. The list is in *Phys.* IV 3.
18. Alexander, *apud* Simplicium, *in Phys.*, 570.1–7.

ander proposes to make the distinction differently, saying that things in contact have extremities that are *one*, whereas things that are continuous actually have no extremity or boundary between them at all. The cost of this move is that a body or line can no longer be regarded as continuous as soon as an intermediate point is mentioned or even considered. There is a continuous line let us say, from Trenton to New York; strictly, however, we cannot say that it passes through Princeton Junction but only that the line from Trenton to Princeton Junction is in contact with the line from Princeton Junction to New York at Princeton Junction. The mention of Princeton Junction actualizes the intermediate point and thus transforms continuity into contact. Although Alexander's analysis appears to demand changes in the Aristotelian definitions, it seems to be in harmony with what Aristotle says in *Physics* VIII 8, where he carries the doctrine of the potentiality of divisibility to an extreme:

> Further, "potentially" is something different from "actually." So, of the points on a straight line between its two ends, any one point is potentially an intermediate, but it is not actually so unless one divides it here and stops and restarts the motion.[19]
>
> If one divides the continuous [line] into two halves, he treats the single point as two; for he makes it both a beginning and an end. The same is true of one who counts, and of one who divides it into two halves. When one divides thus, neither the line nor the motion will be continuous. For the continuous motion is through something continuous, and in what is continuous there are infinitely numerous halves—but potentially, not actually.[20]

According to this line of thought, it is not possible for *two* things to be continuous with each other; at most, they can be in contact or contiguous.

The inconsistency between this chapter of Book VIII and the definitions of Book V, chapter 3, is in fact more apparent than real. In the earlier chapter Aristotle presents the issue somewhat confusingly in that he describes the continuous as the superlative case in a comparison. The point of comparison is the closeness of

19. *Phys.* VIII 8, 262a22–25.
20. *Phys.* VIII 8, 263a23–29.

the union between two things: minimally, they are successive; more closely, they are contiguous; ultimately, they are continuous. But this statement tends to conceal the fact that the last is the limiting case, in which they are no longer two but have become one. The point at which they join, described as *one* in Aristotle's definition, must be regarded dynamically: at the instant of their becoming continuous, the point vanishes.

Alexander's interpretation of Aristotle appears to go in the right direction, then, in the sense that he is faithful to Aristotle's intention. But Simplicius is also right in saying that Aristotle's expression "in the same" must mean "in the same place," since as we have seen, in *Physics* V 3 he makes the same point but uses the word "place" explicitly. He ought not to have used it if he meant to stick to his definition of place. Simplicius's tentative solution, that he meant "in the same place *incidentally*," will not do. When Aristotle said that the parts of a body could be said to be in place incidentally, he meant that we could give an account of where they are by talking about the place of the whole body. But the place of the whole body, according to Aristotle, is the inner surface of the containing body: what a body is in contact with, in other words, *is* its place. If Aristotle wanted to use the concept of place in his definition of *in contact*, he should have said that two things are in contact if each is part of the place of the other, not that their extremities are in the same place.

The positions taken up by Alexander and Simplicius about this passage of Book IV, chapter 4, are maintained consistently in their comments on the definitions of Book V. On the definition of *together* ("those things are together which are in one primary place"), Simplicius quotes a comment from Alexander that treats Aristotle's definition of place seriously, and so concludes that things said to be together must be parts of a single *continuous* body. Simplicius objects to this as an interpretation of Aristotle, quite rightly: things that are together are *less* unified than things that are in contact, and the latter less unified than continuous things. For an example of things that are together in one primary place, says Simplicius, we should be thinking rather of a group of heterogeneous objects huddled together in a city or its surrounding wall. No comment touches on the problem of the place of an extremity at all in this paragraph of Simplicius.[21]

But Alexander's interpretation of "together" leads him into trouble at once, with Aristotle's declaration that things are in contact if their extremities are together. An extremity can be either a part or a limit, he says. In the first sense, however, the extremities of bodies in contact are certainly not in one and the same primary place, since they themselves do not coincide but only touch; and in the second sense, they can only be in the same place incidentally. Alexander suggests, therefore, that in this definition Aristotle is using "together" in a different sense, to mean "exactly fitting" (*epharmozonta*). The earlier definition, he says, was not of "together" simply, but of "together in respect of place."

This term "exactly fitting" is used by Euclid in the sense required by Alexander. One of the "Common Notions" or Axioms states that "things that exactly fit on to each other are equal to each other," and this axiom is used in the proof of proposition 4 of Book I, where the things that exactly fit are the bases of two triangles. (Euclid uses the passive voice of the verb of an area or line being *applied* to another without the implication that they coincide; he uses the active voice intransitively, as Alexander does, in the narrower sense just described.)

Alexander, then, proposes to get Aristotle out of his dilemma by substituting the undefined notion of "fitting together" for "in the same place"—although he offers this as an interpretation of Aristotle rather than an amendment. Simplicius will have none of it, being content to fudge the issue with the formula ". . . in one place, in the sense in which a surface according to its nature is in place."[22] It is a line he can be forgiven for taking, since he is ready, if pressed, to refer to his own corollary on place for a theory that will allow him to speak consistently of the place of a point or a line or a surface. He nowhere works this out explicitly, so far as I have discovered; but it seems to be a feature of the theory put forward in the corollary.

21. Simplicius, *in Phys.*, 868.25–870.8.
22. Simplicius, *in Phys.*, 871.8.

The rest of Simplicius's commentary on the definitions has little of interest for our present purposes.

4. The Argument in *Physics* VI 1–2 to Prove That Every Continuum Is Infinitely Divisible

Simplicius begins his commentary on Book VI, after some general remarks about the arrangement of the *Physics*, with a famous contrast between the early atomic theory of Leucippus and Democritus and the later version of Epicurus[23]—a contrast which I believe to be true to the facts, although most historians reject it. According to the fifth-century atomists, the atoms are not only "impassive" (*apathē*) but also "partless" (*amerē*). According to the Epicureans, they are not partless. And the reason for the change was Aristotle's criticism of partless bodies as components of larger magnitudes. Partless units can make up neither a magnitude composed of parts that are continuous with each other nor one composed of parts in contact. Thus a continuous line cannot be composed of points, since the parts of a continuous magnitude, according to Aristotle's definition, have extremities that are *one*, and points, being partless, have no extremity different from themselves. Similarly, they cannot have extremities that are together and so cannot compose a larger magnitude by contact.

In his own account, Simplicius adds a further argument. It might be objected to the above argument that a limit is not a part, and nothing prevents a partless item from having an extremity that is a limit. He dismisses this objection on the ground that even the distinction between the whole and its extremity is enough to let Aristotle's argument go through, and no such distinction is possible regarding a point.[24] This has some interest in that Epicurean atomists might conceivably have tried this escape route. Although they dropped the thesis that atoms have no parts, they maintained that atoms have parts that are themselves partless; and so they needed to show how partless units could

23. Simplicius, *in Phys.*, 925.13–22.
24. Simplicius, *in Phys.*, 926.12–16.

make up a larger magnitude—namely, an atom. In fact, however, it appears that they chose an alternate way of accounting for this, by supposing that extremities are themselves three-dimensional partless units and that such units can be in contact with each other in some way that does not require that they themselves have extremities. In other words, they substituted for Aristotle's definition of *in contact* something like "next in succession, with nothing between."[25]

Aristotle himself continues, after showing that partless units cannot compose a continuous magnitude either by being continuous or by being in contact with each other, arguing that they cannot do so by being next in succession, either. The argument provokes some debate among the commentators—if we may include in that class Eudemus, the historian of mathematics and younger contemporary of Aristotle. First, Aristotle's argument:

> Nor again can a point be in succession to a point or an instant to an instant in such a way that length can be composed of points or time of instants. For things are in succession if there is nothing of their own kind intermediate between them, whereas that which is intermediate between points is always a line and that which is intermediate between instants is always a period of time.[26]

Simplicius fills out the argument by pointing out that it proceeds a fortiori: if points cannot be next in succession, then a fortiori they cannot touch, and a fortiori again they cannot be continuous. But why does Aristotle imply that there is always something of the same kind between two points? Certainly there is always a *line* between two points. Is a line "of the same kind" as a point in the same sense as pleasure is said in the *Ethics* to be of the same kind as the activity of which it is the limit?[27] But that would appear to entail that the point and the instant must both be quantities. Since that is unacceptable, Simplicius suggests tentatively that the reason why points cannot be next in succession is

25. See Epicurus, *Letter to Herodotus* 58: "We study these [minima] in succession, beginning from the first, and not 'in the same,' nor in contact part with part. . . ." He is actually talking here about perceptible minima, but only to suggest an analogy with the minimal parts of atoms.

26. *Phys.* VI 1, 231b6–10.

27. *Nicomachean Ethics* X 4–5, 1175a20 ff.

that the line between them must contain points, even if only potentially.[28]

Eudemus, however, took a somewhat different view, Simplicius continues. It is not that points must have a line, and therefore a point, between them, but rather that they must have either a line *or a void* between them, and in either case the points do not make up a continuous quantity. In the first case, the successive points are not *in* the line: they are not, therefore, components of it. In the second case, if there is void between them: "the void in continuous things will be more than the components, namely, the alleged successive points; or else there will not be a magnitude at all. For just as two points in contact do not make a length, so neither do a point and a void."[29]

Simplicius says Eudemus may be right in this interpretation; all that Aristotle aims to prove is that points cannot be successive *in such a way as to make a continuous quantity*. Alexander, on the other hand, thought that Aristotle was out to prove the unqualified proposition that there cannot be successive points at all and that he did it by using the opponents' (i.e., atomists') premise that a line and a time are made of partless units—i.e., that points and lines *are* of the same kind. This is a poor interpretation, however, since it gives the argument two incompatible premises—an atomists' premise, that a line is composed of partless units, and an Aristotelian one, that there is a line between any two points.

The difficulty, such as it is, comes from the unsatisfactory notion of potentiality as applied to the points on a line and the uncertainty of the commentators about how to interpret it. There cannot be an *actual* infinity of points on a line: Aristotle and his commentators are agreed about that. That means that every point on the line is potential until actualized by a cut in the line. The actualizing of any point *is* a division of the line at that point. Hence the inference "between any two points there is a line, therefore between any two points there is another point" is a shaky one. But having already shown that points cannot be continuous with each other or in contact, all that Aristotle needs to show is that successive points (if they can be successive—leave

28. Simplicius, *in Phys.*, 928.15–27.
29. Simplicius, *in Phys.*, 928.28–929.9 (= Eudemus, fr. 99 Wehrli).

that open) cannot make a continuous magnitude. So Eudemus is probably right.

What seems to me most interesting in this section of Simplicius's commentary has nothing to do with continuity at all, in any direct way. It is the strange disjunction used by Eudemus, "either a line or a void." Nothing could show more clearly the Peripatetic assumption that mathematical objects are abstracted from bodies, not properties of space. Something like this doctrine is attributed also to Euclid in a recent article by Edward Grant, with the observation that Euclid may perhaps have been familiar with Aristotle's problems about place. "The concept of internal space, whether medieval or early modern, is the physical counterpart of the purely geometric space of Euclid's *Elements*. Where the internal space or dimension of a material body is inseparable from that body, so that whatever its location, a body has its own space, so also does a geometric figure in Euclid's *Elements* possess its own 'internal' space, namely the space of its own configuration, which accompanies it wherever it might be located or moved. There is nothing in Euclid's geometry to suggest that he assumed an independent, infinite, three-dimensional homogeneous space 'in' which the figures of his geometry were located."[30] This is a controversial statement about Euclid, and I do not know whether it is true. But some such distinction between internal and external space is needed to make sense of Eudemus's disjunction "either a line or a void" and is amply justified by Aristotle's discussion of the void in Book IV of the *Physics*.

Although this point is not especially relevant to the concepts of continuity, it may serve to remind us that Aristotle's doctrine is formulated with reference to physical bodies. When he discusses things that are continuous, he thinks primarily of homogeneous natural substances, such as air or water. The distinction between *in contact* and *continuous* is primarily to distinguish a case such as the junction of the upper surface of the sea with the lower surface of the air from the junction of two bodies of water. This is probably why Aristotle defines *in contact* as "having their extremities together," whereas Alexander, thinking more geometrically,

30. Grant 1978, p. 556.

speaks of the extremities of things in contact as being *one*. How could the surface of the sea be one with the surface of the air?

5. Some Problems Concerning Potentiality and the Infinite

Aristotle developed his theory of the potential divisibility of continuous magnitudes ad infinitum in response to an argument derived from Zeno. Attempts had been made to meet this argument by positing indivisible magnitudes, but Aristotle found that solution unsatisfactory and proposed his own theory as an alternative.

The argument leading to indivisible magnitudes can be set out as follows:

> A. If a magnitude is divisible everywhere, then there is no impossibility in supposing it to have been divided everywhere.
> B. But if it is divided everywhere, portions will be produced by the division which must be either (i) magnitudes, or (ii) points or other entities without any magnitude.
> C. If (i), then there are magnitudes left which could be further divided, and that contradicts the hypothesis.
> D. If (ii), then the original magnitude has been shown to be composed of non-magnitudes, which is impossible.
> E. Hence no magnitude is divisible everywhere.
> F. Hence there are indivisible magnitudes.[31]

Aristotle proposes to disarm this argument by distinguishing two senses in which a thing may be said to be divisible everywhere. The argument above takes the statement to mean that the thing is capable of existing in a completely divided state. Aristotle proposes that it may mean that the *process* of dividing the thing may go on ad infinitum, without the possibility of its ever being completed.

There are some features of this solution which Aristotle develops, both in *De generatione et corruptione* I 2 and in *Physics* III 6–8, and which interested the commentators particularly. Those that I have in mind are all closely connected. They concern the

---

31. From *De gen. et corr.* I 2, 316a14 ff.

relation between this proposition about divisibility and Aristotle's doctrine of potentiality, the relation between continuous subtraction ad infinitum in a fixed proportion $(1 - 1/2 - 1/4 - 1/8 - ...)$ and the complementary process of continuous addition ad infinitum $(1/2 + 1/4 + 1/8 + ...)$, the relation between numbers and spatial magnitudes, and the paradox that although it is possible to take a quantity *less* than any assigned quantity of spatial magnitude, it is not possible to take one *greater* than any assigned magnitude, because the cosmos is all that there is.

The solution offered by Aristotle to the Zenonian puzzle depends on the proposition that in a certain sense the infinite exists in potentiality but not in actuality. But that proposition appears at first sight to break the rule that in cases where time is not among the factors to be considered, every potentiality must eventually be actualized. Aristotle explains that the rule is not infringed by his doctrine of infinity. The potentiality in this case is *not* a potentiality for attaining a goal or reaching completeness: it is for a continuing process—the process of taking another step beyond the finite steps already taken. This potentiality *is* actualized whenever the *process* is in effect.[32]

The beginning of Simplicius's commentary on this is interesting:

> He has said that the infinite exists in potentiality in the division of magnitudes ad infinitum; now, since (1) everything that exists potentially must some time emerge into actuality if it is not in vain (*matēn*), and since (2) if actually infinite segments come into being, each having magnitude, an infinite magnitude would result (for that which is composed of infinitely numerous magnitudes is an infinite magnitude, as has often been said), and since (3) it has been shown by many arguments that there is no infinite magnitude, therefore, to solve this problem and demonstrate the nature of the infinite more clearly, he now says that there are two senses of "potentially" as there are of "actually."[33]

The portion of this passage presenting consideration 2 has appeared earlier in Simplicius's commentary,[34] and in one of those

32. *Phys.* III 6, 206a18–24, 206b12–16.
33. Simplicius, *in Phys.*, 492.14–21.
34. E.g., *in Phys.*, 142.10–15, 459.22–26, 462.3–5.

earlier appearances[35] the same thesis is attributed to Eudemus, in the second book of his *Physics*:[36] "To speak of things infinite in plurality of the same form (*homoeides*) is no different from speaking of the infinite in magnitude." The qualification "of the same form" means not "equal in size" but only "such as to be capable of being in contact," as Simplicius explains.

What is interesting about this is that Simplicius appears to apply to a convergent series a consideration that applies only to a nonconvergent one. What has happened?

Aristotle explains that "the infinite in respect of addition" is in a sense the same thing as "the infinite in respect of division."[37] Take a finite line *AB* and divide it in half at *C*. Then divide *CB* at *D*, and add *CD* to *AC*; divide *DB* at *E* and add *DE* to *AD*; and so on (see the illustration below).

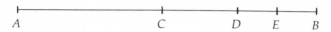

As the division produces an ever smaller portion on the right, it also produces an ever larger portion on the left. This process is the only way, Aristotle claims, in which you can have an "infinite by addition." It is a potentiality that is actualized just by the *process* of subtraction/addition, never by being completed. So there never actually exists an infinite set of parts *AC, CD, DE, ...* . He distinguishes this case from two others. One is the infinite series of units of time or generations of men. This might be thought to produce an actual infinite by addition, in that there must have been infinitely many days before this one or infinitely many generations before this one. But the case is not the same, Aristotle says, as the divided line, in that the earlier days or generations do not persist, and so you still never have an infinite by addition in the sense of an infinite set of things all in existence at once.[38] The second case to be distinguished is that of repeatedly adding to a given magnitude a constant (not diminishing) amount; in that case the sum would exceed any assigned quanti-

35. 459.22–26.
36. Eudemus, fr. 62 Wehrli.
37. *Phys.* III 6, 206b3–26.
38. *Phys.* III 6, 206a25–b2.

ty, and such an infinite by addition does not exist *even in potentiality*. Aristotle takes this to be a consequence of his arguments in *Physics* III 5, showing that there cannot be an infinite perceptible body.

Now, as Aristotle himself states the atomists' argument[39]—the argument that leads to his own theory of infinite divisibility—the ground on which the completion of an infinite division is ruled out is as follows: the resulting segments could neither have any magnitude nor be without magnitude; and his reason for saying they could not have any magnitude is simply that it would contradict the hypothesis that a division *everywhere* had been completed. Simplicius here offers a different reason: if it is completed, there will be infinitely many segments, each having magnitude, and the sum of such segments will be *infinitely large*. I take this to be a mistake made by Simplicius and avoided by Aristotle. Simplicius makes the mistake, perhaps, because of his knowledge of the original argument of Zeno, which he himself reports as containing the same step.[40] The mistake is repeated by Epicurus, Eudemus (as quoted above), and Themistius.[41] Aristotle commits himself to denying that there can ever be an infinitely large spatial magnitude and to denying that an infinitely numerous set of parts can ever be actually produced by dividing a magnitude, but I believe he never makes the former a reason for the latter, as Simplicius does.

In *Physics* III 7, Aristotle takes the infinity of *number* to depend on the infinite divisibility of spatial magnitude; he treats it as parallel to the "infinite by addition." Number and magnitude work in a complementary fashion: magnitude is bounded at the upper end because the cosmos is finite, but there is no lower limit; number, on the contrary, is bounded at the lower end because the number one is indivisible, but there is no upper limit.

> It is always possible to proceed in thought to a larger *number*, since the divisions of *magnitude* are infinite. So this is true in potentiality, not in actuality. But the number taken always exceeds every finite

39. Paraphrased above from *De gen. et corr.* I 2, 316a14 ff.
40. Simplicius, *in Phys.*, 140.34 ff.
41. Epicurus, *Letter to Herodotus*, 57; Eudemus, fr. 62 Wehrli; Themistius, *in Phys.*, 91.29–30.

number. But this number is not separate [from the division],[42] and the infinity does not persist, but is in process, like time and the number of time. But in the case of magnitude, it is the opposite: the continuous is divided into infinite [parts], but there is no infinity in the direction of the greater. For whatever quantity can be in potentiality, that quantity can be in actuality too. Hence, since there is no infinite sensible magnitude, there cannot be one exceeding every finite magnitude, since that would be bigger than the heaven.[43]

Simplicius's comment on this is long and puzzled.[44] He is satisfied with Aristotle's account of the *lower* limit of number. If you divide a group of men, you cannot proceed beyond individual men as units: if you divide individual men, you get parts of men, no longer men. In general, if you divide a unit, you get halves: but each half is *one* half. But Simplicius has much trouble in working out a consistent interpretation of the infinity of number. He does not understand why Aristotle makes the infinity of number derivative from the divisibility of magnitudes. He asks what *division* it is that continually adds to the number of the generations of men or of the revolutions of the heavenly spheres. This thought leads him to a distinction: perhaps it is not all number that gets its potentiality for infinite increase from the divisibility of magnitudes but only the number that "is in subsistence and endures."[45] If you divide up a magnitude, the segments continue to exist, and you actually *have* such and such a number of segments. This number can increase ad infinitum but *only* in potentiality: i.e., you never get an actually infinite number of segments. On the other hand, if you count days or generations, the number exists only in your head (says Simplicius), and there is no number in reality that increases ad infinitum.

Having taken this line, Simplicius is left with a major problem: how to interpret Aristotle's "whatever quantity can be in potentiality, that quantity can be in actuality too." Aristotle applies this principle to spatial magnitude in arguing that because there is no infinite perceptible magnitude in actuality, there is no infinite

42. This phrase is found in the MSS but is omitted by Simplicius and Philoponus.
43. *Phys.* III 7, 207b10–21.
44. Simplicius, *in Phys.*, 504.25–509.20.
45. Simplicius, *in Phys.*, 506.3.

perceptible magnitude in potentiality either, and that means there is no possibility of finding a magnitude that exceeds every assigned magnitude. Now Simplicius asks why the same principle does not apply to number. Given that there is no infinite number in actuality, how is it possible that the number generated by counting the segments produced by dividing a spatial magnitude *can* exceed any given number? In other words, Simplicius is bothered by the following asymmetry that he finds in Aristotle's account:

Whatever quantity can be in potentiality, that quantity can be in actuality too.

[Applied to magnitudes]	[Applied to numbers]
There is no infinite magnitude in actuality.	There is no infinite number in actuality.
Hence, there can be none even in potentiality.	
Hence, it is not possible to exceed every given magnitude.	Nevertheless, it is possible to exceed every given number.

This appears to be a genuine difficulty in Aristotle's account. As a ground for the proposition "It is not possible to have a magnitude that exceeds every given magnitude," he should give "There is no magnitude exceeding that of the cosmos" rather than "There is no infinite magnitude in actuality." Simplicius isolates the problem correctly: "So our indeterminacy [*apeiria*—joke?] has come around to the same point again: how can he say that it is *for this reason* that there is no exceeding every finite magnitude, namely that there is no infinite magnitude in actuality . . . ?"[46] He fails to capitalize on this insight, however. He presents Aristotle with a bogus defense, namely that the only magnitude larger than the largest finite magnitude is an infinite magnitude, and then confesses himself baffled by Aristotle's reasoning about number.

46. Simplicius, *in Phys.*, 508.38 ff.

Chapter II

Atoms and Time Atoms

Richard Sorabji

1. Setting the Scene

It is a familiar idea that there might be atoms of matter.[1] But some Greeks came to postulate that there were atoms of space and of time. Moreover, in recent years, the American physicist J. A. Wheeler has reaffirmed this possibility. In Greek thought (although much Islamic thought and much fourteenth-century Western thought is different), an atom is not the same as a point or instant. Points and instants are indivisible because they have no length at all. They are not short stretches of space or time but instead are merely the boundaries of stretches. Atoms, however, are supposed to be indivisible in spite of having a positive length, perhaps a very short one. How can there be such indivisible stretches of space or time; and why should anyone believe that there are?

It will be clear that I have learned a great deal from David Furley's book (Furley 1967), and my agreement with him on many issues has enabled me to be briefer than I could otherwise have been, particularly in relation to Zeno of Elea, Aristotle, and Epicurus. In revising my paper since the conference at Cornell, I have become especially indebted to three other people. First, David Sedley offered me an invaluable set of comments on Zeno, Diodorus, and Epicurus; and, as recorded above, I found that he had anticipated me in two of my suggestions about the last. Second, I learned that Nicholas Denyer had independently come to one of the same conclusions about Diodorus. Moreover, he has defended our common view in discussion against various objections. Finally, I have depended very heavily on Fritz Zimmermann for information on Arabic sources. I had access only to secondary literature and to the few available translations. He has done his best to inform me on the state of scholarship, to warn me of innumerable pitfalls, and on many occasions to supply me with translations of passages. He cannot be held responsible for the many errors which, I fear, remain.

1. This chapter represents work in progress. It will be incorporated after revision in a book now in preparation on the philosophy of time in antiquity.

Some of the other chapters of this book touch on the ancient reasons for postulating atoms, one of the most prominent of which is Zeno's paradox that we cannot move; for to travel any distance we should first have to go halfway, then half the remaining distance, and so on. In other words, to traverse any distance, we should first have to traverse an infinity of subdistances. Some Greeks thought the paradox had to be solved by postulating atoms. Provided we eventually reach an atomic half-distance, it will contain no further subdistances, and so the number of subdistances to be traversed will after all be finite.[2]

Commentators divide on whether Zeno's paradox has long ago been disposed of or whether it is still full of surprises and lessons which need assimilating. I fancy that among the contributors to this volume Wilbur Knorr belongs to the first camp and Norman Kretzmann (like myself) to the second. At any rate, in chapter X Kretzmann reports a corollary noticed by Richard Kilvington: something occupying the endpoint of the journey, and looking back over the infinity of half-distances, would find itself separated by no gap from odd-numbered half-distances and equally by no gap from even-numbered ones. How can this be, seeing that the odd and the even do not coincide? Another puzzling corollary is this: the infinite series of half-distances, taken as a whole, is not separated by a gap from the endpoint of the journey. How can this be, since every individual half-distance in the series is separated from the endpoint by a gap? The atomist solution would, if it were viable, dispose of all these problems.

A second paradox is mentioned by Wilbur Knorr in chapter IV below. Democritus imagined a cone being sliced by a cut parallel to its base. He then asked whether the upper of the two exposed surfaces will be of the same size as, or smaller than, the lower. If it is of the same size, then, he alleged, what we have is a cylinder, not a cone. But if it is smaller, the cone will ascend in little

2. For the paradox, see Aristotle, *Physics* VI 2, 233a21–34; VI 9, 239b11–14; VIII 8, 263a4–b9. For the atomist solution see Ps.-Aristotle, *De lineis insecabilibus*, 968a18–b4, and perhaps Aristotle, *Phys.* I 3, 187a1–3. But it is a matter of controversy whether the latter passage refers to the half-distance paradox (for this interpretation, see Philoponus, *in Phys.* 81.7–16) or to the paradox of division at every point, and whether it refers to the atomism of Democritus and Leucippus or (as the ancient commentators say) to that of the Platonists.

steps.[3] We are not told what conclusion he drew. One possibility, but only one of many, is that he favored the notches and took them to correspond to the atoms in which he believed.

In chapter I David Furley mentions the paradox of division at every point.[4] If you think that a body or a line is divisible at every point, then imagine it so divided: what would be left? Not little segments, because then the division would not have been made at every point. On the other hand, if only sizeless points or nothings are left, we have the seemingly absurd result that the body or line is made up of points or nothings. Democritus evidently claimed that atoms were needed to solve the paradox. The embarrassing questions could not then be raised, because atomic magnitudes would defy ubiquitous division.

We shall encounter other paradoxes which motivated atomism as we go along. But to say that atomism was to a large extent motivated by its ability to settle paradoxes is not yet to say how there possibly can be indivisible distances. I know of only one ancient attempt to answer this question. Epicurus compared the smallest *thinkable* distance with the smallest *perceptible* distance.[5] If you scrutinize an expanse, say, a blackboard, you will be able to find an area which has a positive size but which is so small that your sight cannot distinguish a smaller within it. By analogy, then, why should there not be a smallest *thinkable* size, just as there is a smallest *perceptible*?

2. The Aim of the Chapter

So much by way of setting the scene; I must now explain what I shall try to do in this chapter. There are different kinds of atomism, corresponding to the different senses in which atoms may be thought *indivisible*. Only some of these senses would encourage one to go beyond atoms of matter and to postulate atoms of space, time, or motion. My task will be to inquire when these various steps were taken. When did atomism of the various kinds, or atomism of any kind, first appear? Above all, who first

3. Plutarch, *Common Notions* 39, 1079E.
4. Aristotle, *De generatione et corruptione* I 2, 316a5–317a17.
5. *Letter to Herodotus*, secs. 57–59.

postulated time atoms? Scholars have been liberal in detecting time atoms in the ancient literature. In six cases, I shall argue that their attributions are mistaken. I shall represent time atomism as quite a short-lived theory among the philosophers of antiquity. It arose with Diodorus Cronus in response to Aristotle's objections, and it continued among philosophers only in the Epicurean school. On the other hand, I shall argue, against some recent skepticism, that Islamic atomism, which revives belief in time atoms, was directly inspired in its earliest stages by Greek atomism.

3. Zeno's Target

The earliest group that scholars have credited with a belief in time atoms are the opponents envisaged by Zeno when he propounded the paradox of the stadium or moving rows, some time around 460 B.C. The hypothesis that Zeno's opponents believed in time atoms was first put forward by Paul Tannery in 1887, and it won widespread acceptance.[6] Tannery's suggestion was that Zeno's atomist opponents were Pythagoreans, while S. Y. Luria later postulated contemporary mathematicians.[7] Soon after Tannery, others maintained that Zeno's paradox of the flying arrow was also directed against atomists.

The independent evidence for atomism among Pythagoreans or mathematicians at this period is weak, and I shall not add to the objections of Vlastos, Owen, Furley, and others.[8] Indeed, to the evidence provided by Zeno's paradoxes, I shall only add a couple of footnotes. Tannery's main contention was that the case of the moving rows, as previously interpreted, was too feeble an argument, whereas it would have had considerable bite if it had been construed as an attack on atomism. On both counts I think he estimated wrongly.

First, Tannery's version of the moving rows paradox could fairly easily be answered by a determined atomist. To put the paradox in modern terms, we can imagine two trains rushing past a

6. Tannery 1887, pp. 247–61.
7. Luria 1932–33.
8. Vlastos 1953, 1959; Owen 1957–58; Furley 1967, chap. 3.

station in opposite directions and at equal speeds. We can assume the trains and the station are of the same length, say, four cars long. The paradoxical conclusion Zeno tries to derive from a consideration of such circumstances is that half the time is equal to double.[9] Tannery's innovation is to treat each car as atomic in length. Suppose that an atomic car of train B passes an atom-length section of the station, A, in one time atom. The question is: how long does that car take to pass an atomic car of train C? Answer: half a time atom; so evidently the time is not atomic after all.

I think Tannery exaggerates the difficulty of answering this. The atomist answer should be that when a car of B passes an atom-length section of A, it passes *two* atomic cars of train C. But it passes these two all at once, simply disappearing from where it was and reappearing farther on. There is no stage at which it has passed only *one* car of C. This involves the surprising idea that motion occurs in a jerk: the moving body is now here, now there, without ever being in between. But an atomist is committed to that in any case: even in passing a *single* atom, a moving body must jerk in this discontinuous way.

Tannery also underestimates, I believe, the force that the paradox would have had without the importation of atomism. The leading car of C will pass all four cars of B in four seconds if it spends one second opposite each. Over the same period, the leading car of B will pass only *two* car-length portions of station A. Suppose now that that car of B also spends one second opposite each car-length portion of A; for Aristotle tells us three times that this is the fallacious assumption: that given the same speed, a thing of the same length will spend the same time opposite a body of the same length, regardless of whether that body is still or moving.[10] Given this fallacious assumption, we get Zeno's paradoxical result: while train C is taking four seconds to pass train B, B is taking two seconds to pass two car-length portions of the station. Four seconds is equal to two seconds.

The paradox, as construed by Aristotle, turns on the relativity of motion: the question whether the body being passed is still or

9. Aristotle, *Phys.* VI 9, 240a1. Aristotle's full report covers 239b33–240a18.
10. Aristotle, *Phys.* VI 9, 240a1–4; a12; a15–16.

moving is ignored. Now in Zeno's time, fallacies about the relativity of motion would not have been easy to detect. We have
Plato's explicit testimony that Zeno was confused about
relativity.[11] He had supposed it would be paradoxical if something
could be both like and unlike, both one and many, both in motion
and at rest. Plato makes Socrates point out to him that there is no
paradox here, provided we specify the different respects and relations in which a thing is like and unlike, one and many, moving
and resting. Confusions about relativity are particularly hard to
clear up. One that had been generated by Zeno's predecessor
Heraclitus was still worrying Aristotle in the following century:
the road from Athens to Thebes may be uphill, while the road
from Thebes to Athens is downhill. Aristotle thinks this is a case
of the roads being identical with each other and yet not having
the same predicates.[12] He does not see that they do have the same
predicates, as would be clear if only the relations were stated
properly. Each road is uphill in the direction of Thebes and downhill in the direction of Athens. Viewed in historical context,
then, there is nothing surprising in the mistake about relativity
which Aristotle ascribes to Zeno.

It has even been suggested to me (by David Sedley) that Zeno
has not made a mistake about relativity, but has rather discovered
the truth that motion is relative and thinks of its relativity as
making it less than real. There would be a parallel with Democritus's argument from the relativity of color and of flavor to their
unreality. Zeno's point will be that if you treat motion as nonrela-
tive, you will get the self-contradictory result that half the time is
equal to double. To avoid this, you should treat it as relative and
hence not fully real.

Be that as it may, the evidence for Tannery's reconstruction is
not strong; moreover, his reconstruction has the disadvantage
that it has no textual support but must on the contrary treat as
mistaken our main source for Zeno's argument, namely, Aristotle's report. What Tannery's reconstructed argument does resemble, if anything, is a certain argument devised by Aristotle himself
against atomism over a century later.[13]

11. Plato, *Parmenides*, 128E–130A.
12. Aristotle, *Phys.* III 3, 202a19–20; b13–16.
13. Aristotle, *Phys.* VI 2, 233b19–33.

In connection with Zeno's flying arrow, I again see no advantage in taking it to be concerned with time atoms. Zeno's idea here might be expressed in modern terms as follows. Imagine a knife stuck in the jam: so long as it does not make a slit wider than itself, it does not move. But at any instant an arrow does not make a slit in the air wider than itself. So at any instant an arrow is not moving. But what is true of an arrow at any instant must be true of it over any period; hence an arrow never moves.[14]

Here Zeno can be construed as talking about perfectly familiar entities: instants. An instant is not a very short period, but the beginning or end of a period. There is nothing obviously startling about the idea that periods have beginnings or ends. An example of an instant would be 2:00 P.M.; and it is unlike the time atom of atomist theory, because, being a mere beginning or end, it does not have a size. There would be no philosophical gain in supposing that Zeno was here talking about those much more puzzling and controversial entities time atoms, which are supposed to be unlike instants in having a size and yet (surprisingly) like them in being indivisible.

One piece of textual evidence might be urged in favor of the view that Zeno is after all envisaging time atoms.[15] For Aristotle expresses the paradox by saying that the arrow stands still (*hestēken*, 239b30). Now, it might be thought that in Aristotle's own view, our arrow could stand still during a time atom, if there were such a thing, but at an instant should be described *neither* as moving *nor* as resting. In that case, will not the Zenonian argument which Aristotle is reporting be envisaging time atoms rather than instants?

I think this argument fails. For one thing, whatever Aristotle thought, Zeno may have allowed talk of rest at an instant, and Aristotle will not have tried to correct him on every point, in the space of his very brief comment. Second, Aristotle's own position is complicated. Some of his arguments that there can be neither motion nor rest at what he calls a "now" would apply to time atoms just as much as to instants, and there are signs that he does so apply them.[16] Admittedly, two polemical passages may be as-

14. Aristotle, *Phys.* VI 9, 239b5–9; b30–33.
15. See Vlastos 1966, esp. p. 9, n. 20a.
16. For the arguments, see *Phys.* VI 3, 234a24–b9; VI 8, 239a10–b4; for reitera-

cribing to atomists belief in rest at a time atom.[17] But that is not a sign that Aristotle thinks such an idea to be in order. On the contrary, the second passage probably takes rest at a time atom to imply something which we know Aristotle rejects, namely, rest at its terminal instant.

For an antiatomist argument like that which has been read into the flying arrow we must again wait a century, until we come to one devised along somewhat similar lines by Aristotle himself.[18]

4. Leucippus and Democritus

I conclude that atomic times are not to be found in the period of Zeno of Elea. If we progress twenty or thirty years to 440 or 430 B.C., we come to the great atomists Leucippus and Democritus. But so far as I know, nobody has suggested that they believed in atomic *times*. What they postulated was atomic *bodies*, and controversy has centered on whether their atomic bodies were merely physically or also conceptually indivisible. This question, I believe, is subject to an unfortunate and unnoticed ambiguity. For in the talk of division being impossible, it matters whether the word "conceptual" qualifies the division or the impossibility. The answer is that when we talk of conceptual indivisibility, it is the *impossibility* which we characterize as conceptual. There is a conceptual impossibility of any kind of division, whether conceptual or physical; for the suggestion is that in this context the idea of parts of any kind has no meaning. But when we turn to physical indivisibility, things may be different. On one conception, the word "physical" characterizes only the mode of *division*. There will be an impossibility, which may be physical or conceptual, of any physical division. If we follow this conception, then what is conceptually indivisible will a fortiori be physically indivisible. But on a commoner conception, for something to be physically indivisible is for there to be obstacles to physical division which

---

tion of the conclusion, VI 6, 237a14; for possible application to a time atom, see VI 8, 239a3–6, where the use of two letters, *AB*, suggests that Aristotle is talking of a temporal item with two ends, i.e., of a time atom rather than of an instant.

17. Aristotle, *Phys.* VI 1, 232a12–17; VI 5, 236a18.
18. Aristotle, *Phys.* VI 1, 231b18–232a17.

are themselves physical, such as hardness and solidity. We might then reserve the phrase *"merely physically indivisible"* to mark off cases in which the obstacles to physical division are *only* physical.

Commentators are seriously divided on the issue of conceptual versus merely physical indivisibility in Democritus.[19] I want here simply to make an alternate suggestion, and I will list very briefly my reasons for making it. The suggestion is that Leucippus and Democritus were not aware of the need to distinguish between physical and conceptual indivisibility. The later atomist Epicurus in the fourth to third centuries B.C. probably made a fairly sharp distinction, and if so, commentators will have asked themselves, in the light of this, what was the intention of the earlier atomists Leucippus and Democritus. If those earlier atomists never made up their minds, it is not surprising that later commentators should have come up with conflicting verdicts. The following are my reasons for this hypothesis.

First, it fits with what I have argued elsewhere about Aristotle. Writing nearly a century later, he did not distinguish between physical and conceptual impossibilities, so I believe, and hence not between the physical and conceptual impossibility of division.[20] If this is true of Aristotle, with his great love of distinctions, it is not at all implausible that it should have been true of the earlier thinkers, Leucippus and Democritus. And this observation, incidentally, removes the value of Aristotle as a witness on this particular issue. Without consciously noting the distinction between physical and conceptual indivisibility, he nonetheless often implies that the indivisibility in question was conceptual. If I am right, however, his evidence is not to be relied on.

The main reason for my hypothesis is that there are several considerations which support one side in the traditional controversy and several which support the other. Each party, therefore, has to discount one half of this evidence. The advantage of the present hypothesis is that it does not have to favor one set of

---

19. For the divisibility as merely physical we can cite P. Tannery, H. Diels, W. Kranz, J. Burnet, T. Heath, S. Pines, G. S. Kirk, A. Mourelatos, J. Barnes; for its being conceptual, J. Mau, D. Furley, H. J. Krämer, W. K. C. Guthrie, D. Konstan.
20. Sorabji 1969, esp. appendix.

considerations rather than the other, but takes them all equally into account. I shall not here catalogue the rival considerations; they are rehearsed often enough in the literature. I shall simply mention a specimen from either side. First, in order that atoms may supply an answer to Zenonian and related paradoxes, which we are regularly told was a major reason for introducing the theory, the atoms will need to be *conceptually* indivisible. On the other hand, the atoms are required to have a great variety of shapes and sizes in order that they may account for the diversity of qualities perceived at the macro level.[21] It is impossible to see, in that case, how they can be conceptually indivisible, since when one is superimposed on another of a different size or shape, one atom is bound to have portions which extend beyond the other.

Only one other hypothesis, so far as I know, tries to take account equally of the two rival sets of considerations, and this is the highly original thesis of S. Y. Luria.[22] He ascribes to Democritus a two-tier theory which others have with more plausibility found later on in Epicurus. According to this theory, atoms are themselves merely physically indivisible, but they contain within themselves minimal parts which are conceptually indivisible. Later sources, not recognizing that there were two distinct tiers, will naturally have given conflicting reports on the Democritean atoms. Luria's evidence is partly the existence of the rival considerations which I too have exploited. But he can cite two passages, one from Alexander and one from Themistius, which do suggest the particular two-tier structure which he proposes. I shall not try to say here why I am not persuaded: David Furley has made an excellent reply to Luria.[23] But I might say that one of Luria's main pieces of evidence, a quotation from Simplicius, seems marginally to favor my own suggestion. Thus Simplicius distinguishes Leucippus and Democritus from Epicurus on the grounds that they made the atoms indivisible not only through imperviousness but also through smallness and partlessness.[24] Why, I should like

21. This theory is most fully described in the treatise *De sensibus* by Aristotle's successor Theophrastus, translated in Stratton 1917.

22. Luria 1932–33, esp. pp. 172–80. See also Luria 1970, comment on his fragment 123 of Democritus.

23. Furley 1967, chap. 6.

24. Simplicius, *in Phys.*, 925.13–17.

to ask, are smallness and partlessness combined? For while part-lessness is a characteristic of geometrical points (as Simplicius says elsewhere) and so suggests conceptual indivisibility, small-ness does not suggest conceptual indivisibility without a lot of extra argument. For what is small. has a positive size, and it would need to be shown why we could not conceive of parts within it.

5. Plato

I come next to Plato (ca. 427–347 B.C.). Aristotle tells us that he believed in the existence of indivisible lines, although the passage has caused difficulty, because there is other testimony that he gave to points the role here given to indivisible lines. "Again, from what will the presence of points in the line be derived? Plato used even to fight against this class of things [viz., points] as being something that geometers believed in, whereas he called indivisible (*atomoi*) lines the origin of the line, and this he often postulated."[25] There is controversy whether Plato's *Timaeus* also expresses a belief in indivisible magnitudes. Plato there describes how the physical world is built out of elementary triangles. There is one piece of evidence that some of the triangles are indivisible, namely, that they seem to come in a finite number of sizes.[26] In that case, there is presumably a smallest size of triangle.

Plato distinguishes among perceptible, mathematical, and ideal entities. Several considerations suggest that it is only in the world of perceptible things that indivisible magnitudes, themselves too small to be perceived, are postulated. A distinct, but related, question is whether the indivisibility is conceptual or merely physical. From the fact that the indivisible entities are physical we cannot infer straight away that Plato intends their indivisibility to be merely physical. But if it is true that *only* physical entities are indivisible, while mathematical entities are *not*, then, in the ab-sence of special argument,[27] we may expect Plato's magnitudes to

25. Aristotle, *Metaphysics* I 9, 992a19–22; but see Sextus, *Adversus mathematicos* X 278; Alexander, *in Metaphys.*, 55.20; Simplicius, *in Phys.*, 454.22.
26. Plato, *Timaeus*, 57C8–D6.
27. For such special argument, consider the modern theory of J. A. Wheeler, described later in this chapter.

be merely physically indivisible. Conversely, if Plato ever treats conceptual indivisibility as impossible, we can infer that his indivisible entities are physical.

Without going into detail, I shall list briefly my four reasons for thinking that Plato's indivisible entities are confined to the perceptible world. (i) The *Timaeus* is discussing the triangles which compose perceptible bodies, and not some ideal triangles. (ii) In the *Parmenides*, Plato argues that a thing lacking parts, i.e., a conceptually indivisible thing, could have neither shape nor location and could not either move or rest.[28] Of course, Plato is here propounding puzzles, and we cannot be sure what he would finally endorse. But the arguments here are particularly good ones, and several were to be taken up in Aristotle's *Physics*. (iii) Plato recognizes that some lines are incommensurable with each other,[29] and these presumably cannot consist of one or more indivisible lengths. The simplest hypothesis is that these are ideal and mathematical lines, while physical lines are the ones which contain indivisibles. (iv) If Plato is the author of the Seventh Letter, he contrasts circles drawn physically (*en tais praxesi*, by our actions), or turned on a lathe, with the ideal circle, on the grounds that the former have straight edges.[30] Why? There is a similar reference elsewhere to the imperfection of the human, as opposed to the divine, circle.[31] We can infer that, if Plato's indivisible lines are straight, then the ideal circle cannot be made up of them. As to why human circles are so made, Plato's idea may be that we draw a circle or turn it on a lathe by depositing particles of charcoal or removing particles of wood, and these particles are not curved and do not have curved edges. The *Timaeus* shows us why not: elementary particles are all rectilinear and, we may add, do not fall below a certain minimum size. In that case, the straight-edged circles, which we know to be physical rather than ideal, will also have edges that do not fall below that size.

My conclusion is that Plato envisages the merely physical indivisibility of items in the perceptible world. There is no suggestion

28. Plato, *Parmenides*, 137D–139B.
29. Plato, *Laws* VII 820A–B.
30. Plato, *Letters* VII 343A5–9. I am grateful to Myles Burnyeat for this point, and for my treatment below of *Lin. insec.*, 968b7–8.
31. Plato, *Philebus*, 62A7–B9.

in the *Timaeus* that we cannot *conceive* of parts in the smallest triangles, or that one triangle could not overlap with another. And this applies whether the triangles are conceived as thin sheets or as something more abstract. Difficulty has been located in Plato's acceptance of infinite divisibility. But what he recognizes as infinitely divisible is not physical body but rather that element in ideal forms and physical bodies which he calls "the great and the small."[32] It may even be significant that he seems to have explained this infinite divisibility by using the example, not of a physical body, but of a mathematical length, the cubit.[33]

If I am right, Plato's idea so far implies nothing about indivisible spaces or times. The shadow on a sundial could glide continuously, part by part, across the indivisible triangles which constitute the face of the dial. A water clock might emit its water one particle at a time, yet the triangles bounding the particle could slide continuously, part by part, out of the aperture. If then, we are to look for evidence of time atoms in Plato, we must turn in a different direction and go to his *Parmenides*. I shall rely here on the findings of a debate between Mills and Strang.[34]

At *Parmenides* 156C–157A, Plato introduces "the sudden" which divides a period of motion from a period of rest. Although Sambursky may see the sudden as an atomic time,[35] it is pretty clearly an instant, as Strang and Mills agree. For Plato says that when something switches from motion to rest, or from rest to motion, it is not then in any time, but it is in "the sudden," which itself is not in any time. In Strang's view (which is the more natural), Plato's idea is that "the sudden" is not a *time* at all, just because it is an instant. Mills suggests that Plato might be willing to call "the sudden" a time and might insist only that it is not *in* any time, on the grounds that, being a sizeless instant, it is not a *part* of time. (Parts must have size, in order to compose a whole.)[36] The dis-

32. See Aristotle, *Phys.*, III 4, 203a9–10; III 5, 206b27. For further explanation of its presence in physical bodies and in Forms, see *Metaph.*, 988a8–14.
33. Porphyry, *apud* Simplicium, *in Phys.*, 453.36.
34. Strang and Mills 1974.
35. Sambursky seems to be comparing "the sudden" with the "leaps" referred to by the Neoplatonist Damascius, which Sambursky construes as atomic in Sambursky 1968; reprinted in Sambursky and Pines 1971 (in which see p. 19).
36. Mills could alternatively have drawn attention to Plato's argument elsewhere in the *Parmenides* that what lacks parts lacks location (138A–B).

advantage of this view is that Mills must invoke a different sense of "in," when Plato says that the thing which is switching between motion and rest is *in* the sudden"; for certainly, it is not *part* of "the sudden." It is simpler to suppose that "in" means throughout something like "coincides with": the switching thing coincides not with any time, but with the sudden, which itself does not coincide with any time.

The implication is that the instantaneous sudden is not a time, and this has consequences for the entity which interests us, namely, the "now," at 152B2–D2. For Plato is willing to call the now a *time* (152B3), suggesting that unlike "the sudden," the now is *not* instantaneous. Nonetheless, it appears to be indivisible; for Plato says of something which is becoming older that when it is at the now time, it already *is* older, and further that it is then not *becoming* older. Why not, if the now time is divisible into parts, so that the aging object is older in the later parts of the now than in the earlier? Plato's presupposition must be that the now time is indivisible. Putting these conclusions together, Strang concludes that Plato's now must be a time atom, i.e., something indivisible like an instant but unlike an instant in being a *time*, i.e., having a duration. Here is the passage in question.

> It *is* older, when, in the course of becoming older, it is at the now-time which is between was and will be. For presumably it will not skip the now when it travels from the once to the after. So when it meets the now, it then stops *becoming* older, and does not *become* but actually *is* then older. For if it were going onwards, it would never be caught by the now, since what is going onwards is so placed as to touch both the now and the after, letting go of the now and grasping the after, becoming between the two, the after and the now. But if of necessity anything that is becoming does not bypass the now, then when it is at the now, it always stops becoming, and then *is* whatever it may have been becoming. [152B2–D2]

Strang's argument does show that there is some reason to construe the now as a time atom.[37] On the other hand, however, it is

---

37. Strang has an additional argument, which I think less satisfactory, for the now's having a duration. Plato implies that a thing does its growing older not at the now but when it is *between* the now and the after and when it is touching both (152C3–6). I take it that the between must be a divisible period in order to leave room for growing older. Strang prefers to construe it as an instant and uses this as

very doubtful that Plato was conscious of this fact. For one thing, he does not make it explicit. Moreover, two things fit badly with the now's being a time atom. First, as we have seen, Plato describes the aging entity as "touching" the now, whereas the now cannot strictly speaking be in contact with anything, if it is really indivisible.[38] For Plato defines contact in terms of occupying the neighboring place (*echomenē chōra*, 148E7–10), while an indivisible thing cannot have any place (138A2–B6).[39] A more serious difficulty, which is raised by Mills, is that the postulation of time atoms fits badly with the postulation of "the sudden." For during an indivisible time atom, there is no time for anything to move. If a thing moves, this must be through its finding itself at different places at successive time atoms. If it comes to a halt, there will be a time atom before which it was at different places, but after which it is in the same place. And it will be at this time atom, if anywhere, that it makes the transition from motion to rest. But Plato wants the transition from motion to rest to be made not at this or at any time atom but at an instantaneous "sudden." Which instant would he then designate as the instant of transition: the one which marks the beginning or the one which marks the end of our transitional time atom? But the one instant seems too early and the other too late. To find a single transitional instant, Plato would need to revert to the more usual view of time as continuous rather than atomic.[40]

I conclude that Plato's now is described in ways appropriate to a time atom but that Plato has not recognized this fact and cannot easily accommodate it. This is not altogether surprising in a context which is concerned to raise dialectical difficulties.

---

a further argument to show that the now cannot be an instant, since two instants cannot be next to each other. His reason for taking the between to be an instant is that otherwise it would be part of the after. But this is not so if the after is a selected time atom somewhat subsequent to the now. Strang's case for treating the now as extended is better supported by his earlier argument.

38. This argument for the divisibility of Plato's now is given by Damascius in his *Dubitationes et solutiones* II 237, in Sambursky and Pines 1971, p. 90.6–14.

39. Admittedly, Plato had not worked out this conclusion about contact, much less applied it to temporal contact as well as to spatial.

40. This is not to deny that there would still be a problem about the instant of transition from motion to rest, namely, whether the body would be moving or resting at the transitional instant. But at least this is a different, and a soluble, problem: see Sorabji 1976, 1979.

6. Xenocrates and the Academy

Xenocrates was the third head of Plato's Academy, from 339 B.C. (four years before Aristotle set up his own school in the Lyceum) to 314. Numerous sources testify that he believed in indivisible lines.[41] The treatise *On Indivisible Lines* (*De lineis insecabilibus*), wrongly attributed to Aristotle but written by someone in Aristotle's school, is an attack on indivisible lines and begins with five arguments that had been used in their support.[42] The fourth argument is associated by one ancient commentator with Xenocrates, and the second and third have ideas and terminology close to Xenocrates' own.[43] Whether or not all five arguments stem from Xenocrates, they do seem to come from Plato's Academy. The second, indeed, concerns an ideal Platonic form.

Versions of two of the arguments are noticed by Aristotle elsewhere. Thus in *De generatione et corruptione* I 2, 316a12, he prefers a certain Democritean argument for atoms to the argument which is elaborated in *De lineis insecabilibus* that the ideal Form of triangle will (absurdly) consist of many parts, unless it is regarded as an indivisible magnitude. He also mentions that somebody posited indivisible magnitudes in order to get out of the argument of the dichotomy (*Physics* I 3, 187a1–3). The ancient commentators identify the person in question as Xenocrates, and one[44] of them gives among other examples of the dichotomy Zeno's paradox that to reach any destination one needs to go first halfway and then half the remaining distance, ad infinitum. This is the paradox which appears as the fourth argument for atoms in *De lineis insecabilibus*, and Aristotle is even aware (*Physics* VIII, 8, 263a25–b3) of the particular version used in *De lineis insecabilibus*, according to

41. See fragments 43–49 in Heinze 1892.
42. Ps.-Aristotle, *Lin. insec.*, 968a1–b22.
43. For the fourth argument, see next paragraph and note; for the terminology of the third (968a14–18: *stoicheion, ameres*: element, partless), compare Heinze, frs. 50–51. The priority of part to whole used in the second and third arguments (968a9–18) is exploited by Xenocrates in a fragment discussed in Pines 1961. The idea of the second argument (968a9–14) that the ideal form of the line is indivisible is ascribed to Xenocrates in Heinze, fr. 46.
44. Philoponus, *in Phys.* 81, 7–16.

which one would need to be able to *count* the infinitely many half-distances.

Between them, the five arguments for indivisibles in *De lineis insecabilibus* go well beyond Plato's original idea, for they would establish indivisible magnitudes in all three worlds, the ideal, the mathematical, and the perceptible. Or if Xenocrates recognized only two worlds, perceptible and ideal, then perhaps it should be said that the arguments would establish indivisible magnitudes in both. Thus the second argument concerns the indivisibility of ideal forms such as the Triangle. The third argument explicitly deals with the indivisibility of the constituents of body in the perceptible world, as opposed to the intelligible world of Forms. The fifth argument belongs with the third, since it makes a point about lines which are actually measured (968b7–8), i.e., presumably about lines in the perceptible world: these at least, it is alleged, will be commensurable with each other. The remaining two arguments, the first and the fourth (which concerns traversing half-distances), ought to be applicable to the mathematical world (if this is distinct from the ideal). Indeed, if the fourth is to answer Zeno's paradox of the half-distances, it will have to involve indivisibility in both the mathematical and the physical worlds. And this argument, like the first and second, calls for a *conceptual* indivisibility. All this creates difficulties for those commentators, ancient and modern, who seek to play down Xenocrates' claim of indivisibility as meaning something unremarkable.[45]

So far none of the five arguments has suggested indivisible times. But Sambursky has ascribed time atoms to Xenocrates, and in a recent book which seeks to emphasize the role of Plato's Academy in the development of atomism, H. J. Krämer offers five arguments to show that Xenocrates and the Academy recognized time atoms.[46] None of these arguments seems to me persuasive. First, *De lineis insecabilibus* opens by asking whether there are indivisible lines and whether in general there is something partless in *all* quantities, as some people say. The five atomist arguments follow immediately. But the reference to *all* quantities need

45. Among those collected in Heinze, frs. 45–47; cf. Pines 1961, p. 19.
46. Sambursky 1956, pp. 151–52; Krämer 1971, pp. 310, 350–51.

not be intended to cover times, as Krämer suggests. The context suggests two other possibilities much more readily: first, and most obviously, the author is likely to be referring to planes and solids as well as lines. Failing that, he is likely to be referring to ideal, mathematical, and perceptible quantities.

Krämer's second point, that the first of the five arguments is general enough to apply to times, does not show that it was thought of as applying to times.

His third point is that Aristotle treats time atoms as analogous to atoms of space and matter and attacks them all. But the question is whether in attacking the Academy's atoms of space and matter, Aristotle is not rather complaining that they have *unwittingly* committed themselves to time atoms. Is there any reason to suppose that they accepted time atoms voluntarily?

Fourth, it is urged, the author of *De lineis insecabilibus* attacks time atoms at 970b9, 971a16–21, and 971b4. But in none of these passages is it implied that the atomist opponent had thought for himself of postulating time atoms. In the first, the anonymous author suggests (borrowing a phrase from Aristotle's *Physics* VI 1, 231b18) that the same argument which composes a line out of atomic lines should compose a time out of atomic times. In the second, his suggestion is that "perhaps" the same argument which composes a line out of points should compose a time out of nows. Here the talk is no longer of atoms but of points, and the "perhaps" makes it clearer still that the atomist opponent had not himself suggested this. Only five lines (971a18–21 and 971b4) are devoted to attacking the suggestions about time, and they are all devoted to attacking the second suggestion, which is not about atoms at all.

Finally, Krämer sees Academic influence in the time atoms referred to at a later date not only by the Platonist Plutarch but even by the Aristotelian Strato. But I shall argue that Strato did not accept time atoms, while Plutarch in his best attested reference to time atoms (*Common Notions*, 41, 1081c), says only that the Stoics had not left themselves free to escape a certain paradox by postulating time atoms. If he is thinking of anyone who did leave himself free in this way, I shall suggest below that it is less likely to be an Academic than Diodorus Cronus followed by Epicurus.

There is a doctrine conjecturally ascribed to Xenocrates that sounds are heard as continuous, though produced by a discontinuous series of instantaneous blows falling on the ear.[47] Even here, however, Xenocrates is not credited with any discussion of a least audible time interval between blows.

7. Aristotle

So far we have not found a conscious postulation of time atoms. The greatest impetus to the theory of time atoms was given, as David Furley argues in chapter I, by Aristotle (384–322 B.C.) in *Physics* VI 1–4 and 10. For in VI 1, 231b18, he says: "The same argument applies to magnitude, time, and motion: either all are composed of indivisibles and divided into indivisibles, or none are." In much of what follows he seeks to substantiate this. He then attacks the atomist theory and assumes that in attacking any one kind of atom, he will be attacking the other two. Subsequent atomists took it for granted that, if they postulated one kind of atom, they would have to postulate another, and the link which Aristotle forged between atoms of magnitude, time, and motion was not questioned at least until Strato.

Aristotle's attacks are relevant only against a theory of *conceptually* indivisible atoms, and Xenocrates and the Academy had just provided him with such a theory. He himself, however (so I have suggested), did not notice the difference between physical and conceptual indivisibility. Furthermore, as references in the *De caelo* show, he thinks his arguments in *Physics* VI valid also against the atomism of Democritus and Plato.[48]

There is, I believe, an unnoticed oversight in Aristotle's argument about time atoms. Sometimes he maintains that if motion, distance traversed, or speed is divisible, so is the time taken;[49] while sometimes he maintains the converse—viz., that, if the time taken is divisible, then at constant speed so are the motion

---

47. See Heinze 1892, pp. 5–10, on Porphyry's commentary on Ptolemy's *Harmonics* (Wallis) p. 213.

48. *De caelo* III 1, 299a9; III 4, 303a20.

49. Aristotle, *Phys.* VI 1, 232a18–22; VI 2, 232b20–233a12; 233b19–33; VI 4, 235a22–24.

and the distance traversed.[50] It is the second claim which introduces indivisible times; for it implies that if there is an indivisible
distance, then, at a given speed, your movement across it (or
rather, as he maintains, your jerk across it) cannot take less than a
certain time. But the words "at a given speed" constitute a most
important qualification. For suppose it is possible to increase indefinitely the number of indivisible spaces traversed per minute;
then the time taken over each space can surely be indefinitely
small, and there will not be indivisible times after all.

In any case, the argument does not seem to concern time itself,
but only the time taken to traverse a given space. In order to
reach any conclusion about time itself, more elaborate considerations would be needed. It might be argued, for example, that the
stars which constitute our heavenly clock are taken as having a
constant speed and that if they had to traverse indivisible spaces,
the time spent in each space would be a minimal time. Perhaps
this is what Aristotle had in mind, although he does not mention
it. But if so, it is not enough for his purposes. For it leaves open
the possibility of adopting additional clocks with faster moving
indicators.

Help might be sought from a claim which Aristotle makes in
another place (*De caelo* II 6, 288b30–289a4). Not only is there a
minimum time and a maximum speed for the revolution of the
heavens; but also for every action, for walking or playing the lyre,
there is a minimum time and maximum speed for actions of that
kind. Perhaps, then, clock indicators cannot move indefinitely
fast. But this will not settle the matter, for it should be possible to
use two more clocks whose jerks are out of phase with each
other by amounts as small as we please. Perhaps Aristotle would
not consider relying on clocks other than the heavenly one, since
he certainly argues for the superiority of the heavenly motion to
all others. But then, that argument presupposes that the heavenly
motion will not occur by jerks.

There is a related oversight in Aristotle's argument at VI 10,
240b31–241a1. For here he supposes that an indivisible body
could perform its jerks only (*monachōs*) if time were made up of

50. Aristotle, *Phys.* VI 1, 232a18–22; VI 2, 233a13–21; VI 4, 235a18–22.

indivisible nows. Why *only*? He has proved very satisfactorily that an indivisible body could move only by jerking. But why should not the time between jerks be indefinitely small, and why should not time itself still be infinitely divisible? What I have been suggesting is that more argument is needed.

Despite these oversights, many of Aristotle's arguments against atomism proved influential. I shall here select only two specimen arguments, which will be relevant to what follows. The first concerns the atomist commitment to jerky motion, which is alleged to be impossible. Moving is not possible either for an indivisible body[51] or across indivisible spaces.[52] For if a body is engaged in moving into an adjacent space, there has to be a stage when part of the body has entered part of the adjacent space, while part of it occupies part of the original space. Clearly, this would be impossible if the body or the spaces lacked parts. In that event, the body could never *be moving* but could at best *have moved*, with a jerk. But such jerky motion would be thoroughly paradoxical. For one thing, a body which was moving by jerks across three indivisible spaces would be not moving but resting in every one of them.[53] (This last point brings us close to a certain reconstruction of Zeno's arrow which was rejected above.)

In attacking indivisible magnitudes here, Aristotle is attacking both indivisible moving bodies and indivisible distances traversed. The former of these two attacks is already formulated in Plato's *Parmenides,* from which Aristotle took it.[54] The response of the later atomists, Diodorus Cronus and Epicurus, was simply to agree that motion must take place in this funny way by jerks.[55]

In the other argument to be cited, Aristotle denies that indivisibles can be so arranged as to build up a continuum.[56] They cannot, first, be continuous (*suneches*) with each other, nor, second, in contact (*haptomenon*), for both these modes of arrangement are defined in terms of *edges*: the edges must either be one or at least

51. Aristotle, *Phys.* VI 4, 234b10–20; VI 10, 240b8–241a6.
52. Aristotle, *Phys.* VI 1, 231b18–232a17.
53. Aristotle, *Phys.* VI 1, 232a12–17.
54. Plato, *Parmenides,* 138D2–E7.
55. For Epicurus, see Themistius, *in Phys.,* 184.9; Simplicius, *in Phys.,* 934.24. For Diodorus, see Sextus, *Adv. math.* X 48; 85–90; 97–102; 143 (cf. 120); *Pyrrhonian Hypotyposes* II 245; III 71.
56. Aristotle, *Phys.* VI 1, 231a21–b18.

be together. But an entity which lacks parts cannot have an edge as distinct from an interior, so Aristotle claims. Contact is an impossible arrangement also, because, for partless entities, it cannot be contact of part with part, nor of part with whole, while contact of whole with whole will not give us spatially separate parts.[57] Third, if the indivisible entities are points or instants, they cannot be in succession (*ephexēs*) to each other, that is, next to each other in an order of first, second, and third, because any two will be separated by further entities of the same kind; and that conflicts with the definition of successiveness.

Quite apart from the other flaws in Aristotle's argument,[58] he has left a big loophole for later atomists, a loophole which Diodorus and Epicurus were to exploit, as we shall see. For he has so far denied only regarding points and instants, not regarding atoms,[59] that they might be arranged successively (*ephexēs*). Indeed, he elsewhere acknowledges that if there were time atoms, they would be so arranged.[60] The Aristotelian author of *De lineis insecabilibus* seems to have felt uncomfortable about the loophole left here.[61] For he first considers the un-Aristotelian

57. Why should contact between atoms not be edge to edge, without involving contact between parts or wholes? Aristotle is probably relying on his mistaken view that edges are parts, but a better argument could be constructed: two atoms will contact each other not along the whole of their peripheries but along only part. But the peripheries can hardly have parts if the atoms themselves do not.

58. Other flaws: (i) From the beginning, Aristotle's attack seems more directed against points than against atoms. For he introduces his arguments (231a24) as showing that, if anything is a genuine continuum, it will not be composed of indivisibles. Atomists could afford to agree and to reply that they do not regard bodies as being genuine continua. Fortunately for Aristotle, some of his objections tend to show that *non*continua cannot be composed of indivisibles either, but others (231b10–12; b15–18) would establish only the more limited conclusion. (ii) Aristotle depends on the mistaken idea that edges are *parts* and so cannot belong to *partless* entities. (iii) Why, further, suppose that continuity, contact, and succession, as here defined, are the only possible arrangements? Aristotle himself mentions that between any two points there are others, without recognizing that this fact might be used for defining the way in which points can be arranged so as to compose a continuum.

59. Aristotle, *Phys.* VI 1, 231b7; 9–10; b13. (The Oxford translation is wrong to refer to parts, instead of points, in the last passage.) Admittedly, Aristotle has a further argument against a successive arrangement (231b10–12 and 15–18), but this argument applies to points more easily than to atoms for the reason given under (i) in n. 58 above.

60. Aristotle, *Phys.* VIII 8, 264a4.

61. Ps.-Aristotle, *Lin. insec.*, 971b26–972a1.

alternative that succession does after all involve contact;[62] but fail-ing that, we are to fall back on one of Aristotle's other argu-ments.[63]

8. Diodorus Cronus

Diodorus Cronus probably overlapped with Aristotle, although his death has recently been brought down from 307 B.C. to ca. 284 B.C., thirty-eight years after Aristotle's.[64] He supported atomism, but he had clearly taken to heart Aristotle's objections, inter alia Aristotle's complaint that if you believe in atomic spaces or bodies, you will be committed to atomic movements or jerks. For Diodorus accepted atomic spaces and bodies and accepted the contention that these entailed atomic movements.[65] His response was to *accept* the resulting atomic movement[66] and to ask what was wrong with it. Admittedly it involves something's having moved (perfect tense) in a jerk, without there ever being a stage at which it *is moving* (present tense). But then there is nothing unusual, he said, about being able to use the perfect without the present: we may be able to say of a woman that she *has had* three husbands, without ever being able to say "she now has three husbands."[67]

Exception may be taken to my saying that Diodorus supported atomism. For he was a dialectician, and this might encourage the belief that he had no doctrines of his own but simply argued on either side of a question and sought to embarrass others. But I do not believe that this can be the case. For Sextus Empiricus pre-sents Diodorus's ideas on atomic bodies, spaces, and movements as his "personal doctrine" (*oikeion dogma*, *Adversus mathematicos* X 86) and as something he "taught" (*edidaske*, X 97; 143). It is the skeptic Sextus who likes to collect arguments on both sides of every case. But Sextus treats Diodorus as a man with a doctrine in

---

62. Aristotle allows this not for succession (*ephexēs*) but only for the different relation of neighboring (*echomenon*; *Phys.* V 3, 227a6–7).
63. 231b15–18 is the original for 971b28–972a1.
64. Sedley 1977.
65. Sextus, *Adv. math.* X 85–86.
66. Sextus, *Adv. math.* X 48; 85–90; 143; *Pyrrh. hyp.* II 245; III 71.
67. Sextus, *Adv. math.* X 91–92; 97–101.

X 86 and contrasts him with the skeptics (*hoi apo tēs skepseōs*). Moreover, he reports no arguments by Diodorus on the other side, against atomism. Diodorus, we have seen, presented the divorce of the perfect tense from the present not as an embarrassment for atomism but rather as something we ought to accept.

It is fairly widely agreed that Diodorus made this contribution to atomist theory, namely, accepting atomic jerks. What I now want to see is what other contributions he made, if any. There is an important argument recorded by Sextus in *Adversus mathematicos* X 119–20. If, as I believe, the original author was Diodorus, then his influence on the development of atomism is likely to have been much greater than hitherto supposed. For what I want to argue is that the passage contains two important, but neglected, atomist ideas, both of them responses to Aristotle. One is the hypothesis of time atoms; the other is the suggestion that atoms can stand to each other in a successive relation of first, second, third. It is not generally accepted that Diodorus believed in time atoms,[68] and indeed Wehrli once suggested that time atoms were later introduced by Strato precisely as a riposte to Diodorus.[69]

The sections leading up to our passage relate arguments by Didorus against the idea that anything ever is moving. *Adversus mathematicos* X 85 introduces a "weighty" argument by him; X 112 presents some "less weighty and more sophistical" arguments of his. Our passage is then introduced, at the end of X 118, by the statement that these less weighty arguments should be set aside and use made instead of "those arguments." The statement admittedly does not explicitly mention Diodorus. But the word "those" supports the suggestion made by Nicholas Denyer that what follows is being viewed as merely a version of the "weighty" argument of Diodorus. It does indeed include an idea which

68. Not even by those readiest to detect time atomism: Sambursky and Krämer. Jürgen Mau remarks in passing that Diodorus has an atomism of time, space, and matter, but this does not look like a considered conclusion, since the texts he cites do not support him as regards time (Mau 1955, p. 107). After I had written this chapter, however, Nicholas Denyer showed me an unpublished work in which he independently ascribes time atomism to Diodorus, on the basis of the same passage. I am grateful to him, moreover, for defending our common interpretation from attack at two points to be recorded below.

69. Wehrli 1944–59, V (first ed. only), p. 63.

forms part of the "weighty" argument and which is repeatedly ascribed to Diodorus, namely, the idea that a thing does not move when it is in either the first place or the second.[70] The following is a translation of X 119–20.

> If a thing moves [present tense], it moves now. If it moves now, it moves in the present (*enestōti*). If it moves in the present, it must move in a partless (*amerēs*) time. For if the present has parts, it will inevitably be divided into a past and a future part, and so will no longer be present.

> If a thing moves in a partless time, it traverses partless places. But if it traverses partless places, it is not moving [present tense—the continuous form of the present is not differentiated in the Greek, but it makes the ensuing argument go better]. For when it is in the first partless place, it is not moving, since it is still in the first partless place. And when it is in the second partless place, again it is not moving but rather *has moved*. Therefore a thing never *is moving*.

There is more than one reason for construing the partless time here not as a sizeless instant but as a time atom. To begin with, the partless places appear to be space atoms, not points, since, first, if they were sizeless points, the author would not allow that one could *have moved* across them; to have "traversed" a sizeless point is not to have made any progress at all. Second, Aristotle had successfully proved for points, but not for atoms, that it is impossible to arrange them successively in an order of first and second, in the way the partless places are arranged here.[71] Third, we have in any case been told a little earlier that Diodorus accepts space atoms. The partless places, then, are atoms; and if so, the partless times, which are cited as putatively adequate for traversing them, will surely be atoms, too. This is confirmed by a further consideration: if the author had been thinking of instants rather than of time atoms, he would have had a quicker proof available that nothing can be moving (present tense). For it is

70. Sextus, *Adv. math.* X 86–90; *Pyrrh. hyp.* II 245; III 71. For further evidence see Sedley 1977, n. 55.

71. Aristotle, *Phys.* VI 1, 231b6–10. The first and second partless places here are meant to be *next* to each other. They are not merely the first and second of two places randomly selected for consideration, for then the argument would be incomplete until it eliminated moving at intervening places.

much more obvious that an instant, being sizeless, leaves no room for moving.

One objection deserves consideration. For it might be thought that the time atoms mentioned here are needed only on the assumption that something "moves in the present" and that this assumption comes to be rejected with the denial that anything ever is moving. But this is not the structure of the argument: the need for partless times does not arise from the assumption that something moves in the present. It is argued on the different ground that a divisible present would be divided into past and future.[72]

The acceptance of time atoms in this context can be set along-side Diodorus's acceptance of atomic motions as constituting a further atomist response to Aristotle, who expected that neither would prove acceptable. By a further irony, the argument for time atoms takes a leaf out of Aristotle's book. For Aristotle had used the same proof that the present must be indivisible (otherwise it would overlap with past and future).[73] But he had taken the indivisible present to be an instant, not an atom.

What I have so far emphasized in the passage X 119–20 is the adoption of time atoms. But it contains another important feature: the suggestion that atomic spaces can be arranged in an order of first and second. This exploits the loophole that we saw Aristotle leaving. When he denied that indivisibles could be so arranged as to form bodies, he omitted, in the case of atoms, to exclude the possibility that they might be arranged successively in an order of first and second. It is just this possibility which X 120 exploits.

If Diodorus is the original source of X 119–20, he will have made three contributions to the atomist reply to Aristotle by accepting atomic movement, atomic time, and the successive arrangement of atoms. But there is yet another contribution he makes, namely by providing new arguments for accepting atomism. One argument is that atomism helps with a kind of paradox first introduced by Aristotle.[74] Aristotle's version concerns an approaching object and the first position at which it is visible as

72. I owe this reply to Denyer.
73. Aristotle, *Phys.* VI 3, 234a9–19.
74. Aristotle, *De sensu* 7, 449a20–31. I have discussed this in Sorabji 1979.

distinguished from the last at which it is still invisible. Any decision about the relation of these two positions to each other seems to make the object simultaneously visible and invisible or, alternately, neither visible nor invisible.

It looks as if there must have been a related paradox which considered not a nearest *position* of invisibility but a largest *size* of invisibility. The question would be the relation of this size to the smallest size at which the object was visible. What I want to suggest is that Diodorus considered these paradoxes in their most general form, and solved them by postulating space atoms.[75] The paradoxes would be solved if the nearest position of invisibility was a space atom adjacent to the farthest position of visibility and, again, if the largest size of invisibility was smaller by one space atom than the smallest of visibility.

The evidence that Diodorus argued for atoms in this way is given by Alexander in his commentary on Aristotle's *De sensu*, where he says: "But if nothing is by its nature the smallest perceptible, nor the largest imperceptible, it could not be shown, as Diodorus thinks he shows, that anything is by its nature the smallest magnitude."[76] Commenting on the paradox concerning the nearest position of invisibility, Alexander says: "It looks for these reasons as if Aristotle was the first to raise and exploit the problem about partless entities, which was raised by Diodorus or someone. But whereas Aristotle invented the problem and made sound use of it, the others took it from him, prided themselves on it, and used it illegitimately."[77]

Others have interpreted Alexander's remarks quite differently.[78] But the advantages of this interpretation are, first, that it takes account of Diodorus's referring to a largest imperceptible size, as well as to a smallest perceptible one and, second, that it takes account of the context of the first quotation from Alexander, namely, a discussion of Aristotle's analogous paradox about distances.

Now that I have considered four atomist responses to Aristotle,

75. The evidence is differently interpreted in Mau 1955 and in Sedley 1977.
76. Alexander, *in Sens.*, 122.21–23.
77. Alexander, *in Sens.*, 172.28–173.1.
78. Sedley 1977; Mau 1955.

it is time to review the historical situation. The new atomist moves are indebted to Aristotle at almost every point. In Sextus's *Adversus mathematicos* X 119–20, Diodorus exploits the loophole left by Aristotle of arranging atoms successively. He borrows Aristotle's argument for the indivisibility of the present. The idea that that present might be an atom rather than an instant was first brought into prominence by Aristotle, even though he rejected it. Diodorus accepts from Aristotle the idea that motion at indivisible times entails motion through indivisible places and that motion through indivisible places entails having moved without ever being in the process of moving. The idea that the perfect tense might be so used in divorce from the present had been raised by Aristotle. And although he rejected it for the case of motion, I shall argue elsewhere that he accepted it for the *ceasing* of instants and points.[79] Diodorus had a similar interest in the problem of *when* things cease to be[80] and may well have followed Aristotle's solution that we can in some cases say that they *have* ceased without its ever being true to say that they *are* ceasing. We have further seen that Diodorus adapted Aristotle's argument about the farthest distance of visibility and nearest of invisibility, in order to produce an argument for atomic sizes. Finally, Diodorus had a famous argument called the Master Argument, which looks like a riposte to Aristotle's treatment of determinism in *De interpretatione* 9.[81] His conclusion is that what is possible will at some time be actual, and Jürgen Mau has suggested that this too could have been used as an argument in support of atomism.[82]

There is a difficulty over the suggestion that Diodorus made all the contributions to atomism which I have been discussing. For certain features of these contributions are common to Diodorus and Epicurus, so that a question of priority arises. We are told, for example, that Epicurus accepted atomic motion, and that his

79. Aristotle, *Metaph.* III 5, 1002a28–b11; VIII 3, 1043b14–16; *Phys.* VI 6, 237b10–11. These passages will be discussed in my forthcoming book on the philosophy of time in antiquity.

80. Sextus, *Adv. math.* X 347–49; there are similar puzzles at IX 269; X 207–11; X 344–50; *Pyrrh. hyp.* III 110–14; 149–50.

81. For the argument, see Epictetus, *Dissertationes* II.19.1. I have summarized the relation to Aristotle's *De interpretatione* 9 in Sorabji 1980, chap. 6.

82. Since nothing will ever be actually divided infinitely, nothing is infinitely divisible (Mau 1954a, pp. 28–31).

motive for accepting it was the same as that which I have ascribed to Diodorus, namely, to accommodate Aristotle's arguments.[83] We shall see also that Epicurus accepted time atoms and the successive ordering of minima. Diodorus was the older man, but, according to Sedley's dating, Epicurus will have joined him in Athens, when, aged thirty-four, he set up his school there in 306 B.C. And he will have remained with Diodorus in Athens until Diodorus moved to Alexandria in the late 290s. Sextus makes clear that it was Diodorus who pioneered the acceptance of atomic motion and devised the arguments to make that palatable, while Alexander reveals that it was Diodorus who adapted Aristotle's *De sensu* to produce an argument for atomism. We also find in Diodorus (*apud* Sextum, *Adversus mathematicos* X 119), not in Epicurus, an argument that the present must be a time atom. Most of the innovation so far discussed seems therefore to belong to Diodorus. But I shall nonetheless argue that, at least in what remains extant, Epicurus does more to make intelligible the idea that particles can be successive without touching. I would claim no more than that Diodorus must be credited with a good proportion of the innovations.

9. Epicurus and His Followers

The two-tier theory of Epicurus (341–270 B.C.), according to which there are minimal parts within an atom, is expounded as part of the summary of his views in his *Letter to Herodotus* 57–59. The majority, though not unanimous, view of scholars is that the minimal parts, unlike the atoms, are *conceptually* indivisible, and I am convinced by this.[84]

Epicurus gives two reasons for believing in conceptually indivisible minimal parts (*Letter to Herodotus* 57). The first reason is modeled on an argument in fragment 1 of Zeno of Elea. We must reject infinite divisibility because infinitely many components, all having a size, would add up to an infinitely large body. Second, if there were an infinity of parts, then, in conceiving the whole, our mind could, *per impossibile*, arrive at infinity. This second difficul-

83. Themistius, *in Phys.*, 184.28; Simplicius, *in Phys.*, 934.18–30.
84. See the arguments in Furley 1967, pp. 21 and 42.

ty is not in Zeno, although the impossibility of counting to infinity is exploited in Xenocrates' elaboration of Zeno's paradox about traversing half-distances.

In the period under discussion, most of the arguments for conceptual indivisibility (as distinguished from merely physical indivisibility) turn on paradoxes, and among the paradoxes exploited those of Zeno are the most popular. So I might choose this moment to survey the examples of his influence. First we have seen that his paradox of traversing half-distances was exploited by Xenocrates and possibly by Democritus. A later Epicurean, Demetrius of Laconia, may also have used this argument in the late second century B.C., since there is a fragment in which he discusses cutting a half and cutting half of the resulting half ad infinitum.[85] Second, we are told by some sources that the paradox of dividing something at every point was Zeno's,[86] and we have seen that this was exploited by Democritus. Third, there was an atomist argument that large would not be distinct from small if both alike had infinitely many parts. This appears as the first argument in *De lineis insecabilibus* in Epicurus's Roman expositor, Lucretius, and as a jibe against the Stoics in Plutarch.[87] It is an adaptation of Zeno's argument in fragment 1 from infinitely many parts to infinite size. Fourth, we have just seen Epicurus exploiting Zeno's fragment 1 in a more direct way. Finally, Diodorus Cronus supports the idea of atomic motions with the argument that a thing can move neither in the place where it is nor in the place where it is not; and this argument is ascribed by some sources to Zeno.[88]

In what immediately follows (57–59), Epicurus introduces an important innovation mentioned earlier in this chapter. We are to understand the idea of a smallest *conceivable* part on the analogy of a smallest *perceptible* part. I am not convinced by Sedley's interesting suggestion that this idea is already in Diodorus.[89] I be-

---

85. Falco 1923, p. 97 (Pap. 1061), further reconstructed in Luria 1932–33, p. 131.

86. See Simplicius, *in Phys.*, 139.26–140.26, citing the authority of Alexander of Aphrodisias.

87. Lucretius, *De rerum natura* I 615–27; Plutarch, *Com. Not.* 38, 1079A–B.

88. Diogenes Laertius, *Lives of Eminent Philosophers* 9, 72; Epiphanius, *Adversus haereses* 3, 11.

89. In Sedley 1977 this is how Diodorus's use of the argument about a largest imperceptible and smallest perceptible size is interpreted. But the interpretation makes no use of the reference to the largest imperceptible.

lieve that Epicurus's discussion has a striking implication: when we try to discriminate a smallest perceptible area within (say) a blackboard, the area we choose is probably too small for us to *perceive* any edge to it and hence any shape. By analogy we should be unable to *conceive* an edge or shape in the smallest conceivable part. There has been much discussion of the shape to be ascribed to Epicurus's minimal parts. My suggestion is that they have no shape at all.

I am glad to find that Sedley (followed by Konstan) has anticipated me in two aspects of the above interpretation. For he too has suggested that Epicurus's minimal parts may be edgeless and shapeless. And he has further construed Epicurus's analogy with sense perception as I do, that is, as intended to show how conceptually indivisible parts are *possible* rather than to prove that they actually exist.[90] This makes Epicurus's argument differ at this point from those of Berkeley and Hume. Both these thinkers argued from a minimum extension in our *ideas* to the conclusion that there must be, not merely that there can be, a minimum conceivable extension in *reality*. Furley is right, however, to bring out the many similarities between Hume's arguments and those of Epicurus.[91]

I should like, however, to take the suggestion of edgelessness one stage further. For if the minimal parts in the atom have no edges, this could be used to show how it is possible for them to be arranged successively next to each other without being in contact. We have seen that Aristotle left the loophole of a successive arrangement without contact and that Diodorus exploited it. What I am suggesting is that by relieving his minimal parts of edges, Epicurus may have been trying to show how it is legitimate to postulate such an arrangement. For a lack of edges will prevent the minimal parts from satisfying Aristotle's definition of contact (they cannot have *edges* together), but not from satisfying his definition of successiveness (two can be arranged so as to have nothing of the same kind in between).

That Epicurus used the loophole of postulating a merely succes-

90. Sedley 1976, n. 2; Konstan 1979, p. 405.
91. Berkeley, *New Theory of Vision* and *Third Dialogue between Hylas and Philonous*; Hume, *A Treatise of Human Nature*, Bk. I, pt. II, secs. 1–4, discussed by Furley 1967, chap. 10.

sive relationship cannot be made certain. Thus the word *hexēs* (in succession), which is applied in *Letter to Herodotus* 58 to the analogous minima in *perception*, may refer only to the order of our *viewing* them and not to the order of the minimal perceptibles themselves. But Lucretius (I 605–6), in describing Epicurus's conceptual minima, talks of them as being arranged *ex ordine* (in order). And the Epicurean Demetrius of Laconia uses the word *hexēs* of Epicurus's successive times without describing these times as being contiguous.[92] Against these occurrences of the words *hexēs* and *ex ordine*, there is no mention anywhere, so far as I know, of conceptual minima being in contact, even though there would have been ample opportunity for such mention in *Letter to Herodotus* 58 and Lucretius I 605–6.

There are many rival hypotheses about how Epicurus arranged his conceptual minima. Mau thinks the relationship is left unclear, Furley that it is edge-to-edge contact. Krämer sees Epicurus's answer in the phrase in *Letter to Herodotus* 58, "measuring in their distinct way," the distinctness (*idiotēs*) being opposed, he suggests, to coalescence. Konstan suggests that the smallest parts of the atom are inconceivable except as parts of a whole and that if follows that no question can arise of how one part attaches to the whole.[93]

When Epicurus says of perceptible minima that we see them neither in the same place nor touching part to part, he is showing, as Mau points out, that he has not fallen into Aristotle's trap (*Physics* VI 1, 231b2–6, discussed above) of postulating contact of whole to whole, which would be amalgamation, or of part to part. My suggestion, in effect, is that Epicurus is also showing that he is not open to Aristotle's other objection against contact. That is Aristotle's argument (*Physics* VI 1, 231a27–29) that since indivisibles lack edges, they cannot have edges together.

The other feature of Epicurus's theory to which I shall draw attention is his acceptance of indivisible times. There is not a two-tier distinction here between time atoms and minimal parts of time. I shall call the minimal times time atoms, because that is

92. Demetrius of Leconia, Herculanean papyrus 1012, col. 31, 4–8, printed in Falco 1923, p. 40, and more recently in Puglia 1980, p. 42.
93. Mau 1954a, pp. 36–37; Furley 1967, pp. 115–16; Krämer 1971, pp. 243–44; Konstan 1979, 398–407.

the expression I have been using in connection with other think-ers. The only contrast is with certain longer periods, namely, the least *perceptible* times. That Epicurus believed in time atoms is attested by a number of sources. Two of them, Sextus and Simpli-cius, ascribe a "least" and "partless" (*elachiston, ameres*) time only to the *followers* of Epicurus (those *peri* or *kata* him).[94] But as Sedley points out, phrases of this kind were commonly used to mean Epicurus *and* his followers. This testimony makes it reasonable to see references to atomic times in various other passages. Lucre-tius says that "in a single time during which we have perception, there are hidden many times whose existence is discovered by reason."[95] This Latin exposition corresponds to the phraseology used by Epicurus himself in the *Letter to Herodotus* 47 and 62, where he speaks of times that are contemplated by reason (as opposed to sense perception). One commentator, while accepting the other testimony, rejects this last, on the grounds that the plural "times" implies that Epicurus is talking of periods of differ-ent lengths, all below the threshold of perception but not atomic because not equal in length.[96] However, the plural is much more easily explained by the fact that in each context Epicurus is con-trasting the times which are contemplated by reason with a long-er period, in one case with a perceptible time, in another with the least *continuous* time. The times contemplated by reason are mentioned in the plural, because it takes a plurality of them to match one of the longer periods mentioned.

There is one more piece of evidence for time atoms in Epicurus, in the passage referred to above from Demetrius of Laconia. According to the last two editors, Falco (1923) and Puglia (1980), the successive times of which Demetrius talks in this passage are also called minimal times. The rolls, however, rescued from the volcanic ash at Herculaneum, are difficult to read, and David Sedley has kindly reinspected this portion for me. According to this reading, the reference is to a minimal *particle* (*to elachiston*) which emerges at the next time, rather than to a particle which emerges at the next minimal time (*chronon elachiston*).[97]

94. Sextus, *Adv. math.* X 142–48; Simplicius, *in Phys.*, 934.26.
95. Lucretius, *De rerum natura* IV 794–96.
96. Boyancé 1974.
97. V. de Falco: *kata ton hexēs chronon, touto[n d' e]lachiston, to echomeno[n] euthus akolouthēsēi.*

I think the evidence for time atoms in Epicurus is good enough, even though the testimony of Themistius seems to me to count against, rather than for, the attribution. Themistius brings it as an objection against Epicurus (an invalid objection, as it happens) that his jerky movement would imply time atoms.[98] This suggests he was unaware that time atomism was actually endorsed by Epicurus. But one recent paper makes a more far-reaching case against time atoms in Epicurus.[99] The main objection is that Epicurus gives to time a low ontological status, making it an attribute of an attribute or even a mere appearance. From this it follows that time is not a substance composed of atoms and void. But I would not agree that it follows that time is not quantized. Nor does the author take account of the positive evidence for time atoms supplied by Sextus and (perhaps) Demetrius of Laconia.

Outside the Epicurean school I know of no subsequent endorsement of time atoms among the philosophers of antiquity; but this will need arguing: for a start, some have found time atoms in Strato.

10. Strato

Strato was head of Aristotle's Lyceum from 288 to ca. 269 B.C. while Diodorus was in Alexandria and Epicurus still teaching in Athens. The difficulty about his view is created by a passage in Sextus Empiricus:

> It remains, then, to consider whether anything can be moving if some things are divided infinitely while others stop at a partless segment. Indeed, the followers of Strato the physicist were drawn in this direction. For they supposed that time stopped at a partless segment, while bodies and places were divided infinitely, and that a thing in motion moved a whole divisible distance at one go in a partless time and not part before part.[100]

E. Puglia: *kata ton hexēs chronon, to[n e]lachiston to echom[[..]]eno[n] euthus akolouthēsē(i)*.
D. Sedley: *kata ton hexēs chronon pou to [el]achiston to echom[[..]]enon euthus akolouthēsē(i)*.

98. Themistius, *in Phys.*, 184.28–185.3.
99. Caujoulle-Zaslawsky 1980. I omit here her case against atoms of space and motion in Epicurus.
100. Sextus, *Adv. math.* X 155.

How can this report be squared with the clear statement of Simplicius that for Strato time was continuous and infinitely divisible? According to Simplicius, Strato departed from Aristotle's idea that time is a kind of number, on the grounds that the whole numbers form a discontinuous series, whereas time is continuous.[101] The phrase "followers of Strato" is not likely to be intended to *distinguish* between Strato and his followers.

Two passages have been or might be misused in the attempt to show that Strato did hold an atomist view of time. A few lines later, Simplicius records one of Strato's objections to the view that time is a number: "Again, the unit and the now will be identical if time is a number, for time will be composed of nows, and number of units."[102] Here Strato is not *endorsing* the idea that time is composed of nows, whether the nows be atomic or instantaneous. Rather he is treating that as an absurd consequence of the view he is opposing. This only confirms that, in his own view, time is continuous.

The other misusable passage comes from Damascius. "Is not time continuous yet separated, as he [Plato] shows? Yes, it is; but it is composed not of partless parts, but of separated lengths. For it consists, as Strato says, of parts which do not stay put; hence of separated parts. Yet each part is continuous, and is, as it were, a measure composed of many measures."[103] Sambursky interprets Damascius, in a way to be contested below, as believing that time comes in atomic jerks, and he translates the word *dihōrismena* as "discrete" rather than separated, taking the reference to be to atomic jerks. Nonetheless, as Sambursky himself recognizes (ad loc.), the word *dihōrismena* does not enter into what is directly ascribed to Strato. It is doubtful that anything more is ascribed to him than the idea that time consists of parts which do not stay put. The last two passages, then, add no further support to Sextus's idea that time was atomic for Strato.

I suggest that a solution may be found in a further report by Simplicius: "But Strato of Lampsacus says that motion is con-

---

101. Simplicius, *in Phys.*, 789.4.
102. Simplicius, *in Phys.*, 789.14–15.
103. Damascius, *Dub. et sol.* II 236.9–13; in Sambursky and Pines 1971, p. 88.5–10.

tinuous not simply because of magnitude, but also in itself."[104] Strato's idea is that although motion is continuous, it does not owe its continuity to that of distance. Perhaps then he argued in the same way about time: although time is continuous, it does not owe its continuity to that of distance. For it would be conceptually possible to have distances continuous, but motion and time discontinuous.

If Strato objected in this way to Aristotle's claim that the continuity of one entails the continuity of the others, this could explain Sextus's taking him (wrongly) to be arguing that time is in fact atomic. How might Strato's argument have gone? Suppose that each moving thing moved in little jerks, reappearing at a distance from where it was before without ever being in between. Suppose, too, that while jerks might occur over infinitely varying *distances*, they were all synchronized to occur only at certain fixed intervals of *time*. Strato might have supposed that, if these intervals were very small, they could in principle be atomic. Certainly, they would not be interrupted by moving things making any progress, since progress is postulated as occurring only at the *end* of an interval. Such a conception is not without difficulty. (Would not these atomic times without motion be undetectable, for example?) But Strato might have supposed such a situation conceivable. He would then conclude that while time is in fact continuous, its continuity is not guaranteed by the continuity of space.

Alternatively, Strato may have been making a simpler point, not about time itself, but about the time any individual takes between jerks. On this conception, the jerks of two different moving bodies could be staggered, so that the time one body spent resting was punctuated by the jerk of another body. Time would not itself be atomic in that case. But there could still be a certain minimum time such that the jerks of an individual body could not be more closely spaced than that. Strato's point would again be that although this does not in fact happen, it is not excluded by the continuity of space.

104. Simplicius, *in Phys.*, 711.9–10.

11. Plutarch

Several authors find time atomism at much later dates in the Platonist tradition—for example, in Plutarch of Chaeronea (ca. A.D. 46–120), who lived over three hundred years after Strato's death, and Damascius, second from last of the great Athenian Neoplatonists, who lived over seven hundred years later. But the gap is bridged by a continuous history of struggle with Aristotle's paradoxes from *Physics* IV 10 about the unreality of time. Aristotle raised the problem that none of the parts of time exist: the past no longer exists, the future does not yet exist, and the present, although it may exist, is a sizeless instant and so not a *part* of time. Soon after Strato's death, the Stoic Chrysippus (ca. 279–ca.206 B.C.) had considered the problem.[105] Plutarch reports Chrysippus's position with contempt and complains that he cannot resuce the reality of time by representing the present as a time atom with a positive size and hence as a *part* of time.

> It is contrary to common conceptions to say that there is future and past time and not present time but that recently and the other day subsist (*huphestanai*), while there is no now at all. Yet this is what happens to the Stoics, who do not allow a minimal (*elachiston*) time and do not want now to be indivisible (*ameres*) but say, whenever someone thinks he has grasped something and conceived it as present, that part of it is future and part of it is past. Thus nothing remains level with now, nor is any part of the present left, if of the time which is said to be present some is assigned to the future and some to the past.[106]

Plutarch goes on to add that the past and future are little better off than the present for Chrysippus, since they are granted mere subsistence (*huphestēkenai*), not full reality (*huparchein*).

Some have thought that, in desiderating a minimal, indivisible time, in other words, a time atom, Plutarch was expressing his own view.[107] But in fact his aim is simply to attack the Stoics, and

105. Plutarch, *Com. Not.*, 41, 1081F; Arius Didymus, in Diels, *Doxographici Graeci*, p. 461.
106. Plutarch, *Com. Not.* 41, 1081C–D.
107. Luria 1932–33, p. 163; Krämer 1971, p. 351.

he does not commit himself on how he would solve the problem. The time atom which Chrysippus had rejected was postulated by Diodorus and Epicurus. It is not an Academic time atom to which Plutarch, as a Platonist, is committed. Indeed, Plutarch tells us that his own teacher retailed the argument that the present gets squeezed out into the past and future and, significantly, does not add that the solution is a time atom.[108]

The other passage where time atomism has been detected[109] seems to me to be concerned with a wholly different topic: spatial, not temporal, indivisibility. The same "now" is found everywhere, in Rhodes and in Athens. If it is thus (spatially) extended, why is it not (spatially) divisible? Evidently because it is incorporeal. This discussion goes back to Plato's treatment of a day as being in many places at once and yet not separate from itself.[110]

12. Damascius

Damascius's teaching in Athens was brought to an end by Justinian's closing of the Neoplatonist school in A.D. 529. He too discussed Aristotle's paradoxes about the unreality of time, and Sambursky sees his solution to the present paradox as resting on time atoms.[111] What Damascius says is that the present is not a mere instant but a whole; and since this has a span, it can be called a *part* of time. Hence one of the parts of time does exist:

> I am impressed by how they solve Zeno's problem by saying that the movement is not completed with an indivisible bit, but rather progresses in a whole stride (*bēma*) at once. The half does not always precede the whole, but sometimes the movement as it were leaps (*huperallesthai*) over both whole and part. But those who said that only an *indivisible* now existed did not recognize the same thing happening in the case of time. For time always accompanies movement and as it were runs along with it, so that it strides along together with it in a whole continuous jump (*pēdēma*) and does not

108. Plutarch, *On the E at Delphi*, 392F.
109. By H. J. Krämer in Krämer 1971, p. 351.
110. Plato, *Parmenides*, 131B.
111. Sambursky and Pines 1971, p. 18, extracted from Sambursky 1968, pp. 153–67.

progress one now at a time ad infinitum. This must be the case because motion obviously occurs in things, and because Aristotle shows clearly that nothing moves or changes in a now but only *has* moved or changed, whereas things do change and move in time. At any rate, the leap (*halma*) in movement is a *part* of the movement which occurs in the course of moving and will not be taken at the now; nor, being present, will it occur in the non-present (*enestōti*). So that in which the present movement occurs is the present time, and it is infinitely divisible, just as the movement is, for each is continuous, and every continuum is infinitely divisible.[112]

The last words make it abundantly clear that Damascius's jump is not atomic but infinitely divisible. How did Sambursky obtain the opposite impression? I believe he construed an earlier line mistakenly when he translated p. 797, line 2 (in his translation p. 78, line 32), as follows: "Those who say that only the Now is indivisible did not grasp that the indivisible is also inherent in time." What Damascius says is that they did not grasp that "the same thing" happens in the case of time. "The same thing" refers, not to the word "indivisible" in the current sentence, but to the preceding sentence where motion was described as involving leaps. Damascius is saying that time too involves leaps and not merely an indivisible, instantaneous present. I translated: "But those who said that only an *indivisible* now existed did not recognize the same thing happening in the case of time."

We can work out how Damascius's idea of an infinitely divisible leap evolved. Aristotle denies Empedocles' theory that light takes time to travel from the sun. Light can fill a whole space simultaneously (*hama*). Similarly, a pond which is not too large can freeze all over its surface all at once (*athroon*) and not "the half before the whole"; and you get the same effect with heat. It cannot happen with motion, but it can happen with qualitative change and with growth or diminution.[113] Theophrastus, Aristotle's successor, reaffirms that this kind of discontinuity is found, and not only in qualitative change. He uses the point in order to show that there can be a first instant of having changed—something

112. Simplicius, *in Phys.*, 796.32–797.13; in Sambursky and Pines 1971, pp. 78.27–80.5. The doctrine of leaps is repeated in *Dub. et sol.* II 236.12–24.
113. Aristotle, *Sens.* 6, 446a20–447a11; *Phys.* VIII 3, 253b13–31.

which is impossible in the case of *continuous* changes.[114] The example of light leaping is offered as an illustration of Theophrastus's point and recurs in Alexander of Aphrodisias.[115]

We hear of a fresh development in Sextus Empiricus.[116] He starts with the view, which he attributes to the Stoics, that space, time, and motion are all infinitely divisible. But he reports that in spite of calling motion infinitely divisible, some had imagined it as occurring all at once and not the half before the whole. Presumably, the moving body disappears from one position and reappears a little farther on, without an intervening time lapse. The leap can be thought of as infinitely divisible because the distance traversed would be infinitely divisible, and another leap could be across a shorter distance, indeed across a distance as short as you like. Evidently these discontinuous leaps had been used in order to solve a version of Zeno's paradox of the half-distances.[117] Thus, provided a person can leap in the way indicated, it is not necessary for him to go first half the distance, and before that half of the half, ad infinitum, in the way that Zeno's paradox threatens.

This is exactly the idea which inspires Damascius, whose new move is to postulate that discontinuous leaps are found also in *time*. But what can he mean by talking of temporal leaps and by calling them infinitely divisible? I suggest we should think of Aristotle's theory according to which time is the countable aspect of change.[118] Time passes only when there are countably different stages in some change, and we notice it passing only when we notice countably different stages. Further, if the stages which we notice are evenly spaced, and if the change progresses at a uniform rate, then by counting stages we will also be *measuring* the

114. Theophrastus, *apud* Simplicium, *in Phys.*, 107.12–16; and *apud* Themistium, *in Phys.*, 197.4–8.

115. Alexander, *in Sens.*, ad loc.; and in a treatise preserved in Arabic, entitled "That to act is a wider expression than to move, according to Aristotle," translated into French in Badawi 1968, pp. 153 ff.

116. *Adv. math.* X 123–42; *Pyrrh. hyp.* III 76–78.

117. Evidence: discontinuous motion by leaps is subjected to various criticisms but not to Zeno's half-distance objection, which is instead reserved for criticizing the idea of *continuous* motion (*Adv. math.* X 139–41; cf. *Pyrrh. hyp.* III 76). This shows that discontinuous motion by leaps had already been recognized as a device for circumventing Zeno's paradox of the half-distances.

118. *Phys.* IV 11, 219a22–b9.

duration of the change. It is this idea which Damascius takes up when he defines time as "the *measure* of the flow of being."[119] If time simply *is* such a measure, then it will contain leaps. For a measure will record only selected stages of a flow, stages which are separated from each other in a discontinuous series. On the other hand, the leaps can be called infinitely divisible, for the discrete stages recorded by the measure can be as close together as you like.

The theory of temporal leaps raises the difficulty that my temporal leaps could surely be punctuated by the termination of yours. Yet any punctuation of my leap would imply that it can after all be caught partway through and so does after all occur part before whole. Such difficulties did not arise with leaps across spatial distances, because there the *distance* I leaped could be punctuated without the *time* of my leap's being punctuated.

I have brought forward Damascius's theory, not because it was a theory of time atoms (on the contrary, the temporal leaps are infinitely divisible), but because the theory of infinitely divisible jumps or leaps was to be revived in Islamic philosophy precisely as a *rival* to atomistic views.

13. Time Atoms in Musical Theory

I believe that there was no revival of the idea of time atoms among the philosophers of antiquity. The idea did reappear, however, in an unexpected quarter: the theory of music. The story has been told by Lasswitz.[120] Aristotle's pupil, Aristoxenus, discussing vocal music, gave the name "primary time" to the smallest unit of measure in rhythmics. And in the third century A.D., Aristides Quintilianus described this time as atomic (*atomos*) and as the least (*elachistos*). It was the least relative to us and was the first to be grasped in perception. The idea was handed on by Martianus Capella in the fifth century, while in the seventh Isi-

119. Damascius, *apud* Simplicium, *in Phys.*, 774.36; in Samburdky and Pines 1971, p. 65.1.

120. Lasswitz 1890, I, pp. 31–37. He cites Aristoxenus *apud* Porphyrium *in Ptolemaei harmonica*, pp. 255–56; Aristides Quintilianus, *De musica* I 14; Martianus Capella IX 971; Isidore of Seville, *Etymologiae* XIII 2 (*De atomis*), sect. 2–3; Bede, *De temporum ratione*, chap. 3 (*De minutissimis temporum spatiis*).

dore of Seville spoke of the year being divided into atomic times, without any longer making reference to music. The venerable Bede, in A.D. 725, gave these atomic times an absolute length. For whereas in musical theory the length of an atomic time had varied with the piece of music in question, Bede assigned exactly 22,560 time atoms to the hour. Tannery has suggested that this number was designed to provide a common measure for the Julian year and the lunar month.[121] Bede further reports that grammarians had spoken of atomic times, assigning two to a long syllable and one to a short, while astrologers had divided the zodiac into atoms so as to be able to state the exact time of birth for predicting a person's fate. None of these time atoms seems to involve conceptual indivisibility, and so they do not raise the same problems as atomic times in philosophy.

14. Atoms and Time Atoms in Islam

It was in Islamic thought that there was a revival of Greek theories. Soon after A.D. 800, there was a controversy between Naẓẓām (died ca. A.D. 846), who said that things were infinitely divisible, and Abū l-Hudhayl al-'Allāf (died ca. A.D. 841) who took the view, which became orthodox, that there were atoms. The most striking difference from Greek atomism was that Abū l-Hudhayl, and most (although not all) Islamic atomists made their atoms extensionless. Even here, however, Wolfson has traced Greek influence through certain misunderstood reports of Democritus's theory.[122]

Greek influence on Islamic thought is universally recognized in respect of later periods. But recently there has been a tendency among some Islamic scholars to play down Greek influence in connection with this early phase of Islamic thought.[123] I think that this approach remains possible only as long as the Greek side of the story is not fully expounded. For I believe that the parallels are more numerous and closer at this early date than has yet been

121. Tannery 1905. I am grateful to Norman Kretzmann for referring me to Tannery and Lasswitz.
122. Wolfson 1976, pp. 472–86.
123. Pretzl 1931; Fakhry 1958, pp. 23–24; see also A. S. Tritton, Montgomery Watt, and A. Wensinck, all cited in Seale 1964, p. 11.

appreciated. Moreover, I think that when the extent of the parallels is brought to light, the Islamic texts may appear to bear a different meaning from that attributed to them by Islamicists who did not have access to all the Greek counterparts.

Naẓẓām postulated that motion occurred by leaps. I presume that these leaps were like those which we have already encountered in Sextus and Damascius. Naẓẓām's motive was to protect his belief in infinite divisibility from a paradox of the Zenonian type, namely, the paradox that to reach any distance you would first have to traverse an infinity of subdistances.[124] The rival atomist view avoided this difficulty anyway. For there was not an infinity of subdistances to be traversed, in atomist theory. But Naẓẓām claimed that believers in infinite divisibility could also avoid the difficulty, just so long as they postulated that motion occurred through a finite number of leaps. The leaps would involve a body's disappearing from one position and reappearing further along. Since Naẓẓām wished to avoid atomism, I presume that his leaps were infinitely divisible, that is, as short as you like. They will not have been of fixed atomic length. This difference between atomic jerks and infinitely divisible leaps is clear in the Greek sources but has not always been appreciated, I think, by the Islamic commentators.[125]

In one source it looks as if Naẓẓām cited the leaping of light as something which could actually be observed and which therefore provided positive support for the thesis that all motion occurs by leaps.[126] Naẓẓām's examples of things that leap, light and coldness, have caused puzzlement.[127] But in fact they are virtually the same as the examples of light, heat, and freezing given in the original source for the idea of leaping, Aristotle's *De sensu*.[128] The inaccessibility of the Greek sources led Otto Pretzl, in an influential article written in 1925, to argue that Naẓẓām's postulation of a

---

124. Baghdādī 1910, pp. 123 ff.; Khayyāṭ 1925, pp. 32 ff. (Khayyāṭ 1957, pp. 19 ff.); Juwaynī 1969, p. 434; Ibn Mattawayh 1975, pp. 169 and 197–98. For modern discussions see Nader 1956, pp. 155–58 and 182–87; Van den Bergh 1969, vol. II, p. 30; Alousi 1968, p. 277; MacDonald 1927; Pines 1936, pp. 10–16; Van Ess 1978.
125. See MacDonald 1927, Van den Bergh 1969, and Van Ess 1978.
126. Ibn Mattawayh 1975, pp. 203–5.
127. Van Ess 1978, p. 9.
128. Aristotle, *Sens.* 6, 446a20–447a11.

leap was actually a sign of his ignorance of Greek discussions.[129] Pretzl considered the leap, along with other ideas of Naẓẓām, to be so unsatisfactory from a philosophical point of view that it was positive evidence that there had been no direct influence from Greek atomist controversy. He suggested instead that any Greek influence must have traveled via Gnosticism. Another part of Pretzl's case was that for the Greeks, the atom had to play the role of what was stable in change. The Greeks therefore had to decide whether atoms were homogeneous and how they behaved chemically or mechanically, to emphasize atomic shapes and hardness and to discuss the role of vacuum. None of this is found in early Islamic theology. What I should like to say is that it is not found, either, in Diodorus, nor in Epicurus's account of the minimal parts within atoms, nor in Xenocrates. It is only one strand in Greek atomism. And quite often, I believe, Islamic controversies over atomism were influenced by other strands which came to the fore in the later, Hellenistic, period of Greek thought after Aristotle's death.

A whole series of arguments by Naẓẓām was recorded by Juwaynī (died A.D. 1085) and by Ibn Mattawayh (first half of the eleventh century).[130] They are often taken as further arguments in favor of the leap. But comparison with the Greek parallels, and considerations of philosophical sense, suggest to me that they are instead arguments against various aspects of atomism. The leaps come in only insofar as Naẓẓām has to show that the infinitely divisible leap will be immune to the objections brought against atomism. Juwaynī is himself responsible for the arguments' being construed differently. For in his polemical report, he introduces them merely as sophisms to which Naẓẓām resorted, when the mindlessness of his leap was pointed out to him. And he often speaks as if the leap had been meant to solve the difficulties for which the atomists are held responsible. Yet several of the arguments do not even mention the leap at all.

One argument has a special position because it looks like an

---

129. Pretzl 1931.

130. The fullest report in English is Van Ess 1978. No English translation has been published, and I am indebted to Fritz Zimmermann for making translations for me.

argument which had been used by the Greeks against atomism and which is repeated by Maimonides (A.D. 1135–1204) as having been used against Islamic atomism.[131] Maimonides reports the antiatomist argument as follows. Since atomic movements do not take up any time, they must occur at the same speed. The Islamic atomists accounted for differences of speed by allowing an atom to *linger* for more or fewer time atoms in successive space atoms. But that in turn raises the problem that the inner atoms of a rotating millstone must linger in their places, while the outer atoms progress, so that the millstone is fragmented. Or at the very least there must be free play in it; for one atom will stay in the same place for two consecutive time atoms, while the next atom farther out from the center moves from one place to another. Maimonides does not mention Naẓẓām, nor how his rival theory escaped the difficulty concerning fragmentation. But that is easy to guess. The beauty of Naẓẓām's leaps will be that we need never have one point in the millstone resting while another moves. All points in the millstone can leap simultaneously, though reappearing at infinitely graded distances round the circle, according to their fixed distance from the center.

Juwaynī does not appreciate the force of Naẓẓām's point. He rests content with the atomist account of how the millstone revolves, some atoms lingering longer than others. But the telltale signs are there. For his central concern is to show how the different parts of the millstone can have different movements. It looks, then, as if the independent movement of parts is what Naẓẓām had objected to, even if Juwaynī does not present his argument that way. And this interpretation is amply confirmed in Ibn Mattawayh. There are other interpretations of Naẓẓām on the millstone, but I have not been able to see how they would make philosophical sense. What is interesting is that the origin of Naẓẓām's argument against atomism, as I have interpreted it, appears in Sextus Empiricus, with the example of a revolving ruler in place of the revolving millstone.[132] (Other texts tell us that Naẓẓām used the example of a revolving spinning top.) The passage

131. Juwaynī 1969, pp. 436–37; Ibn Mattawayh 1975, pp. 198–200; Maimonides, *Guide* I 73, prop. 3.
132. Sextus, *Adv. math.* X 149–54.

in Sextus comes shortly after that which introduces infinitely divisible leaps. Moreover, in Sextus the argument about fragmentation is presented, in the way in which I have presented Naẓẓām's argument, as primarily an objection against atomism. The leap comes into Naẓẓām's argument not as providing the only method for avoiding fragmentation—it does not do that, for the more normal theory of continuous motion also avoids fragmentation. The point about the leap is merely that it avoids the unwanted fragmentation, while atomist theory does not.

Juwaynī and Ibn Mattawayh record many other arguments by Naẓẓām which again I would construe as objections to atomism rather than as positive arguments for the leap. I shall mention only one,[133] because of its influence on fourteenth-century European discussions. If we remember that Abu l-Hudhayl's atoms are sizeless, I think we can see why Naẓẓām saddles him with the view that there are the same number of atoms along the diagonal of a square as along the two sides with which it forms a triangle. For from every sizeless atom on the diagonal, a straight line can be drawn at right angles until it joins a sizeless atom on one of those two sides. When all the joining lines are drawn, they will be parallel and will leave no gaps between them. This is presumably why Naẓẓām can say that each atom in the diagonal has *opposite* it a corresponding atom on the two sides. As I reconstruct Naẓẓām's argument, he is complaining that an atomist ought to expect the route along the diagonal to be no quicker than the route along the two sides, since, after all, it contains the same number of atoms. As a believer in infinite divisibility, Naẓẓām is not faced with the same problem, for it is only *atomist* theory which makes distance a function of the number of atoms. Once again the theory of the leap is not crucial to Naẓẓām's argument; it merely escapes the difficulty which is being pressed against the atomists.

Juwaynī tries to defend the atomists from Naẓẓām's objection by saying that only *some* portions of the two sides are opposite to the diagonal. Ibn Mattawayh, however, suggests some alternate solutions when he discusses a related paradox about the relation

133. Juwaynī 1969, pp. 439 and 441.

of the diagonal to a single side. There may be *gaps*, he suggests, between the atoms along the longer route, or alternately, the atoms there may be arranged lozengewise, corner to corner rather than face to face.[134] Ibn Mattawayh, incidentally, confirms the suggestion about what Juwaynī means by saying that each atom on one line has a corresponding unit "opposite"; for he puts the point by saying that we can produce as many lines from the one as from the other.

For English readers, a more accessible account of Islamic atomism is provided by Maimonides' *Guide for the Perplexed*. In a few pages in I 73, Maimonides summarizes what he calls the common assumptions of Kalām, or Islamic theology. The first of twelve propositions, or premises, is that things are made of atoms, the second that there is vacuum, and the third that there are time atoms and atomic jerks. It is not always remarked that the time atoms and the atomic jerks bring us close once again to later Greek atomism of the Hellenistic period. Maimonides comments that the postulation of time atoms is due to reflection on Aristotle, who holds that atoms of one kind imply atoms of another.

Maimonides goes on, under the third proposition, to report the problem of fragmentation. And there are other objections reminiscent of the Greek ones as well, for example the objection that in a square with atomic sides, the diagonal and side would differ by *less* than an atom.

Other sources provide yet further parallels with Greek controversy. Thus of the various arguments offered in favor of atomism, four at least sound decidedly Greek.[135] One has been encountered already, namely, that atomism avoids the Zenonian problem that traversing any distance would require one to traverse an infinity of subdistances. Evidently this had been put forward as a supposed advantage of atomism as early as the time of Naẓẓām, since Naẓẓām's infinitely divisible leap was intended to cope with the same problem. Another early figure who, although probably not an atomist, seems to have been influenced by Greek atomist

134. Ibn Mattawayh 1975, pp. 192–94.
135. A set of five arguments for atomism, set out by Ibn Ḥazm in the name of the Muʿtazila (*Fiṣal* V 92–98), is recorded in Pines 1936, pp. 10–16. To these I would add an argument recorded in Baghdādī 1910, pp. 123 and 316. Some of these same arguments appear in Juwaynī 1969, pp. 143–48.

thought is Ḍirār (died A.D. 815 or earlier). For he seems to reproduce against Naẓẓām arguments which had earlier been brought
by Lucretius against Anaxagoras's theory that there is something
of everything latent in everything in portions of ever-diminishing
size.[136] Again, Islamic discussions of the number of atoms with
which an atom can be surrounded will remind us of Democritus.[137]
The idea that an atom cannot exist, but can only be thought of, in
separation from a larger whole will remind us of Epicurus's
minimal parts.[138] And the discussion of whether motion super-
venes on a body when it is in its first position or in its second will
remind us of Diodorus.[139]

15. The Fourteenth Century

I will not stray into fourteenth-century Europe except to say
that Islamic atomism seems to have had a profound influence. For
one thing, recent studies[140] have emphasized that one strand,
perhaps the dominant strand, in fourteenth-century atomism
treated its atoms as sizeless. I shall not here try to trace the subsequent history of this tradition, although I would draw attention
to David Furley's discussion of how David Hume in the eighteenth
century is tempted to treat atoms as points.[141] The decisive shift
seems to have come with Islamic atomism.

There are further echoes in fourteenth-century discussions of
the number of directions in which an atom can be surrounded.[142]
And there are objections to atomism strongly reminiscent of objections canvassed in Islam. For example, there are geometrical arguments about the diagonal and side of a square containing the
same number of atoms. There are questions about the absence of
differences of atomic speed. And there are difficulties about the

136. Ashʿari 1969–70, p. 328, 6–11; cf. Lucretius I 830–920.
137. Ashʿari 1969–70, p. 303, 3. For Democritus, see Giordano Bruno, *De triplici minimo* II.11, schol., p. 255; III.11.12; III.11, schol. ad 90, assembled in Luria 1970, fragment 123. See also Aristotle, *Phys.* I 5, 188a22–26; III 5, 205b32–33.
138. Ashʿari 1969–70, p. 316.
139. Ashʿari 1969–70, p. 355; Baghdādī 1910, pp. 144–45.
140. For the fourteenth century see Maier 1949, pp. 155–215; Zoubov 1959; Murdoch 1964, 1969, 1974.
141. Furley 1967, chap. 10.
142. So Gerard of Odo.

case in which the inner of two concentric wheels rests, while the outer moves.[143]

16. J. A. Wheeler

In modern physics, the idea of time atoms has emerged again. I am referring not to standard quantum theory, which quantizes only certain properties such as angular momentum and spin, but to the ideas of J. A. Wheeler.[144]

Talk of differences in length depends for its sense on the presence of some stability. When we take measurements with a ruler, we rely on the marks and the two ends maintaining a fixed distance from each other. When we get down to a certain very small distance, however, 10^{-33} centimeters (a distance related to Planck's constant), we find what might be called turbulence. Indeed, the word "turbulence" understates the situation by suggesting that at any given instant two particles within this distance have a certain (smaller) distance from each other but that this (smaller) distance changes rapidly. In fact, however, the distance between two such particles cannot be ascertained even for a single instant, and so no intelligible application can be given to the idea of a half or a third of one of these Planckian distances or of one and a half times such a distance. Planck's constant thus supplies us with atoms of space.

I hope this layman's exposition of Wheeler does not distort his view. If the view is something like this, then he will have done what only Epicurus did in antiquity, that is, to try and explain how a distance could possibly be conceptually indivisible. At the same time, we can see that the idea of *conceptual* indivisibility is rather a blunt instrument. For we can perfectly well make sense of the idea that our universe might not have exemplified the turbulence that it does, and hence of the idea that there might have been indefinitely small distances. What is inconceivable is not the idea of indefinitely small distances itself nor the idea of indefinitely small distances in mathematical space. At most, if

143. See esp. Maier 1949, pp. 155–215, and Zoubov 1959.
144. See, e.g., Wheeler 1967, p. 242; 1975, p. 538.

Wheeler is right, we would be unable to give clear sense to the idea of indefinitely small distances in our universe as it is.

Wheeler takes it that time as well as space is atomic. This might be thought to follow simply from the atomicity of space. For any clock depends ultimately on the motion of something across a distance, and if the distances are atomic, so, it might seem, will the times be. But in fact matters are not so simple. For we can imagine two clocks out of phase with each other, so that when one has moved ten atomic spaces, the other is found to be one atomic space ahead. One response would be to reopen the question of whether the spaces are genuinely atomic (might not the faster clock be moving a tenth of a space farther on every beat?). But if it is firmly maintained that the spaces are atomic, does it follow at once that the times are atomic? Not at all; for one hypothesis would be that the faster clock rests between beats for a fraction less time than the slower.[145]

I confess that I do not know Wheeler's own ground for treating time as atomic. It will make a difference if he starts from the Einsteinian idea of space time rather than from the simple idea of space. I hope, however, that the above discussion will show that it is not an easy matter to make sense of the idea of time atoms. One further difficulty would be that atomic times would have to be times during which there was no change.

145. It would make no difference to postulate a maximum speed for the moving parts of clocks, for the argument relies not on indefinitely high speeds but only on indefinitely small differences of speed.

Chapter III

Aristotle against the Atomists

Fred D. Miller, Jr.

1. Aristotle's Continuum Thesis

Aristotle is deeply committed to the thesis that physical reality is a continuous plenum. In *Physics* VI he argues that all physical magnitude, and hence every movement, is continuous, with a view to arguing in Book VIII that one unmoved mover is responsible for the perpetual movement of the cosmos. For he bases the existence of an unmoved mover on the claim that there is always movement;[1] and he bases the uniqueness of the unmoved mover on the claims that what always is is continuous and that what is continuous is one, so that there is a single cosmic movement which is due to a single mover.[2] This argument presupposes that a movement which lasts for a period of time is essentially continuous and one. A process might consist of different successive movements, as in the case of a relay race in which different runners carry a torch.[3] But since movements are differentiated in terms of differences of moved thing, type (or path) of movement, and time during which there is movement, and since these are the criteria of continuity and unity, Aristotle claims that (in the strict sense of "movement") "every movement is

I am indebted to the studies of David Furley and Richard Sorabji, in spite of important departures from their interpretations. I benefited greatly from Richard Sorabji's perceptive criticisms of an earlier draft of this chapter. My treatment of *stigmē* and *sēmeion* in *De gen. et corr.* I 2 owes much to David Keyt. I also benefited from discussions of *Physics* VI with Christopher Shields and Victor Ten Brink.

1. *Phys.* VIII 6, 258b10–259a6.
2. *Phys.* VIII 6, 259a13–20; 10, 267a21–24.
3. *Phys.* VIII 6, 259a19–20; V 4, 227b3–229a6.

87

continuous."[4] Hence, Aristotle cannot concede that movement in general is reducible to an unconnected plurality of events without undermining this argument for a prime mover in *Physics* VIII.

The continuum thesis and the arguments with which Aristotle defends it have a philosophical interest apart from the role of the thesis in this argument, "the way *ex motu*," which is open to many familiar objections. In establishing that physical reality is a continuous plenum, Aristotle upholds two principles of fundamental significance for his science of nature: first, the deep structure of movement is the same as that of spatial and temporal magnitude (the thesis of isomorphism); and second, the structure of a continuum, which is shared by movement, space, and time, is not reducible to any deeper structure (the thesis of irreducibility).[5] These principles exerted a long-lasting influence in the history of science, until developments during the last hundred years in subatomic physics and higher mathematics. The possible value of these principles for the future progress of science may not be fully appreciated at present. But in order to understand their true significance for Aristotle, we must take into account the context in which he formed his concept of the continuous: the controversy over the nature and reality of magnitude and movement in which Zeno the Eleatic, the atomists, and the Platonists had become embroiled. In his characteristic manner Aristotle reformulated the old difficulties in his own terms and defined concepts in order to resolve them.

2. The Dilemma of Divisibility

Aristotle's starting point is the arguments of the Eleatics that generation, change, and plurality are unreal. He presents his own theory of the continuum as the only way out of an ancient dilemma which seeks to show the absurdity of continuous magnitudes. In *De generatione et corruptione* I 8 he states the objections of "some ancient men," namely, Parmenides, Melissus, and Zeno, which the atomists, Leucippus and Democritus, had tried to meet. The first familiar objections turn on the alleged unreality of the void,

4. *Phys.* V 4, 228a20.
5. Wieland 1962, pp. 287–88.

but another objection is raised against the view that reality is divisible without containing void:

> In this regard [i.e., in the inability to solve the problem of the one and the many], if one believes that the universe is not continuous but [consists in] what is divided touching, there is no advantage over saying that there are many things, i.e., not one, and the void. For [supposing that the universe is what is divided touching], if it is divisible everywhere, there is no one, and, hence, no many, but the whole is void; whereas if [it is divisible] here but not there, this is like something contrived (*peplasmenō*). For up to what amount [is it divisible], and why is some of the whole thus [indivisible] and a plenum, and part of it divided?[6]

The argument sketched out here, which I shall call "the dilemma of divisibility," presupposes that the theory of the void is set aside. The fundamental question is whether a magnitude is divisible everywhere, i.e., perpetually subdivisible into smaller units, or divisible only down to some atomic magnitude, beyond which subdivision is no longer possible. The first horn of the dilemma starts from the proposition that magnitude is everywhere divisible and argues to the conclusion that the magnitude is thereby reduced to no extension or, more dramatically, to nothing at all. I shall refer to this as "the nihilistic horn" of the dilemma. The other horn, which I shall refer to as "the atomistic horn," starts from the premise that magnitude is not everywhere divisible, leading to the positing of extended but indivisible magnitudes.

What is the sense of "division" at work here? David Furley distinguishes between two different types of division: *physical division*, which is "the division of something in such a way that formerly contiguous parts are separated from each other by a spatial interval," and *theoretical division*, in which "parts can be distinguished within [the thing] by the mind, even if the parts can never be separated from each other by a spatial interval."[7] There is some evidence that Aristotle had an inkling of Furley's distinction between physical and theoretical division at *Metaphysics* IX 9, 1051a21–33: "It is by an activity (*energeia*) also that

6. *De gen. et corr.* I 8, 325a6–12.
7. Furley 1967, p. 4.

geometrical constructions are discovered; for we find them by dividing. If the figures had been already divided, the constructions would have been obvious; but as it is they are present only potentially. . . . Obviously, therefore, the potentially existing constructions are discovered by being brought to actuality; the reason is that the geometer's thinking is an actuality (*energeia*). . . ." (Ross translation). The text presents difficulties,[8] but it does at least suggest that the act by which a geometer divides a triangle in thought into two triangles represents an actualization of a potential, whether or not it is possible to divide the triangle into physical parts.[9] I shall suppose, therefore, that when Aristotle speaks of atoms or indivisibles in the arguments of *Physics* VI, he is thinking of things which cannot be divided even by the geometer in thought.

This dilemma sets the context for much of Aristotle's inquiry into the nature of space, time, and motion. In *De generatione et corruptione* I 2, he recognizes that a reductionist, "punctual" theory of magnitude comes to grief on the nihilistic horn but argues that his own view escapes such difficulties. Throughout *Physics* VI and in some passages in *De caelo* Aristotle presents arguments in keeping with the atomistic horn which show that the hypothesis of indivisible atomism is a contrivance which violates basic assumptions of mathematics. I shall devote the rest of this chapter to the interpretation and criticism of arguments related to this dilemma. My primary concern will be to uncover the underlying assumptions which propel these arguments.

3. The Nihilistic Horn and Aristotle's Escape

In *De generatione et corruptione* Aristotle presents the nihilistic horn of the dilemma as an argument used by the atomists to refute their opponents who hold that magnitude is infinitely divisible. He tries to show that his own theory of magnitude as a continuum escapes the dilemma by distinguishing different senses of the claim that a magnitude is "everywhere divisible." In

8. E.g., *noēsis hē energeia*, which Ross corrects to *hē noēsis energeia*, in Ross 1936.
9. Cf. also *De anima* III 6, 430b20.

one sense, the claim is caught on the nihilistic horn; in the other sense, Aristotle's, the claim escapes.

> Let us now explain that this argument contains a fallacy, and where the fallacy is. Since point is not next to point, there is a sense in which the predicate "divisible everywhere" belongs to magnitudes and a sense in which it does not. When this is asserted [viz., that magnitudes are divisible everywhere], it seems that there is a point anywhere and everywhere, so that the magnitude must have been divided up into nothing—since there is a point everywhere, and so it will be made either of points or of contacts. Yet there is a sense in which there is a point everywhere, in that there is one point any-where, and all of them are there if you take them one by one. But there is not more than one (since they are not consecutive to each other), and so they are not everywhere.[10]

The philosophical assessment of this passage involves difficul-ties which are not fully addressed by recent commentators. Fur-ley, for example, offers the following gloss: "It is impossible to divide a magnitude 'at every point,' because points are not next to each other; between *any* two points there is a magnitude. But this does not entail that these are indivisible magnitudes; every magnitude has points on it, at which it may be divided."[11] This interpretation is unobjectionable, as far as it goes; but Aristotle's refutation has the appearance of a non sequitur. Why should the fact that points in a magnitude are not "next" to each other lead to the conclusion that a magnitude cannot be divided "at every point"? Why could not the proponent of the argument concede that there is a magnitude between any two points and still con-tend that any such magnitude reduces to an aggregate of points at which the line is divisible? Some additional assumptions are required if this argument is to go through. The crucial sentence at 317a7–9, especially, cries out for clarification: "There is a sense in which [this state of affairs] holds everywhere, in that there is one [point] everywhere, and all are everywhere if you take them indi-vidually, but there is not more than one (since they are not con-secutive), so that [this state of affairs] does not hold everywhere"

10. *De gen. et corr.* I 2, 317a1–9; tr. Furley 1967, p. 92.
11. Furley 1967, p. 92.

(my translation). It is not altogether certain from the context whether the omitted words, here represented by "this state of affairs" in brackets, should be understood as *to diaireton einai*, "the magnitude is divisible," or as *to stigmēn einai*, "there is a point." It remains unclear also what Aristotle means by "there is not more than one" (i.e., not more than one point anywhere), and why he should take this to follow directly from the fact that points are not successive and to lead to the conclusion that points are not everywhere. (If there is *at least* one point anywhere, does it not follow that there *are* points everywhere?)

In the restatement of the atomist's argument, Aristotle makes some important distinctions which are not explicitly used in the refutation but which one would expect to be relevant. The first is between actual and potential senses of "divisible" and "indivisible." It says that a magnitude could be actually indivisible (undivided?) and yet potentially divisible (divided?) at any location (*sēmeion*), "but that it should be divisible everywhere simultaneously (*hama*) in potentiality would seem to be impossible. For if it were possible, it would happen. . . ."[12] It is tempting to suppose that Aristotle's own refutation turns in some way upon the distinction between simultaneous and successive division, and this is certainly suggested by Furley's rendering of the compressed expression *pasai hōs hekastē* (317a8) as "all of them are there if you take them one by one." Joachim goes further and gratuitously translates "simultaneously" at 317a9: "Hence it is not simultaneously divisible" for *hōst' ou pantē*.[13] How does this distinction help the refutation? Aristotle's refutation turns on two senses of "divisible everywhere," *diaireton pantē* or *diaireton hotioun*. In the first sense, "divisible everywhere" applies to magnitude, but the nihilistic conclusion does not follow. The nihilistic conclusion would follow from the second sense, but "divisible

---

12. *De gen. et corr.* I 2, 316b19–23. The point of the parenthesis b23–25 is to make clear that the relevant implication of the hypothesis that the line is potentially simultaneously everywhere divisible is not that the line is actually both divisible and divisible simultaneously (*ouch hōste hama einai amphō entelecheia, adiaireton kai diērēmenon*); rather the implication is that the line is [actually] divided at every point [simultaneously] (*alla diērēmenon kath' hotioun sēmeion*). The glossator responsible for this passage uses the verbal adjectives as passive participles.

13. Oxford translation; cf. Joachim 1922, p. 85.

everywhere" does not apply to magnitude in this sense. What are these two senses? The interpretations of Ross and Joachim, which seem to me to be only partly correct, place the principal burden of argument upon the sense of *diaireton,* treating the distinction as one between simultaneous and successive divisibility. Although this interpretation is illuminating, in order to understand Aristotle's argument it is also necessary to distinguish correspondingly different uses of *pantē* or *hotioun.*

"*Successively, not simultaneously* divisible." Ross and Joachim suggest rather different reasons why magnitude is supposed to be "divisible everywhere" in the one sense but not the other. Ross says that a body "cannot be divided everywhere at once, for that would mean that it has a finite number of points such that point could be next to point and that the body could be divided at all these points and dissolved away into nothing; whereas it has potentially an infinite number of points, none next to another."[14] This interpretation introduces a distinction between finite and infinite numbers of points, of which there is no suggestion in the refutation itself. There is, rather, an explicit distinction between "one" and "more than one," which this interpretation does not explain. Aristotle does indicate that the atomists had argued that *neither* could the process of bisecting a magnitude be infinite (*aperios*) nor could the magnitude be divided simultaneously at every location.[15] But the second condition is presented as independent of the first: it is not suggested that the reason that the line cannot be so divided is that such divisions would follow from a *finite* process and would involve a finite number of points. Nor does Aristotle's refutation allude to any false assumptions about the finitude of points on a line. Moreover, Ross's interpretation, so far, does not make it clear why the nihilistic conclusion does not follow. Even if it were impossible to perform an infinite number of divisions upon any magnitude, do there not exist an infinite number of points within the magnitude at which division *could* be performed, and is not this all that is needed for the nihilistic horn?

Joachim's interpretation follows the text more closely. He

14. Ross 1923, p. 100.
15. *De gen. et corr.* I 2, 316b29–31.

makes use of the final sentence of Aristotle's refutation of the nihilistic horn.[16] "For if it is divisible at the center, it will also be divisible at the adjoining point; but [this cannot be the case],[17] for there is no place adjoining place or point adjoining point, but this is division and combination."[18] Joachim interprets this as follows: "If, e.g., the given magnitude has been divided at its center, it cannot also be divided at a point *immediately next* to its center: for there is no such point. On the other hand, the magnitude might have been divided at a point *immediately next* to its center, *instead* of at its center: for a point might have been taken *there*, instead of at the center." Joachim's general interpretation of the refutation is this: ". . . though there is a point 'everywhere' in the magnitude, in the sense that a point can be taken 'anywhere' within it, these points (i.e., 'all the points of the magnitude') are not *immediately next* to one another: i.e., they are not 'everywhere' in the sense that *at all places of the magnitude simultaneously* there are points."[19] Joachim's "i.e." implies that the denial that points are immediately next to each other is equivalent to the denial that points exist simultaneously everywhere in a magnitude. But how has this equivalence been shown? What would be absurd about saying that all the places in a magnitude have points *and* that between any two points is at least one other point? The interpretation seemingly makes Aristotle's argument a non sequitur. Joachim's reconstruction of 317a10–12 seems, moreover, to be internally inconsistent, for he says both "the magnitude cannot be divided, immediately next to the midpoint, for *there is no such point*" and "if the magnitude had not been divided at the midpoint, it could have been divided *at the point immediately next to it.*" The second statement entails the existence of the point whose existence is denied in the former statement! Joachim seems to mean that for Aristotle, if a magnitude is divided at some point, say *m*, then there exist other points of the magnitude, e.g., the point "immediately next" to *m*, at which the magnitude cannot at that time be divided. But the premise that one can describe a point which

16. This sentence is omitted in Furley 1967 (p. 92) for reasons not given; cf. Joachim 1922, p. 85.

17. Cf. Joachim 1922, p. 86, who attributes this reading to T. W. Allen.

18. *De gen. et corr.* I 2, 317a10–12.

19. Joachim 1922, p. 85.

cannot exist in a magnitude (with the description "the point immediately next to *m*") and, hence, trivially, a point at which the magnitude could not be divided, does not support the conclusion that for any points which *can exist* in the magnitude, the magnitude is divisible there. Joachim seems to have been no more successful than Ross in recovering a plausible argument from Aristotle's refutation of the nihilistic horn of the dilemma of divisibility. In order to arrive at a satisfactory understanding of Aristotle's refutation, it is necessary to understand the mode in which he refers to points in the expression "divisible *everywhere.*"

"Divisible at all potentially, not actually, existing points." In our passage Aristotle uses the phrases *pantē* and *hopēoun* ("everywhere," "anywhere") interchangeably with *kata pan sēmeion* and *kath' hotioun sēmeion* ("at every/any location").[20] Aristotle elsewhere uses *sēmeion* in the same sense as *stigmē* (Bonitz cites several passages), and 317a11–12 leaves no doubt that a *sēmeion* is a pointlike location. Nevertheless, Aristotle understands the expression "anywhere" or "at any location" to refer to such points only in a peculiar mode. He does not think of the domain of the quantifier as consisting of actually existing points on a line. For to concede the actual existence of such pointlike locations prior to any process of division would be already to undermine Aristotle's refutation; the crux of this refutation is that all the points in a magnitude cannot simultaneously exist in actuality.

Aristotle's refutation presupposes a special understanding of the point, which is made more explicit elsewhere. He conceives of the point as a cut (*tomē*) or division (*diairesis*) in a line, just as a line is a cut in a surface, which is, in turn, a cut in a solid.[21] A point is a limit (*peras*) of a line;[22] it is the beginning or end of a line segment.[23] Aristotle denies that points have the primary reality of substances, precisely because points exist as divisions or limits.[24] The denial that points are substances rests, in part, upon a consideration of the mode in which points exist. The operations in

20. Cf. *De gen. et corr.* I 2, 316b11, 20, 22, 25, 31.
21. *Metaph.* XI 2, 1060b12–19; III 5, 1002a15–b11.
22. *Metaph.* III 5, 1002b10; XI 2, 1060b16; XIV 3, 1090b9.
23. *Phys.* IV 11, 220a10; Ps.-Aristotle, *De lineis insecabilibus* 4, 971a18.
24. *Metaph.* XIV 3, 1090b8–9.

virtue of which points exist or do not exist are *not* processes of coming to be or ceasing to be:

> . . . points and lines and surfaces cannot either come to be or cease to be, when they now exist and now do not exist. For when bodies touch or are divided, their limits become one at once (*hama*) when their bodies touch and two when they are divided; hence when the bodies are combined, the limit does not exist but has perished, and when they have been divided, the limits exist which did not exist before (or it is not the case that the indivisible point is divided into two), and if then limits come to be or cease to be, from what do they come to be?[25]

Aristotle says, in short, "Some things, like points, either exist or do not exist, without coming to be or ceasing to be."[26] Hence, points have *accidental* being.[27] They exist or do not exist in virtue of operations performed upon substances (or, more precisely, upon magnitudes, which are themselves limits or aspects of substances), such as combination or division. Throughout *De generatione et corruptione* I 2, Aristotle also assumes that points come into existence through certain operations by which a magnitude is subdivided, "whether by bisection (*kata to meson*) or by any method in general."[28] Aristotle envisages a process in which a magnitude is divided at some point "into separable magnitudes which are smaller"; these can actually be separated from each other or rejoined at that point.[29] Aristotle has his attention throughout on bisection, e.g., when he says a point or contact (*haphē*) "is always one contact of two things."[30] When a line segment is bisected, we obtain two segments divided (and capable of contact) at one point. Aristotle also assumes, in another argument, that if we can obtain points by dividing magnitude, we should be able to obtain magnitudes by joining together points. Since we cannot do the latter (two points in contact simply coincide and have no extension), we cannot do the former.[31]

A clue to understanding the use of *hotioun sēmeion* in *De gener-*

---

25. *Metaph.* III 5, 1002a32–b5; cf. XI 3, 1060b17–19.
26. *Metaph.* VIII 5, 1044b21–22.
27. *Metaph.* VI 2, 1026b22–24.
28. *De gen. et corr.* I 2, 316a19–20.
29. *De gen. et corr.* I 2, 316b28–29.
30. *De gen. et corr.* I 2, 316b6–8.
31. *De gen. et corr.* I 2, 316a29–34.

atione et corruptione I 2 is provided in Aristotle's criticisms of Zeno's dichotomy argument in *Physics* VIII 8: "Further, the potential and the actual are different, so that any location (*hotioun sēmeion*) between the two extremes of the straight line is, potentially, a midpoint (*meson*), but is, actually, not [a midpoint], unless [a moving body] divides it by coming to a stand and starts to move again. Hence, the midpoint is a starting-point and ending-point, a starting-point for the later part and an ending-point for the earlier part."[32] When a moving body moves continuously along a continuous path, Aristotle says, the points along which it moves are potential; he contrasts them with the goal at which it comes to a stop and which is thereby made actual.[33] Such language is comprehensible, provided that points are thought of as potential divisions in magnitudes, actualized by bodies coming to a halt and moving again. Aristotle speaks also of producing points by mental acts such as counting.[34] He concedes the point made by Zeno that any finite magnitude can be repeatedly bisected ad infinitum, so that it contains an infinite number of halves; and since the midpoint at which each half is further bisected is a *sēmeion*, the finite magnitude contains an infinite number of pointlike locations. Nevertheless, Aristotle denies that these *sēmeia* need have actual existence, because a *sēmeion* exists as a boundary between two halves, and for the most part, the halves exist only potentially.[35] This is a crucial distinction for Aristotle's refutation of Zeno's dichotomy paradox, since Aristotle concedes to Zeno only that in order to reach a goal a moving body must pass through a *potentially* infinite number of half-distances.[36] If the body were to traverse an *actually* infinite number of halves, it would have to make an infinite number of stops and starts. It is not a part of the essence (*ousia*) of a finite magnitude that it contains an infinite number of subdistances—or of points.[37] Hence, Aristotle understands *kath' hotioun sēmeion* as "at any potentially existing location" when he concedes that a magni-

32. *Phys.* VIII 8, 262a21–26.
33. *Phys.* VIII 8, 262b30–263a1.
34. *Phys.* VIII 8, 262b6–8; cf. 263a25.
35. *Phys.* VIII 8, 263a28–29: *en de tō sunechei enesti men apeira hēmisē, all' ouk entelecheia alla dunamei.*
36. *Phys.* VIII 8, 263b3–5.
37. *Phys.* VIII 8, 263b5–9.

tude can be divided "at any *sēmeion*," in *De generatione et corruptione* I 2. And since he understands the *sēmeion* as becoming actualized only through an operation such as bisection of a line segment, to say that a line is "divisible at any location" is thus to say that any subdivision can itself be further subdivided.

Aristotle refutes the nihilistic horn, used by the atomists, by showing that even though division is possible and a point exists everywhere in the potential mode, it does not follow that magnitude reduces to points. For the existence of every actually existing point is conditional upon the existence of two segments with magnitude into which the subsection is divided. This interpretation makes the best sense of a difficult passage on which both Ross and Joachim founder: "Yet there is a sense in which there is a point [*or*: the magnitude is divisible] everywhere, in that there is one point anywhere, and all of them are there if you take them one by one. But there is not more than one (since they are not consecutive to each other), and so they are [*or*: it is] not everywhere."[38] The words "there is not more than one" mean that in any section of a magnitude *only one* point can be obtained by the process of bisection, viz., the midpoint. There *is* a point "everywhere" in the potential mode: in any section obtained in the process of repeated bisection, a further point can be obtained. But there is *not* a point "everywhere" in the actual mode, because *all* subsections of the given magnitude cannot be simultaneously divided. The latter fact follows from Aristotle's conception of magnitudes and points: at *any* stage a magnitude or section of magnitude is divided only if there are two lesser subsections and a point at which these are divided. Aristotle's reasoning could be evaded only if, at some stage, subsections were divisible not into still smaller subsections but into something else altogether, viz., unextended points. In order to rule out this alternative, Aristotle adds the sentence at 317a10–12: "For, if it is divisible at the center (*kata to meson*) it will also be divisible at the adjoining point; but (this cannot be the case), for there is no location adjoining location or point adjoining point, but this is division and combination." The use of *kata to meson* at 317a10 implies that Aristotle is

---

38. *De gen. et corr.* I 2, 317a7–9.

envisaging a division which is a stage in the recursive process of division *kata to meson* by which the magnitude is divided up.[39] Aristotle denies that the magnitude could consist of pointlike locations or be divided up into points, because neither of these can be "adjoining" (*echomenē*) or "in succession" (*ephexēs*). The latter claim is broader than the former,[40] if the definitions of *Physics* V 3 are relevant here. Since "adjoining" is defined as "in succession" as well as "touching," to rule out "in succession" is to rule out "adjoining" but not vice versa.[41]

A thing in succession to another, by Aristotle's account, is such that (i) between it and its predecessor there is nothing of the same kind as it and its predecessor, and (ii) it is "after" (*husteron ti*) its predecessor.[42] We might take the relationship between the left half, *A*, and the right half, *B*, of a line segment as a paradigm of succession. Both *A* and *B* are segments, and (i) between *A* and *B* there is no segment, and (ii) *B* is after *A*. Both these conditions are relevant to Aristotle's claim regarding the impossibility of constructing a divisible magnitude out of points, as is shown by his criticism in *Physics* VI 1 of the theory that a line is merely a succession of points. He shows that if a pair of points satisfies either one of these conditions, it necessarily fails the other.[43] If *a* and *b* are points on a line segment and we suppose that *b* is in succession to *a*, then we will have to suppose that (i) between *a* and *b* there is no point, in which case the two points, like the two segments *A* and *B*, will touch. But two points that touch would have to do so "as whole with whole" and thus be entirely coincident,[44] in which case *b* cannot be after *a*. If, on the other hand, we stipulate that (ii) *b* is after *a*, there will be a part of the line segment separating *b* from *a*, and in any part of a line segment there are points.[45] So if condition (ii) is fulfilled, condition (i) is violated. In the case of points, then, the two conditions required for succession are incompatible, so that there can be no

39. Cf. *De gen. et corr.* I 2, 316a19–20.
40. Cf. *De gen. et corr.* I 2, 317a9, 11, 15.
41. *Phys.* V 3, 227a17–b2.
42. *Phys.* V 3, 226b34–227a6.
43. *Phys.* VI 1, 231a29–b10.
44. Cf. *Phys.* VI 1, 231b2.
45. Cf. *Phys.* VI 1, 231b9; V 3, 227a31.

operation by which an extended magnitude could be compounded out of points. By the same token there can be no operation by which an extended magnitude is entirely divided into points. A magnitude can be "divided everywhere" *only* by a process in which a subsection is divided into further subsections, but there is never a stage at which there are no more extended constituents.

In conclusion, a magnitude can be "divided everywhere" only by a process in which a subsection is divided into further subsections. There is never a stage at which the division is completed and the line consists exclusively of unextended constituents. For an actually existing point necessarily presupposes the existence of extended magnitudes which have been divided. Hence, the division of a line must be successive rather than simultaneous, and it occurs "at every point" not in the sense of actually existing points but in the sense of points which could mark further subdivisions. Aristotle's refutation of the nihilistic horn relies upon his own "constructivist" conception of a point as an accidental feature of extended magnitudes undergoing operations.

4. The Atomistic Horn

The difficulty which arises for the atomists in the dilemma of divisibility is that their denial that division can go beyond a certain point is "contrived."[46] In *De caelo* III 4, Aristotle contends that atomism so construed is in conflict with basic principles of mathematics.[47] The source of the difficulty is the atomists' commitment to a "smallest magnitude," *elachiston megethos*.[48] The charge is developed more fully in *Physics* VI. It is important to recognize that *this* is the main objection to the atomic theory, rather than the argument that a magnitude is not composed of "indivisibles," which appears in *Physics* VI 1. Critics have complained that this latter argument contains "loopholes" through which an atomist could slip.[49] Aristotle's argument turns on the

46. *De gen. et corr.* I 8, 325a6–12.
47. *De caelo* III 4, 303a20–24.
48. *De caelo* I 5, 271b9–11.
49. See, e.g., Furley 1967, pp. 114 ff.; also Richard Sorabji, who interprets 231b10–15 as directed against atomism (in chapter II, nn. 57–58).

claims that the indivisibles cannot be in contact with or in succession to each other, and allegedly in both cases the argument begs the question against the atomists by assuming that indivisibles have no magnitude. But it is doubtful whether we should interpret this passage as a refutation of atomism. The doctrine under attack explicitly takes the indivisibles as *points*, and the argument turns on the claim that points cannot be continuous, or touch, or be in succession. It is unlikely that Aristotle would confuse atomic magnitudes with points, for in the argument of *De generatione et corruptione* I 2, which we have been examining, he is considering an argument in which the atomists criticize their opponents for reducing magnitudes to points.[50] And the argument which opens *Physics* VI 1 employs many of the same claims as Aristotle's critique in *De generatione et corruptione* I 2, in particular the claim that points cannot be in succession with points.[51] Moreover, Aristotle himself makes the observation that while pointlike entities cannot be successive, atomic times *can be*[52]—and, given the context, he regards this fact as problematic for atomism! Commentators can be excused for construing Aristotle's argument in *Physics* VI 1 as a refutation of atomism, since Aristotle himself says at VI 2 that it has been proven that it is impossible for something to be [made] out of atoms (*ex atomōn*).[53] Aristotle's reasoning about atomism not infrequently appears muddled because he uses the word *atomos* imprecisely. Here, I suggest, the term *atomos* should be taken as meaning simply "indivisible" and as referring to the points under fire in VI 1. Aristotle elsewhere refers to an *atomon nun*,[54] which is a pointlike instant[55] that should not, I think, be identified with the *atomos chronos* of VIII 8.[56] For instants, like points, cannot be successive, whereas atomic times can be. It is important to draw such conceptual distinctions more sharply than Aristotle's loose terminology would seem to warrant; otherwise we lose sight of significant features of Aristotle's argument. In general, when Aristotle

50. The two positions are clearly distinguished at 317a13–16.
51. Cf. *Phys.* VI 1, 231b6–7, with *De gen. et corr.* I 2, 317a9–11.
52. *Phys.* VIII 8, 264a3–4.
53. *Phys.* VI 2, 232a23–24.
54. *Phys.* IV 13, 222b8; VI 9, 241a25.
55. *Phys.* VI 9, 241a5–6.
56. *Phys.* VIII 8, 264a3–4.

speaks of an "atomic magnitude," *atomos megethos*, in the *Physics*[57] or in *De generatione et corruptione*,[58] he has in view something *with magnitude*, as the terminology indicates; it is a mistake to criticize him for assuming otherwise. This is important for an understanding of Aristotle, because his most important criticisms of atomism are criticisms of atomism *as* a theory of magnitude.

The gist of Aristotle's objection against atomism as a theory of magnitude is identified by Simplicius, who reports that Aristotle is alluding to the theorem, "it is possible to take a magnitude smaller than any given magnitude."[59] As I shall try to show, this principle is closely tied to other principles which Aristotle employs in his arguments against atomism in *Physics* VI: e.g., if a given magnitude is traversed by a moving body in a given time, a *smaller magnitude* will be traversed by a body moving at equal velocity in less time or by a body moving at a lesser velocity in the same time. Aristotle is convinced that he can use these principles to establish important conclusions bearing on the atomic theory. First, he believes that he can establish that spatial magnitude, time, and motion are isomorphic, such that either all three of them have an atomic structure, or all three are continua. Second, on the basis of this thesis (and another premise), he thinks he can establish that one can always take a smaller magnitude than any given magnitude and that the attempt of the atomist to deny this leads to incoherence.

5. The Isomorphism Thesis and the Derivation of Atomic Time

The isomorphism thesis is stated in the following terms: "The same argument applies to magnitude, time, and motion: either they [all] are composed of indivisible things and divided into indivisible things, or none [of them] is."[60] Aristotle believes that he can demonstrate a necessary connection between the continuity (infinite divisibility) of magnitude and time, and hence by con-

57. *Phys.* I 3, 187a3.
58. *De gen. et corr.* I 2, 316b32; 317a1.
59. Diels-Kranz 1968, 68A48a; cf. Furley 1967, p. 88, n. *i.*
60. *Phys.* VI 1, 231b18–20.

traposition, between the atomicity (finite divisibility or ultimate indivisibility) of magnitude and time.[61] The mathematical theorem that it is always possible to take a smaller magnitude than any given magnitude holds for spatial magnitude if and only if it holds also for time and movement. He subsequently argues that the theory of atomic time is inferior to the theory of continuous time because it does not permit a coherent analysis of coming to be.[62] Hence, insofar as atomism is committed to such a view of time, it is vulnerable. Aristotle also develops a general argument that atomism is unable to provide a coherent account of motion, but before considering this general argument, we should assess the arguments for the isomorphism thesis.

The thesis that magnitude, time, and motion all have the same structure is presupposed when Aristotle infers that one of the three is continuous because another is: "For because magnitude is continuous, motion is also continuous, and time because of motion."[63] In asserting that they are continua, Aristotle presupposes an account of the continuous which rules out atomism: "Every continuum is divisible into things which are always divisible (*diaireton eis aei diaireta*)."[64] A continuum is always divisible into other continua. But the isomorphism thesis could be, and evidently was, accepted by Aristotle's atomist opponents, including Epicurus.[65] Let us call such a doctrine, which takes motion and time as well as magnitude to be atomic, *pure atomism*. In chapter II Richard Sorabji suggests another, *mixed* version of atomism, according to which magnitude and motion are atomic but time is continuous. According to this theory, as an object moves from atomic magnitude to atomic magnitude, there is a divisible stretch of time during which it occupies, or lingers at, each atomic magnitude. This is a "cinematographic" theory of motion. Sorabji's distinction is a most important one, for it cannot be assumed that a refutation of pure atomism will be a refutation of mixed atomism.

One strong link in the isomorphism thesis is the claim that if

61. Cf. *Phys*. VI 1, 232a18–22.
62. *Phys*. VIII 8, 263b9–264a6.
63. *Phys*. IV 11, 219a12–13; cf. 219b15–16 and VI 2, 233a11–21.
64. *Phys*. VI 1, 231b16.
65. Cf. Furley 1967, chap. 8, and Sorabji, chapter II, section 7.

magnitudes are indivisible, then motion consists of indivisible moves or "jerks" (*kinēmata*). Aristotle's argument goes: "Let it [the atom] change from *AB* to BC . . . and let *D* be the time in which it is changing in the primary sense. Therefore, with respect to the time when it is changing, it must be either in *AB* or in *BC*, or part of it must be in *AB* and part in *BC*; for everything which is changing is thus. But some of it will not be in each of these; for then there would be a part."[66] In Aristotle's view, one can say that the object "is moving," that is, is undergoing a process, only when it is partly in *AB* and partly in *BC*. For when it is wholly in *AB* it has not yet started, and when it is wholly in *BC*, it has already moved. Hence, there will be no *continuous* process of moving out of *AB* and into *BC*. The object simply occupies one place and then another.

Other links in the thesis are rather more problematic, especially those from atomic magnitude to atomic time and from atomic motion to atomic time. For mixed atomism seems to describe a way in which an object can move in jerks across discontinuous magnitudes in a continuous stretch of time. Aristotle provides arguments which would, if successful, rule out such a theory.

6. The Link between Atomic Magnitude and Atomic Time

The first of these links comes at the end of *Physics* VI 1 and continues into VI 2. The argument as Aristotle sets it forth is certainly not free of difficulties. Nevertheless, if some important qualifications are placed upon the argument, it can be shown to have some merit.

As it stands, the principal argument for the isomorphism thesis in *Physics* VI 2 is unsatisfactory because it is circular. The circularity arises in the following way. In the first part of the argument Aristotle shows that certain commonsense theorems about faster and slower things follow from the assumption that magnitude is continuous;[67] and in the second part of the argument he reasons,

---

66. *Phys.* VI 10, 240b20–27; cf. VI 1, 231b18–232a17; 4, 234b10–20; and Plato, *Parmenides*, 138C4–139A1.
67. *Phys.* VI 2, 232a23–b20.

on the basis of such commonsense theorems about faster and slower things, that if magnitude is continuous, then so is time.[68] This reasoning is circular, however, because in the first part of his argument Aristotle tacitly assumes that time is continuous so that he can derive his commonsense theorems from the assumption that magnitude is divisible. Consider the two parts of the argument in reverse. In the second part of the argument Aristotle tries to show that time is continuous.[69] He alleges that it has been proved[70] that if A is faster than B, then if A traverses the same magnitude as B, A will take less time than B. He uses this commonsense theorem to show that the time t_1 in which the slower object traverses a magnitude m_1 can be divided, since the faster object takes less time, viz., t_2. He makes implicit use[71] of his other commonsense theorem, that if A moves faster than B but takes the same time as B, then it traverses a greater magnitude than B,[72] to show that the magnitude m_1 covered by the faster object A in time t_2 can be divided, since the slower object B will cover a lesser magnitude, viz., m_2. And so it goes: the former theorem can be used to divide time, and the latter theorem to divide magnitude, in an unending alternation. Hence, since magnitude is continuous, so is time.

Aristotle proves the commonsense theorem that faster things cover the same ground in less time in the first part of the argument as a corollary of the assumption that all magnitude is divisible.[73] He proves this by first establishing the lemma that if A is faster than B, then given any magnitude which B covers in a given time, A traverses a greater magnitude in a shorter time.[74] Given that A takes less time than B to cover a greater magnitude, it trivially follows, from this and the lemma, that if A is faster than B and covers the same magnitude, then A takes less time than B to do so. But when Aristotle proves the crucial lemma he simply takes it for granted that time is divisible: "The faster thing

68. *Phys.* VI 2, 232b20–233a12.
69. *Phys.* VI 2, 232b24.
70. *Phys.* VI 2, 232b26: *dedeiketai.*
71. *Phys.* VI 2, 232b31–33.
72. *Phys.* VI 2, 232a25–26, 28–31.
73. *Phys.* VI 2, 232a23–27.
74. Cf. *Phys.* VI 2, 232b6–7.

also covers a greater magnitude in less time, for in the time in which *A* comes to *D*, let *B* come to *E*, since it is slower. So since *A* has come to *D* in the entire time *FG*, it will come to *H in less time than this* (*en elattoni toutou*). Let it be in *FI*, and the magnitude *CH*, which *A* has traversed, is greater than *CE*, but the time *FI* is less than the entire time *FG*, so that it covers more magnitude in less time."[75] Since Aristotle is presupposing that magnitude is continuous, he is begging no questions in assuming he can find a point *H* between *E* and *D*. But since he ultimately intends to prove that time is divisible, he is clearly begging the question in assuming here that he can divide the "entire time" *FG* into a smaller portion *FI* (and its complement, *IG*).

Philosophers typically fall into circularity because they try to prove too much. Aristotle could have argued that given our commonsense beliefs about the faster and the slower, the continuity (or atomicity) of magnitude entails that of motion and time. That is, our prescientific or prephilosophical observations about bodies in motion commit us to the isomorphism thesis. This would be to argue from *ta phainomena*, as Aristotle often does. But Aristotle tries to justify these commonsense beliefs about motion on other grounds, and in this he falls into circularity.

7. The Link between Atomic Motion and Atomic Time

In *Physics* VI 10 Aristotle argues that the same reasoning which commits the atomist to an atomic theory of movement will also commit the atomist to an atomic theory of time. In the course of the argument Aristotle claims that there could be movement in the atomists' sense only if time were composed of partless instants (*ek tōn nun*). This claim is an inference in an argument that atomic bodies cannot move in the strict sense: "So the partless thing cannot be moving or be changing altogether; for there could thus be movement of it only (*monachōs*) if time were composed of instants; for always at an instant it would have moved and have changed, so that never would it be moving but always have moved. But this is impossible, as was shown before, for neither is

75. *Phys.* VI 2, 232a31–b5.

time composed of instants, nor a line of points, nor movement of moves."[76] This argument may be recast as follows:

(1) Always at an instant the partless thing has moved or has changed, so that it never is moving but always has moved.
(2) There is movement of the partless thing only if time consists of instants.
(3) Time does not consist of instants.
(4) The partless thing cannot be moving or be changing altogether.

Aristotle's connectives indicate that (1) is a premise from which (2) follows; and that (3) is an independent premise which, together with (2), establishes the first proposition of the passage, viz. (4), as a conclusion. The "time" in the argument, the wider context shows, is "the primary time in which the thing is [putatively] moving."[77] Just before this passage Aristotle has been arguing that an atom cannot *be moving* from place p_1 to (adjacent) place p_2 because it cannot be in both places without being divisible, having a part in each, which is impossible; and when it is at p_2 it already has moved and thus is not still moving; but when it is at p_1 it is not yet moving and thus is at rest, "for what is in the same place for some time is at rest."

Aristotle can be understood as responding to the atomist who says, "The atom is at atomic place p_1 at instant t_1 and then at atomic place p_2 at instant t_2," by asking the following leading questions: "What happens in the interval between t_1 and t_2?" Aristotle here has his sights on the atomist who answers, "There is no interval between t_1 and t_2." Thus, this atomist seeks to atomize movement into jerks by atomizing time into partless instants. It is for this reason that Aristotle thinks that the atomist who asserts

(1) Always in the instant the partless thing has-moved, so that it never is-moving but always has-moved

is also committed to

(2) There is movement of the partless thing only if time consists of instants.

76. *Phys.* VI 10, 240b30–241a4.
77. *Phys.* VI 10, 240b22–23.

For presumably such an atomist would contend that motion exists over an interval so long as at any instant in the interval one can always say that the object "has moved." One can always apply the *perfect* tense of *kineisthai* to the body. This, of course, departs radically from Aristotle's own view, defended in *Physics* VI 6, that a body has moved to p_2 at t_2 only if during some time interval from t_1 to t_2 it is moving across some distance from p_1 to p_2. Aristotle has two different objections to such a theory. The first is suggested by proposition 1: the present tense of *kineisthai*, "is moving," never applies to the body. This objection, developed in *Physics* VI 1, is that since a body cannot at the same time have moved from one atomic magnitude to the next and be moving from the one to the next, the claim that an atom always *has moved* does not establish that it always *is moving*; in fact, Aristotle thinks, it shows that it is not moving at all.[78] The second objection is central to the argument of *Physics* VI 10: the atomist is committed in proposition 2 to an atomic theory of time—hence, this atomist is committed to a *pure* theory of atomism, which Aristotle rejects with proposition 3.

It should be noted that the mixed atomist fares no better who would answer Aristotle's leading question by saying, "The atom is at p_1 at t_1 and lingers there until it jerks to p_2 at t_2." In the first place the mixed theory does no better than the pure theory in meeting the objection that atoms never actually *are moving*: a body is at rest for a period of time and then, suddenly, it *has moved* to p_2. And in the second place, this theory, in avoiding the pitfalls of atomic time, falls into an even worse difficulty, which is suggested by Aristotle's statement that "what is in the same place for some time (*chronon tina*) is at rest." The mixed theory had led to the disconcerting consequence that the temporal interstices between the instants of the jerks into which movement is analyzed will be periods of rest. Thus, there can be no such thing as a stretch of constant movement. The difficulty is that the mixed theory of motion cannot accommodate the criterion stated by Aristotle: "Movement is always other and other" (*hē kinēsis aei allē kai allē*). This criterion is still invoked by modern philosophers. Thus,

78. *Phys.* VI 1, 231b25–232a17.

Donald Williams states, "Motion is . . . defined and explained in the dimensional manifold as consisting of the presence of the same individual in different places at different times." Richard Gale makes the point, in a somewhat more Aristotelian vein, that "motion is defined as the occupation, by one entity, of a continuous series of places at a continuous series of times."[79] The pure theory of atomism can accommodate Aristotle's criterion of movement: the atomic body occupies a different atomic place at each atomic time. But the mixed theory with its "cinematographic motion" does not satisfy this criterion of motion at all. Like modern cinematography, it substitutes an illusion for the real thing. Hence, it is quite reasonable for Aristotle to suppose that an atomic account of motion entails an atomic account of time.

8. The Refutation of Atomism

We are now in a position to consider precisely how, according to Aristotle, the atomist is impaled upon the second horn of the dilemma of divisibility. Aristotle distinguishes atomic units from pointlike entities, although both are described as "indivisible" and "atomic." I have already suggested that it is essential to the atomist theory he is attacking that atoms, unlike points, have magnitude. His objection is that the atomists treat magnitudes in a contrived way, with the contrivance of a "smallest magnitude," which violates the mathematical theorem that one can always find a magnitude smaller than a given magnitude. The theorem is supported by an appeal to commonsense beliefs about relative velocity. For Aristotle thinks of "taking a smaller magnitude" in terms of an actual operation, such as moving a smaller distance.

79. *Phys.* IV 11, 219b9–10; Williams 1951, pp. 104 f.; Gale 1967, p. 3. Aristotle's criterion should be amplified. The criterion includes "always" (*aei*) because it is not sufficient for an object to be moving throughout a time merely if it is at different places at some of the instants, since this would allow intermittent motion. But if "always" implies that at any different instants the object is at different places, the criterion is too strong: it admits rectilinear movement but excludes the circular movement of heavenly bodies, because such movement is periodic. This difficulty can be met, however. Heavenly motion consists of a continuous succession of revolutions, and each of these does satisfy Aristotle's criterion. Thus, constant motion either satisfies Aristotle's criterion or consists of a succession of motions each of which satisfies the criterion. A pure-atomist account of circular heavenly motion would also satisfy this criterion, but a mixed-atomist account would not.

One statement of the objection appears in VI 2.[80] To see the force of the objection one should note that the argument relies upon two sorts of claims: first, the principles of relative velocity, which Aristotle uses to support the isomorphism thesis; second, the general claim that it is always possible to move faster or slower than any given moving body.[81] The second claim, as well as the first, is required in order to establish the theorem that one can *always* find a smaller magnitude. Both sorts of claims are necessary to carry the day. If either sort of claim were withdrawn, one or the other form of atomism would escape refutation.

Pure atomism can avoid difficulty by challenging the *second* claim (not the first, which it endorses). A pure atomist will hold that an atom A moves in an indivisible jerk over an indivisible magnitude in an indivisible time. If this atomist concedes that another atom B could move more slowly than A and agrees that a slower body covers a smaller magnitude in the same time, he will be driven to the conclusion that there is a smaller magnitude than "the smallest magnitude." The pure atomist can avoid self-contradiction only by refusing to concede that it is always possible to move faster or slower than any given moving body.[82] Epicurus seems to have this issue in mind when he denies that atoms traversing atomic magnitudes can move faster or slower than one another.[83]

On the other hand, mixed atomism, with its cinematographic theory of motion, would attack the principles of relative velocity. The second claim can be accommodated by this theory in a way which causes no difficulty. The atom A can move more slowly than B by tarrying for a longer stretch of time at each atomic place than B does. But the phenomena of relative velocity do create problems for this theory. Consider again the principle that the slower of two moving bodies traverses a smaller magnitude in an equal time. According to mixed atomism, the slower A might remain at an atomic unit for two microseconds, while the faster B remained there for only one microsecond, after they had arrived simultaneously at their respective destinations. During two micro-

---

80. *Phys.* VI 2, 233b19–32.
81. Cf. *Phys.* VI 2, 233b19–20.
82. Cf. *Phys.* VI 2, 233b19–20.
83. Epicurus, *Letter to Herodotus,* sects. 61–62. This interpretation is offered by Furley 1967, pp. 120–22 and 130 n. 9.

seconds B traverses two whole atomic magnitudes while A covers only one. But the problem lies with the *first* microsecond, during which A and B traverse the same magnitude: during this same time the slower A does *not* cover less magnitude than B. Hence, mixed atomism generates a counterexample to this principle of relative velocity. Thus, the mixed atomist is forced to reject or severely restrict such principles.[84]

Aristotle bases his argument upon certain beliefs about relative velocity. Although they are grounded in ordinary ways of thinking about the world, opponents might call them into question, especially in view of developments in physics since Einstein. A pure atomist might question the claim that it is always possible to move faster than any given motion. But Aristotle has surely identified some deep assumptions in which his thesis of the continuity of magnitude, time, and motion must be anchored.

84. In section 5 of chapter II Richard Sorabji finds this line of reasoning unconvincing. I am not certain how his suggested distinction between "the time taken to traverse a given space" and "time itself" can save the mixed atomist from the necessity of placing restrictions on commonsense principles concerning relative velocity. Thus, this theory is at variance with the principles advanced by Aristotle.

CHAPTER IV

Infinity and Continuity:
The Interaction of Mathematics
and Philosophy in Antiquity

WILBUR R. KNORR

1. Introduction

The interaction of philosophy and mathematics is seldom revealed so clearly as in the study of the infinite among the ancient
Greeks. The dialectical puzzles of the fifth-century Eleatics, sharp-
ened by Plato and Aristotle in the fourth century, are com-
plemented by the invention of precise methods of limits, as applied by Eudoxus in the fourth century and Euclid and
Archimedes in the third. But does this conplementarity indicate a
causal connection—a direct influence by the philosophers on the
work of the geometers—as is often maintained? I am convinced
that the mathematical studies were autonomous, almost completely so, while the philosophical debates, developing within
their own tradition, frequently drew support and clarification
from mathematical work.

This perspective on the issue contrasts radically with that
adopted in most accounts of the history of philosophy and of the
history of mathematics, in which philosophical debates are
viewed as generating a "crisis" requiring solution by mathematicians. Yet my view conforms to what one may observe as the
usual relation between mathematics and philosophy throughout

The Euclidean *Elements* are cited in the (second) edition by J. L. Heiberg, revised
by E. Stamatis (Leipzig, 4 vols., 1969–73). Works of Archimedes are cited in the
Heiberg edition, 3 vols. (1910–15; reprint ed., Leipzig, 1972). I have used W. D.
Ross's text of Aristotle's *Physics* (Oxford, 1950). All translations are mine unless
otherwise specified.

history and especially recently. Mathematicians form a sort of intellectual elite among members of both the sciences and the humanities; they attained this status, undoubtedly, through the fact that a properly reasoned mathematical argument is incontrovertible by anyone who is accurately informed on the meaning of the terms. Such a consensus is attainable nowhere else in the world of intellectual discourse, although it is approximated to a greater degree the closer one approaches mathematics.[1] The awe in which mathematicians are held is not a purely modern phenomenon. Plato, for instance, admired his teacher Theodorus and his colleague Theaetetus; Eudoxus was an honored member of the Academy, as were his followers. Indeed, Plato framed a critical portion of his program of philosophical education around mathematical studies.[2] Aristotle, while assigning to other sciences vis-à-vis mathematics a relatively greater role than had Plato, nevertheless recognized in mathematics important paradigms of logical method and, as we shall see, adopted mathematical arguments to clarify his viewpoints in physics and cosmology.[3]

I must admit that the argument which follows cannot presume to be confirmed explicitly by our documentary evidence. Indeed, even if our sources on pre-Euclidean mathematics had survived in more ample condition than the meager fragments we now have, this situation would not be altered. For we are searching for an interpretative viewpoint, and our documents are not likely simply to hand us one. Given that mathematical and philosophical writers treat of related issues, the question remains open as to which, if either, influenced the thought of the other. Correspondences in their treatments of those issues have resulted in familiar views that, for instance, the Eleatic paradoxes on plurality and motion instigated radical changes in the deductive format of mathematical proof;[4] or, again, that Democritean atomism played a key role in the formation of a heuristic style of analysis based on

1. Can one deny that this is a factor in the current debate over the use of quantitative methods in historical and social studies?

2. On Plato and mathematics, see Brumbaugh 1954, Wedberg 1955, and Knorr 1976, chaps. III/VII.

3. A useful survey of Aristotle's mathematical discussions is provided in Heath 1949.

4. Introduced in one form in Tannery 1887, this view has been expanded by A. Szabó, e.g., in Szabó 1969. (See section 2 below.)

infinitesimals.[5] My reasons for adopting the contrary position—that mathematical studies owed nothing of significance to such philosophical efforts—rest on the following observations.

1. In the period of the fifth and early fourth centuries we can perceive no sign that mathematicians adopted any caution in those areas which should have been rendered suspect by the foundational troubles raised through dialectical inquiries; I refer, for instance, to the use of infinity after the time of Zeno and the use of proportions in geometry after the discovery of irrationals.

2. If the thoroughgoing adoption of elaborate deductive forms, including the attempt to axiomatize geometry on the basis of fundamental definitions and postulates as we find them in Euclid, was the result of philosophical stimuli—how can we reconcile this with the indubitable fact that philosophy itself, even at the hands of such masters as Plato and Aristotle, remained at such an inadequate level of systematization?

3. Along similar lines, how can we reconcile this with the fact that the philosophers of antiquity are, with no exception I know of, so inept in the management of mathematical arguments?

4. The concepts we shall consider—the infinite and the infinitesimal—are never introduced at all within mathematical arguments of a formal sort (but see n. 22 below). Whatever considerations induced this result among the mathematicians seem to have missed the philosophers—especially Aristotle—who introduce and consider these concepts over and over again.

5. These philosophical arguments invariably turn on other than mathematical aspects of the problems. Indeed, Aristotle sometimes admits that a given difficulty might not be a matter for the geometer to trouble himself over. Surely, the ancient mathematicians did not react far differently from moderns in the analogous situation: why should philosophical difficulties peripherally related to mathematical work interfere with research? If, ultimately, these difficulties do raise the possibility of admitting actual tech-

5. This is most prominently argued by S. Luria and by J. Mau (section 4 below). Indeed, Luria has attempted to interpret the whole of Archimedes' work as a development of atomism; see Luria 1945, 1948.

nical errors, then they will be taken seriously—although such counterexamples usually emerge only much later and through the elaboration of techniques, not the inquiry into methods.[6] Of course, the philosophers might then say—and frequently do say—that the mathematicians would have been better advised to take their criticisms seriously earlier. Nevertheless, the fact seems clear that philosophical studies do not directly—or even indirectly—affect the course of mathematical research.

These observations will be developed in the remainder of this chapter, as I assess the claim that philosophical considerations affected mathematical work and as I explore the interpretative possibilities of my view of the mathematicians' autonomy. In an earlier essay I have examined this issue in the context of the question of the origins of formal methods in the pre-Socratic geometry.[7] The present study will concentrate on two issues in fourth-century geometry: the study of infinity and the use of indivisibles.

2. The Mathematical Aspect of Zeno's Paradoxes

Zeno's paradoxes on motion turn on difficulties in the understanding of infinite processes. Just such processes are essential for the proofs of the measurement of the circle, the cone, and the sphere, as presented in Euclid's Book XII. The limiting techniques used there derive from Eudoxus, Plato's contemporary (ca. 395–340 B.C.) and commonly go under the name of the "method of exhaustion."[8] This correspondence between the ideas of Zeno and the techniques of Eudoxus has encouraged some to view the latter as a sort of mathematical solution to the Eleatic paradoxes—in

6. For a critique of the hypothesis of ancient foundations crises, see Knorr 1976, chap. IX. References appear there to the studies by H. Hasse and H. Scholz, B. L. van der Waerden, and H. Freudenthal. On more recent episodes in the development of mathematical foundations, one may consult Kline 1972. The mathematical view of foundations is well summarized in Bourbaki 1960, pp. 9–63. A useful, if dated, survey appears in Hankel 1874, pp. 111–27.

7. Knorr forthcoming; this article was presented in an earlier version at the second conference of the International Union for the History and Philosophy of Science, at Pisa, September 5, 1979.

8. See n. 23 below.

effect, assigning to the geometers the specific motive of avoiding and resolving philosophical difficulties.[9] As I shall argue here, however, this view seriously distorts the origins and purpose of these geometric methods.

According to Plato (*Parmenides* 128D), Zeno's writings had the purpose of defending Parmenides on the indivisibility of being by deriving contradictions from his opponents' assumptions, such as the existence of plurality. Such appears to be the motive behind not only the paradoxes on plurality but also those on motion, as reported by Aristotle in the *Physics*.[10] Two of these latter paradoxes relate to the description of infinite processes: the "dichotomy" asserts that no motion can be completed, for this would require completing the half, then the half of what remains, then the half of that remainder, and so on—that is, the completion of an infinity in finite time (*Physics* VI 2); the "Achilles" asserts, for much the same reasons, that no runner, however swift, could overtake another, however slow, for when the pursuer arrives at the leader's present position, the leader will have advanced further ahead (*Physics* VI 9). One should observe at once that the difficulty lies not with any mathematical aspect of the procedure, but with the physical and philosophical implications. There is no question that any finite magnitude can be viewed as the sum of its half, quarter, eighth, sixteenth parts, etc.—a sequence with an unlimited number of terms. But a difficulty seems to enter when we speak of actually moving across the magnitude, in effect completing an infinite set of acts in a finite span of time. Aristotle's analysis and explanation are basically sound: we are dealing with *two* magnitudes—distance and time—both of which are infinite with regard to their divisibility. In this sense, an infinity of spans of time *is* accessible to us for completing this motion, so that the paradox vanishes.[11]

9. One such statement, "This method was invented by Eudoxus . . . in answer to Zeno's dilemma about the infinitely small," appears in Maziarz and Greenwood 1968, p. 239.

10. The paradoxes on motion and on plurality are brought together in Owen 1957–58.

11. In a later account, Aristotle sharpens the paradox (*Physics* VIII 8, 263a4–b9): by completing any span we might be viewed as in a sense counting it, so that completing the whole entails actually having counted an infinite number in finite time. This is clearly impossible—under the further assumption, which Aristotle

Nevertheless, if we consider Aristotle's discussion of this paradox in the light of his discussions, elsewhere in the *Physics* and in the *De caelo*, of the nature of the infinite (i.e., of the impossibility of infinite magnitude, body, force, etc.) we recognize that his analysis here falls noticeably short of a complete technical account of the issue. Without doubt, Aristotle himself sensed this, for he next provides an extensive mathematical argument on infinite motion.[12] To my knowledge, the discussions of this text do not indicate that it is intended to amplify the refutation of Zeno. But this intent is clear not only from the point made in the argument but also from the fact that it is unrelated to the subject of the chapter proper, viz., that motion, time, and magnitude are all alike continuous and divisible without limit.[13]

Aristotle's argument amplifying his account of Zeno's paradox runs as follows. It is asserted that no infinite can be traversed in finite time, nor any finite in infinite time. He takes up the latter: suppose the time to be infinite, the distance traversed finite. Next choose a finite portion of the time; in that finite time a finite distance will be traversed in accordance with the assumed motion. Aristotle then supposes that in times equal to that time, equal distances will be traversed (i.e., uniformity of motion). For simplicity, he assumes that this distance is a proper measure of the whole given distance. As a finite number of these distances sum to the whole distance, so also the same number of the corresponding times sums to the whole time required to traverse this distance. As these times are each finite and there are finitely many of them, the whole time is thus finite. This establishes that the time to traverse a finite distance cannot be infinite.

At first glance this argument seems a labored way of establishing a simple point. For if a given finite distance D is traversed in a time T according to a given uniform motion, and if in a time t

would appear to admit, that any such single act of counting requires some minimal finite time. He answers this paradox by pointing out that we have altered the character of the motion: it is now discontinuous, since the act of counting each subinterval amounts to stopping and then beginning to move anew. It is thus no longer paradoxical that this mode of motion might not admit of completion. We observe that here, as before, the element of paradox does not touch on the purely mathematical concept of magnitude.

12. *Phys.* VI 2, 233a32–b15.
13. *Phys.* VI 2, 233a11–21, b15–32.

the distance d is traversed according to the same motion, then the proportionality $T : t = D : d$ establishes that the time T required to traverse D is finite. For the historian of ancient mathematics, however, Aristotle's method is of considerable interest, for it reflects the techniques being developed in his time in the examination of proportion theory.[14] Nevertheless, we may perceive several aspects of his argument which are less than satisfactory.

For instance, although here and in related arguments Aristotle introduces principles fundamental for the geometry of his time and frequently employs the technical vocabulary of the geometers, his phrasing of these principles is all too frequently obscure and his framing of proofs imprecise. One assumption crucial for the present argument is that any finite magnitude through finite multiplication can be made to exceed any other finite magnitude. This is found in the *Elements* (Book V, definition 4) and is a pillar of the Euclidean proportion theory. While stated by Aristotle in a number of variants,[15] it is not given explicitly here and has to be supplied.

Again, Aristotle presents the same argument on infinite motions later in *Physics* VI.[16] He there allows for a more general situation, covering not only the case of uniform motion but also the cases in which the motion may be accelerating or decelerating. In this he commits a plain error, however. In subdividing the given distance into equal parts, he assumes that the time required for traversing each such part—while not necessarily equal to the time for any other part, since the motion is now nonuniform—is nevertheless finite. His justification, if it can be called such, is that

14. I have begun such an examination of these Aristotelian arguments in Knorr 1978b, pp. 198 f. Besides the arguments on infinite motion in *Phys.* VI 2 and 7, one may add those in IV 8 on the void, VIII 10 on forces, and *De caelo* I 6 and 7 on weight. These all apply a pre-Euclidean technique of proportions. Commentary on these passages has not been particularly useful. On *De caelo* I 6, for instance, Heath remarks: "The chapter is very long, and the wording very involved, not to say slipshod" (Heath 1949, p. 165). The commentary on the *Physics* in Ross 1936 offers little of interest, nor have I discovered much in the commentary of Simplicius on this material. In the light of my findings on the pre-Euclidean proportion theory, I would expect these passages to contribute to our understanding of the chronological development of Aristotle's physical writings.

15. See *Phys.* III 6, 206b3–12; 7, 207a32–b13; and VIII 10, 266b2–4. These are discussed in Knorr 1978b, pp. 210 f.

16. *Phys.* VI 7, esp. 237b34–238a18 and 238a20–35. The arguments are technically identical, differing only in terminology.

the time for traversing the part cannot be infinite, as he has assumed the whole time is infinite, and the time for traversing the part must be less than that for the whole.[17] It is hard to believe that a geometer could have been the ultimate source of Aristotle's treatment here; for a geometer would certainly understand that an infinite whole might have an infinite part. Indeed, Aristotle has proved as much in his earlier discussion in the *Physics* (VI 2), and this principle seems to have been grasped even by some of the pre-Socratics, notably Anaxagoras.[18] In the present case, having admitted nonuniform motion, we might easily construct a decelerating motion which requires some fixed time to traverse each successively diminishing proportional part of the distance; then the time to traverse the whole would indeed be infinite.

More significantly, Aristotle has failed to isolate the essential logical difficulty with Zeno's argument. Having determined the time T (as from our earlier argument) to traverse the given distance D, we are compelled by Zeno's argument to admit that in no time less than T will the entire distance D have been traversed. But there is no difficulty in making this admission; it is certainly *not* equivalent to the assertion that the motion will *never* be completed, as Zeno appears to infer. To obtain that result, one must deny an important assumption for Aristotle's whole argument, but one which he appears to slip in without due notice: that there exist *some* time (t) and *some* distance (d) such that t suffices for traversing d. But notice that the denial of this—i.e., that there do not exist a time t and a distance d such that t suffices for traversing d—is equivalent to the impossibility of motion; thus, admitting this as an *assumption* renders circular Zeno's alleged *derivation* of the inconsistency of the concept of motion.

These aspects of Aristotle's treatment of the motion paradoxes reveal that far from groping toward the invention of geometric principles appropriate for the resolution of these paradoxes, he was *applying*—often imprecisely—certain principles from the geometry of his day which he perceived to be relevant to his

17. *Phys.* VI 7, 238a10.
18. Anaxagoras (fr. 3) asserts that there is no smallest; that the large and the small are equal with regard to number. See Kirk and Raven 1960, pp. 368–77. Such ideas were fundamental in the continuum theory of the Stoics, see Sambursky 1959, pp: 96–98.

discussion.[19] The awkwardness of this and related technical discussions would be especially remarkable, if we assumed that Aristotle had access to geometers' discussions specifically directed
against the Eleatics.[20] While it is clear he did have access to a
general technique of proportions—that of Eudoxus and his followers—the use of this technique in the context of the Eleatic
debate must surely be his own.

This inference is strengthened when one considers the Euclidean treatment of the principle of unlimited bisection. In *Elements*
X 1 Euclid proves that for any two given magnitudes, if from the
larger more than its half is subtracted, and from the remainder
more than its half, and so on, eventually a remainder is left which
is less than the smaller given magnitude. The proof is reminiscent
of Aristotle's discussion of infinite motion and may be summarized as follows: taking the two given magnitudes, Euclid multi-
plies the smaller (A) to obtain a magnitude (C) greater than the

19. I believe that Aristotle possessed in Eudoxus's work *On Speeds* a source for
the geometric techniques applied in the *Physics*. According to Simplicius (*in De
caelo*, ed. Heiberg, p. 494) this was the work in which Eudoxus presented his
geometric system of nested spheres for the description of planetary motions. As
the title indicates, the geometry of motion was a necessary element in this study.
The definition of uniform motion given by Aristotle—the equal magnitude is always traversed in equal time (*Phys.* VI 2, 233b5)—is surely that of Eudoxus; it is
still taken as the definition by Autolycus (*De mota sphaera*, preface). Thus, Eudoxus
would have to establish as a *theorem* that in a uniform motion the distances
traversed are proportional to the times. (This is taken as an assumption by Autolycus; but, of course, it may be derived as a theorem on the basis of the definition
he has given.) Now, a proof of this theorem may be cast according to the techniques of the pre-Euclidean proportion theory discussed in Knorr 1978b. In such a
proof, one first establishes the commensurable case, then proves the incommensurable case via an indirect argument which reduces to the commensurable case.
The argument given by Aristotle in *Phys.* VI 2 conforms to the proof we would
produce for the commensurable case of Eudoxus's theorem. Moreover, when Aristotle says (ibid., 233b3) "this [magnitude] either measures *AB* or exceeds or falls
short," he can be seen as conforming to the pattern of the proof of the incommensurable case in which an auxiliary magnitude is introduced, either greater or less
than a given. Thus, Aristotle appears to apply techniques developed earlier in the
Eudoxean astronomy. (For texts and discussion, see Lasserre 1966, pp. 67–74 and
198–212.)
20. According to Simplicius (*in Phys.*, ed. H. Diels, p. 138), Aristotle's contemporary, the philosopher Xenocrates, following a doctrine of Plato, posited the
existence of indivisible lines in order to avoid the dichotomy paradox of Zeno. (See
also the Peripatetic tract, *On Indivisible Lines*, 968a23–b4, and Sambursky 1959, pp.
91 f.) Xenocrates' surrender would appear to indicate, first, the novelty of the
geometric techniques by which Aristotle at this very time was refuting Zeno and,
second, the absence of any precedents for such refutations among geometers
themselves.

larger (*B*), in accordance with *Elements* V, definition 4. He then subtracts from *B* more than its half and from *C* a part equal to *A*. Since *B* is less than *C*, and more than half of *B* has been removed, while less than half of *C* has been removed, it follows that the remainder of *B* is less than the remainder of *C*. This procedure of subtraction is continued until there remains of *C* only one part equal to *A*. The corresponding remainder of *B* is thus less than *A*, as was to be proved.

Reading this theorem from Euclid makes clear its affinity with the Aristotelian arguments on the infinity of motion in *Physics* VI 2 and 7. But more striking than their similarity is this fundamental difference: in contrast with Aristotle's intent to explicate the nature of the infinite and his uninhibited use of the term "infinite" (*apeiron*) throughout these discussions, Euclid uses neither the term nor the concept of the infinite anywhere in this proof. Indeed, save for the context of parallel lines, "infinite" has been eliminated from the geometers' vocabulary altogether. Surely this is a serious difficulty for any view which assigns the philosophical debate over Zeno's arguments a major role in the development of the formal geometric theory of limits. For how can one explain the geometers' abandonment of the infinite per se, when Aristotle himself neither advises nor follows this course?

In fact, it appears to me more plausible to view Aristotle's discussions in the *Physics* as an effort to *save* the concept of the infinite, in the face of a movement among the geometers of his day to give up that concept. This view helps to account for the fundamental problems in his theory of the infinite. In particular, while he insists that one must deny the *actual* existence of any infinite, whether as magnitude or as multitude, he still wishes to allow its existence in certain *potential* senses—i.e., as the unlimited sequence of the integers or as the unlimited divisibility of continuous magnitude. Even this weaker concept of the infinite is dispensable for the purposes of geometry, however, where only finite magnitudes need be taken into consideration. Even within Aristotle's theory, the retention of the potentially infinite is unfortunate. For by his own definition, a thing is *potentially* such-and-such only if a state of affairs is possible in which it can *actually* become such-and-such. As the infinite is in no sense capable of existing actually, the potential infinite must stand as a major exception to Aristotle's schemes for describing being and change.[21] It is ironic that Aristotle denies one specific sense of the infinite in which it *is* in fact indispensable for geometry: on cosmological grounds he maintains that no line can be infinite, or even indefinitely extendible; for the cosmos is bounded, so that no line can exceed in length the diameter of the universe. While this is purely a physical argument, Aristotle carries it over into the abstract field of geometry. But his claim that geometers can do without it is an error, and non-Euclidean systems are readily constructible on the denial of the unlimited extendibility of magnitude.[22]

In view of these difficulties, the fourth-century debate over the arguments of the Eleatics, as presented in Aristotle's *Physics*, hardly supports the view that this debate was a factor in the formal work in geometry at that time. Aristotle's mathematical arguments make clear that he had access to formal terminology and techniques, as in proportion theory; but by their awkwardness they reveal that he did not possess any explicit mathematical precedent for the refutation of Zeno. Aristotle's theory of the infinite shows remarkable insensitivity to the issues which must have occupied the geometers of his generation. If Euclid and his predecessors knew of this theory, they chose wisely to disregard it. In all, Aristotle's treatments appear to be the *application* within philosophical contexts of techniques drawn from the mathematics of his time. They do not represent the context within which those techniques were invented; nor do they reflect the motives behind their invention.

21. Heath 1949, pp. 102–13, presents a survey of Aristotle's remarks on the infinite and perceives his notion of the potential infinite as an exception to his general view of potentiality. See also Wieland 1962.

22. Euclid retains the infinite only in the sense that any given line may be extended indefinitely (*eis apeiron*; see, e.g., Book I, postulates 2 and 5 and definition 23). At *Phys.* III 7, 207b27 Aristotle argues that geometers do not actually require this sense of the infinite; but Jaakko Hintikka has clearly shown his error here (Hintikka 1966). T. L. Heath misses this aspect of the issue, however, relating it instead to the Eudoxean analysis (Heath 1949, p. 111). The opinion of M. G. Evans on this point is unfortunate but perhaps all too often encountered: "In this passage, Aristotle has summarized admirably the prevailing Greek attitude in mathematics. Aristotle shared the Greek horror of the infinite" (Evans 1964, pp. 49 f.).

3. The Origins of the Method of Exhaustion

The principle of bisection, discussed above in connection with Zeno's paradoxes, is an essential feature in the "method of exhaustion" presented by Euclid in *Elements* XII.[23] From Archimedes we learn that this technique derives from Eudoxus, that is, from the mid-fourth century.[24] But while Eudoxus introduced this formal method, the results in whose proofs it is applied were known before him: the quadrature of the circle (XII 2) was stated in very nearly its Euclidean form by Hippocrates of Chios, ca. 400 B.C., and the volumes of the pyramid and of the cone (XII 3–7 and 10) were known to Democritus. In this and the next section of the chapter I propose to trace the origins of the Eudoxean method and to recover the form in which the earlier geometers treated these theorems.

The importance of the bisection principle for Eudoxus's method and the supposed link between this principle and the debate over Zeno's paradoxes have led to the familiar view of a corresponding philosophical influence on Eudoxus's work. The argument of the previous section, however, has revealed that the geometric study of this principle did not depend on such philosophical efforts but, on the contrary, was most probably a source for them. In regard to Eudoxus, moreover, it seems clear that the principle of bisection in its Euclidean form was not yet a feature of his method. This statement may seem surprising, for it denies the view maintained in all standard accounts of this material. But my study of

---

23. The term "method of exhaustion"—whose inappropriateness is often noted—was coined for the classical formal analysis by seventeenth-century geometers. Gregory of St. Vincent used it to denote his own method of indivisibles (1647), despite the fundamental differences in logical structure between his and the ancient method. (See Boyer 1949, p. 136.) One should observe that Gregory also expounds a technique of summing infinite series, which he applies to explicate the paradoxes of Zeno. Here, again, the term *exhaustus* appears; it renders into Latin forms of *anaireo* and the like in Aristotle. This indicates a relation between discussions of geometric method and studies of philosophical problems in the seventeenth century.

24. Archimedes in the prefaces to *Quadrature of the Parabola, Sphere and Cylinder I,* and *The Method.* For a review of the historical implications of these passages, see Knorr 1978b, pp. 194–97; Van der Waerden 1954, pp. 184–87; and Neuenschwander 1974–75.

the Euclidean proportion theory and the forms which preceded it has led me to realize, on the basis of both technique and terminology, that the theory in *Elements* V represents a revision of the version introduced by Eudoxus.[25] A little-noted but important question so came to have a natural answer: why doesn't Euclid employ in Book XII the basic principles used in Book V? This incongruity, despite the great utility for streamlining the proofs which these principles could afford, must have resulted from the facts that Euclid presented Book XII largely in its early Eudoxean form but incorporated the later revised versions of proportion theory into Book V.[26]

Euclid's form for the bisection principle in X 1 relies, as we have seen, on axioms drawn from Book V (in particular, on the multiplication principle in V, definition 4). It is enunciated in this form: "Two unequal magnitudes being set out, if from the greater there is subtracted greater than the half and from the remainder greater than the half, and this happens continually, there will be left a certain magnitude less than the lesser magnitude set out."[27] By contrast, in the theorems of Book XII as well as in theorems of Archimedes and other authors, appeals to this principle are made according to a different formula: "Cutting the larger given magnitude in half, and cutting the remainder in half, and doing this continually, we shall be left with a certain remainder less than the lesser given magnitude."[28] While the difference might seem slight to us, its significance cannot be denied. For verbatim quotation is Euclid's standard way of calling attention to an appeal to prior theorems in his proofs. His failure to reproduce the wording of X 1 in these theorems thus indicates that these proofs originally admitted the bisection principle in a different form. Indeed, Archimedes tells us that the early geometers had appealed to this

25. See Knorr 1978b, pp. 191–200, 213–20.
26. O. Becker, recognizing the discrepancy between Books V and XII, attempted an explanation on the assumption that Eudoxus produced the "exhaustion" theorems before developing his general proportion theory (Becker 1934–36b). See also Scholz 1928.
27. My translation from the text of Heiberg.
28. This is a paraphrase and composite of several applications of the bisection principle in Euclid, Archimedes, and others. See the specimens presented in Knorr 1978b, appendix IV.

principle as a "lemma," which in his terms means an axiom or unproved assumption.[29]

Thus, it appears that Eudoxus admitted this principle as obvious and not requiring proof. This accords with our earlier observation that in the Aristotelian discussion of Zeno's problem, the constitution of a finite magnitude as the sum of its infinitely many proportional parts did not present difficulty; it was the element of motion which demanded explanation. It accords also with the fact that the study of infinite series, to which Zeno's paradoxes have the strongest affiliation, received little attention among ancient geometers. Indeed, we have but one example from the ancient mathematical literature of the summation of an infinite series.[30] Admittedly, on my view Eudoxus has employed without proof a principle which we—and, in fact, his ancient successors, Euclid and Archimedes—would perceive as needing proof; nevertheless, this is not a difficulty. The equivalent situation obtains for several other principles, for instance, the assumption of the fourth proportional in the proofs of Book XII, as well as in Archimedes and other authors.[31] While we might demand that such a principle be justified, and while it may be argued that this or comparable principles received some attention among philosophers such as Bryson,[32] the fact remains that they were not taken up in the mathematical literature, nor was any effort made to find intuitively more obvious forms for them.

Since I deny that Eudoxus actually attempted to demonstrate the bisection principle, and since I thereby undermine the effort to detect philosophical precedents for his methods, what account can be given of the background from which his methods developed? To address this question, it will be helpful to consider the Euclidean theorem on the circle (XII 2), which I will take to be characteristic of Eudoxus's method.[33]

29. Archimedes, preface to *Quadrature of the Parabola*; see my discussions in Knorr 1978a, pp. 251–55, and 1978b, pp. 205–13.

30. Archimedes, in *Quadrature of the Parabola*, prop. 23, established in finite form the equivalent of the summation $1 + (1/4) + (1/4)^2 + (1/4)^3 + \ldots = 4/3$.

31. See Becker 1932–33b, 1934–36b. The same assumption figures in the pre-Euclidean proportion theory discussed in Knorr 1978b, p. 198.

32. The circle quadrature by Bryson is examined in Becker 1934–36a. It is also discussed by Ian Mueller in chapter V.

33. For a justification of this assumption, see Knorr 1978b, pp. 194–97.

The theorem to be proved is that "circles are as the squares on their diameters." The proof employs an indirect argument. If the circles (A, B) do not have the same ratio as the squares on their diameters $(C, D$, respectively), then if $C : D = A : X$,[34] X will not equal B. Suppose first that X is less than B. We inscribe in B a regular polygon (say, a square), bisect each of the arcs (in this case, four) and connect all the points of section, so obtaining the inscribed polygon having twice as many sides (here, the octagon). Now, the difference between the two polygons consists of a set of equal triangles, one for each side of the initial polygon. Each of these triangles is the half of a rectangle having the same base and height as the circular segment which contains the triangle; as the segment is itself contained within this rectangle, it follows that the triangle is greater than the half of the segment. Therefore, in passing from the first polygon to the one having twice as many sides, we have diminished the difference between the circle and the polygon by more than its half. Proceeding in this way, we will eventually obtain an inscribed polygon differing from the circle by less than the difference supposed between B and X; that is, this polygon will exceed X.[35] We designate this polygon as E and inscribe in circle A a polygon F similar to E. Now, similar polygons are as the squares of the diameters;[36] thus, $F : E = C : D$. It follows that $A : X = F : E$. Since F is inscribed in A, F is less than A. From the proportionality, it follows that E is less than X. But by construction E is greater than X. Thus, the initial assumption that X is less than B has led to contradiction. One next shows that the assumption that X is greater than B also leads to contradiction.[37] This establishes that X equals B, and so the theorem has been proved.

34. Here the existence of the fourth proportional is assumed without proof; see n. 31 above.

35. The existence of such a polygon follows from the bisection principle. In Euclid's text there follows here a verbatim citation of X 1, but this has been identified as an interpolation; see Knorr 1978b, pp. 200 f.

36. By appeal to XII 1.

37. Eudoxus might have established this step by means of the analogous argument based on circumscribed polygons, as Archimedes does in *Dimension of the Circle*, prop. 1. But since in Eudoxus's theorem proportions are involved, he can finesse this: by inverting the ratios and assuming again the existence of the fourth proportional, this case of the theorem may be reduced to the previous inscribed case.

The Interaction of Mathematics and Philosophy

The use of indirect reasoning tends to make proofs in this style somewhat difficult to follow. But the essential idea here is straightforward: the circle may be viewed as the limit of the regular polygons inscribed in it. Given two circles and similar polygons inscribed in each, one readily establishes via the theorems on similar rectilinear figures (as presented in *Elements* VI) that the polygons are as the squares on the diameters of their respective circles. As this proportionality holds for all such inscribed figures and the polygons themselves can be constructed as close to the circles as desired, it follows that the circles too must have this ratio. What Eudoxus has achieved in his indirect method is a way of establishing the limiting condition via demonstrated properties of constructible rectilinear figures only. The instrument for this is the bisection principle, which we have seen removes the need to appeal to naive notions of limits or of infinite processes.

The search for a precedent for Eudoxus's procedure is unusually fortunate, for Simplicius has preserved in his commentary on the *Physics* two substantial documents, the circle quadratures by Hippocrates of Chios and by Antiphon, the former a major geometer, the latter a Sophist from the late fifth and early fourth centuries B.C. Simplicius asserts that he draws the fragment of Hippocrates verbatim from the history of geometry compiled by Aristotle's disciple, Eudemus of Rhodes; conceivably, the materials on Antiphon have the same provenance. We are thus in a good position to view some of the work of Eudoxus's precursors in the very field of his geometric activity.

The Hippocrates fragment deals with the construction and quadrature of "lunules," crescent-shaped figures bounded by arcs of circles. Simplicius's account begins as follows:

> He made a beginning, and of the things useful for these [constructions] he first set out that [1] similar segments of circles have to each other the same ratio as their bases in power. This he proved from the proof that [2] the diameters have in power the same ratio as the circles, which Euclid placed second in the tenth book of the *Elements*, giving its protasis thus: [2a] Circles are to each other as the squares on the diameters. [3] For as the circles are related to each other, so also the similar segments. [4] For similar segments are those which are the same part of the circle, for instance, the semicircle to the

semicircle and the third part to the third part; because [5] also similar segments admit of equal angles. Now, [6] those [angles] of semicircles are right, and those of greater [segments] are less than right, and by as much as the segments are greater than the semicircles; and those [angles] of lesser [segments] are greater and by as much as the segments are less [than the semicircles]. Having proved this first he then proved that [7] if a lunule has a semicircle as its outer arc, its quadrature might be effected in a certain way.[38]

Eudemus thus asserts that Hippocrates prefaced his quadratures of the lunules with the proof of theorem 1. This theorem does not appear in Euclid, but a proof has been preserved by Pappus in Book V of his *Collection*, and it conforms to the structure outlined by Eudemus.[39]

Hippocrates' proof of [1] would proceed in the order [4], [3], [2], [1]. Doubtless he took [4] as a *definition* of similar segments, while Simplicius viewed it as a derived property and so inserted at [5] the statement of the Euclidean definition (from *Elements* III, definition 11). Comparison with Pappus reveals a certain confusion at [4]. As a property of *segments* (*tmēmata*), it is useless. But the analogous assertion for *sectors* (*tomeis*)—that sectors of the same circle have the same ratio as the arcs which subtend them— is proved by Pappus by means of the technique of proportions which I have identified as due to Eudoxus.[40] Hippocrates' elucidation of the notion of similarity via proper parts (i.e., the halves and the thirds) foreshadows this technique in that the latter characteristically provides first a proof for the commensurable case of a theorem, then proves the incommensurable case by means of an indirect argument based on the commensurable case. In [3] *tmēmata* must mean *segments*, despite what I have just said about [4]. This necessary fluctuation of the sense of the term has been noted

38. Simplicius, *in Phys.*, ed. H. Diels, pp. 60–69. The translation is mine; numerals have been added. Complicating the interpretation of this text is the problem of separating Eudemus's words from Simplicius's glosses. Several efforts have been made, e.g., by Bretschneider, Diels, Tannery, Rudio, and Becker. I have found Rudio's notes frequently quite perceptive (Rudio 1907).

39. *Collection* V 13, pp. 340–42.

40. *Collection* V 12, pp. 336–40. Pappus repeats the proof in his commentary on Book VI of the *Almagest* of Ptolemy; see my translation and discussion in Knorr 1978b, pp. 189–91, 227–30.

by F. Rudio.[41] While geometric terminology at Hippocrates' time may not yet have become fixed precisely as we find it in Euclid, it seems incredible that a competent geometer would ever have used the same term to designate two such different figures as *segments* and *sectors*. Presumably, then, an error has entered the text in the course of its transmission from Hippocrates via Eudemus to Simplicius, not to mention the numerous intermediate transcriptions during this 1,000-year period. Conceivably Simplicius himself, encountering an unfamiliar term and not perceiving that a distinction had to be made between [4] and [3], amended the received text. At any rate, the confusion is easily recognized and corrected.

The results stated in [6] do not figure in the proof of [1] but do apply in the constructions of the lunules which follow. Hippocrates' terminology differs from that of Euclid in Book III: his "angle *of* a segment" is Euclid's "angle *in* a segment" (III, definition 8), for Euclid takes the "angle *of* a segment" to be that bounded by the arc and the base of the segment (definition 7). The expression of the relations in [6] is rather loose; but it appears that a direct proportionality is intended: the angle of a segment exceeds a right angle by an amount proportional to the amount by which the arc of the segment is exceeded by a semicircle. These assertions may be compared with Euclid's III 31 and VI 33.

These comparisons indicate that Hippocrates had already mastered a significant part of plane geometry, very nearly in its Euclidean form. Discrepancies in terminology merely increase our confidence in Simplicius's fidelity to the text of Eudemus. This is of special interest at [2]. Here we have the theorem on the circle, equivalent to Euclid's XII 2 but expressed in accordance with the archaic "power" (*dunamis*) terminology familiar in the fourth century although increasingly replaced by locutions using "square" (*tetragōnon*) from the third century onward.[42] What is important to note is that Hippocrates certainly possessed what he took to be a *demonstration* of this theorem. Eudemus says as much: that

41. See Rudio 1907, pp. 41–46.
42. On uses of *dunamis*, see Knorr 1976, chap. III/I and Knorr 1978a, pp. 240, 254, 264.

WILBUR R. KNORR

Hippocrates had proved [1] from the fact of having proved (*deixai*) the theorem on circles [2].[43] Moreover, the careful deductive ordering, evident in these opening remarks on the proof of [1], as well as in the whole of the treatment of the lunules which follows, persuades one that Hippocrates produced a justification of the principal underlying theorems. Whether his proof of [2] was included in his preface or whether he could refer to its prior demonstration in another work such as his compilation of the "elements," we of course cannot say.[44]

What was the form of his proof? Clearly, it could not have been the complete Eudoxean (Euclidean) version, since credit for the precise formal proof goes to Eudoxus, a half-century later. But we may perceive the lines of Hippocrates' approach by considering another circle quadrature preserved in this passage from Simplicius, that of Antiphon.[45] According to this account, Antiphon inscribed a polygon, such as a square,[46] in the circle; bisecting each side and drawing perpendiculars from the midpoint to the circle, he thus produced a triangle on each side to obtain the inscribed octagon. In the same way, he obtained the inscribed 16-gon. "And then in the same way cutting the sides of the 16-gon and joining the lines and doubling the inscribed polygon, and doing this always, so that at some time, the area being exhausted (*dapa-*

43. It might look as if Hippocrates must not have proved [1]; for this theorem amounts to a quadrature of the circle, and it is this problem which the quadrature of the lunules is intended to solve. But first, this objection would apply with even greater force, had Hippocrates admitted [1] merely as an assumption. Again, the theorem on the ratios of circles would have been viewed as asserting a property, not a construction, of the circle and so would not have been viewed as a solution to the quadrature problem. Moreover, while it appears to be Aristotle's opinion that Hippocrates' quadrature of the lunules was supposed to apply toward the quadrature of the circle, this has been doubted by many scholars (see, e.g., Heath 1921, I, p. 199). The fragment as we possess it reveals a profound sense of proof technique on Hippocrates' part; it seems hardly credible that he could then go on to commit the patent logical error entailed in extending his theorems to the case of the circle. Indeed, Simplicius himself suspected this was a misinterpretation based on a confusion of "segment" for "lunule" (*in Phys.*, ed. Diels, p. 69).

44. Proclus names Hippocrates as the first writer of "elements" of geometry (*in Euclidem*, ed. G. Friedlein, p. 66).

45. Simplicius, *in Phys.*, pp. 54 f. Cf. Ian Mueller's discussion of Antiphon's quadrature in chapter V.

46. In an alternative version, preserved by Themistius, the figure is an isosceles triangle (*in Phys.*, ed. Schenkl, pp. 3 f.).

nōmenou), a certain polygon would be inscribed in this manner in the circle whose sides on account of smallness would coincide with the arc of the circle."[47] This portion of the argument may be compared with a line in the Euclidean proof of XII 2: "Next, cutting in half the remaining arcs and joining the lines and doing this always, we will be left with certain segments of the circle which will be less than the excess by which the circle exceeds the area *S*." It is evident that both in the general conception of the construction and in the terminology for expressing it, the two passages conform closely to each other. Is this merely a consequence of Simplicius's paraphrasing his source in Euclidean terms, or has he preserved for us another sample of pre-Euclidean usage? I subscribe to the latter view. For, first, Simplicius had access to Eudemus's history, as we know from his discussion of Hippocrates. Moreover, Simplicius is aware of Eudemus's analysis of Antiphon's argument. In the passage of the *Physics* which gave rise to this commentary,[48] Aristotle charged Antiphon with committing a fallacy which undermines a basic geometric principle. Which principle was this? Simplicius refers to Alexander's opinion that it was the fact that a straight line and a circle meet at a point; the line cannot coincide with the arc, as Antiphon would claim. But Simplicius then cites, with his approval, Eudemus's view—that the principle involved is the unlimited divisibility of magnitude; that is, since each polygon will have a finite difference in area from the circle, the process of subdivision can always be continued, and the difference will never be exhausted, as Antiphon seems to believe it might. Thus, Simplicius has in Eudemus a source for his discussion of Antiphon. Further, he requires such a source other than Euclid; for there are aspects of the argument, the construction, and the terminology which are not to be obtained from the *Elements*. For instance, Antiphon constructs triangles on each side of his polygons in order to obtain the figure of doubly many sides; Euclid effects this by bisecting the arcs.

---

47. Simplicius, *in Phys.*, p. 55. Diels suspects that *hōste* ("so that") in the text is a mistranscription of *ōieto* ("he thought"); see his note in Diels-Kranz 1968, II, p. 341.

48.. *Phys.* I 2, 185a14.

Most important, of course, is the appearance of "exhaustion"; the Euclidean method is designed to avoid any such direct appeal to limits.

Viewed as geometry, Antiphon's argument displays a remarkable incongruity. The conception of approaching the circle through the sequence of successively doubled polygons is sound, a major step toward the Euclidean proof. For this, Antiphon has gained an honorable mention in histories of mathematics.[49] Yet the second part of the argument is a disaster. It would be bad enough to view the circle as attained at the end of the infinite process, but Antiphon makes the preposterous assumption that the circle is attained after *finitely* many steps.

Antiphon's defense is that his argument is not intended as an effort in geometry. Antiphon was numbered among the Sophists; indeed, were it not for the remark by Aristotle and the comment on it by Simplicius, we should not have known of a single mathematical contribution by him—his absence from Proclus's list of pre-Euclidean geometers is noteworthy.[50] Antiphon's interests were centered on ethics and epistemology; the distinction between convention (*nomos*) and nature (*physis*) was a pivotal element in his thought, as it was for the Sophists in general.[51] In the argument on the circle, Antiphon explains the coinciding of the line and the arc on the grounds of their *smallness*. It is not difficult to detect in this the influence of atomist doctrines. Democritus, in particular, supposed a fundamental distinction between the realms of cognition and sense perception.[52] If Antiphon had such a view in mind, the purpose of his argument becomes clear: in constructing the sequence of polygons, it is evident *to thought* that the polygons always fall short of the circle which bounds them; but if the figures are actually drawn, it eventually becomes impossible *by sense* to distinguish polygon from circle, because of the

49. See, e.g., Heath 1921, I, p. 222.

50. Proclus, *in Euclidem*, pp. 66–68; this list is generally accepted as based on Eudemus's history of geometry. Diels appears to assign the Antiphon fragment to Antiphon's *On Truth* (Diels-Kranz 1968, 87, B13).

51. On this debate among the pre-Socratics, see Guthrie 1969, chap. IV; on Antiphon's role in this debate, see Guthrie 1969, pp. 107–13, 202.

52. In fr. 11 Democritus considers two kinds of knowledge: the genuine (*gnēsiē*) and the obscure (*skotiē*), the latter based on the physical senses, the former, presumably, based on thought (Kirk and Raven 1960, p. 422).

smallness of the sides. In this way, an argument which is geometric nonsense actually makes a valid and significant epistemological point.

Antiphon's lack of mathematical credentials permits us to doubt that he originated the geometric part of the argument. We may plausibly suppose that he was able to draw this example from the geometry of his time and, consequently, we may identify Hippocrates as the source—for it is clear that Antiphon's argument has the most direct bearing on Hippocrates' theorem on the circle.

On this basis, we can readily construct an argument by which Hippocrates could prove that theorem. Given the two circles, let similar polygons—say, squares—be inscribed in each. As described in Antiphon's account, let triangles be erected on each side of both polygons. Now, the triangles constructed in the one circle are each similar to those constructed in the other, so that they have the ratio of the power (or square) of their homologous sides.[53] Thus, the triangles are each in the ratio of the squares on which they have been erected, for their bases are the sides of those squares. The same applies for the triangles erected on the sides of the resulting octagons by which the 16-gons are obtained: these also are in the ratio of the powers of the sides of the initial squares. Now, the area of each circle can be constituted from the initial square and all the triangles which are constructed on it in unlimited sequence. Each triangle in the one circle has the same ratio to the corresponding triangle in the other, namely, the ratio of the square inscribed in the first to the square inscribed in the second. The sums of all the figures in the one circle and the other thus have this same ratio (via a standard theorem on the ratio of sums of terms in constant ratio).[54] As these sums comprise the whole areas of their respective circles, and as the initial squares

---

53. Via VI 19–20.

54. Euclid proves in V 12 that if $A : B = A' : B' = A'' : B'' =$ etc., then $A + A' + A'' +$ etc. $: B + B' + B'' +$ etc. $= A : B$, where, of course, the As and Bs are finite in multitude (cf. also VII 12 for the equivalent assertion for numbers). This theorem is essential for Archimedes' quadratures of conoids in a more general form proved as *Conoids*, prop. 1 (cf. also *The Method*, lemma 11). This theorem is cited by Aristotle in the *Nicomachean Ethics* V 7, 1131b14: "whole is to whole what each part is to each part" (see Heath 1926, II, p. 160).

have the ratio of the squares on the diameters of the circles (each is the half of the square of its diameter), it follows that the circles also have the ratio of the squares of their diameters. This was the theorem to be proved.

Scholars are already aware of an ostensibly similar reconstruction of Hippocrates' argument,[55] according to which Hippocrates could see that the squares, the octagons, the 16-gons, and so on, had to each other the same ratio of the squares on the diameters; thus, the circles which bound the respective sequences of polygons had this same ratio. The passage from the polygons to the limiting circles would thus be founded on a naive inductive step. Of course, the general use of induction in this form is invalid.[56] One might argue that the appreciation of logical rigor in geometry at Hippocrates' time had not yet reached the level of forbidding such steps. But the argument as I have presented it proceeds somewhat differently. Each circle is built up as the sum of a square plus four triangles (yielding the octagon) plus eight more triangles (yielding the 16-gon) and so on. Just as any finite magnitude might be conceived as the sum of its half, quarter, eighth, sixteenth, and so on, so also the circle could be viewed as this sort of sum. The exhaustion of the whole via the infinite sequence might well enter as an unstated axiom, just as we have seen that the closely related lemma on bisection entered into Eudoxus's proofs. Once the circle is taken as such a sum, the proportionality of the circles and the squares follows from appeal to a theorem on the ratios of sums. Framed thus, the argument was well within the reach of a geometer like Hippocrates; centering on the constituent triangles rather than the resultant polygons, it conforms to the pattern presented in the Antiphon fragment; and the manner of passing to the limit is such as to satisfy the prevailing standard of rigor.

To a later geometer like Eudoxus, however, with the benefit of a half-century of work on the formal organization of the *Elements* begun by Hippocrates, aspects of such an argument would be found unacceptable. While the summation might pass—especially

55. See Toeplitz 1925.
56. One might in this way "prove" that the circle is constructible or that it is an inscribed polygon.

if it is shown that the remainders decrease faster than successive bisection, as is done in *Elements* XII 2—the application of the theorem on ratios would be seen as suspect, for it is here required for an infinite set of terms. The Eudoxean form of the proof would thus arise by way of the removal of this step, through restructuring the overall argument in the indirect mode and rendering unnecessary the consideration of infinite sets of magnitudes by a careful manipulation of finite magnitudes.

This review of the origins of the principle of bisection and of the Eudoxean method of limits challenges the familiar view presented in the histories of mathematics. In brief, it is commonly maintained that the early geometers, left to themselves, would have persisted in their naive heuristic methods had not the critique of the philosophers, beginning with Zeno and continuing through Plato and Aristotle, forced upon them the awareness that many of their concepts—such as those of the infinite and the limit—were logically incoherent and that their proofs ought to satisfy stringent criteria of logical precision. This view is not merely an oversimplification; it seriously distorts the pre-Euclidean evidence available to us. The mathematical aspect of Zeno's paradoxes—in essence, the principle of bisection—posed no difficulty either for geometers like Eudoxus or even philosophers like Aristotle. The roots of the "exhaustion" method of Eudoxus lie not in mathematicians' distress over philosophical puzzles but in the evolution of techniques such as those of Hippocrates. This view of an autonomous development within the geometric field is surely more plausible than the gratuitous assumption of external influences.

4. The Heuristic Analysis by Indivisibles

In the philosophical literature of the fourth century, the question of infinity is closely related to another issue: the constitution of continuous magnitudes from indivisible elements. The same chapter in which Aristotle presents his geometric analysis of Zeno's paradox of the "dichotomy" contains a geometric refutation of the notion of the indivisible.[57] Thus, while the first stages

57. *Phys.* VI 2.

of the study of indivisibles in the work of the fifth-century atomists, Leucippus and Democritus, had been predominantly physical at base, by the fourth century the doctrine had acquired an unmistakable theoretical dimension.[58]

The device of the indivisible is a significant feature of the heuristic mechanical method which Archimedes expounds in *The Method* for the measurement of the areas, volumes, and centers of gravity of curvilinear figures. By this method, a figure is viewed in a certain way as the aggregate of its constituent indivisibles. For instance, given two plane figures, corresponding indivisibles are marked off by the section of each. These two sections are next shown to satisfy a condition of proportionality, which under the principle of equilibrium means that they balance each other. This being true of any associated pair of sections, the condition of balance will hold for their aggregates, namely the given figures. Thus, knowing the magnitude and center of gravity of one of the figures, one can compute these values for the other.

The appearance here of indivisibles suggests that the atomist theories may have influenced the development of Archimedes' technique. This would appear to be supported in a passage from Plutarch drawn from an account by the third-century Stoic leader Chrysippus containing a discussion of a puzzle posed by Democritus:

> If [said Democritus] a cone were cut by a plane parallel to the base, what must we think of the surfaces forming the sections? Are they equal or unequal? For, if they are unequal, they will make the cone irregular as having many indentations, like steps, and unevennesses. But, if they are equal, the sections will be equal, and the cone will appear to have the property of the cylinder and to be made up of equal, not unequal, circles, which is very absurd.[59]

58. David Furley has argued that Democritus himself viewed the atoms as indivisible in a theoretical sense (Furley 1967). But judgments are divided, tending more to view the theoretical sense as a fourth-century elaboration.

59. Translation in Heath 1921, I, pp. 179 f., of Plutarch, *Common Notions*, 1079E: for text and discussion see the *Moralia* (Loeb Classical Library), XIII, pt. II, ed. H. Cherniss, pp. 818–22. For Chrysippus's analysis, see also Sambursky 1959, pp. 92–96. Chrysippus does not know of any solution by Democritus. But it is difficult to comprehend what the difficulty could have been for Democritus. The division of the physical cone must stop at the atomic level, after a finite number of steps; thus the physical cone must be irregular at this level. But between any two sec-

Whatever Democritus's own position on this paradox was—Chrysippus maintains that Democritus did not have an answer—it is clear that his notion of constituting volumes like the cone and the cylinder out of circular sections could be adapted for geometric purposes. Since Archimedes himself, in the preface to *The Method*, assigns to Democritus the statement of theorems on the volume of the cone and the pyramid, at least a circumstantial case seems possible for the claim that Democritus had worked out some form of analysis of the Archimedean type.

On this basis a reconstruction has been proposed for the theorem on the cone, namely, that it equals in volume one-third the cylinder of the same height and base.[60] In its general line it follows the Euclidean proof: (1) it is established that pyramids of the same height have the ratio of their bases (XII 5–6); (2) given a triangular prism, its diagonals are used to dissect it into three equal pyramids, so that the pyramid is seen to equal the third of the corresponding prism (XII 7); (3) from this it follows that any pyramid of polygonal base is the third of the corresponding prism (XII 7 Porism); (4) by now considering the sequence of polygons converging to the circle bounding them, it is shown via the usual "exhaustion" method that the cone is the third of the corresponding cylinder (XII 10). Within this structure, the proof of (4) would have to be revised so as not to employ the full "exhaustion," for the same reasons as those behind our previous examination of Hippocrates' proof of the circle. But it is in the proof of (1) that the use of indivisibles might replace the Euclidean version, which also applies the "exhaustion" technique. In such an alternate treatment, two solids are taken, each having a plane figure as base and tapering to a point as vertex (e.g., a pyramid or a cone). If a section is made in each by a plane parallel to its base at the same distance from the base, the sections formed will have the

---

tions of the geometric cone another section may be made; the division may be continued ad infinitum, so that one cannot designate the contiguous sections at all. Democritus's apparent failure to grasp this latter aspect speaks poorly for his expertise as a geometer. He may, however, merely have wished to point out by means of this puzzle the difference between physical and theoretical conceptions (cf. n. 52 above). See also the discussion of this puzzle by Richard Sorabji in chapter II.

60. This argument may be compared with the versions given in Luria 1932–33 and Mau 1954a. A brief account is given in Van der Waerden 1954, pp. 137 f.

same ratio, each to its respective base. By alternating the ratios, it follows that the sections will have to each other the same ratio as the bases. This holds for all sections of the solids, so that it will apply also to their aggregates.[61] Thus, the solids of this form and of equal height will have the ratio of their bases, as claimed.

In some such form the hypothesis of a Democritean analysis by indivisibles has gained a relatively wide acceptance.[62] But for a number of reasons I reject the view either that Democritus devised any geometric technique of indivisibles or that such a technique served as a specific influence on Archimedes' method.

First, although Archimedes does employ indivisibles in his proofs in *The Method,* his remark on Democritus in the preface says nothing about the method Democritus used, but only "of those theorems whose proof Eudoxus was the first to discover, about the cone and the pyramid, . . . one might assign no small credit to Democritus, who was the first to make the assertion about the figure mentioned, although he stated it without proof."[63] Of course, the words "without proof" might be supposed to mean that Archimedes wished to deny to Democritus's method the status of *formal* proof, just as he does in connection with his own mechanical method. Still, it is odd that he should have failed to make any more specific comment on the connection between Democritus's method and his own, if in fact he knew of such a connection. Moreover, in the preface to another work, *Sphere and Cylinder I,* Archimedes does not mention Democritus even in this limited role. Indeed, he there says of the theorems on the cone and the pyramid, "Of the many geometers worthy of note prior to Eudoxus, it happened that these things were unknown by them all, nor were they recognized by anyone." This passage is in evident contradiction to the remark in *The Method* but it is not difficult to explain. *The Method* was communicated late in Archimedes' career, many years after *Sphere and Cylinder.*[64] Pre-

61. Note that this involves an application of V 12; cf. n. 54 above.
62. This view, developed by Luria and Mau (see n. 60 above), was known and supported earlier in Heath 1921, I, p. 180, and in Philippson 1929. It is proposed as a possibility in Boyer 1949, p. 22, in Van der Waerden 1954, p. 138. Carruccio 1964, p. 41, cites, e.g., Enriques and Mazziotti 1948 as support. But Guthrie expresses doubts (see n. 65 below).
63. Archimedes, *Opera,* ed. Heiberg, II, p. 430.
64. On the ordering of these works, see Knorr 1978a, pp. 258–68.

sumably, then, in the time between writing these works, Archimedes first learned of Democritus's contribution to these theorems and so revised his judgment on Eudoxus's absolute priority in their discovery. What Archimedes' source of information was we of course cannot say for certain. While he appears to have studied this material in a version close to that produced by Eudoxus, he hardly gives evidence of any direct knowledge of Democritus's treatment. Democritus is not even mentioned in Eudemus's long list of pre-Euclidean geometers, and he must have written little, if anything, of interest to the professional mathematician.[65] The fragment on the cone was drawn from a work on questions in natural philosophy, as Chrysippus says, so that this probably would not have gained Archimedes' attention. But works by Democritus were still extant and were surely accessible to Archimedes' correspondents, the scholars at Alexandria. It seems plausible to me to suppose that Archimedes' remark in the *Sphere and Cylinder* was noted by one of these scholars, who then sent back some statement of Democritus's contribution. But one must recognize that even when Archimedes acknowledges this in *The Method,* he shows no awareness of the character of Democritus's treatment. Further, as Archimedes was already applying his own method prior to the writing of *Sphere and Cylinder* (it is an implicit basis of the proofs in his earlier work, *Quadrature of the Parabola*), Democritus could not have been a factor in the invention of the Archimedean method.

Second, against the hypothesis of a Democritean analysis of indivisibles is the fact that the critiques of the notion of indivisibles, such as those in Aristotle's *Physics* VI, never introduce difficulties in the mathematical sense of these entities. Aristotle's objections are physical: that the existence of faster and slower motions will necessitate the subdivision of any hypothesized atomic elements of time or of distance; or that these elements, defined as partless, cannot be in contact with each other and thus cannot by any sort of sequential placement be made to add up to

65. See n. 50 above. This embarrassment has been explained via the incredible argument that Platonist prejudices against Democritus induced Proclus to omit all mention of his name. For a balanced account of Democritus's mathematics, see Guthrie 1969, pp. 483–88.

a finite magnitude. Even in the Peripatetic tract *On Indivisible Lines* (*De lineis insecabilibus*) the geometric objections raised are of a trivial sort: that there would be no distinction between commensurable and incommensurable; that the diagonal of an indivisible unit square must equal its side.[66] These objections reveal not a glimmer of awareness of the sophisticated difficulties which a geometric method of indivisibles actually poses: for instance, that through a one-to-one correspondence of constituent points or of constituent lines one could argue the equality of all line segments or of all triangles, respectively.[67] Such gaps in the fourth-century philosophical debate give no encouragement to the advocates of a Democritean analysis.

Third, on the hypothesis of the Democritean method, one might expect that the Euclidean treatment of the cone would betray some sign of a prior use of indivisibles, just as do the Archimedean proofs of the parabola and the conoids. But there are no such signs. Essential to the indivisibilist approach is the division of the cone into parallel circular sections. But in the proof that the cone is one-third the cylinder of equal height and base, one does not need the division of the cone, only that of the pyramid.[68] And for the division of the pyramid Euclid does not take parallel sections at all. Instead, he views the pyramid as comprised of two smaller pyramids (each of its dimensions being half the corresponding dimension in the given pyramid) together with two triangular prisms; the two smaller pyramids amount to less than half the volume of the given pyramid. Thus, via the principle of convergence (X 1) the pyramid can be successively bisected, where at each stage the prisms formed are removed, eventually to leave a remainder of small pyramids which sum to an arbitrarily small volume. By means of an indirect argument he can then establish that pyramids of equal height are in the ratio of their bases.

Thus, the Democritean conception of parallel sections is absent

66. The arguments are summarized in Heath 1949, pp. 255–57.

67. Such difficulties were examined in the debate between Cavalieri and Guldin in the seventeenth century; see Baron 1969, pp. 133–35.

68. The proof of XII 10 (on the volume of the cone) depends on XII 5 (on ratios of pyramids); XII 11 (on the ratios of cones) uses a limiting argument comparable to that in XII 2 (on circles).

from the Euclidean treatment. If we can take the latter as, in essence, the Eudoxean form of the proof, then this failure to influence geometric method will be all the more striking. Now, there is a slight indication that the Euclidean text has incorporated revisions on the original versions; in particular, the manner of wording the convergence lemma in XII 5 is a bit different from the wordings used elsewhere in the book.[69] Further, the conception of parallel sections is common in Archimedes' theorems on the conoids and appears in a treatment relating the cone and the spiral, preserved by Pappus.[70] Thus, one might entertain the view that Eudoxus had indeed used a method of parallel sections but that his followers chose to modify his proof. One might even perceive their motives for doing this: following the Democritean pattern, one would inscribe in the pyramid solids made up of prisms, where at each stage the heights of these prisms are to be bisected. But it happens that this does not reduce by half or more the difference between the pyramid and the former inscribed solid.[71] This method, if used by Eudoxus, would thus not conform to the conditions of the criterion of convergence (X 1) as set out by his followers, so that they would be compelled to devise an alternative method, namely, that now extant in the *Elements*. This is a possible, if only remotely possible, view; it suggests how a prior method of indivisibles, implicit in the demonstrations of Eudoxus, might have influenced Archimedes in the invention of his mechanical method. But even with this, it does not necessarily entail support for a Democritean origin. For, as we have seen, geometric aspects are of minimal significance within the philosophical discussions about indivisibles.

As for Archimedes, it is remarkable that he has nothing to say relative to the questions on indivisibles which so vexed the philosophers. Having established a certain relation among circular sections, for instance, he posits that "the figure be filled out" and so passes from "all the circles in the cylinder" to the cylinder itself. But how do the sections actually constitute the solid? Or again, if,

69. See Knorr 1978b, p. 236.
70. I have discussed this theorem of Pappus (*Collection*, IV, 21–25), arguing an Archimedean provenance, in Knorr 1978c.
71. For further details of this proof, see Knorr 1978b, p. 202.

as he supposes, the sections have weight, how is their infinite aggregate to avoid having infinite weight? Archimedes does not address such issues. Unlike the philosophers, he is not concerned over adopting and defending an ontological position. Rather, he is applying a heuristic technique for which he presumes no deductive force; it is a source of tentative results whose formal demonstration must be given, in accordance with the usual strict criteria, before these may be accepted as established. In fact, a review of Archimedes' statements on the status of his "mechanical method" and his applications of it reveals that it was the appeal to mechanical principles, not the use of indivisibles, which inspired his caution.[72] One can easily see how a grasp of the Eudoxean formal method might suggest indivisibles; as rectangles diminish in width or cylinders in height, without limit, they come to resemble lines or circles. The use of indivisibles thus arises as a convenient simplification of the rigorous treatment based strictly on finite magnitudes. This was the view of infinitesimals commonly held among seventeenth-century geometers[73] and appears the most straightforward view to ascribe to Archimedes. But it also renders superfluous any assumption that philosophical debates influenced him in the development of his method of indivisibles.

5. Philosophy and Geometry in Antiquity

Throughout this chapter I have argued that alleged philosophical factors actually had minimal significance for the development of pre-Euclidean geometry. In an earlier study[74] I argued to similar effect that the elaboration of deductive structures of demonstration within geometry did not result from specific philosophical admonitions; that, on the contrary, the efforts of fourth-century geometers served as a model for philosophical inquiries. The three topics examined in the present study point to the same autonomy of mathematics. The physical theories of the atomists appear to have had no role in the geometric use of indivisibles,

72. See Knorr 1978a, pp. 247 f.
73. Knorr 1978a, p. 245.
74. Knorr forthcoming.

most notably by Archimedes. Eudoxus devised his "method of exhaustion" not for the resolution of philosophical difficulties but as a refinement of the techniques employed by predecessors such as Hippocrates of Chios. Zeno's paradoxes exercised the physicists, not the geometers; the "exhaustion" of a magnitude through successive bisection entered into Eudoxus's proofs as an *assumption*,[75] while the Euclidean *proof* of the principle (X 1) handles the concept of the infinite altogether differently from the Aristotelian way.

Having argued that Eudoxus himself did not prove the principle of bisection, we have yet to account for the motives among his successors leading them to work out a proof, namely, in the manner presented in the *Elements*. The familiar hypothesis of a "horror of infinity" among the Greek geometers is a preposterous myth whose demise can only be welcome. To be sure, the salient feature of this proof is its meticulous avoidance of any direct use of the notion of the infinite; all assertions are made with reference exclusively to finite magnitudes. But this is a consequence of the geometers' ambition to satisfy stringent criteria of deductive form. The standards set by the model of Hippocrates' work were already high, and Eudoxus pitched these at a yet higher level. As the recognized starting points (axioms) for proofs appeared not to extend directly to constructions resulting from an infinite process, an alternative indirect procedure was sought.

Thus, an account of the Greek geometers' methods for treating infinity and continuity will depend not on the consideration of the potential influence of specific philosophical doctrines but on the identification of the sources of the geometers' commitment to the ideology of strict demonstration. Might not the encouragement of philosophers, in particular those within the circle of Plato's Academy, have been a major factor responsible for this deductive commitment? A problem in supposing the affirmative is that philosophers in the fifth and fourth centuries were by no means unanimous in their views on method. While Plato might insist on a strict adherence to the deductive mode, others made

75. "Exhaustion" is of course to be taken here in its indirect and finite sense: that the successive bisection of a given finite magnitude will eventually reduce it to less than another given finite magnitude.

different recommendations. Protagoras, for instance, observed that geometers, in subscribing to idealized constructions, were at variance with physical reality.[76] We have seen how other philosophers, such as Antiphon and Democritus, proposed views which pitted the facts of experience against the abstract notions of geometry. Hence, it was by their *choice* that geometers accepted the commitment to deductive method, not their passive response to philosophical criticisms.

Why, then, did they make this choice? Was it a historical accident, the result of the affiliation of a few key individuals like Eudoxus with a specific philosophical outlook, the theories of Plato? Or was there something intrinsic in mathematics itself which made the adoption of the deductive ideal especially appropriate?

While one can accept affirmative answers to both questions, I have inclined primarily to the latter alternative in this chapter. Admittedly, there are difficulties in maintaining this position exclusively. For one thing, other mathematical traditions failed to make such a commitment, as inquiries into the mathematics of ancient Egypt, Mesopotamia, India, and China reveal. Indeed, all formal traditions of mathematics, including our own, can trace their adoption of deductive standards back to the Greek model. Further, one may well question whether strict deductive method is altogether desirable. Informal procedures, such as Archimedes' mechanical method, are the usual route by which new discoveries are made to advance the field. An emphasis on proof techniques, to the detriment of the extension of heuristic methods, can lead science into stagnation, as happened to geometry in the later Hellenistic period.

But as the alternative source of deductive method, the philosophers stand condemned by the tenuousness of their own commitment. Parmenides, the would-be father of the deductive mode, availed himself of at least two radically different techniques for compelling acquiescence: by logical procedures and by mantic pronouncement. How else can we comprehend his fram-

76. According to Aristotle (*Metaphysics* III 2, 997b35–998a4), Protagoras observed that the circle met its tangent line not at a point, as supposed by geometers, but in a line. See the discussion in Heath 1949, pp. 204 f.

ing of his philosophical arguments in dactylic hexameters, the language of the inspired seers? For all their emphasis on logical techniques, Plato and Aristotle frequently stumble in the actual practice of these techniques.

Insight into the evolution of logical method, both in mathematics and in philosophy, may be gained through a consideration of the general cultural climate in Greece, Athens in particular, during the fifth and early fourth centuries. This was a society experiencing a crisis of authority, both intellectually and politically. Theoretically at least, every citizen had independent political standing and had the opportunity, indeed the necessity, of presenting his own cause before the assembly. Analogously, the Sophists, teachers of logic and rhetoric, provided training in techniques in argument under the ideology that what was true was relative to each individual and that good technique might lead even the weaker cause to victory. Philosophers like Plato, of a conservative inclination, were concerned with recovering a consensus on values by describing the absolute bases of true belief and knowledge. Certainly, mathematicians must merely have been put off by pretensions to expertise on the part of the uninformed;[77] but they could hope to curtail inappropriate criticism by framing their proofs according to strict deductive procedures. Their success in doing this became a model for Plato as the solution to the correlated crisis in philosophy.

Under this view the parallel adoption of rigorous logical procedures in both philosophy and mathematics in classical Greece arose as the common response to the special open cultural climate of that time. If anything, the fourth-century philosophical development, moving back into an absolutist position, drew from mathematical advances, rather than conversely. But it is the unique character of this social environment which exerted a real, if subtle, influence on the direction of the development of mathematics, leading it into the strongly formalist and deductivist manner we now take as the hallmark of the classical geometry.

77. Plato portrays the geometer Theodorus as vexed by such ingnorant critics (*Theaetetus* 170D–E).

CHAPTER V

Aristotle and the Quadrature of the Circle

IAN MUELLER

1. Introduction

In the section of his *History of Greek Mathematics* devoted to the squaring of the circle, Heath mentions the people whom ancient authors associated with this problem: the Pythagoreans, Anaxagoras, Hippocrates, Antiphon, Bryson, Hippias, Dinostratus, Archimedes, Nicomedes, Apollonius, and Carpus. Heath rightly rejects as valueless assertions about Pythagorean accomplishments in this area and is constrained to do no more than refer to Anaxagoras because the only relevant information concerning him is Plutarch's statement that Anaxagoras described (*graphein*) a quadrature of the circle while he was in prison.[1] Heath, like most historians of mathematics, considers Hippocrates' alleged quadrature to be a misattribution originating in Aristotle's misunderstanding of Hippocrates' work, and he contrasts the procedures of Antiphon and Bryson with the work of the remaining men, which he characterizes as "real rectifications or quadratures of circles effected by means of higher curves, the construction of which is more 'mechanical' than that of the circle."[2] Of these remaining men, only Hippias of Elis and Dinostratus are pre-Euclidean. Moreover, the evidence suggests that although Hippias invented the curve later called the quadratrix and used by Dinostratus to square the circle, Hippias himself used it only to divide angles in various ratios.[3] Dinostratus is described by Pro-

1. Plutarch, *De exilio*, ed. W. Sieveking, 607F.
2. Heath 1921, p. 225.
3. Heath (1921, pp. 225–26) suggests that Hippias did square the circle but later

clus as the brother of Menaechmus, a student of Eudoxus and Plato.[4] Clearly Dinostratus was alive when Aristotle was, but it is not possible to determine whether Aristotle knew of his quadrature. However, since Aristotle mentions only the problematic quadratures of Antiphon, Bryson, and (apparently) Hippocrates, and since he seems to believe that quadrature has not been accomplished and, perhaps, that it cannot be accomplished,[5] it seems reasonable to suppose that Aristotle did not know of Dinostratus's work, which would then presumably have been done relatively late in the fourth century. The hypothesis that Aristotle knew of no "real" quadratures is of interest not only for the history of Greek mathematics but also for understanding Aristotle's attitude toward the problem. A casual reference to quadrature in Aristophanes' *Birds* (1001–5) makes it almost certain that the problem was already of major concern in the last quarter of the fifth century, so that Aristotle would be looking back at a seventy-five-year period during which great strides had been made in mathematics but the problem of quadrature had not been solved. He suggests, perhaps not surprisingly, that the problem is unsolvable, and he uses purported solutions to it to illustrate shortcomings in argument.

Before discussing these purported solutions, it is well to say a few words about Hippocrates, Antiphon, and Bryson. Hippocrates of Chios was a geometer of great distinction whose theory of comets is preserved by Aristotle in the *Meteorology*.[6] From his position in Proclus's catalogue of geometers,[7] it is to be inferred that he flourished toward the end of the fifth century. His quadrature of lunes, plane figures contained by two circular arcs curved in the same direction, is described in great detail by Simplicius,

---

appears to change his mind. See Heath 1949, p. 19. Becker (1957, p. 95) affirms that Heath's second opinion is correct. Knorr (1978c, p. 74) postulates a second Hippias from the late third century.

4. Proclus, *in Euclidem*, ed. G. Friedlein, p. 67.9–11.

5. *Categories* 7, 7b27–33; *Eudemian Ethics* II 10, 1226a28–30; cf. *Physics* VII 4, 248b4–6 (aporematic passage).

6. *Meteorology* I 6, 342b29–343a20. The texts relating to Hippocrates, other than Simplicius's description of his quadrature of lunes, are collected in Diels-Kranz 1968, I.

7. Proclus, *in Euclidem*, p. 66.4–6; Hippocrates is grouped together with Theodorus, before Plato and after Anaxagoras and Oinopides.

who quotes from and adds to the report from Eudemus's history of mathematics.[8] Simplicius also describes Antiphon's quadrature, and here too he appears to depend upon Eudemus.[9] It has been customary to identify Antiphon the circle-squarer with Antiphon the Sophist, an acquaintance of Socrates and the author of a work *On Truth* in which epistemological and cosmological questions are treated, and to distinguish him from the well-known politician and orator Antiphon, who died in 411.[10] Morrison has recently revived the theory that the Sophist and the orator are identical. In any case Antiphon would be a fifth-century figure, possibly somewhat older than Hippocrates. There is no evidence of any work in mathematics other than his purported quadrature, a fact which suggests that the quadrature may not have been mathematically sophisticated. The evidence on Bryson has been collected and discussed by Döring, according to whom Bryson was born in approximately 400.[11] In the *History of Animals* Aristotle twice refers to Bryson as a Sophist,[12] and in the *Rhetoric* he ascribes to him a defense of obscenity: one of two ways of saying the same thing cannot be worse than the other, since they both say the same thing.[13] Again, there is no evidence of mathematical activity other than his attempted quadrature; so Bryson, too, may be a mathematical amateur.

Thus, of the three quadratures mentioned by Aristotle, one is associated with a prominent mathematician of the late fifth century, another is most likely to be from the same period but by a person not otherwise connected with mathematics, and the third is by a person of the same kind from the mid-fourth century. Since Aristotle gives no exact information about these quadra-

8. Simplicius, *in Phys.*, pp. 61.1–68.32.

9. Simplicius, *in Phys.*, pp. 54.20–55.11.

10. This distinction is made by Diels-Kranz, for example. In the Pauly-Wissowa *Realencyclopädie der klassischen Altertumswissenschaft*, a natural philosopher and circle-squarer Antiphon is distinguished from both the Sophist and the orator and is said to have written shortly before Aristotle. This view has not found wide acceptance. Morrison 1972 provides an English translation of all the materials associated with the major Antiphons.

11. Döring 1972. In Becker 1932–33b, p. 374, Bryson is called a late fifth-century Pythagorean, and in Becker 1934–36a he is called an older contemporary of Plato. In neither case is there an attempt to justify the description.

12. *History of Animals*, VI 5, 563a7; IX 11, 615a10.

13. *Rhetoric* III 2, 1405b9–11.

tures, and since interest in them has largely been confined to historians of mathematics, discussion has tended to focus on the commentators' explanations of what Aristotle is talking about. The point of view adopted here is that, where possible, the remarks of Aristotle and of his pupil Eudemus should be given priority in the account of these quadratures, and the commentators' reports made subsidiary. In the next section of this chapter I shall therefore discuss the four passages in which Aristotle refers critically to one or another of the quadratures,[14] and then I shall turn to the commentators' accounts in a third section.

2. Aristotle's References to Specific Quadratures

Physics I 2

At the beginning of the *Physics* Aristotle is concerned to rule out of consideration the contentious (*eristikos*) arguments of the Eleatics against the existence of change. "It is not our task to refute every [wrong conclusion] but only those which someone demonstrates falsely (*tis edeiknus pseudetai*) from first principles, and not others, just as it is the geometer's task to refute the quadrature by means of segments, but it is not his task to refute Antiphon's quadrature."[15] The ancient commentators Alexander (*apud* Simplicium), Simplicius, Philoponus, and Themistius all take the quadrature by means of segments to be a fallacious inference made by Hippocrates from his successful quadrature of lunes. It seems likely that Aristotle intends to refer to lunes with the word "segments," but as will be seen, there are reasons for doubting that he ascribes this quadrature to Hippocrates. I shall therefore refer to the author of the quadrature by means of segments or lunes as "Hippocrates." In the *Physics* passage, then, Aristotle tells us that "Hippocrates" reasoned incorrectly from bona fide first principles, whereas Antiphon did something else. Since Aristotle says, a few lines before the passage quoted above, that the physicist has to deal with Eleatic arguments no more than the

14. I do not, then, deal with Aristotle's use of the quadrature by means of lunes as an illustration of reduction in *Prior Analytics* II 25, 69a30–34.

15. *Phys.* I 2, 185a14–17.

geometer has to deal with those of someone who abrogates (*anai-rein*) *his* first principles,[16] the commentators assume that Aristotle's criticism of Antiphon's argument is that it is based on geometrically false ideas. I accept this assumption and shall attempt to support it in the sequel.

On Sophistical Refutations 11

In this chapter of Aristotle's there are two passages which contrast "Hippocrates" and Bryson; the second of these also contains a cryptic reference to Antiphon. In the first the contrast is again between proving falsely (*pseudographein*) and arguing contentiously or sophistically. Aristotle describes as a kind of eristic argument paralogisms which are not in accordance with the method of inquiry but seem to be. He continues: "For false proofs are not contentious (for the paralogisms are in accordance with what falls under the art); nor is it contentious if something is a false proof about what is true, e.g., the false proof of Hippocrates or the quadrature by means of lunes. However, the way in which Bryson squared the circle is sophistic, even if the circle is squared, because it is not in accordance with its subject."[17] The second passage begins with an analogy. "In a sense the person who argues contentiously is to the dialectician as the person who proves falsely is to the [true] geometrician; for the contentious person argues fallaciously (*paralogizetai*) from the same [premises] as the dialectician, and the false prover argues fallaciously from the same as the geometer."[18] Rather than developing the analogy, however, Aristotle explains a difference between the contentious person and the false prover, and illustrates the difference by reference to quadratures.

> However, the false prover is not contentious, because he proves falsely from first principles and their consequences which fall under the relevant art; but since the contentious person proceeds from what falls under dialectic, it is obvious that he will be contentious concerning other things. For example, the quadrature by means of lunes is not contentious, whereas Bryson's is. It is not possible to

16. *Phys.* I 2, 184b25–185a3.
17. *On Sophistical Refutations* 11, 171b13–18.
18. *Soph. Ref.* 11, 171b34–37.

transfer the former argument, but it applies only to geometry because it is based on principles peculiar to geometry (*ek tōn idiōn archōn*); but the latter applies to many [people], to anyone who does not know the possible and the impossible in a subject. For it will be suitable. (Or as Antiphon squared the circle.)[19]

Notice that in the first passage Aristotle explicitly distinguishes the quadrature by means of lunes from the false proof of Hippocrates.[20] Aristotle does not tell us what this false proof is, and the comments of pseudo-Alexander and the anonymous paraphraser, whom I shall call Sophonias, add no information. Both writers assign the quadrature by means of lunes to Antiphon, but the *Physics* passage already quoted makes this assignment seem unlikely.

The first passage might lead one to suppose that Aristotle's criticism of Bryson is the same as his criticism apparently directed against Antiphon, namely, violation of geometric principles. This impression is strengthened by the cryptic last sentence of the second passage, which is most naturally read as classifying Antiphon's and Bryson's quadratures together. However, the point of this classification may simply be that both quadratures convince only the nongeometer who does not know the possible and the impossible in geometry. The idea of transferability to many things, which is brought out in the second passage, suggests a different kind of criticism of Bryson. The criticism is perhaps clarified by the example Aristotle gives following the passage. The refusal to assent to the assertion that it is better to walk after

19. *Soph. Ref.* 11, 171b38–172a7.
20. So Ross (1949, p. 491), in disagreement with Heath (1949, p. 34), who very hesitatingly reads the "or" as explicative. Ross, however, accepts Diels's athetization of the words "or the quadrature by means of lunes" as a later but correct gloss, although he retains the words in his edition of the *Topics* and *Sophistical Refutations*. In the context of Ross's commentary, "correct" appears to imply that Hippocrates did attempt a circle quadrature, but in his note on the *Physics* passage Ross implies the opposite. "Correct," then, means that the gloss conveys correctly Aristotle's incorrect conception. But if the words are a gloss which provides historically false information, it seems preferable to assign the mistake to the glossator rather than put ourselves in the position of second-guessing Aristotle. But then, we might just as well leave the text as it stands and free Aristotle from the charge of misunderstanding Hippocrates' work. We would then not know what Hippocrates' false proof was, but this position of ignorance seems to me preferable to thinking either that Hippocrates did produce a fallacious quadrature or that Aristotle was mistaken.

dinner on the basis of Zeno's arguments against the possibility of motion is, Aristotle says, a contentious rather than a medical position. Clearly an analogous position could be adopted on many subjects, and Aristotle seems to think the position irrefutable. And why should anyone admit the value of exercise or advise a person to undertake it if he knows exercise to be impossible? On the other hand, Aristotle is surely right that medical people will be unimpressed by the position, since it has nothing to do with what might be called the medically possible and impossible. In this sense one might say the argument is correct but medically uninformative. Before considering how an analogous situation may have arisen in the case of Bryson's quadrature, I want to introduce the remaining Aristotelian reference to specific quadratures, which again is a reference to Bryson.

Posterior Analytics I 9

Since it is evidently not possible to demonstrate that anything which is shown holds as such except from the first principles of the thing, knowing is not just a matter of proving from undemonstrated and immediate truths. It is possible to prove in this way, as Bryson does in his quadrature. Such arguments prove in accordance with what is common, which will also belong to something else; therefore, the arguments will be applicable to other things in other genera. Hence one does not know what is proved as such but indirectly (kata sumbebēkos); otherwise the demonstration would not also be applicable to another genus.[21]

Here Aristotle gives a relatively positive assessment of Bryson's procedure. Like all correct arguments, it is ultimately based on immediate truths, but because the argument has broader applicability, the result established is known only indirectly and hence does not constitute true scientific knowledge. It emerges rather clearly from the rest of chapter 9 and from chapter 5 of Book I that there is for Aristotle an appropriate level of generality for the proof of any proposition. For any demonstrable property P there is a maximally general kind or genus K of which P can be scientifically demonstrated. If S is a species of K, a correct demonstration that S is P does not yield genuine scientific knowledge, nor does a

---

21. *Posterior Analytics* I 9, 75b37–76a3.

proof that K is P which proceeds by establishing that all species of K are P.[22] Aristotle is less specific about the possibility of a correct proof which, like Bryson's quadrature, is too broad, but he explicitly asserts that with some exceptions which are not relevant here, a single scientific demonstration applies to a single genus.[23] Bryson's quadrature appears to have violated this principle, but we are not told how. Nor does Aristotle indicate how one decides when an appropriate level of generality has been reached. Indeed, he admits the difficulty of reaching such a decision: "It is difficult to determine whether or not one knows; for it is difficult to determine whether or not we know a thing on the basis of its first principles. We think that we know when we have a syllogism based on primary truths, but we do not; rather the syllogism must be of the same kind as the primary truths."[24] In the light of other passages in the *Posterior Analytics* it is natural to suppose that Aristotle's criticism of Bryson is that his quadrature involves considerations which somehow extend beyond plane geometry, and indeed, this is how the criticism has generally been interpreted. Pseudo-Alexander and Sophonias both take this view and say that Bryson's argument will apply to other things, like numbers, times, places, and solids. Since I am going to argue that this interpretation is unsatisfactory and that the generality to which Aristotle objects is extendibility to plane geometric objects other than circles, I want to point out now that what Aristotle says about Bryson is compatible with my interpretation and even suggests that the standard view is false. For, first of all, it is not necessary to suppose that when Aristotle refers to other genera in the *Posterior Analytics* passage in which he mentions Bryson, he means genera other than that of geometric objects; he could just as well mean kinds of geometric objects other than circles. And, although in *Sophistical Refutations* 11 Aristotle contrasts Bryson's quadrature with that of "Hippocrates," which he characterizes as in accordance with what falls under its art and as applicable only to geometry, he refrains from ascribing to Bryson's argument the antithetical features; instead he says that it is not in accordance

22. *Post. An.* I 5, 74a17–32.
23. *Post. An.* I 7.
24. *Post An.* I 9, 76a26–30.

with its subject, the thing it treats (*to pragma*, i.e., the circle), and that it will be applicable to (i.e., successful with) ignorant people.

In any case we can say that in Aristotle's opinion Bryson argued too generally to give the appropriate scientific knowledge of the result he established, whereas "Hippocrates" committed a fallacy in the course of a geometric argument. Aristotle's criticism of Antiphon is not so easily determined, but it seems to be either the same as the charge against Bryson or, somewhat more probably, the claim that Antiphon violated geometric principles. With these criticisms in mind we can now consider the content of the arguments criticized.

3. The Reports of the Commentators

Antiphon

The principal sources for Antiphon's quadrature are the commentaries on the *Physics*.[25] Simplicius, whose account seems to be derived from Eudemus, says that, given the side *AB* of a polygon inscribed in a circle *ACB*, Antiphon proceeded to erect the perpendicular bisector *CD* of *AB*, thus bisecting the segment *ABC*; he then connected the straight lines *AC*, *BC* (see diagram below).

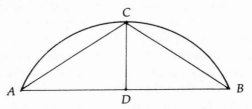

Doing this continually, he thought that he would at some time exhaust the area of the circle and inscribe a polygon the sides of which would coincide with the circumference because of their smallness; the square constructed equal to this polygon would then also be equal to the circle. According to Simplicius, Alexan-

25. This section should be compared with Wilbur Knorr's discussion of Antiphon's quadrature in chapter IV above.

der criticized Antiphon for having violated the truth that a straight line and a circle are tangent at a point only (and hence cannot coincide).[26] Simplicius modifies this criticism by making what is violated the principle that a straight line and a circle can never coincide, a criticism also adopted by Philoponus.[27] After giving his own criticism, Simplicius continues:

> Thus if one divides continually the surface between the straight line and the arc of the circle, he will not exhaust this surface, nor will he reach the circumference of the circle at some time since the surface is divisible ad infinitum. If he does reach it, a geometric principle has been abrogated, the one which says that magnitudes are divisible ad infinitum. And Eudemus also says this principle is abrogated by Antiphon.[28]

Eudemus, then, objected that Antiphon's quadrature is incompatible with the fact that the segment $AB\overset{\frown}{C}$ is divisible ad infinitum into smaller areas. Themistius apparently follows Eudemus on this point since, without a clear explanation, he speaks of the abrogation of the hypothesis of division ad infinitum, which the geometer accepts.[29]

Although different authorities give different criticisms of Antiphon, it is clear that they all take him to have thought of geometric magnitudes as in some sense composed of finitely many minimum parts. The unanimity of the authorities in this respect makes it reasonable to suppose that Aristotle has the same kind of criticism in mind, in whatever form he might have expressed it. Antiphon may have been motivated by the kind of empiricism often associated with Protagoras on the basis of Aristotle's remark about Protagoras's conception of the relation of circle and straightedge;[30] that is to say, Antiphon's quadrature may have turned on the fact that there is no perceptible difference between

---

26. Simplicius, in Phys., pp. 54.20–55.11. The suggestion in Wasserstein 1959, pp. 94–95, that Alexander's criticism has a point only if Antiphon used both inscribed and circumscribed polygons, depends on the supposition that *haptesthai* (meet) means "touch" or "be tangent to"; but it does not. See Heath 1926, vol. II, p. 2.
27. Philoponus, in Phys., ed. H. Vitelli, p. 31.21–23.
28. Simplicius, in Phys., p. 55.19–24.
29. Themistius, in Phys., ed. H. Schenkl, p. 4.7–8.
30. Metaphysics III 2, 997b32–998a4.

a circle and a polygon with sufficiently many sides. Or Antiphon may have used a mathematical atomism of the kind Luria ascribes to him and especially to Democritus. But in either case there is no genuine notion of infinitesimals or infinite processes involved,[31] so that it is difficult to attach much credence to Heath's attempt to rescue Antiphon from the criticisms of the commentators. Heath writes:

> But the objection to Antiphon's statement is really no more than verbal; Euclid uses exactly the same construction in XII, 2, only he expresses the conclusion in a different way, saying that, if the process be continued far enough, the small segments left over will be together less than any assigned area. Antiphon in effect said the same thing, which again we express by saying that the circle is the *limit* of such an inscribed polygon when the number of its sides is indefinitely increased. Antiphon therefore deserves an honorable place in the history of geometry as having originated the idea of *exhausting* an area by means of inscribed regular polygons, an idea upon which, as we said, Eudoxus founded his epoch-making *method of exhaustion*.[32]

With his constructions Antiphon, no doubt, did intend to exhaust the circle in a literal sense. But despite the traditional designation "method of exhaustion," there is no literal sense in which Eudoxus purports to exhaust the circle; indeed, his method is based on the recognition that it is impossible to exhaust the circle for precisely the reasons adduced by the commentators. The undeniable analogy between Antiphon's and Eudoxus's methods makes it possible to imagine some kind of influence, but the fundamental opposition between the mathematical and the atomist or empiricist points of view makes such a hypothetical influence seem more accidental than essential. One would hardly want to say, as Heath seems to suggest, that Eudoxus simply reformulated Antiphon's argument or that Antiphon "laid the foundations of what we now call the calculus."[33]

31. It is to some extent misleading for Luria (1932–33) to call the theory he assigns to the atomists and Antiphon an infinitesimal theory, since according to the theory any finite magnitude is composed of finitely many indivisibles of finite size.

32. Heath 1921, p. 222.

33. Wasserstein 1959, p. 95. Wasserstein's view of Antiphon's achievement is not entirely clear to me. In addition to making the quoted remark and the asser-

"Hippocrates"

Simplicius's discussion of the quadrature by means of segments[34] provides the most extensive and reliable information we have about early Greek mathematics, but its interpretation is not completely unproblematic. He first assigns to Hippocrates a circle quadrature which was apparently ascribed to Hippocrates by Alexander.[35] The fallacy in the argument is pointed out by Simplicius. It consists in the unjustified assumption that the quadrature of one particular kind of lune, that contained by a half-circumference of one circle and a quarter-circumference of a circle of twice the area of the first, enables one to square another type of lune. Simplicius describes a second, similar quadrature without ascribing it to Hippocrates; it too may come from Alexander. After some further discussion, which need not be rehearsed here, Simplicius reports what he has found concerning Hippocrates in Eudemus's history of geometry, namely, three quadratures of particular lunes with outer boundaries greater than, equal to, and less than a semicircle, and a quadrature of a circle plus another particular lune. It seems clear that Simplicius has found no trace of an attempted circle quadrature in Eudemus and that he is baffled because he rightly considers Eudemus a more reliable source than Alexander. He says:

> But if it is accepted (dokei) that Hippocrates has supplied a general quadrature of a lune (for every lune has as its outer arc either the arc of a semicircle or that of a segment greater than a semicircle or that of one less), someone might say that it is possible to produce a square equal to a circle by itself by subtracting from the square equal to a circle plus a lune a square equal to the lune and squaring the remaining rectilineal figure.[36]

Simplicius is uncomfortable with this suggestion because he assigns to Aristotle the view that the circle had not been squared. In a hesitating way Simplicius makes the correct point that

---

tion that Eudemus's criticism "is not really as damaging as it may look at first sight," Wasserstein also calls the criticism valid and relevant (p. 94).

34. Simplicius, in Phys., pp. 55.25–69.34.

35. Ross (1936, p. 465) shows that there is some reason to think that Aristotle is referring to this quadrature at Pr. An. II 25, 69a32–33.

36. Simplicius, in Phys., p. 69.12–18.

Hippocrates' quadratures are of particular lunes and hence do not permit such a quadrature of the circle.

It is clear that Simplicius could find no reliable information concerning the quadrature by means of segments, not even the name of its author or the nature of the segments. *Sophistical Refutations* 11 makes it likely enough that the segments in question are Hippocrates' lunes, but nothing Aristotle says implies that the alleged circle quadrature belongs to Hippocrates. Indeed Aristotle's failure to connect the quadrature with any person suggests that he does not know to whom to assign it and perhaps that the quadrature was never "published" but merely put forward for discussion. We cannot, of course, be certain about the nature of this quadrature, but given Eudemus's account, the last argument suggested by Simplicius seems a plausible candidate.

We would presumably call the shortcoming of this alleged quadrature logical rather than geometrical, since it turns on the ambiguity of an expression like "to square a figure," which may refer to squaring either a particular figure or any figure at all. The possibility of confusion here is illustrated by the assertion that Hippocrates squared a circle plus a lune; for what Hippocrates demonstrated was how to square an arbitrary circle together with a particular lune defined in relation to the circle. It does not seem to me unreasonable to suppose that Aristotle has in mind Simplicius's logical objection to the quadrature by means of lunes, even though he assigns the task of refuting the quadrature to the geometer. For first of all, Aristotle's general description of a false proof as based on (true) first principles makes it necessary that the shortcoming of such a proof be ultimately a matter of bad logic. Moreover, Aristotle's own theory of inference, syllogistic, would not be adequate to explain the shortcoming in the quadrature described by Simplicius; and, in any case, a geometer seems more likely to notice the shortcoming than a dialectician.

Before leaving Hippocrates, it is well to say a word about the controversial first part of Simplicius's presentation of Eudemus's report, which runs as follows:

> He [Hippocrates] took as first principle and laid down as primary among the things useful for his quadratures that similar segments of

circles have the same ratio to one another as their bases have in square. He showed this on the basis of having shown that diameters of circles have the same ratio in square as the circles. [Simplicius points out that this latter proposition amounts to *Elements* XII 2.] For as circles are to one another, so are the similar segments. For similar segments are those which are the same part of a circle, as semicircle is similar to semicircle and third of a circle to third of a circle. Therefore, also, similar segments admit equal angles. And, indeed, the angles of all semicircles are right, those of greater segments less than right and as much less as the segments are greater, and those of smaller segments greater and as much greater as the segments are smaller.[37]

Scholars have generally been puzzled by the assertion that Hippocrates proved the equivalent of *Elements* XII 2, since in the rest of Eudemus's report Hippocrates appears as a logically rigorous mathematician, and it is believed on good grounds that Eudoxus provided the first logically rigorous proof of XII 2 some fifty years after Hippocrates' *floruit*. One might then wish to speculate that Hippocrates used some kind of intuitive argument involving an infinite process of the kind discussed in connection with Antiphon. However, it seems unlikely that a Peripatetic like Eudemus would think such an argument had any demonstrative force at all. In addition, it is hard to see why Hippocrates would have been willing to use a procedure like Antiphon's to establish XII 2 or its equivalent but not to use it to square lunes or even the circle.

The last part of the preceding quotation includes a very unsatisfactory derivation of the proposition that circles are to one another as similar segments of them, along with what is at best a plausibility consideration to show that similar segments admit equal angles. If the words describe Hippocrates' own work,[38] there is reason to think that he might have adopted the equivalent of XII 2 on grounds of plausibility, arguing that since similar polygons have the same ratio to one another as their corresponding sides in square, similar segments must, too, without thinking

37. Simplicius, *in Phys.*, p. 61.5–18. I have not discussed Wilbur Knorr's interesting interpretation of this passage (chapter IV), because to do so adequately would require another chapter as long as this one.
38. For discussions of the source of these words, see Heath 1921, pp. 187–91, Dijksterhuis 1929, pp. 33–38, and Becker 1934–36a.

of segments as limiting cases of polygons. Eudemus's report is itself somewhat curious in this respect. The first sentence in the quotation would normally mean that Hippocrates adopted the proposition about similar segments as a hypothesis without proof. Only in the second sentence does Eudemus suggest a derivation of the proposition, a derivation from a proposition which Eudemus presumably knows to have been proven by Eudoxus. However, it has often been pointed out that Eudemus arbitrarily credits to Thales mathematical propositions and proofs simply because in Eudemus's conception of mathematics they are presupposed by other propositions credited to Thales.[39] It seems quite possible that Eudemus is proceeding in the same way with Hippocrates.

Bryson

The commentators' descriptions of Bryson's quadrature vary considerably and show no indication of reliance on Eudemus. I am inclined to think that there are no direct historical, mathematical, or philological grounds for preferring any one of them[40] but will argue that a version of Bryson's quadrature given by Proclus fits best with Aristotle's criticism. The most extended discussion of the quadrature is in Philoponus's commentary on the *Posterior Analytics*.[41] Philoponus describes Alexander's epitome of the argument. It rests on the principle ABP (Alexander's Brysonian principle):

Things greater and less than the same thing are equal to each other,

and proceeds as follows:

A circle is greater than every rectilineal figure inscribed in the circle and less than a circumscribed one; a rectilineal figure drawn between

---

39. See Dicks 1959, p. 302 ff.
40. Heath (1949, pp. 48, 50) seems equally skeptical about the reliability of the reports. Their unreliability does not, however, justify purely conjectural accounts such as Wasserstein's suggestion that Bryson gave no real argument at all but merely "suggested that there exists a sort of proportion in which what we now call π was the middle term between circumscribed and inscribed figures as extreme terms . . ." (Wasserstein 1959, p. 100). For criticism of this suggestion see M. Brown 1972, p. 26.
41. Philoponus, *in An. post.*, ed. M. Wallies, pp. 111.6–114.17.

an inscribed and a circumscribed rectilineal figure is also less than the circumscribed one and greater than the inscribed one; therefore, the circle is equal to the rectilineal figure drawn between an inscribed and a circumscribed one.

The notion of drawing a figure between two figures is not clarified, but Sophonias[42] and pseudo-Alexander[43] say that Bryson simply inscribed and circumscribed a square, drew a third square of intermediate size, and claimed on the basis of ABP that this square is equal to the circle. Each source gives a numerical counterexample to ABP. Pseudo-Alexander points out that 8 and 9 are not equal, although both are greater than 7 and less than 10.

Alexander's account does not really seem to be compatible with Aristotle's criticism of Bryson. For the problem with Alexander's argument is not its generality, but the fact that ABP is false and, indeed, false not only of numbers but also of the plane figures involved in the argument itself. However, Becker[44] has claimed that the argument Alexander has in mind is a more interesting one which is more adequately represented by Themistius,[45] according to whom Bryson's principle is TBP:

Things than which the same things are greater and less are equal to each other;

and his argument is

A circle is greater than all inscribed polygons and less than circumscribed ones; the polygon drawn between those incribed in and circumscribed about the circle is greater than all inscribed ones and less than all circumscribed ones; therefore, this polygon and the circle are equal to one another.[46]

This formulation comes remarkably close to treating the quadrature of the circle as a matter of taking the limit of the infi-

42. Sophonias?, *in Soph. el.*, ed. M. Hayduck, p. 30.1–7.
43. Ps.-Alexander, *in Soph. el.*, ed. M. Wallies, p. 90.12–17.
44. Becker 1932–33b, pp. 370–72.
45. Themistius, *in An. post.*, ed. M. Wallies, p. 19.13–20.
46. I am inclined to think that Becker's motivation for assimilating Alexander's and Themistius's versions of Bryson's quadrature is to be able to use Alexander's authority as a basis for asserting the historical reliability of Themistius's version. Becker is able to argue plausibly that, taken by itself, ABP can be read as equivalent to TBP, but he can do nothing with the fact that whereas Alexander's account makes ABP and Bryson's reasoning uninteresting, Themistius's does not.

nite sequences of inscribed and circumscribed polygons. Of course, there is no sense in the notion of drawing this limit as a polygon between the two sequences. Indeed, if one imagines the sequences as existent, their limit would be the circle, and Proclus's criticism of Alexander's reconstruction as a repetition of Antiphon's argument would seem appropriate.[47] A similar criticism applies to Heath's use of Themistius's version to argue that Bryson's procedure is simply a refinement of Antiphon's, in which inscribed and circumscribed polygons rather than just inscribed ones are used.[48] Such a view is also difficult to reconcile with the apparent difference between Aristotle's objections to Bryson and Antiphon.

According to Philoponus, Proclus himself made the suggestion that Bryson did not attempt to draw an intermediate polygon but, using an inscribed and circumscribed rectilineal figure, applied the principle PBP:

> There is something equal to that than which there is a greater and a less

to conclude that there must be a rectilineal figure equal to the circle. PBP gives clear expression to an intuition about continuity, namely that there are no "gaps" in the areas of rectilineal figures intermediate in area between two given ones. A similar intuition can be read into TBP,[49] but Proclus's version of Bryson's argument has the advantage of simplicity over Themistius's, and it eliminates the awkward reference to drawing a figure equal to the circle. In addition, although there do not seem to be any formulations of TBP in early texts, Becker points to passages in Plato and Aristotle

47. Philoponus, *in An. post.*, pp. 111.31–112.6.
48. Heath 1921, pp. 224–25.
49. Becker (1932–33b, pp. 373–74) uses Themistius's version to claim that Bryson argued for the uniqueness but not the existence of a rectilineal area equal to a given circle and maintains that Proclus was the first to argue for existence. This claim is prima facie implausible, since application of Euclid's first common notion ("Things equal to the same thing are equal to each other") to the assumption that there are two areas equal to a given circle leads immediately to contradiction; and it is highly unlikely that a proof that there is at most one square equal to a given circle would be called a quadrature. Moreover, Becker gives no grounds for reading an expression like "the intermediate polygon" as "the intermediate polygon, if there is one."

in which the content of PBP is expressed.[50] Moreover, it is possible to argue that Proclus's version fits quite well with Aristotle's criticism of Bryson.

I have already mentioned that pseudo-Alexander and Sophonias locate the difficulty with Bryson's argument in its applicability to numbers, times, places, and solids. However, insofar as PBP is an attempt to express the idea of continuity, it would presumably not be intended to apply to numbers. And insofar as Bryson's argument is a quadrature, times, places, and solids would not seem to be relevant either. For the issue is the generality not of the single premise PBP used in the argument but of the argument as a whole. Aristotle is fully cognizant of the fact that in geometric arguments one uses "common axioms" such as "Things equal to the same thing are equal to each other."[51]

Because of the apparent irrelevance to Proclus's version of Bryson's quadrature of the criticism assigned to Aristotle by pseudo-Alexander and Sophonias, I am inclined to adopt the alternative interpretation of Aristotle's criticism mentioned earlier, namely, that the problem with Bryson's argument is its applicability to any plane figure. This fault would be the inverse of proving that K is P by proving that all species of K are P. It is to be noticed that this kind of fault is not logical in our sense but might instead be called epistemological. Although it would be difficult to characterize this epistemological fault precisely, there does seem to be a kernel of truth in Aristotle's position. To use his examples, the person who knows Euclid's general proof that the sum of the angles of a triangle is equal to two right angles does seem to know or understand more than the person who can only prove the result separately for equilateral, isosceles, and scalene triangles; and a single

50. Becker 1934–36a, pp. 236–39. The passages are Plato, *Parmenides* 161D7–8, and Aristotle, *Nicomachean Ethics* V 5, 1131a9–12, and *Phys.* VII 4, 248a24–25.

51. Themistius (*in An. post.*, p. 19.19–20) suggests that the problem with Bryson's quadrature is that the general principle on which it relies cannot be restricted to a specific genus as, according to Aristotle, a common principle should be. (See *Post. An.* I 10, 76a37–b3, and Barnes 1975, comment ad loc.) According to Themistius, the difficulty is that Bryson's principle has to be applied to a circle and a polygon simultaneously, but to make his point he has to deny implicitly that a circle is a magnitude. Such a view would undermine a great deal of the geometry of the *Elements*.

proof that proportionals alternate is more informative than separate proofs for numbers, lines, solids, and times.[52]

Constructivist philosophers of mathematics have sometimes argued that nonconstructive proofs convey too little information to count as genuine additions to knowledge, and as Philoponus insists,[53] Proclus's version of Bryson's argument is nonconstructive; it shows that there can be a square equal to a circle but does not show how to construct it. However, one need not suppose that Aristotle is a conscious constructivist in order to justify assigning to him the belief that Bryson's quadrature does not provide real knowledge. One need only look at the elaborate but constructive Euclidean argument that any rectilineal figure can be squared (*Elements* II 14) to understand why Aristotle might think that Bryson's argument is as useful mathematically as a Zenonian argument against walking is useful medically. Bryson's quadrature, if scientific, would do as well for a rectilineal figure as for a circle, but I think anyone can agree that such a quadrature does not convey the information contained in Euclid's.

Thus, Proclus's version of Bryson's argument makes good sense of Aristotle's prima facie puzzling view that the argument is a valid derivation from true first principles but is nevertheless inadequate. PBP, properly understood, represents a sound intuition about continuity, but intuitions do not constitute genuine knowledge except in the context of a theory in which they can be exploited systematically. More than 2,000 years were required for Bryson's intuition to find such a context, and by that time the problem of circle quadrature was sufficiently well understood to make Bryson's attempt at a solution a triviality.

52. *Post. An.* I 5, 74a17–32.
53. Philoponus, *in An. post.*, p. 112.25–34. Philoponus goes on to produce a geometric counterexample to PBP and says that it is only true for homogeneous things and not for heterogeneous things like circles and rectilineal figures. On this material see Becker 1932–33b, pp. 378–87, and 1954, pp. 46–52. Becker's assignment (1934–36a, p. 243) of an analogous criticism of Bryson to Aristotle seems to me unsatisfactory because the criticism amounts to saying that Bryson, like Antiphon, argued from a false principle.

CHAPTER VI

William of Ockham and the Logic of Infinity and Continuity

JOHN E. MURDOCH

1. Introduction

Although the characterization of Aristotle as *il maestro di color che sanno* was derived from reflection upon his fundamental position within thirteenth-century philosophy, there is no doubt that he was also *talis magister in philosophia naturali* in the fourteenth century, including those parts of natural philosophy that concerned themselves with infinity and continuity. Still, this is not to say that all matters of this sort were but interpretations and elaborations of things said or implied by Aristotle. Many were; but there were also elements within the fourteenth-century analysis of the infinite and the continuous that went well beyond what one could appropriate from the Philosopher.

Indeed, as one reads through the literature relevant to this particular problem area in late medieval philosophy, at least five such new elements make a rather striking appearance. There is, first of all, considerable effort spent in examining the problem of the *existence* of indivisibles within continua, something that Aristotle, for all his analysis of the continuous, did not much trouble himself with, at least not directly.

Secondly, although Aristotle had indeed devoted a great deal of attention to the refutation of the composition of continua out of indivisibles, the kind of mathematical argument so often put to this task in fourteenth-century literature is not something characteristic of his attack on indivisibilism. These *rationes mathematicae* were given a substantial impetus toward effectiveness and respectability when they were employed by Duns Scotus at the very beginning of the century, his authoritative example apparently urging all manner of authors ever thereafter to bring such arguments to bear on the problem of the composition of continua, although they reached their most extensive and developed display but some twenty years after Scotus in Thomas Bradwardine's *Tractatus de continuo*.[1]

The third new element that entered into the fourteenth-century investigation of continuity had to do with what might be called, in our terms, the ascription of limits to a continuous sequence or series. In medieval terms, the issue was that of assigning first and last instants, or "beginnings" and "endings," to continuous changes or processes or to states of affairs occurring within continuous time. This issue in its most developed treatments furnished prime ground for the exercise of sophismata and of reasoning *secundum imaginationem*.[2]

A fourth un-Aristotelian factor in our subject matter was a specific puzzle concerning the infinite: namely, the occurrence of some infinites that clearly seemed to be greater than others, despite the fact, or the axiom, that all infinites must be equal. This problem of the equality of infinites appears first to have been brought to the fore within debates concerning the possible eternity of the world, the prime mover in this respect seemingly being St. Bonaventure.[3] The problem was not mentioned by Aristotle (although some saw items of relevance in his works) and, being little debated anywhere in available ancient sources, was something of a medieval creation.[4]

So was, in another way, our fifth and final new element, the question of which infinites might be logically possible under

1. John Duns Scotus, *Opus Oxoniense*, Bk. II, dist. 9, Q. 2. The text of Bradwardine's *Tractatus* has been edited in Murdoch 1957. For a brief sketch of *rationes mathematicae* in analyzing continua in the later Middle Ages, see Murdoch 1974.

2. On the problem of the ascription of limits see Wilson 1956, chaps. 2–3; Kretzmann 1976b; and Murdoch 1979.

3. St. Bonaventure, *Comm. sent.*, Bk. II, dist. 1, p. 1, art. 1, Q. 2.

4. The paradox of the equality of infinites is treated briefly in Plutarch, *De comm. not. adv. Stoicos*, 1079a; Philoponus, *De aeternitate mundi* I 3, and *apud* Simplicium, *Phys. VIII* 1, ed. Diels, p. 1179, 1.15–26; Alex. Aphrodisias, *Quaest. naturales* III, p. 12; Proclus, *Comm. in Euclidem*, def. 17, and *Elem. theol.*, prop. 1; Lucretius I, 615–26. Treatment of the paradox was more extensive in Islamic material: see, for example, Al-Sharastānī 1934, chap. 1; Averroës 1954, pp. 9–10, 14, 162–63; and Pines 1965.

God's absolute power. Aristotle was, for example, adamant in his opposition to actual, completed infinites, but might not such be allowable *de potentia Dei absoluta*? This, too, was a development that to an appreciable extent took place within the discussion of the eternity of the world, but it also found expression in deliberations over the limitations that might be set upon God's power itself and, stemming from such theological contexts, in works on natural philosophy as well.

If these five relatively new factors do characterize an important part of the map of the fourteenth-century treatment of infinity and continuity, concentrating upon the deliberations of William of Ockham in this regard will then be somewhat unrepresentative, since he does not bear witness to these new factors in anything near the measure one might expect. Thus, although he did speak out on the puzzle of the equality of infinites and also treated the problem of the existence of indivisibles, the attention he paid to the issue of the kinds of infinite possible under God's absolute power is decidedly less than what one finds in many of his contemporaries. More than that, Ockham was clearly far from the main stream in his neglect of *rationes mathematicae* in treating problems of continuity or limits.[5]

Instead, he was far more concerned with interpreting and developing inherited (largely Aristotelian) notions and doctrines, although he often carried out this development to a degree that makes the offspring most unlike the parent.[6] In fact, even when there is little in Aristotle himself of direct relevance to the point at issue—such as, to cite a prime example, the existence of indivisibles—Ockham was concerned to treat the implication of this point for issues that *are* in Aristotle. The subdivisions of the general

5. Ockham did, however, take notice of these then popular mathematical arguments in his *Quodlibet* I, Q. 9 (*Utrum linea componatur ex punctis*) and in various places in his *Expositio Physicorum* (for example, Lib. III, t. 61; MS Merton 293, 71r), yet with nothing like the assiduousness of so many of his contemporaries. He also seems to have regarded of little importance much of what his contemporaries struggled with in the problem of beginning and ending limits (see, for example, Ockham 1974, II, cap. 19).

6. Like Ockham, John Buridan spends less time than one would expect in discussing the new elements mentioned above and concentrates more upon the development and criticism of the Aristotelian fabric at hand. I hope to publish the relevant material on Buridan soon.

problem area of infinity and continuity that seem to have been of greatest interest to Ockham are, on the one hand, the existence of indivisibles and the necessity of considering them in natural philosophy and, on the other hand, the infinite divisibility of continua. But this infinite divisibility as well as the necessary consideration of indivisibles *within* the continuous magnitudes and processes involved in nature are to the mark Aristotelian concerns. And if to this one adds Ockham's treatment of the equality of infinites, one has, I believe, a proper roster of the three aspects of the infinite and the continuous that most occupied him. As such, these aspects will form the structure of our investigation.

With the exception of Ockham's discussion of the equality of infinites, I shall concentrate my attention almost entirely upon one work: his *Expositio super libros Physicorum.*[7]

2. The Equality of Infinites

Although a wide variety of conceptions and arguments were applied within late medieval discussions of the equality of infinites, one can, I believe, reasonably distinguish three different traditions at play within these discussions. The first, and certainly oldest, of these traditions utilized the paradox of equal yet unequal infinites to reject the antecedent that gave rise to the paradox in the first place. Thus, thirteenth-century Franciscans were all but unanimous in using this paradox to establish the impossibility of an eternal world. If, the argument frequently read, one considers the actually infinite past time that would be entailed by an eternally existing world, then during that infinite past time there would be twelve times as many revolutions of the moon as there would be

7. Ockham, *Expositio Physicorum*, unedited; I have used the following MSS: Oxford, Merton College 293, 1r–149v; Berlin SB lat. fol. 41 (Rose 974), 86r–209r; Bruges 557, 104r–185r; Vienna NB 5364, 1r–120r. No manuscript of the *Expositio* covers all eight books of the *Physics* (the most complete containing I–VII, or—as is the case with Merton 293—through the beginning of VIII; Bruges 557 covers only I–IV). I have only rarely appealed to Ockham's *Quaestiones Physicorum*, since they are in large part taken from parts of his *Expositio*. However, F. Corvino has edited the *quaestiones* treating of continuity (in Corvino 1958), and I have on occasion made reference to his edition for passages parallel to those in the *Expositio*. On Corvino's edition, see note 21 below.

revolutions of the sun; yet both would also be infinite in number and hence—on the grounds that all infinites are equal—both equal and unequal. One can only conclude, then, that the hypothesized eternity of the world that initially generated such a contradiction must be rejected. And the same sort of thing can be seen to be true if one compares the actually infinite past time up to today with the infinite past time up to yesterday.[8]

The second tradition was solidly fourteenth-century, apparently Parisian in concentration and perhaps even in origin. In sum, this tradition argued *both* that no infinite is greater or less than another *and* that some infinites are not equal to one another, inferring on the basis of these two *conclusiones* that "no infinite compared, *per imaginationem*, with another is less than, equal to, or greater than that other infinite, but every infinite is incomparable with every other."[9] The "rejectionism" of this second tradition was quite different from that of the first tradition: in place of denying the existence of infinites that gave rise to the paradox of their simultaneous equality and inequality, one now removed the paradox by denying the applicability of equality and inequality to such infinites.

By contrast, the third tradition did not deny this applicability but instead attempted to resolve the paradox by making the strategic focus of the attack upon it the whole-part axiom that governed occurrences of greater than and less than in mathematics and then asking just what new kinds or senses of such excess or defect might be permissible for infinites (which were, by the

---

8. See the reference to St. Bonaventure in note 3 above; cf. Peter John Olivi, *in Sent.* II (ed. B. Jansen), Q. 3, esp. pp. 36–43.

9. Nicole Oresme, *Quaestiones Phys.* III, Q. 12, concl. 3 (MS Sevilla, Bibl. Colomb. 7–6–30, 38r): "Nullum infinitum alteri comparatum per ymaginationem est ipso minus vel aequale vel maius, sed omne omni est incomparabile." Oresme was followed, conclusion by conclusion, by Albert of Saxony: *QQ. De caelo* (ed. Paris, 1518), I, Q. 10. Although John Buridan does not explicitly urge the "incomparability thesis" for infinites, some of what he does urge (in his *Quaest. Phys.* [ed. Paris, 1509] III, Q. 18) concerning the impossibility of actual infinites looks like reasonable background for the position maintained by Oresme and Albert. Note might also be made of the fact that both Galileo (*Discorsi*, ed. naz., p. 79) and Newton (Letter to Richard Bentley, 1693, in Cohen 1958, pp. 293–99) also deny comparability when faced with the paradox of the equality of infinites, something that does not, of course, imply their knowledge of similar views in fourteenth-century Paris.

other horn of the dilemma, at least in one sense clearly equal). This tradition was, by and large, English,[10] and William of Ockham was one of its adherents. The most notable of his predecessors in this regard were the atomist Henry of Harclay and his critic William of Alnwick; they may be described as trying to formulate a more general whole-part (or set-subset) axiom that would be applicable to infinites.[11]

What appears to be a first stage in Ockham's own treatment of this issue is to be found in an *additio* to Book II of his *Commentaria sententiarum*. The context is that of the possibility of an eternal world. Ockham concedes that in the infinite past time entailed by such a possibility, the infinity of the revolutions of the moon *would* be greater than the infinity of the revolutions of the sun.[12] Moreover, in response to a more complicated argument operating with both past *and* future infinite times, which concludes that the part (all past time up to the beginning of today) is *greater* than the whole (all past time up to the end of today), Ockham replies that the whole argument is based upon a false proposition: namely, that all infinites are equal.[13]

10. Gregory of Rimini, however, is a notable adherent to this "English" tradition. His *Comm. sent.* contains what can properly be regarded as the most successful resolution of the paradox along the lines of this tradition. See Murdoch 1965.

11. See Murdoch 1965.

12. "Rationes probantes quod [mundus] non potuit fuisse ab aeterno . . . Tertia est quia infinita essent excessa actualiter, quia secundum te infinitae revolutiones sunt praeteritae, sed plures sunt revolutiones actualiter lunae quam solis; ergo sequitur quod plures erunt revolutiones in infinitum actualiter lunae quam solis; sed quod exceditur non est infinitum ex quo est excessum. . . . Ad tertiam concedo quod infinita essent excessa, sicut probat ratio, et quod unum infinitum esset maius alio, sicut revolutiones lunae excedunt revolutiones solis." *In Sent.* II, Q8 (ed. Lyon 1495, ad sig. B & D).

13. The argument Ockham is answering is given in outline in note 20 below. His reply is (op. cit., ad sig. H): "Ad aliud argumentum principale dico quod illud argumentum fundatur super falsum, scilicet quod omnia infinita sunt aequalia, quod falsum est posito ypothesi. Patuit enim prius quod revolutiones solis pertransitae sunt infinitae si mundus fuisset ab aeterno, et similiter infinitae revolutiones lunae quae sunt plures quam revolutiones solis. Et ideo posita ypothesi debet concedi quod infinitum est maius infinito et exceditur ab infinito, et hoc sive comparetur infinitum ad infinitum pertransitum sive ad infinitum pertranseundum. Patet enim manifeste, si mundus fuisset ab aeterno, quod totum tempus praeteritum copulatum ad principium huius diei esset infinitum actualiter et similiter totum tempus praeteritum copulatum ad finem huius diei esset infinitum actualiter, et tamen esset maius quam totum tempus praeteritum copulatum ad principium huius diei, ad minus per unum diem esset maius. Eodem modo dico quod totum tempus praeteritum copulatum ad principium huius diei et totum

Although thus allowing inequality between infinites, Ockham does not here push further to inquire into the precise nature of that inequality. For such an inquiry we must turn to other works of his. In his *Quodlibeta,* for instance, he asserts that unequal infinites and the consequent apparent violation of the stipulated relation between parts and wholes are among those difficulties frustrating the possibility of an eternal world.[14] To circumvent these difficulties we should, Ockham maintains, realize that they are due to an equivocation in the use of the term "more numerous." On the one hand, one set of things is said to be more numerous than another when it contains as many elements as the other and still more in some definite number (*plura in aliquo certo numero*). This kind of excess is not, however, relevant to infinites. On the other hand, a second sense of excess does apply to infinites: one in which we again have as many elements in the one set as in the other, but where the one set contains still more elements not contained in the other, although *not* more in some definite number.[15]

This admissible kind of excess for infinites automatically removes the first difficulty facing the possibility of an eternal world, since that difficulty was simply that one infinite *would* exceed another,[16] a state of affairs that is now no longer problematic. A second difficulty, however, is more complex. It claims that because one infinite would *not* be greater than another (the reason

tempus futurum copulatum ad principium huius diei non sunt aequalia, sed unum est maius alio; sed quod est maius et quod minus difficile est nos iudicare. Cum ergo illa tota deductio fundetur super istam totam propositionem: 'omnia infinita sunt aequalia,' quae falsa est, ut probatum est, manifeste patet quod non sequitur quod pars sit maior toto."

14. Ockham, *Quodl.* II, Q. 5 (Ockham 1980, 129.11–29): "Secundo dico probabiliter quod Deus potuit fecisse mundum ab aeterno, propter hoc quod nulla apparet contradictio manifesta. Sed tunc hic sunt duae difficultates: una, quia aliquae rationes concludunt quod mundum fieri ab aeterno includit contradictionem . . . Tum quia infinita essent plura infinitis, et essent excessa. Patet de revolutionibus solis et lunae. Tum quia pars esset aequalis toti, quia unum infinitum non esset maius alio."

15. Ockham, *Quodl.* II, Q. 5 (Ockham 1980, 131.73–132.79): "Ad aliud dico quod aequivocatio est de 'pluribus': uno modo dicuntur aliqua esse plura quando tot sunt in istis quot in illis, et adhuc plura in certo numero. Et sic infinita non sunt plura infinitis, quia neutrum excedit aliud in certo numero. Alio modo dicitur: quot sunt illa tot sunt ista, et adhuc sunt multa alia in illis, non tamen excedunt in certo numero. Et eodem modo dico ad illud de excessu."

16. See text in note 14 above.

for this being that all infinites are equal), it follows that a part would be equal to its whole.[17] One can remove this latter difficulty, Ockham holds, if one realizes that (as he had already maintained in his *Commentaria sententiarum*)[18] it is false that all infinites are equal. Indeed, one would think that the admissible excess that Ockham had just claimed for infinites would have provided sufficient grounds for establishing that falsity.[19] But Ockham did not take that tack. Rather, he established that it is false that all infinites are equal because neither of the two possible senses of equality can be applied to the actual infinites in question. Thus, since the whole "difficulty" at hand rests upon all infinites being equal, the difficulty, or paradox, disappears.[20]

17. Again, see text in note 14 above. Although Ockham is not explicit here about the fact that the crucial premise in this argument is the one asserting the equality of all infinites, this becomes absolutely clear when one proceeds to his reply to this argument (for which, see note 20 below). He is also silent here concerning any instantiating argument for this "second difficulty" (unlike the case of the first difficulty, where he noted that what was involved would be evident from the well-known example of the disparate number of the revolutions of the sun and the moon under the assumption of an eternal world). He must have had in mind, however, some such argument as that comparing an infinite past up to yesterday with an infinite past up to today, where the former is part of the latter yet equal to it because all infinites are equal.

18. See note 13 above.

19. In the text quoted in note 13 above, Ockham seems to allow that such a consideration is sufficient to prove that "All infinites are equal" is false.

20. Ockham, *Quodl.* II, Q. 5 (Ockham 1980, 132.81–96): "Ad aliud dico quod aliquid potest dici aequale dupliciter: uno modo, quando totum est in uno quod est in alio et non plus, vel cuilibet in uno correspondet tantum in alio et non plus. Et sic unum infinitum non est semper aequale alteri, immo maius, quia frequenter quantum est in uno, tantum correspondet in alio, et aliud. Sed tunc haec est falsa secundum istum intellectum 'quidquid est maius uno aequalium, est maius reliquo.' Aliter dicitur aliquid aequale alteri quando est dare certam quantitatem unius et tantam alterius et non plus. Et de tali aequali verum est quod quidquid est aequale uni aequalium, et reliquo est aequale. Et isto etiam modo unum infinitum non est aequale alteri. Unde (immo VA3075) primo modo loquendo, dico quod unum infinitum potest esse maius alio. Et quia super hoc fundatur illud argumentum, quod omnia infinita sunt aequalia, quod falsum est, ideo non concludit."

There are several problems with this text. To begin with, in Ockham's account of the first sense of "equal" it is not immediately clear just what relevance the principle that "whatever is greater than one of [two] equals is also greater than the remaining one" has to the matter at hand. Although it is not present in the quodlibetal question quoted here, Ockham probably had in mind an argument similar to that in his *Comm. sent.* concerning both past and future infinite times (see note 13 above). (The fact that Ockham neglects to mention such an argument should occasion no surprise, since throughout his *Quodlibeta* he often omits the arguments to which he is replying.) The argument to which the text given in note 13 replies is, in outline, the following (*Comm. sent.* II, Q. 8, ed. cit. sig. B):

Ockham and the Logic of Infinity and Continuity

Although in his other treatments of apparently unequal infinites Ockham does not broach the question of what kind of equality is or is not applicable, he does invoke a distinction about possible excesses or greater numerosities among infinites that is similar to that just cited from his *Quodlibeta*. He does so, however, within a context other than that of a possible eternal world: to wit, the greater infinity of parts in a whole continuum than in any of its parts. Thus, in both his *Expositio Physicorum* and in another quodlibetal question he claims that we can solve the paradox in this instance by once again seeing that the term *plura* (or a phrase containing it) can be taken in two senses. In one, *plura* entails being greater by some definite number (which, as in the parallel case cited above, does not apply to infinites). Alternatively, infinites can be covered by a second sense of *plura* wherein one thing contains as much or as many as another but also contains something else in addition.[21]

"Praeterea, si sic [scil. mundus fuit ab aeterno], sequeretur quod pars integralis esset maior toto. Probo: sit A totum tempus praeteritum terminatum ad principium huius diei et B totum futurum terminatum ad principium huius diei, et C totum praeteritum terminatum ad finem huius diei et D totum tempus futurum terminatum ad finem huius diei. Tunc arguo sic: A et B sunt aequalia, quia totum tempus praeteritum terminatum ad principium huius diei . . . et totum tempus futurum terminatum ad principium huius diei sunt aequalia; ergo A est maius C. Antecedens est verum per positum, quia tam A quam B est tempus infinitum. Consequentiam probo . . . B est maius D, quia totum tempus futurum terminatum ad principium huius diei est maius quam totum tempus futurum terminatum ad finem huius diei; ergo quod est aequale B [scil. A] est maius D, quia *si unum aequale sit maius alio, reliquum erit maius eodem*. Ultra D est aequale C . . . , quia ambo sunt infinita; et si A est maius D, ut probatum est, sequitur etiam quod *A est maius C, quia maius suo aequali* [scil. D] sed A est pars C . . . ergo sequitur quod pars integralis est maius suo toto, quod videtur inconveniens." It is evident that the second set of italicized words amounts to an application of the principle cited in the above quodlibet text (*quidquid est maius . . . reliquo*), while the first set of italics bespeaks the application of an equivalent principle if *minus* is substituted for *maius*. But it is just such applications that Ockham meant to castigate in his *Quodl.* II 5, when he claimed that the principle in question was false when applied to infinites. Thus, it seems highly probable that he had in mind an argument like that in his *Comm. sent.* when he wrote *Quodl.* II 5.

The second problem with the quodlibet text quoted above cannot, as far as I have been able to determine, be similarly solved by appealing to another of Ockham's works: namely, why Ockham denies that the *second* sense of "equal" is also inapplicable to infinites. However, it is likely that his denial was related to the fact that infinites do not have the *certa quantitas* demanded by this alternative sense of equality.

21. *Exp. Phys.* VI, t. 79 (239b18–30), MSS Mert. 293, 137r; Berlin lat. fol. 41, 197v: "Et si proterviatur contra ista [scil. infinitae partes continui] primo quia nulla sunt plura infinitis, sed plures partes sunt in aliquo toto quam in sua medietate quia omnes partes quae sunt in una medietate sunt in toto et non econverso, igitur

If we allow ourselves to put all of this into modern terms, we could say that in both his *Quodlibeta* and his *Expositio Physicorum* in differentiating two meanings for *plura* Ockham had come close to formulating, on the one hand, a notion of unequal cardinality (which is not applicable to infinites) and, on the other hand, a notion of set-subset (which is applicable to infinites). In this he appears to have marked an advance over his predecessors who also attempted to delineate new notions of excess and defect for infinites.[22] Yet in his determination to establish that it is false that all infinites are equal, Ockham seems to have gone too far. He provided no sense in which one infinite *is* equal to another. Although, as the relevant texts stand, one might argue that Ockham would allow that *some* infinites were equal,[23] one certainly has to admit that he does not explicitly recognize that infinite sets

---

plures partes sunt totius quam medietatis, igitur partes unius medietatis non sunt infinitae. . . . Et ad primum istorum dicendum est quod iste terminus 'plura' accipitur stricte et large. Stricte dicuntur aliqua plura aliis quando in aliquo certo numero sunt haec et illa, sed in maiori numero sunt haec quam illa. Et sic accipiendo 'plura' nulla sunt plura infinitis. Aliter accipitur iste terminus 'plura' quando scilicet illa quae sunt ex una parte sunt ex alia et aliqua alia et non econverso. Et sic accipiendo 'plura' concedo quod aliqua sunt plura infinitis, et isto modo accipiendo hoc vocabulum 'plura' procedit argumentum, non primo modo." Cf. *QQ Phys.*, ed. in Corvino 1958, pp. 198–200.

Quodlibeta I, Q. 9 (Ockham 1980, 59.226–60.240): "Si dicis: accipiatur aliqua pars caeli eiusdem quantitatis cum grano milii. Tunc illa pars caeli habet tot partes eiusdem quantitatis et similiter proportionis sicut granum; sed totum caelum habet plures partes eiusdem proportionis quam illa pars millesima, aliter totum non esset maius sua parte. Respondeo: haec propositio 'totum habet plures partes quam pars' potest dupliciter intelligi: uno modo, quod pars habeat aliquem certum numerum partium et quod partes totius excedant illum numerum in aliqua certa multitudine; et isto intellectus est falsus, quia implicatur quod pars habet certum numerum partium, quod falsum est. Alio modo, quod pars caeli habeat partes non tot in aliquo certo numero quin plures quia infinitas habet, et quod totum caelum habet tot partes et adhuc alias; et sic concedo quod totum caelum habet plures partes quam pars."

The question (*Utrum in forma maiori sint plures partes quam in forma minori*) edited in Corvino 1958, pp. 203–08, also treats of the equality of infinites, but it appears in only one of the three MSS of Ockham's *QQ Phys.*, and it contains things that are inconsistent with some of what Ockham says in unquestionably genuine works. I believe, therefore, that this particular question is not authentic, a judgment with which, I am pleased to report, Stephen Brown, who has prepared the *QQ Phys.* for publication, agrees.

22. I have in mind, in particular, Henry of Harclay and William of Alnwick. See note 11 above.

23. Would he not allow that the set of all odd numbers was equal to the set of all even numbers, or that given an actual infinity of (physically whole) men, the set of all right hands would be equal to the set of all left hands? The *posito ypothesi* in note 13 above above suggests that he might. Still, the measure of Ockham's

can be equal to their infinite proper subsets,[24] let alone provide an explanation of how that equality obtains—features of the infinite that were duly noted by some of his near contemporaries.[25] Nevertheless, what he had accomplished surely reduced some of the difficulties besetting a proper treatment of the problem of the equality of infinites.

3. The Existence of Indivisibles and Their Occurrence in Natural Philosophy

In dealing with the issue of the existence and nature of indivisibles, Ockham approached his task under the assumption of a particularist ontology which urged him to base all *scientia realis* upon a world of macroscopic individuals or, as Ockham would call them, *res permanentes*. Thus, to cite a familiar example, just as motion for Ockham must be accounted for only in terms of the individual *res permanentes* constituting nature—that is, in terms of the relevant mobiles and places or forms occupied or possessed by (or not yet occupied or possessed by) such mobiles[26]—so such indivisibles as points, lines, and surfaces must be accounted for, ultimately, in terms of three-dimensional bodies.[27] Simply put, indivisibles are not properly things (*res*) at all, something that

---

determination not to permit the equality of infinites can be seen from his claim (in note 13 above) that an actually infinite past time up to some moment is either greater or less than the actually infinite future from the same moment, although he cannot say which.

24. When treating, for example, the number of revolutions of the moon compared to that of the revolutions of the sun under the assumption of an eternal world (notes 12–14 above), or the number of parts in a whole continuum relative to the number of parts in one of its parts (note 21 above), he gives no indication that, in some sense, the infinite sets involved *are* equal.

25. To cite but a single instance, in the early 1340s Thomas Bradwardine clearly sees that infinite sets can be put in one-to-one correspondence with their infinite subsets (see Murdoch 1962, pp. 18–19) and others before him were aware of much the same. Further, also in the early 1340s, Gregory of Rimini did explain what was involved in the "equality" of such one-to-one correspondence between infinite sets and subsets (see note 10 above).

26. See Ockham 1944 and Shapiro 1957.

27. "Ultimately" because points were to be accounted for in terms of lines, lines in terms of surfaces, and surfaces in terms of three-dimensional bodies. Similarly, instants were to be accounted for in terms of extended temporal intervals. To cite a single illustrative example, "a point" was to be regarded as equivalent to "a line of such and such length," the point in question being the terminus of that line and determining that it was in fact of such and such a length. For the relevant texts in Ockham, see note 28 below.

Ockham spends a seemingly inordinate amount of time establishing.[28] What is more, we do not need indivisibles as things, in spite of the fact that they are everywhere present in some sense in natural philosophy (to say nothing of mathematics). Thus, to speak merely of points, the all-important presumed function of points in terminating lines or in continuing the parts of lines could—indeed, must—be accomplished by the existing lines themselves. For such duty we need no separately existing indivisibles at all, a critical point of view in which Ockham found a substantial number of followers in the fourteenth century.[29]

Given such strictures against the existence of the likes of points and instants, it occasions no surprise to see Ockham insist that Aristotle and Averroës agreed with this denial of the existence of indivisibles. To be sure, both the Philosopher and the Commentator do speak of points, but they do so only *secundum opinionem famosam* and do not intend their existence as indivisible things really distinct from lines.[30] Further, even taking the nonexistence of indivisibles into account, it was not superfluous for Aristotle to devote so much time to arguing that a continuum cannot be composed of indivisibles, since his reasoning was *conditional*: *if* there were such indivisibles, then they could not compose continua.[31]

28. Indeed, the amount of time Ockham spent in discussing the existence of indivisibles makes it impossible to give anything like a proportionally adequate treatment of this issue here. A fair amount of attention is paid to the problem in his *Expositio Physicorum* (VI, t. 3), but his most extensive treatment of it is the very lengthy introductory section of his *De sacramento altaris* in Ockham 1930. The short shrift given here to Ockham's investigations of these matters may also be partially excused by the fact that I have treated them on two previous occasions, in Murdoch forthcoming b and Murdoch forthcoming c. See also Eleonore Stump's discussion of the material in *De sacramento altaris* in chapter VII.

29. Thus Ockham was followed in his criticism of the existence of indivisibles as separately existing things by, e.g., Thomas Bradwardine, William Heytesbury, John Buridan, and Albert of Saxony. See Murdoch forthcoming b and forthcoming c.

30. *Exp. Phys.* III, t. 24 (202b30–36), MS Mert. 293, 63r: "Tertio notandum quod non intelligunt Philosophus et Commentator quod punctus sit quaedam res distincta a linea quae nec sit finita nec infinita, quia nulla res est in istis inferioribus inanimatis quin sit extensa; sed loquuntur secundum opinionem famosam quae ponit tales res indivisibiles." *Exp. Phys.* III, t. 35 (204a8–14), MS Mert. 293, 65r: "Tamen sciendum est quod nec Commentator in isto commento nec in commento 34 intendit quod punctus sit aliqua res indivisibilis distincta realiter a linea et corpore, sed loquitur secundum opinionem famosam quae ponit talia indivisibilia; vel per talem propositionem: 'punctus est indivisibilis' intelligit istam propositionem: 'quando aliquid finitur, non habet partem ulteriorem.'"

31. *Exp. Phys.*, VI, t. 3 (231b10–18), MSS Mert. 293, 125v; Berlin lat. fol. 41, 187r: "Dico quod Philosophus non frustra probat continuum non componi ex indivisibil-

Authoritative passages in Aristotle that at first glance seem to imply the existence of indivisibles can clearly be saved without any such implication.[32]

In addition to the "saving" of such *texts* in Aristotle and Averroës, one can (by a similar maneuver) account for all *doctrines* or *conceptions* in natural philosophy that appear to require the existence of indivisibles. Here, more often than not, Ockham characteristically turns to propositional analyses (that is, analyses in which the very elements of analysis are propositions and the terms contained within propositions, these terms and propositions in turn standing for things and events *in rerum natura*). Thus, in dealing with the occurrence of the indivisibles involved in motion or change, Ockham explains Averroës' reference to motion at an instant by saying that what he really meant was that the proposition *Motus est* is true at an instant.[33] Similarly, when Aristotle maintains that that into which something has first changed is indivisible (which is to say that something has changed in an instant), Ockham explains all he intends: that when something has changed from one thing to another, at some instant one can truly say "This has already changed" in such a way that previously it was not true to say "This has changed into

---

ibus, et hoc propter duas rationes quarum prima est quia, ex habundanti posito quod essent talia indivisibilia in rerum natura, probat quod non possent esse partes alicuius continui. Alia ratio quia Philosophus principaliter intendit probare quod tempus et motus non componuntur ex indivisibilibus, et quia aliquo modo in illis concedendum est quod sunt aliqua indivisibilia sub bono sensu quamvis nulla sit talis res indivisibilis, ideo non probat quod nihil sunt, sed probat quod, posito quod essent, adhuc ex eis non componeretur continuum."

32. *Exp. Phys.*, loc. cit.: "Continua sunt illa quorum ultima sunt unum . . . intentio Philosophi . . . est ista: continua sunt illa quae constituunt aliquod unum. . . . Per istam: illa tangunt se quorum ultima sunt simul, intelligit istam: illa tangunt se quae distincta non faciunt unum totum inter quae tamen nihil quantum est medium. . . . Quando dicit punctum esse indivisibile, magis dicit secundum opinionem aliorum quam secundum opinionem propriam; unde et sub conditione dicit illam propositionem. . . . Quando dicit Philosophus partes lineae copulari ad punctum, non intendit aliud quam partes longi, dum est unum longum, non possunt esse quaedam tota non facientia unum totum, quod tamen requiritur ad partes quantitatis continuae permanentis."

33. *Exp. Phys.* VI, t. 7 (231b28–232a6), MSS Mert. 293, 126v; Berlin lat. fol. 41, 188r: "Sciendum est hic quod Commentator dicit commento 7 quod 'instans in quo movetur per magnitudinem est aliud ab instanti in quo perficitur motus' et post dicit quod 'instans in quo dicitur ambulare est aliud ab instanti in quo dicitur ambulasse,' quod non est intelligendum quod (quasi *Berl.*) motus sit in instanti, sed intelligit quod haec propositio est vera in instanti: 'motus est,' sicut haec est vera in instanti: 'aliquid habet unam partem et caret alia quam habiturum est.'"

that," although it might have been true to say "This is changing into that."[34] In both of these cases Ockham has, he believes, succeeded in removing the problematic indivisible instants from view, from the world of *res*, while preserving the meaning of what Averroës or Aristotle unquestionably (for Ockham) had in mind.

Following the traces of indivisibles even further, one can see that they are needed entities in mathematics as well as in natural philosophy. For Ockham, one manner of accounting for this need was simply to claim that, like infinite lines, points are only *imagined* by mathematicians; such imaginary entities suffice for their purposes.[35]

But a second manner of providing for the indivisible entities needed in mathematics was a function of Ockham's view of mathematical theorems in general: they are conditional propositions. Applying this to our problematic indivisibles, one can circumvent the difficulty of the existence of any such things by always placing the term standing for the indivisible in question in the antecedent of a conditional proposition. Then the mathematician is merely claiming that *if* there were such and such an indivisible, then this or that state of affairs would ensue. One is therefore committed to the existence of indivisibles only *sub conditione*.[36] More than that, one can find explicit appeals in Ock-

34. *Exp. Phys.*, VI, t. 44 (235b32–236a5), MSS Mert. 293, 132r; Berl. lat. fol. 41, 193r: "In ista parte Philosophus declarat secundum praeambulum necessarium ad propositum, videlicet quod illud in quo aliquid primo est mutatum est indivisibile, id est quod aliquid est mutatum in instanti, nihil aliud intendens nisi quod quando aliquid est mutatum ab uno in aliud contingit in instanti vere dicere: 'hoc iam mutatum est' ita quod prius non erat verum dicere: 'hoc mutatum est in hoc,' quamvis prius fuit verum dicere: 'hoc mutatur in hoc'; et ita mutatum esse est in instanti."

35. *Exp. Phys.*, VI, t. 3 (231b10–18), MSS Mert. 293, 125v; Berlin lat. fol. 41, 187r: "Et si dicas quod linea est longitudo sine latitudine cuius extremitates sunt duo puncta, dicendum est quod mathematici imaginantur talia puncta sicut imaginantur lineam infinitam, quae tamen est impossibilis; et iuxta illam imaginationem mathematicorum datur praedicta descriptio et assimilatur illi diffinitioni linearum aequedistantium: lineae aequedistantes sunt illae quae in infinitum protensae non concurrent, cum tamen impossibile sit aliquas lineas protrahi in infinitum. Debet tamen sic intelligi quod, si in infinitum protraherentur, non concurrerent, sic ista diffinitio: 'linea est longitudo' debet sic intelligi: 'si esset aliqua longitudo et non latitudo et haberet puncta talia indivisibilia, tunc quaelibet linea haberet duas extremitates quae essent duo puncta.'"

36. *Exp. Phys.*, III, t. 70 (207b21–27), MSS Mert. 293, 75v–76r; Bruges 557, 166r: "Sciendum est quod mathematici in demonstrationibus suis utuntur frequenter propositionibus conditionalibus in quibus ponuntur tales termini: 'linea infinita,'

ham to this *sub conditione* technique when it is a question of the existence of indivisibles in natural philosophy as well as in mathematics. One can, for example, explain Aristotle's talk about the *per accidens* motion of an indivisible by maintaining that he was speaking only *conditionaliter*.[37]

All of this, however, leaves unsaid one major way in which Ockham went about "saving" the indivisibles that were relevant to natural philosophy. This saving amounted to yet another manner of accounting for the intent of propositions in which some such term as "indivisible," "point," or "instant" occurred by framing other propositions in such a way that the term in question was no longer used, the resulting new proposition, or propositions, then being an accurate mirror of a world in which there were no separately existing indivisible things. Part of the propositional analysis we have already seen Ockham use to cover the nonexistence of needed indivisibles, this major "new way" consisted in a distinct technique: the application of the successive verification of contradictory propositions.

To begin with, we should note the connection Ockham makes between succession and contradictories. We should realize that

---

'corpus infinitum,' nec unquam utuntur tali termino nisi in propositione conditionali nisi errantes et nescientes mathematicam; sicut mathematici non accipiunt talem propositionem categoricam: 'lineae rectae aequedistantes in infinitum protensae nunquam concurrunt,' sed accipiunt talem propositionem: 'si lineae rectae aequedistantes in infinitum protendentur, nunquam concurrerent.' Et si aliquando auctores ponant vocaliter talem propositionem categoricam, per eam intelligunt unam ypotheticam. Nunc autem ad veritatem conditionalis non requiritur veritas antecedentis, et ideo ad mathematicas non requiritur quod aliquod infinitum sit, sed requiritur quod ex tali propositione in qua ponitur iste terminus 'infinitum' sequatur alia vel sequatur ex alia, et hoc potest contingere sine hoc quod infinitum possit esse. Et sicut est de infinito, ita est de puncto, linea et superficie. Et recte sensientes in mathematica et non transgredientes limites mathematicae non asserunt quod punctus sit quaedam res indivisibilis distincta a linea nec linea a superficie nec superficies a corpore, sed ponunt conditionales aliquas in quibus subiicitur 'punctus' vel 'linea' vel 'superficies' sic accepta. Unde non habent dicere quod punctus sit quoddam indivisibile distinctum a linea terminans ipsam lineam, sed debent dicere quod, si sit res alia a linea, quod terminat lineam, ex quo non potest esse sine linea et non est pars lineae."

37. *Exp. Phys.* VI, t. 86 (240b8–20), MSS Mert. 293, 138v; Berlin lat. fol. 41, 198v: "Et sciendum est hic primo quod Philosophus non intendit quod sit aliquod indivisibile in istis inferioribus distinctum realiter a divisibili, et ideo quando dicit quod indivisibile movetur per accidens, vel loquitur secundum opinionem famosam quae ponit talia indivisibilia, vel loquitur conditionaliter ponendo illam propositionem cathegoricam pro ista conditionali: 'si esset aliquod indivisibile in istis inferioribus, illud moveretur per accidens et non per se'."

"real succession" can be accounted for without there being a succession of different *things* which requires the corruption of one distinct thing after another; we need only the truth of a negative *proposition* in which *esse* is negated of some subject of which it was previously verified, or vice versa.[38] But this entails, as Ockham puts it in another passage, that succession can occur only if two contradictory propositions can be verified. To cite Ockham's own illustrative example: "We say that a son succeeds his father because the father exists and the son does not exist, while the son does exist later in the sense that first this is true: 'The son does not exist,' and later this: 'The son does exist,' and therefore the son succeeds his father because the son's existence succeeds his nonexistence."[39]

It is a development of this connection between succession and contradictories which afforded Ockham the new technique of saving the intent of propositions that speak of indivisibles. Stated abstractly, this development amounts to combining the fact that contradictories cannot be true at the same time, even at the same instant, with the additional fact that propositions speaking of indivisibles do occur in important discourse about *res successivae* such as time and motion. Because we know that contradictories *can* be verified if there is any succession or *res successiva*, in terms of such verification we can "take care of" the references to indivisibles in those propositions talking about such successive things.

We can, for example, account for Aristotle's belief that it is impossible for motion to occur in an instant without appealing to

38. *Exp. Phys.* III, t. 57–58 (206a18–b3), MSS Mert. 293, 70r; Bruges 557, 162r: "Et ideo sciendum quod ad successionem realem non requiritur semper quod aliquid vere et realiter corrumpatur secundum se totum ita quod sit ibi aliqua res quae secundum se totam non sit postquam fuit (sicut est quando aliquid de nigro fit album), sed sufficit veritas negativae in qua esse negetur ab aliquo subiecto de quo verificabatur (sicut est in divisione reali magnitudinis)."

39. Ockham, *QQ Phys.*, Q. 28, MSS Vat. lat. 956, 36v; VlDom 187/153, 184v: "Sed dubium est ratione cuius accidit successio motuum. Respondeo quod nunquam esset successio nisi quia duae partes unius contradictionis possunt verificari. Unde si nulla contradictoria possent esse vera sed semper esset una pars contradictionis cuiuslibet vera et alia semper falsa, nulla posset esse successio; sed quia contradictoria possunt esse vera, et manifestum est quod non possunt simul esse vera, ideo oportet quod contradictoria sint successive vera, primo una pars et postea alia pars. Exemplum: dicimus quod filius succedit patri quia pater est et filius non est et post filius est ita quod primo est ista vera: 'filius non est' et postea ista: 'filius est', et ideo filius succedit patri quia esse filii succedit suo non esse."

instants themselves. For we merely say that while any mobile is in motion, two contradictory propositions can be successively verified. No instant has been mentioned, but we can see the effectiveness of Ockham's procedure when we realize that since no two contradictories can be verified in the same instant, it follows that no mobile can be in motion at an instant.[40] Thus, put in general terms, if a given mobile is in motion during X and both A and not-A are true during X, then X is not indivisible. And the same technique will allow us to give a proper Ockhamist interpretation of what Aristotle meant by saying that an instant is indivisible. For given the fact that time is the motion of the primum mobile (although the motion of other mobiles could be made to suffice),[41] we should be able to account for a proposition asserting the indivisibility of an instant in terms of the fact that the primum mobile occupies a given place for but an instant.[42] But we can express the latter without mentioning instants by saying that no two contradictory propositions can be successively verified while the proposition "The primum mobile is in this place" remains true.[43]

40. *QQ Phys.*, Q. 13, MS Vat. lat. 956, 34r; VlDom 187/153, 179r: "Sed haec est impossibilis: 'motus est in instanti', et similiter haec: 'aliquod mobile movetur in instanti', quia impossibile est quod mobile moveatur quando ista contradictoria sint vera successive dum mobile movetur: 'hoc instans est', 'hoc instans non est'; sed contradictoria non possunt verificari in instanti, igitur et cetera." Q. 17, MS cit. 35r, 180r–v: "Si motus esset una res absoluta cuius omnes partes essent simul adquisitae mobili, tunc posset esse in instanti. Sed quando motus non est talis sed importat unam rem adquisitam mobili et aliam immediate adquirendam, sicut ego pono, tunc non potest motus esse in instanti propter contradictionem quae sequitur, quia dum mobile movetur possunt duo contradictoria sibi succedentia verificari, puta 'hoc instans est',' 'hoc instans non est', quae non possunt in instanti verificari."

41. See the texts quoted and paraphrased in Baudry 1958, pp. 265–66.

42. That is to say, since time is the motion of the primum mobile (or something equivalent in function) for Ockham, all intervals of time and all "points" in time are determined by its successive occupation of different places. Thus, if the primum mobile were to *remain* in a given place, then the "instant" determined by the primum mobile's occupation of that given place would be an "extended" and "divisible" thing (it would be, for example, 4:30 P.M. throughout the primum mobile's occupation of that place).

43. *Exp. Phys.* VI, t. 24–25 (233b33–234a5), MSS Mert. 293, 128v–129r; Berlin lat. fol. 41, 190r: "Dicit [scil. Aristoteles] instans esse indivisibile non quia sit quaedam res existens in rerum natura carens omni parte, sed quia aliquod mobile indivisibiliter est in aliquo loco, hoc est quia est in aliquo loco in quo secundum se totum non fuit nec erit ita quod Philosophus per istam propositionem: 'instans est indivisibile' intelligit istam: 'mobile primum est alicubi'—illo modo accipiendo hunc terminum 'esse alicubi' quomodo vere praedicatur de primo mobili—'et tamen prius fuit in aliquo loco sibi aequali et non in isto et post erit in aliquo alio' ita

This successive verification of contradictories was also brought to bear by Ockham in analyzing conceptions and doctrines in which no "indivisible term" like "instant" appeared—such conceptions, for example, as a continuous motion. Thus, to account for the fact that a given local motion is continuous, in place of saying that such a motion is one in which the mobile does not rest for a single *instant*, one should merely maintain that in a continuous motion the occupation of a given place by the mobile in question does not "coexist" with the successive verification of any two contradictory propositions.[44]

In all these examples Ockham has attempted to replace talk about instants with talk about the successive verification of contradictory propositions. One might note, however, that when he applies this technique he does not mention—indeed, did not need to mention—the fact that contradictory propositions are those which cannot be true at the same instant. Yet it should not be imagined that this meant that Ockham's use of the technique of the verification of contradictory propositions entailed the existence of those very instants he was trying to "remove" by this

---

quod nulla contradictoria possunt verificari simul cum ista: 'hoc mobile est in hoc loco.' "

44. *Comm. sent.* (ed. Lyon, 1495; reprint London, 1962), II, Quaest. 9, ad sig. mg. J: "Alia est continuatio qua unum succedit alteri sine medio. Et talis continuatio requiritur necessario in motu . . . talia autem successiva sunt in duplici genere, quia aliquando successiva non possunt manere simul naturaliter, licet per potentiam divinam possint, sicut in motu locali . . . Loquendo de primis successivis, tunc est motus continuus quando nullum eorum potest coexistere duobus contradictoriis sibi invicem succedentibus; et hoc non tantum loquendo de contradictoriis intrinsecis motui quae sunt de ratione motus, sed etiam de extrinsecis. Exemplum: ad hoc quod aliquis moveatur localiter continue non tantum requiritur quod ubi non tantum coexistat simul cum affirmatione et negatione alterius ubi naturaliter, quia contradictio est quod ubi iam acquisitum existat cum affirmatione et negatione alterius ubi [this much accounts for the local motion itself, but not its continuity], sed requiritur quod illud ubi non coexistat naturaliter cum aliis contradictoriis sibi continue succedentibus, puta cum istis: 'rex sedet', 'rex non sedet', vel cum istis: 'Sortes est', 'Sortes non est'. Si enim utrumque istorum potest verificari manente eodem ubi naturaliter, non est motus localis eius, sed necessario est quies intercepta. Sed si unum praedictorum contradictoriorum verificatur de uno ubi et aliud cum alio ubi, et contradictoria sibi continue succedant ita quod unum statim succedit alteri, et sic est motus continuus. Secus est si ista contradictoria non continue sibi succedant. Quia si unum contradictoriorum maneant per tempus, puta quod 'rex sedet', potest tunc mobile habere unum ubi et post quiescere, . . . tunc iste motus non est continuus, quia quiete intercipitur." Cf. Ockham 1944, pp. 62–63.

technique. For although one might indeed define contradictory propositions as propositions which cannot be true at the same instant, a more general and adequate definition would appeal to the inability of either contradictory being true in any part of the interval of time throughout which the other is true, thus avoiding the awkward reference to instants.[45]

4. The Infinite Divisibility of Continua

Although, as we have seen, Ockham did express concern (mostly in his theological works, one might note) with the problem of the equality of infinites, his main interest in the infinite was in the model kind of infinity furnished by the divisibility of continua. In that he was being quite Aristotelian, since there is little question but that that was the kind of infinity of most concern to Aristotle in the *Physics* as well.

As one would expect from Ockham, the first thing that he claims about this infinite divisibility is that it is not something totally distinct from finite permanent things but merely entails a succession of permanent things. In this it is like the infinite generally and like all successive things (of which the division of a continuum is an instance).[46] Secondly, the division of a con-

45. Although not in the context of the application of Ockham's technique, it was in fact later maintained that the existence of instants was required in order to explain the nonsimultaneous verification of contradictories. Brought up as an *argumentum principale* in one of John Buridan's questions on the *Physics*, his reply amounts to that given above, basing the nonsimultaneous verification on intervals of time: Buridan, *Quaest. Phys.*, VI, Q. 4 (ed. Paris, 1509), 96v, 98r: "Item regula concessa ponitur quod impossibile est contradictoria esse simul vera et oportet per simul intelligere vel idem tempus divisibile vel idem instans indivisibile. Si instans indivisibile, habeo propositum. Si tempus divisibile, regula est falsa, quia quantumcumque parvum tempus sumatur, tamen in illo possent esse vera ambo contradictoria, scilicet unum in una parte et alterum in alia. . . . Ad aliam dico quod regula sic intelligitur: quod impossibile est in quo toto tempore verum est unum contradictoriorum, aliud est verum in aliquo illius temporis." I have not been able to find a similar text in Ockham himself. For a discussion of the successive verification of contradictories in a different context, see Norman Kretzmann's chapter X.

46. *Exp. Phys.* III, t. 58 (206a29–b3), MSS Mert. 293, 69v; Bruges 557, 161v: "Concludit Philosophus unam conclusionem: quod infinitum non est ponendum tanquam 'hoc aliquid sicut est homo vel domus,' hoc est infinitum non est aliqua res distincta secundum se totam a rebus finitis, sed est 'sicut dies et agon,' quae non ideo dicuntur esse quasi sint quaedam substantiae vel res secundum se totas distinctae ab aliis rebus, sed dicuntur esse eo quod semper sit aliqua res per-

tinuum is not one that takes place through the real separation of the things divided; that would render the continuum in question no longer a whole continuum. It is, rather, a division grounded upon the action of the mind, since it is in such a way that one "takes" the parts in a continuum.[47] It is, finally, a *processus* of determining parts, but one that occurs *sine certo numero*.[48]

These contentions about the infinite divisibility of continua would likely have been accepted in one form or another by most fourteenth-century thinkers. But Ockham's next point does not seem to have received the same measure of support. Basically, this point has to do with the way in which the parts of a continuum are related to, or exist in, the whole continuum to which they belong. Beginning from a report that some philosophers believe that Aristotle had resolved Zeno's paradoxes by appealing to the traversal of an infinite, not *in actu,* but only *in potentia,* Ockham claims that these philosophers have misunderstood Aristotle's (and Averroës') intentions when they have said that the infinitely many parts of a continuum are not actually but only potentially existent. As a matter of fact, Ockham continues, Aristotle *does* intend to posit an infinity of parts in a continuum

---

manens et corrumpitur alia ita quod semper est alterum post alterum. Et ita est hic intentio Aristotelis expressa quod nec infinitum nec dies nec agon nec tempus nec aliquod successivum sit aliqua alia res distincta secundum se totam a rebus permanentibus."

47. *Exp. Phys.* III, t. 57 (206a18–29), MSS Mert. 293, 70r; Bruges 557, 162r (text following that in note 38): "Nam post divisionem [scil. divisionem realem] haec est vera: 'hoc totum non est,' quae tamen prius fuit vera. Et non est modo ista vera: 'hoc totum non est,' quia est aliqua res secundum se totam destructa, sed quia una pars est separata ab alia. Sed de tali divisione non loquitur Commentator [scil. in commento 57], sed de divisione qua anima accipit plures partes realiter distinctas in eodem toto. [There follows the relevant quotation from Averroës] . . . sed ista divisio non fit per realem separationem, quia contingeret devenire ad aliquam magnitudinem quae non posset realiter dividi propter aliquod impedimentum. Sed ista divisio fit per hoc quod anima vere sine mendacio dicit quod in isto toto continuo sunt duae medietates et in utraque illarum medietatum sunt duae et utraque illarum secundarum medietatum habet duae medietates et sic sine fine ita quod nunquam contingit animam accipere aliquam partem istius totius quin vere et realiter potest affirmare semper quod illius sunt duae medietates."

48. *Exp. Phys.* III, t. 61 (206b27–33), MSS Mert. 293, 71r; Bruges 557, 162v: "Circa istam partem de processu in infinitum tam in appositione quam in divisione est primo sciendum quod tota ratio quare Philosophus ponit talem processum in infinitum est quia ponit infinitas partes in continuo ita quod non est ibi certus numerus partium nec possunt signari tot in aliquo certo numero quin sint plures."

which actually exist *in rerum natura*.[49] In establishing that there really is such an infinity of actually existent parts, Ockham offers as evidence the fact that all parts of actually existent things (among which are continua) themselves actually exist *in rerum natura*. The fact that the parts in question are in some sense infinite in number does not exclude them from this "rule." Surely one would agree that the half of some actually existent whole is actually existent, so by a parity of reasoning why not also the half of that half, and so on with respect to any half?[50] Of course, given Ockham's view of the nature of points, it would seem to follow that the "points" in a continuum would also be actually existent *in rerum natura*[51] (and the same thing is explicitly said to be true of number as tied to the division of continua).[52]

49. *Exp. Phys.* VI, t. 79 (239b18–30), MSS Mert. 293, 136v; Berlin lat. fol. 41, 197r; VI 5364, 107r: "Sciendum est quod aliqui ponunt hic quod Philosophus solvit praedictas rationes [scil. per quas Zeno nitebatur probare quod nihil movetur] per hoc quod contingit pertransire infinita in actu sed in potentia. Sed quia multi ponentes istam distinctionem errant circa intentionem Philosophi et Commentatoris dicentes quod partes infinitae non sunt nisi in potentia, non in actu quasi non sint actualiter existentes, sed in potentia tantum, cum tamen hoc sit contra intentionem Philosophi; ideo ad declarationem solutionis Philosophi est primo declarandum quod Philosophus intendit ponere infinitas partes continui actualiter existentes in rerum natura."

50. Ibid. (directly following text in note 49 above): "Et potest probari haec conclusio primo sic: omnis pars alicuius existentis actualiter est vere actualiter existens in rerum natura; sed omne continuum est actualiter existens; igitur quaelibet pars sua est vere existens in rerum natura. Sed partes continui sunt infinitae quia non tot quin plures; igitur partes infinitae sunt actualiter existentes. Maior principalis patet, tum quia nihil componitur ex illo quod non est, tum quia a toto ad partem respectu existere est bona consequentia. Si ergo continuum est, quaelibet pars continui est. . . . Item medietas alicuius totius existit actualiter in rerum natura, ergo eadem ratione medietas illius medietatis existit actualiter et per consequens quaelibet medietas existit actualiter. Sed medietates sunt infinitae quia non sunt in aliquo numero certo, igitur infinitae partes existunt actualiter."

51. That is, because (1) points are, for Ockham, lines of such and such a length, where the point is not to be considered as distinct from the line whose specific length it determines but is that line itself as so determined, and (2) line lengths or segments are parts of continua (viz., longer lines), it would seem to follow that, like these parts, the "points" determining them would also be actually existent *in rerum natura*. Cf. the following text of Ockham (whose purpose, however, is to refute the *potential* existence of points as *distinct from* divisible entities like lines), *Exp. Phys.* VI, t. 3 (231b10–18), MSS Mert. 293, 125v; Berlin lat. fol. 41, 186v: "Nec valet dicere quod illa puncta media non sunt in actu sed in potentia, quia illud quod non est in rerum natura non potest esse continuativum aliquorum existentium realiter; sed punctus secundum sic opinantes ponitur realiter continuare partes lineae, ergo est in rerum natura."

52. *Exp. Phys.* III, t. 41 (204b7–10), MSS Mert. 293, 66r; Bruges 557, 159v:

185

A major problem remains for this particular contention of Ockham's, however: how can one maintain that it is also Aristotle's contention that this infinity of parts *actually* exists in nature if both he and Averroës clearly say that the infinite divisibility of a continuum and consequently these parts exist *in potentia et non in actu*?[53] One minor reason is, Ockham claims, that the terms *esse in actu* and *esse in potentia* are used equivocally in different passages. But the heart of the matter is that Aristotle really claims *in potentia* existence for the parts of a continuum because (1) these parts are not separately existing wholes that constitute the single continuum of which they are parts and (2) there is among them no first part, no second, no third, and so on, but rather before any part there is always some other part.[54] It is, then, this lack of separate existence and this lack of order, this lack of there being an absolutely first part that one can take, which justifies one in saying that the parts of a continuum exist only potentially, factors that Ockham emphasizes in several passages.[55]

"Numerus potest dupliciter accipi [the second sense is that of *numerus discretus* and need not concern us here]: Vel pro omni multitudine qualitercumque distinctorum, et talis numerus est infinitus; hoc est, talia sunt infinita actualiter existentia in rerum natura. Nec talem infinitatem negat Philosophus sicut ostendetur inferius; nam talem infinitatem ponit in quolibet continuo quia non possunt accipi tot partes quin plures."

53. *Phys.* III, t. 57 (206a18–29); cf. *Phys.* IV, t. 44 (212b3–7).

54. *Exp. Phys.* VI, t. 79 (239b18–30), MSS Mert. 293, 137r; Berlin lat. fol. 41, 197r; VI 5364, 107r: "Ideo dicendum quod intentio Philosophi est quod infinitae partes sunt actualiter existentes in rerum natura. Dicit tamen Philosophus et similiter Commentator eas esse in potentia et non in actu, quia non sunt quaedam tota separata non constituentia aliquod unum nec est ibi dare primam partem, secundam et tertiam et sic procedendo, sed ante omnem partem est dare aliam partem. Et ita aequivoce in diversis locis utitur istis vocabulis 'esse in actu' et 'esse in potentia.' Et si dicatur quod impossibile est aliquod finitum componi ex infinitis in actu, si igitur partes continui sint infinitae in actu, non componunt aliquod finitum; dicendum est secundum intentionem Philosophi quod partes infinitae quarum quaelibet secundum se totam est extra aliam et quarum quaelibet est accipere primam non componunt aliquod finitum; sed partes infinitae actualiter existentes quarum nulla est prima nec quaelibet earum secundum se totam est extra aliam, quas dicit Philosophus esse in potentia quia non sunt quaedam tota separatim existentia, bene possunt componere aliquod finitum, immo valde parvum finitum. Et huiusmodi sunt partes continui, actualiter tamen existentes, quamvis non sint a toto divisae." The objection cited in note 21 above directly follows this text.

55. *Exp. Phys.* I, t. 35 (187b7–13), MSS Mert. 293, 13r; Bruges 557, 114r: "Nec est dicendum sicut aliqui dicunt quod illae infinitae partes non sunt in actu sed in potentia tantum. Vere enim sunt in actu, sicut caput hominis est in actu, non tamen sunt in actu separatae ab invicem, sicut nec caput hominis separatur a

Matters are, however, more complex than that. For Ockham employs these notions of "separate existence" and "order" (really, consecutiveness) not merely to explain why Aristotle and others have said that the parts in a continuum exist only potentially, but also to explain more exactly just what kinds of infinitely numerous parts can obtain in a continuum. Thus, an infinity of parts all of which are separate from one another and of which there is an absolutely first part will not yield a finite continuum. However, if there is no absolutely first part and the parts overlap or are parts of each other, then such an infinity of parts can compose a finite continuum.[56] Indeed, if these conditions of no first part and overlapping are observed, the infinity of parts can even be all of the same size;[57] in fact, in one passage Ockham emphasizes this point by claiming that a two-foot quantity can contain an infinite number of one-foot quantities.[58]

Pushing matters a step further, we learn that the condition of there being no first part is more fundamental than that of overlapping. A finite continuum can be composed of an infinity of parts all of which are wholly separate from one another, provided that

---

corpore. Sed propter hoc non sequitur quin sint actualiter existentes in rerum natura. Philosophus tamen vocat eas aliquando in potentia, non quin sint vere existentes, sed quia non sunt actu separatae ab invicem." Cf. *QQ Phys.*, Q. 68, ed. in Corvino 1958, p. 196.

56. *Exp. Phys.* III, t. 61 (206b27–33), MSS Mert. 283, 71r; Bruges 557, 162v: "Secundo sciendum est qualis est ista infinitas partium. Et est sciendum quod in eodem continuo possunt dari infinitae partes quarum una sit pars alterius sicut una medietas est pars totius et medietas illius medietatis est pars illius et medietas alterius secundae medietatis est pars illius et sic in infinitum. Sed quod in eodem continuo sint partes infinitae quarum quaelibet secundum se totam sit extra aliam ita quod sit ibi prima, secunda et tertia, hoc est per se impossibile quia hoc necessario concluderet totum compositum esse infinitum."

57. *Exp. Phys.* I, t. 37 (187b22–35), MSS Mert. 293, 14r–v; Bruges 557, 114v: "Sciendum est quod impossibile est in aliquo finito esse infinita secundum numerum quorum quodlibet sit secundum se totum distinctum ab alio, sicut duae medietates secundum se totas distinguuntur, et quae habent ordinem determinatum ad invicem, ut scilicet unum sit primum, aliud secundum, aliud tertium et sic in infinitum. Quod tamen in eodem sint infinitae partes, etiam eiusdem quantitatis, quae tamen non secundum se totas distinguantur vel quae non ordinentur secundum primum, secundum et tertium et sic de aliis, non est inconveniens; immo hoc est necessarium in omni continuo."

58. *Exp. Phys.* III, t. 61 (206b27–33), MSS as in note 56 above: "Similiter in corpore continuo finito possunt esse infinitae partes eiusdem quantitatis secundum omnem dimensionem, sicut in quantitate bipedali possunt esse infinitae partes quarum quaelibet sit pedalis, sicut posset manifeste probari." Cf. *QQ Phys.*, Q. 71, concl. 6, ed. in Corvino 1958, p. 203.

there is no absolutely first part to be taken in that infinity. The division of a finite continuous line segment according to parts of the same proportion furnishes such a case.[59]

To summarize and to put all of this into its proper Aristotelian framework, we should be careful to note that Ockham is speaking of the kind of existence the parts of a continuum have and of the kind of relation these parts can bear to one another. It is, first, the kind of relation they may bear to one another (namely, no separate existence and no consecutiveness) which affords Ockham what he believes to be the proper interpretation of Aristotle's ascription of potential existence to these parts.[60] But the kind of relation these parts have to one another does not speak to the kind of existence they have. As we have seen, Ockham is firm in claiming that the parts in an actually existent continuum actually exist *in rerum natura*. In separating this kind of *existence* from the kind of *relations* these parts (as so existing) have, Ockham has

59. *Exp. Phys.*, loc. cit.: "Quod tamen sint infinitae partes quarum quaelibet secundum se totam sit extra aliam inter quas tamen nulla est prima nec secunda nec est inconveniens. Ita enim est in quolibet continuo. Nam accipio corpus quadratum, puta ABCD sint isti quatuor anguli illius; tunc inter AB et CD sunt infinitae partes quarum quaelibet est extra aliam secundum se totam. Quia dividatur in duo aequalia; illae duae medietates secundum se totas distinguuntur. Iterum dividatur una illarum; tunc prima medietas, quae vocetur E, et secunda medietas alterius primae medietatis secundum se totas distinguuntur. Iterum dividatur alia medietas et una illarum differret secundum se totam a primis, scilicet secunda et tertia. Et iterum alia dividatur et una illarum secundum se totam differret a prima, secunda, tertia et quarta; et sic in infinitum. Et inter istas partes. quamvis sit dare primam medietatem, non tamen est dare primam partem, quia adhuc illius primae medietatis est aliqua pars prior illa medietate." Cf. *QQ Phys.*, Q. 71, concl. 2, ed. in Corvino 1958, p. 202.

Ockham pushes the permissible kinds of infinitely numerous parts even further in a text directly following that in note 58 above (which itself directly follows that just quoted from the *Expositio*): "Sed quod in aliquo continuo sint infinitae partes eiusdem quantitatis secundum omnem dimensionem quarum quaelibet secundum se totam sit extra aliam est impossibile, quia tunc necessario sequeretur quod totum resultans ex eis esset infinitum. Verumtamen in eodem continuo possunt esse infinitae partes aequales in longitudine et infinitae partes aequales in latitudine quarum quaelibet sit extra aliam secundum se totam, sicut in quadrato inter A B possunt ymaginari infinita puncta et similiter inter C D; et ita possunt esse et sunt infinitae partes aeque longae, tamen illae non erunt aequales in aliis dimensionibus." This is indeed curious. It is difficult to see what grounds Ockham could have for allowing an infinity of nonoverlapping parts of the same quantity in one dimension but not in all dimensions. The parallel text from the *QQ Phys.* (Q. 71, concl. 3, ed. in Corvino 1958, p. 202) offers no help in resolving the puzzle.

60. Aristotle speaks more often of the potential (infinite) divisibility of continua than he does of the potential existence of parts, while Ockham focuses on the latter in his account of Aristotle's view.

neatly made his own claim of actual existence for these parts independent of, and hence consistent with, Aristotle's claim for their potential existence, since the latter is, as just noted, tied only to their possible relations.

The second point to note about Ockham's assertion of the actual existence of the infinity of parts in a continuum is that it does not bear on the kind of infinity in question. Above all, to say, with Ockham, that there is an infinity of actually existing parts is not in any way to say that there is an actual infinity of parts. Indeed, his idea of the kind of infinity these actually existent parts have is that they are not so numerous but that they can be more numerous (*non tot quin plures*)[61]—that is, that they are potentially or syncategorematically infinite, not actually or categorematically infinite.[62] Thus, in spite of his conviction that the parts actually exist in continua, there is no question at all but that Ockham firmly believed that the divisibility of a continuum was only potential. This means that we should not look to the actually existing parts as somehow being generated by carrying out or actualizing, by means of division, the potential infinite divisibility of a continuum. On the contrary, when we are faced with an actually existing continuum, we already—one might even say automatically—have before us the infinity of actually existent parts of which Ockham speaks. Given any continuum, without its being actually divided, we are also given its halves, the halves of these halves, and an infinity of all manner of parts, all of which are actually existent *in rerum natura* in Ockham's sense. It follows, of course, that when a mobile traverses (with continuous motion) a continuous magnitude, infinitely many such actually existent parts are traversed. Indeed, that is Ockham's view of the proper interpretation of Aristotle's reply to Zeno's paradoxes.[63] And all this

61. See texts in notes 48, 50, and 52 above.
62. On the expressions "syncategorematic" and "categorematic" as applied to the infinite, see Maier 1949, p. 157.
63. *Exp. Phys.* VI, t. 79 (239b18–30), MSS Mert. 293, 137r; Berlin lat. fol. 41, 197v; "Istis visis dicendum est quod intentio Philosophi est solvere rationes Zenonis per istam modum: quod, quia non sunt ibi partes infinitae quarum quaelibet secundum se totam sit extra aliam ita quod sit accipere primam, secundam et tertiam, sed sunt ibi partes infinitae quarum nulla est prima, ideo non est inconveniens per illas partes infinitas moveri. Unde ad primam rationem Zenonis quando accipit quod impossibile est pertransire infinita, verum est si illa infinitae sint secundum

obtains without any consideration of realizing the potential divisibility of the continua involved.

Thus far, in treating of the infinite divisibility of continua and their parts, Ockham has shown little of his usual penchant for propositional analysis, which he applied so assiduously in dealing with issues concerning the presence of indivisibles within continua. The problems attending the infinite divisibility of continuous magnitudes receive propositional analyses all their own, however. The first such problem is how one should come to grips with this potential infinite divisibility itself.

An appropriate way to approach this topic is to begin with Ockham's analysis of Aristotle's claim of the difference in the kind of potentiality involved in the infinite as compared with that involved in the creation of a statue out of bronze.[64] Ockham begins his analysis of this claim by distinguishing *esse in potentia* from *esse in actu* in terms of a difference in predication: the one involves predication by means of the verb *est*, the other by means of the verb *potest*. Each of these sorts of predication is itself twofold, but the important distinction for the so-called potential infinite and hence for the potential infinite divisibility of a continuum is the double sense he stipulates, not for *est*,[65] but for *potest* or *potentia*.

The first of these two senses occurs when, given a proposition

---

se tota distincta ita quod sit accipere aliquod de illis quo nullum sit prius; sed talia non sunt in aliquo continuo. Si autem illa infinita non sint secundum se tota distincta ut non sit aliquod primum distinctum inter ea, possibile est talia infinita pertransire, immo necesse est talia infinita pertransire quandocumque aliquod spatium pertransitur." Ockham's solution to Zeno's second argument (*quod velox nunquam attinget tardum*) is too long to give here, but see the shortened version in *QQ Phys.*, Q. 70, ed. in Corvino 1958, p. 201.

64. *Physics* III, chap. 6, 206a18–20. The medieval text (t. 57) reads: "si possibile sit hoc statuam aes esse, quod et erit hoc statua."

65. *Exp. Phys.* III, t. 57 (206a18–29), MSS Mert. 293, 68v; Bruges 557, 161r: "Aliquando enim aliquid praedicatur de aliquo mediante hoc verbo 'est' ita quod non includit aequivalenter aliquam aliam propositionem in qua idem praedicatur de illo vel de alio mediante hoc verbo 'potest' vel mediante verbo de praeterito vel de futuro cum negativa de praesenti vel de praeterito vel de futuro . . . hoc est, per istam propositionem 'homo est,' non denotatur nisi quod res est et non denotatur quod una res est et alia res erit quae non est vel quae non est in tali, vel aliquid consimile. . . . Aliter dicitur aliquid esse, vel praedicatum mediante hoc verbo 'est' praedicari de aliquo, ita quod includat alias propositiones sunt quasi exponentes eam quae sunt de praeterito vel de futuro vel de possibili vel etiam negativas, et isto modo dicitur esse de omni illo quod importat motum."

in which *potest* or *potentia* appears, there corresponds to this proposition another *single* proposition in which *esse* occurs without the appearance of *potentia* or anything equivalent to it. The key factor here is, moreover, that the single correspondent proposition does not have a plurality of exponents (*propositiones exponentes*), that is, propositions which, taken together, explain the proposition being expounded and are equivalent to it. The example Ockham gives of this first sense of *potest* is precisely that given by Aristotle himself in the passage from which this exposition began: "The bronze is the statue in potentiality," and the single correspondent proposition is: "The bronze is the statue."

On the other hand, a second type of proposition in which the term *potest*, or *potentia*, occurs is one to which there corresponds an assertoric proposition that *does* have a plurality of exponents. The examples given for the second sense are directly related to our infinite-continuum problem area: "The division of a continuum is infinite," "A continuum can be divided in infinitum," "Number can increase in infinitum."[66]

Ockham does not at this point explain these examples further. In particular, he does not go into detail specifying just what sorts of exponents fall under this second sense of *potest* or *potentia*. For enlightenment of that sort we can conveniently turn to his interpretation of Averroës' assertion that the infinite involves an act mixed with potentiality.[67] First of all, we should realize that Ockham takes this particular conception of Averroës to apply not only to the infinite, but to any successive thing, motion being the prime example of the latter. Yet in all cases of such an *actus mixtus* what we really have is a proposition that is equivalent to a present-tense proposition together with one or more other proposi-

---

66. *Exp. Phys.*, loc. cit., MSS Mert. 293, 69r; Bruges 557, 161v: "Et sicut dictum est quod esse multipliciter accipitur ita etiam potentia multipliciter accipitur. Aliquando enim propositioni in qua ponitur 'potentia' vel 'potest' vel aliquid aequivalens correspondet una propositio in qua ponitur 'esse' sine tali 'potentia' vel aequivalente quae non habet tales exponentes, sicut est de ista: 'aes est in potentia statua,' cui correspondet ista: 'aes est statua,' quae non habet tales exponentes. Aliquando autem propositioni in qua ponitur 'potentia' correspondet propositio de inesse sine 'potentia' quae habet multas tales exponentes, et tales propositiones sunt istae: 'divisio continui est infinita in potentia,' 'continuum potest dividi in infinitum,' 'numerus potest crescere in infinitum' et huiusmodi."

67. Averroës, *Comm. in Phys.* III, t. 57 (ed. apud Junctas, Venice 1562–74; reprint, Frankfurt, 1962), vol. 4, 111v–112r.

JOHN E. MURDOCH

tions *de possibili,* negative propositions, or propositions in the past or future tense, all of which are to be considered as the relevant exponents. Thus, the proposition "Local motion exists" is true only if something like the following *plures exponentes* are true: "This is not in a place other than that place, and yet this will be in a place other than that place."[68] Alternatively, to bring the matter home to our topic, the propositions "The division of a line is infinite" and "A line can be divided in infinitum" are equivalent to such exponents as the following: "A line is divided or can be divided, and after the division of any part another part can be divided."[69]

In sum, the touchstone of the potential infinite divisibility of a continuum is that the *de possibili* proposition asserting that divisibility has a plurality of *propositiones exponentes.* In contrast, a finite thing—indeed, even that finite *acceptum* which, for Aristotle, is the result of each step in the continuous process of accumulating an infinite—can be characterized propositionally as that which has *esse* verified of it in a proposition that does *not* entail a plurality of exponents.[70]

Finally, to make his propositional analysis of the infinite divisibility of a continuum as consonant as he can with the topic of *de possibili* propositions, Ockham confronts his analysis with two "rules" governing such modal propositions.

68. *Exp. Phys.* III, t. 57 (206a18–29), MSS Mert. 293, 68v–69r; Bruges 557, 161r (directly following text in note 65): "Et tale esse vel talem actum vocat Commentator actum mixtum cum potentia, et hoc quia talis propositio aequivalet copulativae ex aliqua propositione mere de praesenti et alia vel aliis de possibili et aliquando de praeterito et de futuro. Et sic dicitur motus esse quia haec propositio est vera: 'motus est,' quae aequivalet istis tanquam pluribus exponentibus: 'aliquid est in aliquo vel habet aliquid et immediate ante habuit aliud et est in potentia ad aliquid immediate habendum' ita quod multae tales propositiones tam de praeterito quam de futuro, quam etiam negativae, requiruntur ad veritatem talium propositionum. . . . Sicut haec non potest esse vera: 'motus localis est' nisi aliqua talis sit vera: 'hoc non est in alio loco ab hoc et tamen erit in alio loco ab hoc.'"
69. Ibid., "Quando esse praedicatur de aliquo important successionem, requiruntur multae propositiones tanquam exponentes illud quarum aliqua erit de praeterito, aliqua de praesenti, aliqua de futuro et aliqua negativa; et sub tali sensu conceduntur tales propositiones: 'divisio lineae est infinita,' 'linea potest dividi in infinitum,' quae aequivalent talibus: 'linea est divisa' vel 'potest dividi et post cuiuscumque partis divisionem potest alia pars dividi.'"
70. *Exp. Phys.,* loc. cit., MSS cit., 69v; 161r: "Et vocat hic acceptum illud de quo verificatur esse vel esse tale in propositione non includente plures exponentes."

192

The first rule is that for the truth of any *de possibili* proposition[71] it is required that it is possible that there be some assertoric proposition in which the very same property involved in the initial *de possibili* proposition is predicated of a pronominal subject denoting that for which the subject of the *de possibili* proposition stands. (For example, "Socrates can be musical" is true only if it is possible that "This is musical" is true, where "this" denotes Socrates.) However, Ockham cautions, the proposition "A continuum can be divided in infinitum" or any similar *de possibili* proposition does not fall under this rule.[72] This is, unfortunately, all he has to say on the matter. But if we fill out the logic in question, especially in terms of what he says in the relevant place in his *Summa logicae*,[73] his intention becomes evident. For if "A continuum can be divided in infinitum" is to be true—and as a "postulate" of natural philosophy it is known to be true—then it is required that it be possible that "This is divided in infinitum" is true, where "this" denotes a continuum. But no specific continuum ever *is* divided in infinitum, for that would entail its actual or completed infinite division, which never occurs. Therefore, propositions asserting the infinite divisibility of continua are exempted from this particular rule concerning modal propositions.

It is the failure to satisfy a second rule about *de possibili* propositions, however, which affords Ockham a fulcrum for establishing a propositional interpretation of yet another fact about the divisibility of continua. Whereas exclusion from the first rule was related to the fact that no continuum is ever completely divided in infinitum, the failure of such propositions to be governed by the second rule provides a propositional equivalent to the fact that the potentiality involved in the division of continua is, unlike

71. More exactly, a *de possibili* proposition *sine dicto,* where the modal term is not predicated of the whole proposition as such but verbally or adverbially in the proposition itself.

72. *Exp. Phys.*, loc. cit., MSS cit. 69v; 161r: "Et est hic sciendum quod tales propositiones de possibili: 'continuum potest dividi in infinitum' excipiuntur ab illa regula de qua dictum est alibi: quod semper ad veritatem propositionis de possibili requiritur quod aliqua propositio sit possibilis in qua ipsummet praedicatum praedicatur de pronomine demonstrante aliquid pro quo subiectum supponit."

73. Ockham 1974, II, chap. 10, p. 276.

other potentialities within nature, one that never is, indeed never can be, realized. What is more, in this instance, Ockham explains why propositions asserting the infinite divisibility of a continuum do not satisfy the rule in question.

The rule is that every possible can be reduced to being (*omne possibile potest poni in esse*). Beginning from this rule, he agrees that most *de possibili* propositions can be governed by it. Thus, from the (true) *de possibili* proposition "Socrates can sit" one can, by this rule, move to the (possible) affirmative assertoric proposition "Socrates sits." In the case of the *de possibili* proposition that asserts the potential infinite divisibility of continua, however, there must be something peculiar about the proposition that will *not* allow one to formulate the corresponding affirmative assertoric proposition. Quite so. It is because it is to be expounded into other propositions; Ockham's usual procedure again. But one of these exponents is a *negative* assertoric proposition ("Some part of the continuum has not been divided"), and this particular proposition frustrates the transfer of the whole *de possibili* proposition into an affirmative assertoric one.[74] Yet this is but a propositional way of expressing the fact that the potential infinite divisibility of a continuum bespeaks a potentiality that can in fact never be realized.

This is, however, certainly not the end of Ockham's propositional analysis of the divisibility of continua. Thus far we have

---

74. *Exp. Phys.* III, t. 61 (206b27–33), MSS Mert. 293, 71r; Bruges 557, 162v: "Istis visis, videndum est tertio de modo loquendi. Et primo videndum est an haec sit concedenda: 'continuum potest dividi in infinitum,' vel ista: 'secundum omne signum potest continuum dividi.' Et dicendum est quod concedenda est haec: 'continuum potest dividi in infinitum' secundum intellectum philosophorum. Et si dicatur quod omne possibile potest poni in esse, igitur ponitur in esse quod continuum sit divisum in infinitum, quod est impossibile, dicendum quod quamvis omnis propositio de possibili quae non exponitur per aliquam propositionem alterius modi vel de inesse possit poni in esse, quamvis vario modo quando sumitur in sensu compositionis vel est aequivalens sensui compositionis, et quando sumitur in sensu divisionis vel est aequivalens sensui divisionis, sicut alias ostendi. Quando tamen propositio de possibili exponitur per aliam propositionem, non oportet poni in esse, sicut in proposito. Nam ad veritatem istius: 'continuum potest dividi in infinitum,' requiritur veritas istius tamquam exponens eam: 'nulla est pars continui quae non potest dividi,' et similiter ista: 'aliqua pars continui non est actu divisa,' quae est una negativa de inesse. Et propter hoc tota propositio de possibili non debet poni in unam affirmativam de inesse." Ockham follows this text with an objection and reply, for which see the shortened version in the parallel passage in *QQ Phys.*, Q. 66, ed. in Corvino 1958, p. 193.

observed his attempt to analyze this potential infinite divisibility in terms of *de possibili* propositions and their exponents. But Ockham brought a different logical doctrine to bear in the analysis of what results from the infinite divisibility of continua, that is, of what relations obtain for the parts that derive from this divisibility.

The logical doctrine in question has to do with the difference made when one had certain "logical words" within certain propositions occupy *different positions* relative to the nonlogical terms in these propositions and relative to one another, all else in these propositions being the same. Yet before we examine the relevance of this doctrine to the problem of the infinite divisibility of continua and the relations of parts within continua, it will be instructive to begin with an especially simple example having to do with the infinite pure and simple. *Infinitum can* function as a syncategorematic term.[75] But it is often the *position* of *infinitum* within a proposition which reveals whether it is functioning as a syncategorematic term or not. Thus, if it precedes the term it "modifies" or, as it was sometimes put, if it is posited *a parte subiecti,* then it functions distributively as a syncategorematic term and means merely that that which it modifies is "not so great or numerous but that it could be greater or more numerous" (*non tantum quin maius sive non tot quin plura*). In this sense the proposition *In infinitum continuum est divisibile,* where *in infinitum* precedes the subject, is true and properly expresses the kind of potential infinite divisibility we have been speaking of above. In contrast, when *infinitum* follows the term it modifies, it functions as a categorematic term, its sense then being equivalent to the modified thing's having no end or being actually infinite. In this sense the proposition *Continuum est divisibile in infinitum* is false, since it means that a continuum can be completely divided into an actual infinity of parts.[76] Exactly why one or the other position of a term like *infinitum* had one result rather than another was, more often than not, a matter of convention.

The particular doctrine of "positional difference" as applied to the problem of the parts in a continuum was, however, some-

---

75. See note 62 above.
76. Cf. Albert of Saxony, *Quaestiones in octo libros Physicorum* III, Q. 9 (ed. Paris, 1518), 37r and Wilson 1956, p. 16.

what more complex than the foregoing case of the term *infinitum*. It had to do with the difference caused by the different relative positions of *two* logical terms within a single proposition (all else in the proposition again remaining the same). The two logical terms in question were almost always "every" (*omnis*) and "some" (*aliqua*), although the latter at times did not expressly appear in the proposition at hand but was tacitly understood.[77] Our interest in this particular kind of "positional-difference" logic lies in the fact that, at some point early in the fourteenth century, it was realized that its application could bring out with unprecedented clarity certain crucial features involved in the infinite divisibility of continua. In particular, it was seen that it could provide certain new and effective "tests" of what could, and what could not, be true about that infinite divisibility and that it could reveal in an especially incisive way what contradictions or impossibilities would ensue if one were in error about that infinite divisibility.

Perhaps the earliest application of this positional-difference technique to the issue of the divisibility of continua occurs in William of Alnwick's reply to one of Henry of Harclay's arguments that continuous magnitudes are composed of an infinity of indivisibles immediately in contact with one another.[78] The technique was used, then, to refute one of the few genuine atomists of the later Middle Ages.[79]

Although when Ockham employed the technique he was not arguing against some specific atomist opponent, the substance of what he believed he had accomplished was all but identical with that of Alnwick's reply to Harclay. Beginning from Aristotle's point that, although there is, even potentially, no greater magnitude in infinitum, one can have a smaller magnitude in infinitum,[80] Ockham wends his way toward a clarification of the latter half of this claim by rigidly distinguishing two different propositions:

(1) Than every magnitude there is [some] smaller magnitude.
    (Omni magnitudine est [aliqua] magnitudo minor.)

77. Alternatively, the term "any" (*quodlibet*) could take the place of "every."
78. See Murdoch 1969, pp. 220–21.
79. For other late medieval atomists, see Murdoch 1974.
80. *Physics* III 6, 206b18–22.

(2) Some magnitude is smaller than every magnitude.
(Aliqua magnitudo est minor omni magnitudine.)

The first proposition is true, the second false. But the only difference in these two propositions which accounts for the different truth values is that of the relative positions of the two syncategorematic words "every" and "some." The second proposition is false because it means that there would be some *smallest* magnitude within a continuous magnitude. Ockham confirms this by invoking the doctrine of supposition: when in proposition 2 we assert, "Some magnitude is smaller than every magnitude," since the first occurrence of the term "magnitude" is preceded only by the word "some," it has *determinate* supposition. But if we turn to our logical primer, we can see that as in the case of any term having determinate supposition, we can logically descend from it to its singular inferior terms as presented in a disjunctive proposition. In the case at hand, this means that we can descend to: "*This* magnitude is smaller than every magnitude, or *that* magnitude is smaller than every magnitude, or *that other* magnitude is smaller than every magnitude," and so on. But this in turn means that some one of these magnitudes specified in this disjunction is the *smallest* magnitude within a continuous magnitude, something that violates the Aristotelian contention, followed by Ockham, that all continuous magnitudes are infinitely divisible into always further divisible magnitudes.

On the other hand, the first proposition, in which the relative position of "every" and "some" is reversed, is true because it means merely that given any magnitude no matter how small, one can always find a smaller one, which is precisely what is required by the standard Aristotelian view of the infinite divisibility of continua. Once again, however, Ockham appeals to supposition in order to explain just how this is guaranteed: when we assert that, "given any magnitude, there is a smaller magnitude," the term "smaller magnitude" has *merely confused* supposition because it is preceded by the universal sign "every" *a parte subiecti.* However, looking again to our logical primer, we learn that this means that one *cannot* make a logical descent to a disjunctive proposition constituted of relevant singulars, which in turn means that we cannot specify some one smallest magnitude within a continuous magnitude.[81]

Thus, two strictly opposed views of the divisibility of continua, and consequently of the relations of parts in continua, have been distinguished from one another and have had their mutual relations spelled out with unprecedented preciseness. And the means for accomplishing this lay in the utilization of the difference effected by the variant positions of key logical terms, a difference that was based upon, indeed really amounted to, a difference in the supposition of the terms, a difference in what the terms stood for.

In terms of modern logic, we can say that the difference in position to which Ockham called attention amounted to a difference in the order of quantifiers in two otherwise identical propositions when these propositions contained relational predicates connecting the variables bound by these quantifiers. In fact, this modern translation of medieval results helps explain, and confirms the correctness of, another move made by Ockham in the passage we have been examining. Restricting ourselves to Ockham's second proposition, another reason why it is false is that if it were true that there were "some magnitude smaller than every magnitude," then there would be a magnitude that would be smaller than itself (*minor seipsa*).[82] In our terms this is to say that if there is no restriction on what "every magnitude" in this second proposition can stand for, then one possibility is that it can stand

---

81. *Exp. Phys.* III, t. 61 (206b27–33), MSS Mert. 293, 71v; Bruges 557, 163r. "Est autem istis adiciendum quod quamvis haec sit vera: 'omni magnitudine est minor magnitudo,' haec tamen est impossibilis: 'aliqua magnitudo est minor omni magnitudine.' Ista enim est vera: 'omni magnitudine est minor magnitudo,' quia est una universalis cuius quaelibet singularis est vera. Haec tamen est falsa: 'aliqua magnitudo est minor omni magnitudine,' quia est una particularis cuius quaelibet singularis est falsa. Et est simile sicut de istis duobus: haec est vera: 'omnis homo est animal,' et haec falsa: 'aliquod animal est omnis homo.' Et ratio diversitatis est quia in ista: 'omni magnitudine est minor magnitudo' ly 'minor magnitudo' supponit confuse tantum propter signum universale praecedens a parte subiecti, et ideo ad veritatem sufficit quod ista magnitudine sit una magnitudo minor et illa magnitudine sit una alia magnitudo minor et sic de aliis. Sed in ista: 'aliqua magnitudo est minor omni magnitudine' ly 'magnitudo' supponit determinate, et ideo oportet quod aliqua una magnitudo numero esset minor omni magnitudine, et per consequens esset minor seipsa." Note that Ockham dispenses with the unnecessary *aliqua* in the first proposition; it was included in other treatments.

82. See the final sentence of the text cited in note 81 above.

for the same thing that "some magnitude" stands for in the same proposition, which, given what the proposition claims, means that there would be some magnitude smaller than itself.[83]

If this were the only instance in which Ockham applied the positional-difference technique, that would be significant enough in itself. The truth of the matter is, however, that he employs the technique in a good number of other instances of analyzing infinity and continuous magnitudes or processes. He properly sees, for example, that just as, given any magnitude in a continuum, from the fact that we can always find a *smaller* magnitude in that continuum we cannot infer that there is some magnitude *smaller* than every magnitude, so from the fact that, given any magnitude, there is always another *greater* than it, we cannot infer that there is some magnitude *greater* than every magnitude. Since the latter would imply the existence of the actual infinite, this positional-difference technique is one way to show the impossibility of obtaining such an infinite.[84]

Turning to the field of continua, we find Ockham employing the same technique in proving that there can be no first part in a continuous magnitude[85] and in establishing a sharper interpretation of Aristotle's contention that everything that is *in* motion must *have been* moved before,[86] a dictum that Ockham phrases as *ante omne mutari est mutatum esse*. Maintaining that, Ockham cautions, certainly should not lead one to adopt the atomist view that there is some first moment of change preceding the whole process of change in question. The positional-difference cast of Ockham's argument is evident even without inquiring into its specific details.[87]

---

83. In symbols, given $(\exists x)(y)\ x < y$, if there is no restriction on the value y may assume, one may infer $(\exists x)\ x < x$.

84. In place of the relevant *Exp. Phys.* text, see the shorter version in the *QQ Phys.*, Q. 67, ed. in Corvino 1958, pp. 194–95. Note that Ockham takes the false proposition "There is some magnitude greater than every magnitude" to represent Aristotle's denial (in note 80 above) of the existence, even potentially, of a greater magnitude in infinitum.

85. *Exp. Phys.* VI, t. 79 (239b18–30), MSS Mert. 293, 137r; Berlin lat. fol. 41, 197v: "Ad aliud quod non est ibi prima pars nec sequitur igitur 'aliqua pars est ibi prior omni parte,' sed bene sequitur ista: 'quod omni parte est aliqua pars prior.'"

86. *Physics* VI 6, 236b32–34.

87. *Exp. Phys.* VI, t. 52 (236b32–237a3), MSS Mert. 293, 133v; Berlin lat. fol. 41, 194v: "Tertio sciendum est pro sophisticis quod ista propositio de virtute sermonis

To cite one last specific instance of Ockham's utilization of this technique, we can turn to his analysis of Zeno's arrow paradox. The heart of the paradox is, Ockham claims, the postulate that anything that is in a place equal to itself is at rest. Of course, if something is in such a place throughout an interval of time, then it is at rest. But then it is false that Zeno's arrow, or anything in motion, is always in a place equal to itself. On the other hand, Zeno could have meant that a mobile is in a place equal to itself *per instans*. But then it is false that the mobile would be at rest. This is so because, although a mobile, while it is in motion, is *per instans* in a place equal to itself, it is *in motion* because it is in no one designatable place equal to itself through an interval of time.[88] However, *pro sophistis*, it might be wise, Ockham feels, to explain with greater precision just how a mobile is in a place equal to itself *per instans*, and it is for this explanation that Ockham again appeals to positional difference. Now the two propositions embodying this positional difference read:

(3) This mobile in any instant is in the same place equal to itself.
(Hoc mobile in quolibet instanti est in eodem loco aequali sibi.)

(4) This mobile is in the same place equal to itself in any instant of this time.
(Hoc mobile est in eodem loco aequali sibi in quolibet instanti illius temporis.)

Once again, the first proposition is true because the term "in the same place" has merely confused supposition because it is pre-

est concedenda: 'ante omne mutari est mutatum esse,' quia quaelibet singularis est vera, scilicet ista: 'ante hoc mutari est mutatum esse' et 'ante illud mutari' et sic de singulis. Sed ista falsa est: 'aliquod mutatum esse est ante omne mutari,' quia est una indiffinita cuius quaelibet singularis est falsa. Nec sequitur: 'ante omne mutari est mutatum esse, igitur aliquod mutatum esse est ante omne mutari,' quia in prima 'mutatum esse' stat confuse tantum propter hoc quod sequitur signum universale affirmativum mediate; in consequente autem stat determinate, quia praecedit signum, et ideo est fallacia figurae dictionis et etiam fallacia consequentis."

88. *Exp. Phys.* VI, t. 76 (239b8–9), MSS Mert. 293, 136v; Berlin lat. fol. 41, 196v: "Ad formam ergo rationis Zenonis dicendum est, quando accipit quod omne quod est in loco sibi aequali quiescit, quod ista est distinguenda. Quia vel intelligit quod sit in loco sibi aequali per tempus et tunc vera est, sed tunc est haec falsa: 'omne mobile est semper in eodem loco aequali sibi'; vel intelligit quod sit in loco aequali sibi per instans et tunc falsa est, quia mobile dum movetur per instans est in loco sibi aequali, movetur tamen quia in nullo eodem loco aequali sibi est per tempus."

ceded by the universal sign "any," and this allows us to claim only that the mobile in question at *this* instant is in one and the same place equal to itself, at *that* instant is in one and the same place equal to itself, and so on. Yet, as expected, the second proposition is false because there the term "in the same place" has determinate supposition, since it precedes the universal sign "any." If the second proposition were true, there would be some given place equal to the mobile regarding which it would be true to say: "This mobile is in this place equal to itself in any instant." But that is demonstrably false, hence so is proposition 4. Save for the fact that Ockham goes on to draw a corresponding distinction *secundum amphibologiam* that obtains between propositions like (3) and (4), the pattern of argument is quite the same as in the first instance we examined of his applying positional difference. He concludes, of course, by maintaining that Aristotle and Averroës had the second, false proposition in mind when combating Zeno's arrow.[89]

Finally, before we leave Ockham and positional difference, it is worthy of remark that apart from these applications of this technique in his *Expositio Physicorum*, in his *Summa logicae* he gives a veritable litany of fallacies of affirming the consequent which can occur if insufficient attention is paid to positional difference.[90]

89. Ibid., "Est autem sciendum pro sophistis quod de virtute sermonis haec est concedenda: 'hoc mobile in quolibet instanti est in eodem loco aequali sibi,' quia quaelibet talis est vera: 'hoc mobile in hoc instanti est in loco eodem aequali sibi' et 'in illo instanti est in eodem loco aequali' et sic de singulis. Haec tamen falsa est: 'hoc mobile est in eodem loco aequali sibi in quolibet instanti illius temporis,' quia quocumque loco demonstrato haec est falsa: 'hoc mobile est in hoc loco aequali sibi in quolibet instanti illius temporis.' Nec sequitur ex prima, sed est fallacia consequentis et figurae dictionis propter hoc quod in prima iste terminus 'in eodem loco' supponit confuse tantum eo quod sequitur mediate signum universale affirmativum et in secunda supponit determinate eo quod praecedit signum universale affirmativum. Verumtamen pro protervis ista: 'hoc mobile in quolibet instanti est in eodem loco sibi aequali' potest distingui secundum amphibologiam. Unus sensus est iste qui dictur est, alius est iste: 'hoc mobile in aliquo eodem loco est in quolibet instanti' et iste sensus falsus est, et sic accipit eam Aristoteles hic et etiam Commentator."

90. Ockham 1974, p. 828. For a more extended example of applying positional difference where infinity or continuity is not involved, see Ockham 1974, I, chap. 71, p. 213.

5. Conclusion

There are, to be sure, other facets of infinity and continuity that were discussed by Ockham, but those which have received our attention here were, I believe, the central ones. To put it in other terms, they were those which were most "Ockhamist" in the treatment they received, because their investigation by Ockham fairly bristled with the application, at times perhaps intrusion, of convictions and methods he exhibited in all the other corners of his philosophy and theology.

Hence, his severely critical approach to "what there is" baldly revealed its restrictive character in his refusal to grant any kind of proper existence at all to indivisible entities as such. Yet this critical approach also found expression in a much less obvious way, I believe, in his admission of actual existence for the parts of continua. One feels that once he had granted (with all his contemporaries) the actual existence of finite continua, the only way these continua could have parts which could effectively play out their roles in natural philosophy was for the parts as well to possess the actual existence of the continua to which they belonged.

Natural philosophy deals with what there is *in rerum natura*, and the mere potential existence of parts of continuous quantities will not qualify them for that status. In no sense do we "construct" these parts; they are already there. True, the process of dividing a continuum is something Ockham ascribes to our minds; but the mind only "takes" (*accipit*) the already existent parts involved in this division, it does not create them. Of course, we have to be able to give an account of what responsible tradition says about these parts (that they exist only *in potentia*, for example), but that can be done simply by pointing to things that are true about these parts as actually existing. It seems fair to conclude, therefore, that the status Ockham granted the parts of continua was a function of his ontological convictions.

So also, one could maintain, was almost everything else he had to say about infinity and continuity, with the difference that "everything else" (excluding his treatment of the problem of the equality of infinites) almost always allowed, indeed required, the appropriate exercise of Ockham's methodological predilection: the application of conceptions and techniques bound up with logic to the problem or doctrine at hand—what I have been calling "propositional analysis."

At the more elementary end of the scale of such analyses, one explains or interprets doctrines simply by pointing out which proposition or propositions need be true and under what circumstances they are true. (The explanation of motion or change at an instant is a case in point.) Alternatively, one might focus upon what *kind* of propositions are involved in accounting for some situation (as conditional propositions, for example, are invoked to explain the existence of points or infinite lines), or one might appeal to specific permissible relations between propositions (as in Ockham's appeal to the successive verification of contradictories).

Moving still further up the scale of complexity in propositional analysis, we have seen Ockham attack the central problem of the infinite divisibility of continua by invoking the logic of *propositiones exponentes,* where not just which, but which kinds of, or how many, exponents are called for proved to be the telling factor in the analysis at hand. At times the initial propositions receiving such an "exposition" were modal—specifically, *de possibili*; but that is to be expected if one is set upon giving a propositional analysis of the fact of the *potentiality* of the infinity or the infinite divisibility, being interpreted. These logical moves seem to have been directed more toward taking account of the characteristically Aristotelian contentions about continua than does Ockham's technique of positional difference; for the latter seems to be more *generally* applicable in the analysis of continua. It is, for example, an instructive tool that can be, and was, used to bring out that which was implied by various views concerning the division and composition of continua.

In any event, if one attempts to encapsulate the basic characteristics of Ockham's treatment of the infinite and the continuous, the predominance of propositional analysis suggests that Ockham was bent on displaying what one might reasonably call the "logic" of infinity and continuity. Indeed, one recent scholar of

Ockham has remarked that, when it comes to natural philosophy, Ockham's *Summa logicae* was a kind of "code book leading to a different Aristotelian message."[91] This remark is, I believe, felicitous and true. One can, that is, find the relevant "operating instructions" in the *Summa logicae* for almost all of the important moves Ockham made in natural philosophy, including the problem area of the infinite and the continuous.

But why believe that one can best do—perhaps even only do— natural philosophy by having such a code book at hand? In particular, why was propositional analysis regarded as such an effective method? One reason was undoubtedly that it produced results. It gave more rigorous solutions to traditional problems and was remarkably efficient in developing this or that area of philosophy (or even theology) in terms of uncovering, and then resolving, new problems. Another reason may have been that indulging in propositional analysis was a natural corollary of the decision made by Ockham and others that although science or natural philosophy is about things *in rerum natura*, it consists in, is made up of, propositions. Additionally, a more historical reason can be found in the rise and signal position of logic itself in the later thirteenth as well as the fourteenth century.

All these factors undoubtedly counted. But there may very well have been another factor that was influential in the rise of propositional analysis. Begin from the fact that most natural philosophy in the later Middle Ages dealt with inherited notions. A major task of medieval natural philosophy was, then, to interpret these inherited notions. The question was: how to do it? As a start, regard these interpretations as having a conditional form; something like: if p (inherited notion), then q (interpretation). Now the best way to test these implications or inferences is to concentrate upon the fact that they are inferences between propositions and then ask what one knows about these propositions as propositions which will tell one about the propriety of these inferences; and to do that is to practice propositional analysis.

This is indeed a quite speculative account of one way in which

91. Brown forthcoming.

the application of logic in general and propositional analysis in particular may have come to assume the dominant positions they held in the fourteenth century. But it does, I believe, fit some of the relevant facts. The fit is very good, for example, in much of what has been said above of Ockham's analysis of infinity and continuity. Further, in natural philosophy in general, the appeal to the doctrine of exponible propositions bespeaks more than an occasional match with the speculative thesis I am here suggesting. Similarly, this thesis fits well with many of the applications of supposition theory that one finds in later medieval natural philosophy, where it very often functioned as a check on inferences from some doctrine or conception to a proposed interpretation or analysis of that doctrine or conception. It told one what kind of inference tickets were permissible, and that became an increasingly important part of the enterprise of natural philosophy.

One additional question might be raised, however, with respect to Ockham's procedure in this regard, and that is how one might attempt to square his method with that of Aristotle. Aristotle in his natural philosophy surely did not concentrate to such an extent, or in such a fashion, on propositions, and Ockham was aware of that fact. At times he excuses the contrast between his procedures and those of Aristotle by claiming that Aristotle was fond of using shorter propositions in place of longer ones (where these longer propositions would be the *propositiones exponentes* arising in appropriate propositional analysis). Nevertheless, in Ockham's eyes Aristotle certainly did intend logic to be applied in natural philosophy, and even applied as Ockham applies it. Hence we find Ockham claiming that "not caring much about words," Aristotle merely assumed that those doing or learning natural philosophy would possess enough logical expertise to tell when he was using one proposition when he really meant another. Ockham felt, however, that Aristotle's assumption was too optimistic. As far as Ockham's own contemporaries were concerned, many tried to do natural philosophy before they knew enough logic, something that left them holding erroneous views and attributing to Aristotle and others a multitude of things con-

JOHN E. MURDOCH

trary to what they obviously intended.⁹² Was it not, perhaps, for such contemporaries that Ockham wrote his code book?

92. *Exp. Phys.* III, t. 61 (206b27–33), MSS Mert. 293, 72r; Bruges 557, 163r: "Verumtamen aliquando Philosophus ponit unam pro alia [scil. one of two different propositons] non curans multum de verbis et supponens quod addiscentes istam scientiam sunt sufficienter exercitati in logica per quam sciant discernere inter propositiones et advertere quando una ponitur pro alia et quando non. Quod tamen multi moderni ignorant, et ideo, quia frequenter audiunt alias scientias antequam perfecte sciant logicam, multas opiniones erroneas inveniunt et imponunt multa Aristoteli et aliis philosophis quorum contraria ex intentione demonstrant."

CHAPTER VII

Theology and Physics in
De sacramento altaris:
Ockham's Theory of Indivisibles

ELEONORE STUMP

1. Introduction

Ockham's theory of indivisibles was very influential in four-teenth-century natural philosophy, accepted even by scholastics who rejected other Ockhamist positions.[1] In articles either recent-ly or about to be published, John Murdoch has presented an account of this theory which leaves it open to serious philosophi-cal objections.[2] Murdoch's interpretation of Ockham's theory has both a metaphysical and a semantic component. According to Murdoch, Ockham maintains that indivisibles such as points are nonexistent and that one way of dealing with a term referring to an indivisible is to replace it by an expression which does not refer to that indivisible; thus, for instance, the term "point" is said to be equivalent to the expression "line of such and such a length." If we take this account at face value, it is not hard to see how this interpretation makes Ockham's theory of indivisibles appear incoherent. By definition, it is true that

(1) A point is indivisible

I am indebted to Norman Kretzmann and John Boler for their many helpful comments and suggestions, and I am grateful to John Crossett, whose efforts on my behalf made this paper possible.

1. See, e.g., Murdoch forthcoming a, forthcoming b, and forthcoming c. Cf. also Eldredge 1979, pp. 95–97.

2. See, e.g., besides the two papers mentioned in n. 1 above, chapter VI. Although I take a critical attitude toward Murdoch's interpretation, I have learned a great deal from his writings on these subjects.

and that

    (2) A line (of such and such a length) is divisible;

but if we make the appropriate substitutions warranted by the apparently Ockhamist analysis of the term "point," it will also be true that

    (1') A line is indivisible

and that

    (2') A point is divisible.

And there are other, similar sorts of serious difficulties with Ockham's theory as Murdoch presents it.[3] In the face of such difficulties, it seems worthwhile to reconsider what Ockham says about indivisibles to determine whether his theory really is as open to philosophical objections as Murdoch's account makes it seem. I propose to do so by looking carefully at Ockham's *De sacramento altaris*. However surprising it may at first seem, this treatise contains one of his most elaborate discussions of indivisibles, and Murdoch has relied heavily on it in his account of Ockham's theory.[4]

There are two obstacles to a consideration of Ockham's treatment of indivisibles in that treatise, however. The first has to do with the state of the text and with uncertainties about its historical context. In the only modern edition of *De sacramento altaris*,[5] which is not a reliable critical edition,[6] T. Bruce Birch has pre-

3. Some of these are pointed out in Kretzmann forthcoming.

4. There are, of course, other works besides *De sacramento altaris* in which Ockham discusses the nature of indivisibles. Because I am examining Murdoch's interpretation as well as Ockham's theory here, it seems to me important to analyze in detail Ockham's discussion in the work which has more than once constituted the major source for Murdoch's interpretation. For a consideration of Ockham's discussion of the nature of indivisibles or of quantity in works other than *De sacramento altaris*, see, e.g., Weisheipl 1963; Sylla 1975; Buescher 1950, pp. 67 ff.; Shapiro 1957 (esp. pp. 24 ff.); Maier 1955, pp. 176 ff.; Leff 1975, pp. 584 ff.; Zoubov 1961, pp. 48 ff.; and esp. chapter VI.

5. Ockham 1930.

6. For critical reviews of Birch's edition, see, e.g., Anonymous 1932 and 1929–32.

sented as one work what are really two independent treatises,[7] and he has given mistaken or at least confusing titles to the two treatises which in his edition constitute two portions of one work. Sorting out the relationships between the two treatises and determining their titles will have to await a critical edition of the texts,[8] but something tentative can and must be said here.

It is not improbable that only the treatise printed second in Birch's edition is correctly titled *De sacramento altaris* and that the treatise printed first (the one that contains Ockham's elaborate discussion of indivisibles) should be titled *De corpore Christi*.[9] Simply for the sake of convenience I will refer to the treatises under those titles in the remainder of this chapter. Whether the treatises were written before or during Ockham's stay in Avignon is not clear.[10] But the many references to malicious or sophistical attackers, the frequent citation of ecclesiastical authorities, and the explicit, scrupulous submission to the Church indicate plainly that they were written when Ockham was already under attack for his account of the Eucharist;[11] and in fact, Ockham claims that he is writing *De sacramento altaris* not in order to spread novel doctrines about the Eucharist but in order to defend himself from charges made against him on the basis of his earlier writings on the sacrament.[12] There is some suggestion that *De sacramento altaris* was written before *De corpore Christi*;[13] simply on the basis of the content

7. Cf. Baudry 1936 and Brampton 1964.

8. A critical edition is being prepared as part of the Franciscan Institute edition of Ockham, and I am very grateful to Carlo Grassi for his kindness and generosity in allowing me to see the collations of the manuscripts on which his critical edition will be based. In what follows, the citations to the two treatises will be to Birch's edition; but I have checked Birch's text against Grassi's collated manuscripts, and the Latin given in the footnotes is a corrected version of Birch's edition. See also Solá 1966.

9. See Junghaus 1968, pp. 83–84. What I am calling *De corpore Christi* occupies pp. 1–156 in Birch's edition; what I am calling *De sacramento altaris* runs from p. 158 through p. 500.

10. Junghaus 1968, pp. 84–85.

11. See, e.g., Ockham 1930, pp. 6.13–25; 116.16–18; 126–128.4; 154.13–29; 210.21–22. I have cited only a few of many such passages.

12. *De sacramento altaris*, Ockham 1930, p. 160.8–12.

13. Cf., e.g., Baudry 1936, p. 141, and Maier 1955, pp. 176–77. It has been suggested (in Brampton 1964) that *De corpore Christi* is the precursor to *De sacramento altaris* because in the former Ockham defines terms he means to use in the latter; but this view is mistaken and results from a failure to appreciate the contents of the two treatises.

of the treatises, that suggestion seems plausible. In *De sacramento altaris* Ockham argues for a certain account of transsubstantiation which depends on a particular theory of the nature of quantity. Ockham defends his theory of quantity at length in this treatise, but in a general sort of way, taking into consideration various arguments about the implications of his account for theories of the sacrament and trying to show the philosophical and theological respectability of his position by citing and discussing numerous authorities. It is clear from John Lutterell's accusations, however, and from subsequent fourteenth-century discussion[14] that one of the weakest or most controversial parts of Ockham's account of transsubstantiation is his theory of the nature of quantity. And *De corpore Christi*, which is a short treatise (about half the length of *De sacramento altaris*), is devoted exclusively to a thorough, detailed examination of the nature of quantity, so that (to judge only from its content) it is not implausible that *De corpore Christi* was written to buttress the controversial part of *De sacramento altaris*. But whether or not *De corpore Christi* was written after *De sacramento altaris* and for the sake of supporting it, it is clear from the prologue of *De corpore Christi* that the purpose of its treatment of quantity is to provide a foundation for Ockham's theory of the Eucharist.

Ockham's account of indivisibles, then, is developed within the context of his discussion of the sacrament, and so it is helpful for analyzing Ockham's treatment of indivisibles to know something of his account of transsubstantiation.[15] Indeed, it is the fact that his discussion of indivisibles is deeply enmeshed in his account of transsubstantiation that constitutes the second obstacle to a consideration of Ockham's doctrine of indivisibles in these treatises.

2. Transsubstantiation

The first ten chapters of *De sacramento altaris* are devoted to a presentation of a theory of transsubstantiation current in Ockham's day, a theory Ockham explicitly accepts before going on to present his own interpretation of it. Before the priest's consecra-

---

14. Cf., e.g., Maier 1955, pp. 199 ff.; and Buescher 1950, pp. xxv–xxvi and 145 ff.
15. Cf. the discussion of the relationship between theology and Ockham's theory of the nature of quantity in Maier 1955, pp. 176 ff., and in Sylla 1975, an excellent paper.

tion of the bread, Ockham explains, the host consists in the substance of the bread and the accidents (such as taste, color, size, and shape) which inhere in that substance. When the bread is consecrated, the substance of the bread is annihilated, being converted into the substance of Christ's body only—i.e., not into the substance of his blood, or into his soul, or into the accidents inhering in his body, although insofar as these are all natural concomitants of the substance of the body of Christ, when the substance of the body of Christ is present in the host, these are also concomitantly present. But even though the substance of Christ's body is then present in the host, it is not "circumscriptively" but "definitively" present. Ockham means that it is not the case that the whole of Christ's body is present in the whole of the space occupied by the host, each part of his body occupying a part of that space, but rather that the whole of his body is in every part, no matter how small, of the host. Piety alone dictates such a conclusion, since otherwise, for example, in the breaking of the host, the body of Christ would be broken. But there are philosophical reasons for it as well: for instance, it is part of Christian doctrine and experience that the body of Christ in the host is not accessible to human senses, but if the body of Christ were *circumscriptively* present in the host, it is hard to know what would prevent its being seen or otherwise perceived by the senses.

While this doctrine of the definitive rather than circumscriptive presence of Christ's body in the sacrament obviates some problems, it produces a variety of others. For example, if the whole body is present altogether in every part, will there not be a confusion of the parts and of the functions of the body, a result which is philosophically and theologically unacceptable? Of all such problems, the one most focused on by philosophical theologians was a twofold problem having to do with the quantity of the body of Christ in the sacrament. In the first place, since a body is constituted by a certain quantity of matter, and since matter is three-dimensionally extended,

(3a) How can Christ's body in the host be unextended?

as it must be if it is only definitively present there. In the second place, it is part of Christian doctrine that Christ's body is in the host with all the perfections it has in heaven, so that the body of Christ in the sacrament is in no way less good or complete than it is in heaven. Now, the body of Christ as it is in heaven is extended and so has the characteristic (or accident) of having a certain quantity; hence the body of Christ in the sacrament apparently must also have quantity. But if its presence there is noncircumscriptive and hence unextended,

(3b) How can Christ's body in the host have quantity?

A separate but philosophically related set of issues arises in connection with the substance and accidents of the bread. Doctrine and experience agree in the view that the accidents of the bread remain after the consecration. But if the substance of bread is annihilated when the bread is consecrated,

(4) How can the accidents of the bread exist without their natural subject?

To postulate that the accidents of the bread persist but inhere in no subject requires postulating a number of divine interventions in the natural order, so that God causes each of the remaining accidents to exist independently, as if it were a substance. To postulate that the accidents might inhere in the substance of the body of Christ was considered impious and entails philosophical problems as well.[16] In the face of these difficulties, a solution which had become common by Ockham's time was to say, as Thomas Aquinas had said, that the qualities of the bread after consecration inhere in the quantity of the bread as in a subject, so that one of the accidents serves as the subject in which the other accidents inhere. In that way only one divine intervention in the natural order need be postulated, the one that causes the accident of quantity to exist independently, as if it were a substance.[17]

Of these two fundamental problems raised by theories of transsubstantiation, it is clear that it is the one expressed in (4) which is Ockham's central concern in both his treatises on the Eucharist.

---

16. *De sacramento altaris*, Ockham 1930, pp. 202–4.
17. Cf. the discussion in Buescher 1950, pp. 122 ff.

He says as much in various places,[18] and the table of contents in *De sacramento altaris* also makes it plain. After expounding the basic theory of transsubstantiation in chapters 1–10 (I am using Birch's numbering of the chapters) and certain principles fundamental to his account in chapters 11–15, he presents in chapters 16–22 the conclusions he wants to support in the treatise. These all have to do with the quantity of the bread after consecration, and this section of the treatise concludes in chapters 21–22 with an elaborate attack on the notion that after consecration the qualities of the bread inhere in the quantity as in a subject. Ockham's own view is the one requiring more rather than less divine intervention, the view that each of the qualities of the bread remaining after consecration exists independently, without inhering in a subject; and the rest of the treatise, from chapter 23 to the end, is an elaborate defense of this view and the philosophical presuppositions about the nature of quantity on which it rests.[19]

3. Ockham's Theory of Quantity

It is Ockham's view that quantity is not an absolute thing, distinct from substance or quality; but, as he points out, this view is not equivalent to the claim that there is no such thing as quantity.[20] According to Ockham, something is "an absolute thing" (*res absoluta*) just in case God by his absolute power can make it exist independently of every other thing (always excepting God himself, of course).[21] Given this definition, motion, for example, is not an absolute thing, since it is logically impossible for motion to exist independently of some moving thing; therefore, even God in his absolute power cannot bring it about that

18. See, e.g., *De corpore Christi*, Ockham 1930, p. 4.9–19; and *De sacramento altaris*, Ockham 1930, p. 240.1–10.

19. Edith Sylla espouses Maier's suggestion that Ockham first developed his theory of quantity in *De sacramento altaris* but thinks that Ockham's theory of quantity was developed to solve problems connected with the quantity of Christ's body in the Eucharist (Sylla 1975, p. 364) rather than with the quantity of the bread; she gives no reasons for her view.

20. See, e.g., *De sacramento altaris*, Ockham 1930, chap. 35, in which Ockham explains how there can be a separate category for quantity even though quantity is not distinct from substance or quality.

21. See Weisheipl 1963, pp. 157–58.

motion exists independently of every other thing, and so motion is not an absolute thing. According to Ockham, only substances (which for Ockham include not only composites of matter and form but also matter as well as form) and qualities are absolute things. It is not unlikely that if it had not been for the doctrine of the Eucharist, Ockham would have admitted only substances as absolute things.[22] But in either Aquinas's or Ockham's theory of the sacrament, after consecration at least one accident remains and exists independently of every other thing. And if in the Eucharist the qualities, say, of the bread *do* exist independently, then obviously it is within God's absolute power to bring about their independent existence, and Ockham by his own principles must allow qualities as absolute things.

On Ockham's view, it is not logically possible for any quantity to exist independently of a substance or a quality, and so no quantity is an absolute thing—hence Ockham's claim that quantity is not a thing distinct from substance or quality. Nonetheless, quantity is not to be taken either as identical with substance or quality or as simply nothing. In general, Ockham understands quantity as the condition of having parts capable of local motion toward one another, so that quantity is nothing more than a certain characteristic of a substance or a quality, namely, its extension.[23] Terms of quantity, consequently, are connotative rather than absolute; they signify a substance or a quality and connote that it has parts capable of moving toward one another. On the other hand, though a term of quantity signifies a substance or a quality, a proposition such as

(5) A substance is a quantity

is false because a quantity is not predicable per se of a substance or a quality. Ockham here takes a proposition (or predication) to be per se only in case the subject connotes just whatever the predicate connotes. In the case of a proposition such as (5), the predicate connotes something, namely, that the parts of whatever

22. Ibid.; cf. Sylla 1975, p. 371.
23. See, e.g., *De sacramento altaris*, Ockham 1930, pp. 432.27–434.27. For a fuller treatment of Ockham's theory of the nature of quantity, see, e.g., Buescher 1950, pp. 67 ff., and Maier 1955, pp. 176 ff.

is denoted (by the predicate term) are capable of motion toward one another, which is not connoted by the subject. Though quantity is not a real thing distinct from substance or quality, the terms "substance" or "quality" are not always interchangeable, *salva veritate*, with the term "quantity."[24]

Ockham has many arguments for his view of quantity, perhaps the most frequently cited of which is that having to do with condensation and rarefaction. Richard of Middleton had argued that quantity and substance must be really distinct, since in condensation quantity alters, though there is no loss of substance.[25] In reply, Ockham maintains that condensation is simply the moving closer together of the parts of some substance, so that the change in quantity is nothing more than a change in the degree of separateness among the parts of a substance. But this separateness is not a real thing distinct from substance, and so neither is quantity. Ockham maintains instead that this separateness of parts is simply a natural, concomitant condition of something's being material—natural but not necessary, since God by his absolute power could condense a material substance to such a degree that it had all its parts in one place, no matter how small.[26]

Although Ockham's account of quantity in his treatises on the Eucharist is developed as a response to (4), "How can the accidents of the bread exist without their natural subject?" it is plain that it has important implications also for both (3a) and (3b): "How can Christ's body in the host be unextended?" and "How can Christ's body in the host have quantity?" Given Ockham's account of quantity as a natural but not necessary condition of material things, it is possible for God by his absolute power to bring it about that all the parts of Christ's body exist in every part, no matter how small, of the space occupied by the host, so that it is perfectly possible for Christ's body to be only definitively present in the host. This leads Ockham to maintain bluntly, against the Thomistic view, that Christ's body in the host has no

24. See *De sacramento altaris*, Ockham 1930, pp. 464–70; cf. Buescher 1950, pp. 76–77.
25. See Maier 1964, pp. 191 ff. Ockham's discussion of Richard's objections occurs in *De corpore Christi*, Ockham 1930, pp. 116.21–142.13.
26. *De corpore Christi*, Ockham 1930, pp. 128.10 ff. and 142.14 ff.; *De sacramento altaris*, Ockham 1930, pp. 188–96. Cf. Weisheipl 1963, p. 161.

quantity. But, he argues, this claim does not entail that the body of Christ in the host lacks one of the perfections it has in heaven because, in Ockham's view, quantity is not a real thing distinct from substance or quality, and all of the substance and the qualities of Christ's body in heaven are also present in the host.[27]

4. Ockham's Theory of Indivisibles: Metaphysics

Ockham's theory of indivisibles in *De corpore Christi* is part of his argument for his theory of quantity and needs to be understood in that context. In *De corpore Christi* he begins by briefly presenting an orthodox account of transsubstantiation and then posing two problems, the first having to do with the existence and distinction of the accidents of the bread after consecration and the second having to do with their separation from a subject. Conceding (as universally acknowledged) that the qualities of the bread are really distinct from one another and from a substance, he narrows his investigation to a consideration of quantity and its relation to quality and substance. To do this in a thorough and orderly way, he focuses on three major questions in turn, intending to establish the truth or falsity of these propositions:

(6) A point is an absolute thing really distinct from a line;
(7) (a) A line is an absolute thing really distinct from a surface;
    (b) A surface is an absolute thing really distinct from a body;
(8) A body (which is a quantity, on Ockham's view) is an absolute thing really distinct from substance.

He devotes seven or eight times as much space to (6) as to (7), relying heavily in his discussion of (7) on arguments presented in his rejection of (6); and it is plain that in his treatment of indivisibles in this work Ockham is laying the foundation in particular for his subsequent rejection of (8) and in general for his theory of the nature of quantity.

The basic issue in Ockham's discussion of an indivisible, as in his discussion of quantity, is the question whether it is an absolute thing[28]—that is, whether an indivisible such as a point is

27. See, e.g., *De corpore Christi*, Ockham 1930, pp. 148.4 ff.
28. See, e.g., *De corpore Christi*, Ockham 1930, pp. 6.1–12, 8.1–5, 16.26–30, 22.5–9, 24.25–29, 24.30–26.16, 28.3–25, 28.26–30.11, 72.12–28.

something which God by his absolute power could cause to exist independently of every other thing. There is something at least misleading, then, in characterizing Ockham's discussion of points here as a discussion about the *existence* of points.[29] Ockham himself does not put the issue in those terms here. As he explains it, what is at stake in his treatment of points is not so much whether there are such things as points as what the nature of a point is. The case of a point is in this respect similar to the case of quantity: a demonstration that there is no such thing would entail many absurdities for mathematics and the sciences as well as for ordinary discourse, and Ockham intends no such demonstration. His aim is rather to show that a point, like quantity, is not an absolute thing, an entity which could without logical contradiction be postulated to exist separately from every other entity.[30]

Ockham understands a point primarily as a limit of or a cut in a continuum.[31] There are such cuts or limits, just as there are absences from loved ones; but a cut or a limit, like an absence, must not be thought of as an independently existing thing. This continues to be Ockham's general strategy also with lines and surfaces—he takes each to be a kind of limit which is not an entity in its own right[32]—until he reaches his general conclusion about quantity, namely, that a substance or a quality is not quantified by the addition to it of a separate, independently existing entity which is quantity but instead is quantified simply by itself, by a certain condition and arrangement of its parts.[33]

29. As Murdoch does in, e.g., chapter VI as well as in Murdoch forthcoming a and forthcoming b.

30. That this is Ockham's aim is made plain throughout the entire *De corpore Christi* and can be seen even in the basic structure of the treatise, which consists in the treatment of three different but related issues concerning whether or not something is an absolute thing. Furthermore, the overriding purpose of the treatise, as he makes plain in the prologue (Ockham 1930, p. 4.13–19), is to come to some conclusions about the nature of quantity. The principal conclusion he reaches is that quantity is not an absolute thing (see, e.g., p. 92.20–21), and his method for reaching that conclusion is to show that a point is not an absolute thing really distinct from a line, that a line is not an absolute thing really distinct from a surface, that a surface is not an absolute thing really distinct from a body, and that a body (which, he says, *est quantitas*, p. 92.6) is not an absolute thing really distinct from substance and from quality.

31. Cf., e.g., Ockham's two discussions of the meaning of "point" in *De corpore Christi*, Ockham 1930, pp. 36.22–38.5 and pp. 40.18–42.11.

32. See, e.g., *De corpore Christi*, Ockham 1930, p. 82.12–18, p. 84.1–7, and p. 84.16 ff.

33. See, e.g., *De corpore Christi*, Ockham 1930, p. 92.13–15 and p. 94.4 ff.

In his discussion of points, Ockham is so concerned to demol-
ish the view of points as absolute things that he says repeatedly
what at first glance is misleading, namely, that a point is no more
a privation than it is a positive entity.[34] But if one looks more
closely at Ockham's denials in these passages, it becomes apparent that he is trying to guard only against the notion of a point as
a hypostasized privative entity which, for instance, must be
added to a line in order to terminate it. Thus he says, for example, that "one must not think that a point is some privation totally
distinct from a line, as men commonly imagine, because it is
impossible to imagine that a point *is* something, whether privative or positive, a distinct whole in its own right, or not the same
as a line."[35] Or, again,

> this is not to be granted: "A point is a privation," "A line is a
> privation," "A surface is a privation"; and this in accordance with
> correct [ordinary] usage and the imagination of those who imagine
> that a privation *is* something, considered as a thing, in any way
> whatever distinct from positive things. Therefore, [these arguments
> are presented or made] against that imagination which imagines that
> a point, considered as a thing, is a certain privation distinct in any
> way imaginable from a line as a whole in its own right.[36]

And he goes on to add in this same section that although a point
is not a privative thing, nonetheless in any nominal definition of
the term "point," some negative word or concept must always be
included.[37] These repeated claims of Ockham's that a point is not
a privation do not conflict, then, with his general view of points

34. *De corpore Christi,* Ockham 1930, p. 64.17 ff.

35. *De corpore Christi,* Ockham 1930, p. 64.17–22: "Nec est tamen intelligendum
quod punctus sit aliqua privatio distincta totaliter a linea sicut homines communiter imaginantur, quia impossibile est imaginari quod punctus sit aliquid vel privatum vel positivum secundum se totum distinctum vel non idem cum linea."

36. *De corpore Christi,* Ockham 1930, p. 70.1–9: "illa non est concedenda, 'punctus est privatio,' 'linea est privatio,' 'superficies est privatio' et hoc secundum
proprietatem sermonis et secundum imaginationem illorum qui imaginantur quod
privatio sit aliquid a parte rei quocumque modo distinctum a rebus positivis. Unde
[argumenta illa sunt recitata sive facta] contra illam imaginationem quae imagina-
tur, quod punctus sit a parte rei, quaedam privatio distincta quocumque modo
imaginabili secundum se totum a linea."

37. *De corpore Christi,* Ockham 1930, p. 70.12–15: "Sed non sic ponit illa opinio,
nec magis ponit quod punctus est privatio quam positivum; quamvis in diffini-
tione exprimente quid nominis ipsius debeat poni unum nomen negativum vel
conceptus negativus."

as cuts in or limits of a continuum. Rather they are another part of his attempt to show that such a cut or limit is not an entity in its own right, not even some fancied privative entity.[38]

Ockham uses many different sorts of arguments to show that points are not absolute things; but his basic strategy, which he uses also in connection with his discussion of lines and surfaces, is to show that there is no absolute entity which a point could be, and he constructs a lengthy argument which exhausts the possibilities. He begins by saying that if a point were an absolute entity, it would be either a substance or an accident,[39] since in Aristotelian metaphysics these two types exhaust the possibilities for entities. Now, if a point were a substance, Ockham says, it would have to be one of the following: (a) matter, (b) form, (c) a composite of matter and form, or (d) a form abstracted from matter. Three of these possibilities—(a), (c), and (d)—are quickly ruled out, because while points are indivisible, matter is divisible, and so consequently is any composite of matter and form, or any form abstracted from (and thus imposable on) matter. Ockham's reason for ruling out (b) as the sort of substance a point might be is not made clear until later in the treatise in connection with a different argument where Ockham says that the only unextended form is the rational soul.[40] If a point were a form, it would have to be an indivisible and hence unextended form; consequently if the only unextended form is the rational soul, a point would have to be a rational soul, which is an absurd conclusion and shows that a point cannot be a form. (Ockham gives no hint here why he thinks that the only unextended form is the rational soul; and in the context to assume that the only unextended form is the rational soul is tantamount to begging the question.)

Having disposed in this quick way of the possibility that points are substances, Ockham goes on to consider in great detail

---

38. It is misleading, then, to claim as Murdoch does, that Ockham intends to reduce points to "macroscopic individuals" or "three-dimensional bodies" (in chapter VI and Murdoch forthcoming a, nn. 29 and 31), since this suggests the erroneous view that Ockham is willing to admit points as real things if we will only take them to be bits of matter, a view that is, moreover, inconsistent with Murdoch's claim that for Ockham indivisibles are nonexistent.
39. *De corpore Christi*, Ockham 1930, p. 8.11 ff.
40. *De corpore Christi*, Ockham 1930, p. 14.16–25.

whether they can be accidents.[41] It seems likely that if it were not for the influence of theology on Ockham's physics, he might have ended his argument with the conclusion that points are not substances. To show that points are not absolute things, however, he is obliged to go on to consider accidents, since in his own view *some* accidents are absolute things because God by his absolute power can make the qualities of the bread after consecration exist independently.

Miracles aside, any accident, Ockham says, must inhere in a subject, and it must do so in one of three ways. Either (i) the whole of the accident exists in the whole of its subject and in every part, no matter how small, of that subject; or (ii) the whole of the accident exists in the whole of its subject and each part of the accident exists in some part of the subject; or (iii) the accident inheres in an indivisible subject. Most of Ockham's arguments are directed against the first and third of these possibilities; the second is easy to rule out, since it requires the accident in question to be divisible into parts, and a point is indivisible. His basic strategy for dispensing with the third possibility is the same as the one he uses in showing that points themselves cannot be substances. If a point is an accident inhering in an indivisible subject, what is the nature of that indivisible subject? It must be (a) matter, (b) form, (c) a composite of both, or (d) form abstracted from matter; but it cannot be (a), (c), or (d), since these are divisible. And it cannot be (b) because, as in the earlier argument, the only indivisible form is the rational soul, but it is absurd to suppose that the rational soul is the subject in which points inhere as accidents. Hence there is no indivisible thing which can be the subject for a point, and the third possibility for points as accidents is eliminated.

Possibility (ii) poses no problem for Ockham because it is the case of a *divisible accident* inhering in a divisible subject; possibility (iii) is that of an indivisible accident inhering in an *indivisible subject*, and its rejection derives straightforwardly from Ockham's views about indivisible substances. But possibility (i) is more diffi-

---

41. *De corpore Christi*, Ockham 1930, p. 8.25 ff. In what follows, for the sake of brevity I am giving only the skeleton of Ockham's argument, which is more complicated than is indicated here.

cult to dismiss; it is a mixture of the other two cases, and rejecting it requires demonstrating that a point cannot be an *indivisible accident* inhering in a *divisible subject.* To reject it, Ockham takes as his example of a divisible subject a line (segment) *A,* and considers whether it can be a subject for a point *B* which terminates it. If it can be a subject for *B,* he says, then by parity of reasoning it can also be a subject for a point *C,* which terminates *A* at its other extremity. Consequently, *B* and *C* would be in the same subject. But Ockham maintains that accidents which are in the same (primary) subject are not in different places. So if *B* were in *A* as its subject, *B* and *C* would not be in different places—which is absurd. Therefore *B* cannot inhere in *A* as its subject, and so a point cannot be an indivisible accident inhering in a divisible subject. To the natural objection that *B* does not inhere in the *whole* of *A* as its subject but only in a part of *A,* Ockham replies in this way. Let the relevant part of *A,* which is to be the subject for *B,* be called *D.* Then we ask if *B* inheres in *D* as its subject. If it does, then for the same reasons so does point *E,* which terminates part *D* at its other extremity—and the argument continues as before, to the same conclusion. Since there is no divisible part of *A,* no matter how small, for which a similar argument cannot be made, it seems clear that a point cannot be an accident inhering in a divisible subject.

Hence all the possibilities for points are rejected; they can be neither substances nor accidents and consequently cannot be absolute things. As in the case of quantity, which is also not an absolute thing, such a conclusion does not compel us to maintain that there are no points, only that a point is not an independently existing thing.

5. Ockham's Theory of Indivisibles: Semantics

Ockham's theory of the nature of points combined with certain features of his philosophy of language requires him to give a special analysis of terms for indivisibles.[42] These give him more trouble than do terms for quantity generally, because although he

42. For discussions of relevant portions of Ockham's philosophy of language, see, e.g., Moody 1935 and Loux 1974, esp. pp. 1–46.

denies that any quantity is an absolute thing, he nonetheless does understand quantity as something positive, namely, the extension of an absolute thing; thus he takes "quantity" to signify a substance or a quality and to connote that it has parts which are capable of moving toward one another.[43] A point, however, he takes to be simply a certain sort of privation; and it is a privation not even in respect of a substance or a quality but only in respect of a line, which is itself not an absolute thing.

Ockham suggests two methods of dealing with terms for indivisibles. The first he explains in this way.[44] Some people, he reports, would deal with an abstract term such as "privation" by saying that it is equivalent in signification to the phrase "deprived subject" (*subiectum privatum*). In accordance with this method, as we grant the truth of this proposition

(9) A deprived subject is material (*materia*),

so we ought to grant the truth of this one:

(10) A privation is material.[45]

If any sense is to be made out of this way of dealing with a nonreferential term, I think it must be understood in the following way. A term which appears to signify a privation is to be taken as nothing more than an abbreviated way of signifying a deprived subject. Consequently, talk which is ostensibly about a privation is really only talk about the subject of a privation. Thus in accordance with this method (10) is true, and so the proposition

43. See, e.g., *De sacramento altaris*, Ockham 1930, p. 434.15–27.

44. Ockham's exposition of the first method begins on p. 36.21 of *De corpore Christi*, where he introduces it by saying that we can suppose the term "point" to have the force of a name and not to be equivalent to a composite expression. This exposition continues to p. 40.5, where he introduces the second method by suggesting that we can also suppose the term "point" to be equivalent in signification not to a name but to some composite expression of such a sort that it renders any proposition containing the term "point" figurative. For places in which he speaks of the two methods together, in order to compare or contrast them, see, e.g., *De corpore Christi*, Ockham 1930, p. 66.19–23 and p. 70.16–20.

45. *De corpore Christi*, Ockham 1930, p. 38.13–17: "Unde sicut dicunt aliqui quod hoc nomen 'privatio' aequivalet in significando huic toti 'subiectum privatum'; et propter hoc, sicut concedunt istam, 'subiectum privatum est materia,' ita concedunt illam 'privatio est materia.'"

(11) A privation is immaterial

is *false,* not because this method involves a peculiar view of privation, but because it takes the term "privation" as nothing more than a potentially misleading substitute for the longer phrase signifying a subject which is (Ockham evidently thinks) always material. This first method, then, in effect removes the word "privation" from our vocabulary and makes it impossible to mention privation itself by insisting that any occurrence of the term "privation" is simply a disguised occurrence of the phrase "a deprived subject."

If we use this method to construct an analogous account of the term "point," we can say that "a point" is equivalent in signification (*in significando aequivalet*) to "a line not further extended." In accordance with this first method, then, Ockham explains, the proposition

(12) A point is a line

is true, and so is the proposition

(13) A point is divisible.[46]

This method does not provide an analysis of the term "point," however.[47] The replacement of an analysandum by its analysans

46. *De corpore Christi*, Ockham 1930, p. 38.17 ff: "Ita si hoc nomen 'punctus' in significando aequivalet isti toti 'linea non ulterius protensa' vel alicui consimili . . ., sicut haec conceditur, 'linea est divisibilis,' ita illa conceditur de virtute significationis, 'punctus est linea,' 'punctus est divisibilis.' Immo quicquid verificatur de hoc nomine 'linea' sumpto significative, verificatur de hoc nomine 'punctus' sumpto significative. . . ."

47. Cf. chapter VI above. See also Murdoch forthcoming a, where he says: "the term 'point' is equivalent to the expression (*complexum*) 'a line of such and such a length' or something of that sort. . . . Of course, the term 'point' occurs everywhere in the propositions of natural philosophy, and there is nothing wrong with using the term 'point' in these propositions; we should merely realize that in so doing we are but employing the term in place of more complex expressions or propositions in which the term 'point' does not appear. . . ." Such an interpretation is not warranted by the text, and it leaves Ockham's theory open to very serious objection. In this interpretation, for example, Ockham's theory has disastrous consequences for both geometry and Aristotelian physics because it will be true to say, for instance, that the center of a circle is a line of such and such a length, and contrary to Aristotle, motion will be possible in an instant, since "instant" (on the analogy of "point") will be equivalent to "temporal interval of such and such a length." Even the laws of logic are altered in drastic ways, in this

within an open context preserves the truth value of the proposition within which the replacement is made. But if we apply this putative analysis within the ordinarily accepted proposition

(14) A point is indivisible,

we produce

(15) A line not further extended is indivisible,

which is absurd. But this method of Ockham's does not *analyze* terms for indivisibles; rather, it is equivalent to removing such terms from our language by insisting that any occurrence of, say, "point" is just a disguised occurrence of the phrase "a line not further extended." Hence, in accordance with this method, ordinarily accepted propositions such as (14) or

(16) Between any two points there is always another point

are actually *false*—not because of some radical Ockhamist geometrical doctrine, but because "point" is simply an abbreviation for "line not further extended," and it is false that a line is indivisible, or that between any two lines (segments) there is always another line (segment).

This is a drastic, even primitive way of dealing with a nonreferential term; and while Ockham does not reject it, he clearly does not favor it, either. Instead he proposes a second method for dealing with the term "point"; and it is this method to which he devotes the most attention and on which he relies throughout the rest of his discussion of points.[48] It would indeed be peculiar if he were really to adopt the first method, because, as he himself recognizes,[49] it ultimately entails the truth of propositions such as

(17) A point is an absolute thing.

---

interpretation, because the law of noncontradiction becomes "Contradictories cannot be true within the same temporal interval (of such and such a length)." But there is no need to saddle Ockham with such a bizarre theory of indivisibles.

48. *De corpore Christi*, Ockham 1930, p. 40.5 ff.

49. See, e.g., *De corpore Christi*, Ockham 1930, p. 66.13–15, p. 66.20–22, and p. 70.16–20.

That is, if we adopt this first method for dealing with the term "point," we must, to be consistent, adopt it also for "line" and "surface," since lines and surfaces, too, are indivisibles in certain respects. "Line" will then be replaced by "surface not further extended," and "surface" by "body not further extended," so that if we make all the appropriate replacements, it emerges that we are ultimately to replace "point" by "body not further extended." Since in Ockham's view a material object is an absolute thing, (17) would then be true in accordance with this method. Proposition 17, however, is just what Ockham's whole treatment of indivisibles is designed to reject. And Ockham must have recognized that there is something at least confusing and inelegant about adopting a semantic account of "point" which requires us to accept (17), although we are required to reject it in accordance with the metaphysics for points.

According to Ockham's second method for dealing with terms for indivisibles, the term "point" is not properly speaking a name at all and is not equivalent to any noun phrase such as "a line not further extended" but rather does duty for an independent clause such as "a line is not further extended." Hence, it cannot function as a subject term in a proposition. Consequently, propositions containing the term "point" as a subject term must be regarded as metaphorical or figurative and cannot be taken literally in any investigation of the truth.[50] To illustrate this method, Ockham gives the following example.[51] Suppose that we let *A* stand for the phrase "then correctly" (*tunc bene*). On that hypothesis we are to consider the proposition

(18) *A* is something.

---

50. *De corpore Christi*, Ockham 1930, pp. 40.5–44.21. Murdoch tends to conflate Ockham's two methods of analyzing terms for indivisibles. In Murdoch forthcoming b, for example, he says, "to give the nominal definition of the term 'point' is to say that the term 'point' signifies the same thing as the phrase 'a line of such and such a length' . . . . whenever the term 'point' occurs in a proposition or *oratio*, then the *oratio* is a *locutio figurativa*, not one that functions *secundum proprietatem sermonis*. Still, such *orationes* or propositions can be conceded once we realize that . . . the term 'point' is being used in place of its nominal definition, in place of a phrase equivalent to it."
51. *De corpore Christi*, Ockham 1930, p. 52.16 ff.

Such a proposition has the appearance of being grammatically and logically well formed, but its appearance is deceptive because (18) is simply an abbreviation for

(19) Then correctly is something.

But (19) is neither grammatically nor logically well formed, and it makes no sense to ask about its truth or falsity. The best we can do is to take (19) as figurative and interpret it as if it were

(19') This, which is then correctly, is something

or some equivalent formulation.[52] According to this second method, then, a proposition in which a term for an indivisible occurs as the subject term is not well formed. In consequence, neither

(20) A point is something

nor

(21) A point is nothing

is either true or false;[53] and this claim does not violate the law of noncontradiction because despite appearances, (20) and (21) are not contradictories, any more than (19) and

(22) Then correctly is not something

are contradictories.

In general, in accordance with this second method Ockham tends to understand the term "point" as equivalent in sense to

(23) A line is not further extended,

52. It looks as if the referent of the demonstrative pronoun in (19') is intended to be *the expression* "then correctly," so that the problem here is a use-mention ambiguity in the interpretation of the arbitrarily assigned designation A. His choice of *tunc bene* is probably associated with the fact that it is a familiar expression in medieval disputational exchanges, indicating the correctness of a reply in certain circumstances.

53. *De corpore Christi*, Ockham 1930, p. 58.17 ff. and pp. 64.25–66.6.

rather than to the noun phrase "a line not further extended," as in the first method. But his explicitly stated, theoretical principle is that a proposition including a term for an indivisible must be translated into a well-formed proposition (which can be taken literally) not on the basis of any simple formula but instead on an ad hoc basis, in accordance with the intentions of the author in whose writing the figurative proposition occurs.[54] Thus, when Aristotle says that

(24) The parts of a line are joined at a point as at a common terminus,

this proposition is to be treated as a figurative expression the literal meaning of which is conveyed in this conjunction:

(24') There is nothing intermediate between the parts of a line, and they themselves form one line per se.[55]

And the proposition

(25) A coming-to-be is in an instant

is to be understood literally as

---

54. *De corpore Christi*, Ockham 1930, p. 40.18–24: "Sed illae propositiones et consimiles non sunt concedendae secundum proprietatem sermonis, tamquam propriae non excusandae per aliquam figuram grammaticalem; et per consequens non est ex eis arguendum in investigatione veritatis, nisi ipsis acceptis secundum sensum quem habent ex intentione auctorum. . . ."

p. 54.7–12: "Et ideo sicut multa dicta in metris et ornato modo loquendi non sunt recipienda nisi excusentur et glossentur, ita multa dicta causa brevitatis non sunt recipienda secundum proprietatem sermonis, sed secundum intentionem auctorum dicentium ea qui figurative propter dictam causam loquebantur."

55. *De corpore Christi*, Ockham 1930, p. 74.5–21: "Et ideo philosophus per illam propositionem, 'partes lineae copulantur ad unum terminum communem,' intelligit illam propositionem, 'inter partes lineae nihil est medium et illae faciunt per se unum,' ita quod duo requiruntur ad hoc quod linea sit continua, videlicet, quod inter partes lineae nihil est medium situaliter. Et propter hoc, quando unum corpus est in uno situ et aliud corpus in alio situ et inter illa corpora est aliquod medium situaliter, illa duo corpora non continuantur. Secundum requiritur, videlicet, quod faciant per se unum et propter hoc contigua non sunt continua, et ita per illam propositionem 'partes lineae copulantur ad punctum tamquam ad terminum communem,' et per consimiles intelligit philosophus illam copulativam: 'inter partes lineae nihil est medium et ipsae faciunt per se unam lineam.'"

(25') When something comes to be, it is not the case that one part comes to be before another, but rather the whole comes to be at once.[56]

It is important to see here that Ockham is concerned to remove talk of indivisibles by understanding (24) as (24') and (25) as (25') not because of some belief which requires that indivisibles not be mentioned but rather as a consistent complement to his metaphysical theory of indivisibles. Any accurate helpful gloss on "at once" in (25') will have to mention a cut in the temporal continuum. And if Ockham's concern were to show that all talk of indivisibles is dispensable in virtue of his conviction that indivisibles do not exist,[57] then such a gloss on "at once" would be embarrassing counterevidence to Ockham's view. But what Ockham wants to demonstrate with his interpretation of (25) is not that instants do not exist and therefore should not be mentioned but rather that semantic considerations do not force us to consider an instant as some sort of real entity *within* which coming-to-be occurs. That this is Ockham's aim is clear from the text:

> I say that this proposition "A coming-to-be is in an instant" is not to be understood as it sounds, as if one thing were in another, as the proposition "Water is in a vase" denotes that one thing is in another distinct thing.[58] Similarly, the proposition "Motion is in time" ought not to be understood as it sounds, according to the form of the proposition, namely, that one thing is in some other thing really distinct from it. Rather it ought to be understood [in the following way]: "When something is moved, it acquires one part before another" [or something similar]. . . .[59]

---

56. *De corpore Christi*, Ockham 1930, p. 54.16–27: "Unde dico quod illa propositio 'generatio est in instanti,' non est recipienda sub intellectu quem sonat, quasi una res sit in alia; sicut per illam propositionem 'aqua est in vase' denotatur quod una res est in alia re distincta; unde discurrendo per omnes modos quibus aequivoce accipitur haec praepositio 'in,' de quibus loquitur philosophus, IV. Physicorum, patet quod secundum nullum illorum potest dici quod generatio est in instanti; sed illa propositio 'generatio est in instanti' sub illo intellectu debet recipi 'quando aliquid generatur, non generatur pars ante partem sed totum simul generatur'. . . ."
57. As Murdoch suggests in chapter VI and Murdoch forthcoming a and forthcoming b.
58. *De corpore Christi*, Ockham 1930, p. 54.16–20 (cf. note 56 above).
59. *De corpore Christi*, Ockham 1930, p. 56.3–8: "Consimiliter illa propositio 'motus est in tempore' non debet recipi sub illo intellectu quem sonat secundum

Ockham's theory of indivisibles, then, is more sophisticated and less open to objection than it has been made to seem. It is part of Ockham's general treatment of quantity, which is itself part of his argument for his account of transsubstantiation, and it is influenced by Eucharistic doctrine. Ockham understands indivisibles as privations, as cuts in or limits of various kinds of continua; and what he is principally concerned to demonstrate is that, like quantity, an indivisible is not an absolute thing, so that (for example) a point is not a positive, independently existing entity which must be added to a line in order for that line to be terminated or continued. His semantic theory for indivisibles is meant to show that the presence of terms for indivisibles in ordinary language does not require us to understand indivisibles as independently existing entities. In his view, we can in more than one way construct a semantic theory which avoids commitment to the ontological position he repudiates. We can simply remove terms for indivisibles from our language by considering them nothing more than convenient abbreviations for longer phrases in which the indivisible in question is not mentioned. Or as Ockham prefers, we can claim that terms for indivisibles are not really names at all, so that any proposition in which such a term occurs as the subject term is not well formed, although such a proposition can be translated into one which is well formed and which does not commit us to a belief in indivisibles as absolute entities, on the basis of considering the intentions of the author in whose writings the proposition occurs and understanding the nature of indivisibles as limits of various kinds of continua.

It should be clear, however, that to say Ockham's theory of indivisibles is more sophisticated and less open to objection than it has been made to seem is not yet to say it is a good theory of indivisibles. Even in the version I have argued for, the theory is still open to objections. The most important of these, I think, is that Ockham's account of indivisibles in the treatises on the Eucharist is basically negative; it tells us what indivisibles are not. Indivisibles for Ockham cannot be absolute things; they are priva-

---

formam propositionis, scilicet, quod una res est in re alia distincta realiter ab ea, sed debet recipi sub illo intellectu, 'quando aliquid movetur, acquirit unam partem ante aliam'. . . ."

tions, cuts in a continuum. But what is a privation? Given that it is not an absolute thing, we might be inclined to suppose that it is a property of something which is an absolute thing. A surface, for example, we might take to be a property of some body—namely, its being extended so far and no farther. But on Ockham's account indivisibles cannot be accidents of absolute things either. Indivisibles, then, cannot fit into any of Aristotle's ten categories. Still, as I have argued, Ockham does want simply to reject the notion of an indivisible as meaningless or incoherent. But what positive account of indivisibles he has in mind or could provide is not clear in these treatises.

CHAPTER VIII

Infinite Indivisibles and Continuity in Fourteenth-Century Theories of Alteration

EDITH DUDLEY SYLLA

1. Introduction

Following Aristotle, most fourteenth-century natural philosophers assumed that there were three or four basic categories of natural motion or change. Not only was there local motion, a change in the place of a body, there was also the motion of augmentation or diminution, a change in the quantity of a body, and the motion of alteration, a change in the qualities of a body. And if alteration was pushed far enough, a fourth kind of change resulted, the generation or destruction of a body. Most fourteenth-century natural philosophers also assumed, again following Aristotle, that within a single motion of any of the first three kinds the place, quantity, or quality acquired or lost was continuous, as was the motion itself. Concerning alteration in particular, the fourteenth-century addition-of-part-to-part theory of alteration made a special point of emphasizing the continuity of the qualities acquired or lost, sometimes carrying this emphasis to the extent of denying altogether the existence of indivisibles in quality.[1]

All this is as one might expect, given the foundation of fourteenth-century natural philosophy in Aristotle's works. There was, however, one fourteenth-century theory of alteration, the so-called succession-of-forms theory, which asserted that the

---

1. See Sylla 1973, pp. 230–32, 251–62.

qualities acquired in alteration were not continua with parts that could be taken on gradually. According to this theory, every qualitative form that exists in a body is indivisible with respect to degree. When a body is altered, the theory claimed, it takes on an infinite series of indivisible degrees, each old degree in turn being destroyed to be replaced by a new one. This succession theory for qualitative change had similarities to the theories of substantial forms and substantial change propounded by Thomas Aquinas. It was applied to the explanation of change in the Eucharist by Godfrey of Fontaines, and it was elaborated most thoroughly by Walter Burley.[2]

There were in the fourteenth century some "atomists" who asserted that the physical world contains indivisible entities and accepted the deviations from Aristotelian orthodoxy that such an assertion entailed.[3] Walter Burley and the other exponents of the succession-of-forms theory, on the other hand, were not such atomists. While attempting to explain alteration in terms of indivisible degrees of quality, they simultaneously aimed at saving the continuity of motion.

In this chapter I explore some of the problems that emerged in these fourteenth-century efforts to reconcile continuity of motion with indivisible degrees. I will devote most of the chapter to examining selected texts from the works of Walter Burley and of Richard Kilvington insofar as these texts are directed to issues regarding indivisibles and the continuity of motion. Burley's concerns clearly arise from the succession-of-forms theory. His best solutions make use of the generally applicable tools of logic rather than deriving specifically from physics or mathematics. Kilvington, in the texts I will be using, never explicitly states his views concerning theories of alteration—never, for example, supporting either the addition theory or the succession theory. Nevertheless, his work fits well with Burley's and casts light on it because of the similar logical tools Kilvington employed. In addition to directing attention to some fourteenth-century problems of continuous motion and indivisible degrees in the realm of alteration, I hope in

2. Sylla 1973, pp. 230–31, 233–38. For Godfrey of Fontaines, see Sylla forthcoming a.

3. See Murdoch 1974, pp. 11–32. Also Murdoch and Synan 1966, pp. 212–35.

this way to provide a representative case study of fourteenth-century logic in action in the service of natural philosophy.

2. Indivisibles and Aristotelian Continuity

Before turning to the works of Burley and Kilvington, I should make clear a difference between Aristotelian and modern views. When Aristotle's definition of continuity is adhered to, it is impossible to produce a continuum directly from indivisibles. As has been shown in earlier chapters of this volume, Aristotle defined continuity in terms of a nested set of conditions. Entities of a certain sort might have between them other entities of the same sort or of a different sort. If two given entities had no entities of the same sort between them, Aristotle said, they were called "successive"; thus, for instance, houses standing in a row or integers used in counting might be called successive. If successive entities touched each other, they were called "contiguous"; thus, for instance, the air over a lake is contiguous to the water, or muscles are contiguous to bone in the body. If successive contiguous entities had limits that coincided, he said, the entities were called "continuous" and, indeed, "united" or "one"; thus, for instance, one-half of a stick or of a body of water is continuous with, or united to, or one with, the other half.[4]

Two comments might be made about these definitions from a modern point of view. First of all, it should be clear that Aristotle's definition of continuity is physical rather than mathematical. Physical entities such as air and water or bone and muscle can be contiguous without being continuous according to Aristotle's definitions. It is questionable, however, as Averroës very nicely pointed out, whether there can be any difference between continuity and contiguity with respect to mathematical entities, since in mathematics there is no difference of substance that might allow identity of position without physical identity.[5] Thus, from a

4. For these Aristotelian classifications, see *Physics* V 3.
5. See Burley 1501, f. 160ra, "Notanda sunt hic duo secundum Commentatorem. Primo quod contiguatio est duplex, scilicet contiguatio naturalis et contiguatio mathematica. In contiguatione naturali duo ultima remanent duo demonstrata, sed in contiguatione mathematica duo ultima revertuntur in unum. Unde breviter in mathematica duo contigua non habent duo ultima sed unum ultimum.

modern or mathematical point of view, we might consider that Burley has demonstrated mathematical continuity when, from his point of view, he has only argued for contiguity.

A second comment concerns Aristotle's nested criteria for continuity insofar as these might have any applicability to the relations of indivisibles. In Aristotle's view, bodies approach nearer to continuity as they are first successive and then contiguous before they finally become continuous. When one considers the infinitely numerous points of a line in light of these criteria, it is notable that the points not only do not fit the last criterion for continuity but also fail to meet the criteria of contiguity or even of successiveness. The proponents of the succession-of-forms theory assumed that the degrees of quality were extensionless and therefore indivisible, that they were infinite in number, and that they were "mediate,"—i.e., that between any two degrees there were other degrees. So the relation of indivisible degrees to one another was analogous to the relation of points on a line to one another. On the basis of Aristotle's definitions, then, most medieval scholars concluded that entities such as points or indivisible degrees cannot be continuous with each other, since they have no limits or extremes that could possibly touch or become one as required by the definition of continuity.[6] Nevertheless, as modern mathematics represents a line as an infinite set of mediate points, so, from a modern point of view, one might conclude that Burley's infinitely many mediate indivisible degrees form a continuum even when he believes they do not.[7]

Et sic in mathematicis contingua sunt idem quod continua." There is also much else of interest in nearby passages. See also ibid., f. 161rb.

6. See Aristotle, *Physics* VI 1, 231a24–29: "nothing that is continuous can be composed of indivisibles: e.g., a line cannot be composed of points, the line being continuous and the point indivisible. For the extremities of two points can neither be *one* (since of an indivisible there can be no extremity as distinct from some other part) nor *together* (since that which has no parts can have no extremity, the extremity and the thing of which it is the extremity being distinct)." Cf. Burley 1501, f. 172va.

7. As I understand it, modern mathematics uses infinite sets of mediate indivisibles (e.g., points) to represent continua, but these sets of indivisibles must also meet stronger criteria, since mediateness or density alone is recognized as an insufficient condition for continuity.

3. Walter Burley on Continuity and Indivisibles in Alteration

With these comments in mind, then, let me turn to Walter Burley's efforts to reconcile continuity of motion with indivisible degrees. Because of Aristotle's definition of continuity, Burley did not directly assert that indivisibles could be continuous with each other. He did assert, Aristotle to the contrary notwithstanding, that continuous motion could occur over discontinuous magnitudes:

> But a doubt is raised, because the Philosopher in the Sixth Book of this work says that motion takes its continuity from the magnitude over which the motion occurs, therefore motion cannot be continuous unless the magnitude is continuous. I say that we can understand two things by "continuous," namely either that of which the parts are united at a common terminus (and speaking this way of continuity it is not true that motion takes its continuity from magnitude); or in another way we can understand by "continuous" that which is infinitely divisible . . . and in this [second] way it is true that motion takes its continuity from magnitude, because motion is infinitely divisible because the magnitude over which the motion occurs is infinitely divisible. . . .[8]

Thus, according to Burley, for motion to be continuous in the sense of being infinitely divisible, the magnitude over which it occurs must be similarly divisible,[9] but motion can be continuous

---

8. Burley 1501, f. 160vb, "Sed dubitatur quia Philosophus sexto huius dicit quod motus capit continuitatem a magnitudine super quam est motus, ergo motus non potest esse continuus nisi magnitudo sit continua. Dico quod per continuum possumus duo intelligere, scilicet vel illud cuius partes copulantur ad terminum communem et isto modo loquendo de continuitatem non est verum quod motus capiat continuitatem a magnitudine. Alio modo per continuum possumus intelligere illud quod est divisibile in infinitum per continuitatem divisibilem in infinitum et isto modo est verum quod motus capit continuitatem a magnitudine, quia motus est divisibilis in infinitum propter hoc quia magnitudo super quam est motus est divisibilis in infinitum. Unde concedo quod ad continuitatem motus requiritur continuitas magnitudinis, hoc est divisibilitas magnitudinis in infinitum, et talem continuitatem habet illud quod est unum unitate contiguationis tantum." Cf. ibid., ff. 136va, 173va.

9. In the case of alteration, this infinitely divisible magnitude would be the "latitude of degrees." See Sylla 1973, pp. 226–28, 233–38; see also Burley 1501, f. 163va.

in terms of the unification of its parts when the magnitude over which it occurs is not continuous. Motion, for instance, through air into water can be continuous in Aristotle's sense, according to Burley, even though the air and water are themselves only contiguous.

The problem of alteration was, however, even more difficult for the succession-of-forms theorists, because in alteration there were not even contiguous magnitudes to be traversed, but as I have said, infinitely many mediate indivisible degrees. One context in which Burley attempted to preserve continuous or at least contiguous alteration when infinitely many mediate indivisible degrees were acquired was in his commentary on Aristotle's *Physics*. Aristotle had argued that of all motions only the uniform circular motion of the heavens can be eternal. If any motion is to be eternal, he argued, it must be continuous. But motion is continuous only if the magnitude over which it occurs is continuous. Since an unlimited continuous magnitude over which motion occurs is available only in circular motion, only circular motion can be eternal. Alteration cannot be eternal because continued alteration must eventually or occasionally reverse direction. There is, for instance, a maximum possible degree of heat or of cold, so if continued motion with respect to temperature were to be possible, it would have to involve heating for a while, followed by cooling and then reheating, and so forth. But such reversals would, Aristotle argued, render the motion discontinuous.[10]

In commenting on such an argument, Burley concedes that reversed alterations cannot be continuous, but he maintains that they can be contiguous, something that, as I have commented above, might be considered equivalent from a mathematical point of view. He says:

. . . when it is said that contrary motions can be contiguous (*habiti*),[11] so that nothing is between them, this may be conceded. And when it

10. *Physics* VIII 7–8.
11. The terms which Burley uses in this context are *habitus* and *sese* or *sesse*. He takes the term *sese* from Averroës' commentary on the *Physics*. In his own translation Burley had *habitus* where Averroës (in Latin translation) had *sese*. Burley understands *sese* and *habitus* to have meanings similar to "contiguous," implying that the things referred to are successive and touching, but implying further that

is said that then they have the same extreme, I say that this is not true—indeed, they have different extremes. And when it is asked whether these are measured by the same instant or by different instants, I say that they are measured by the same instant. And when it is said that then the extremes of contraries will be in the same thing together (*simul*) at the same instant, I say that the extremes of contraries of which one is intrinsic to one motion and the other is extrinsic to the other, can well be together in the same subject at the same instant, but the extremes of contraries which are intrinsic to them cannot be together at the same instant.

For the understanding of this it should be known that no extreme is intrinsic to motion except the extreme at the end of motion (*ex parte post*) or some changed state (*mutatum esse*) acquired by this motion. Thus, no beginning of motion beginning from rest is intrinsic to that motion. But [by definition] a changed state joining the parts of motion to each other is intrinsic to either part. And then I say that if, when heating is ended, cooling should immediately begin, the extreme of heating and the beginning of cooling are measured by the same instant. And this is possible because the extreme of heating is intrinsic to heating and the beginning of cooling is extrinsic to cooling. Therefore, these can be in the same [thing] at the same instant.[12]

Burley's argument in this passage is that if a body is heated and then cooled, the motions of heating and of cooling can be temporally immediate to each other. This can happen, he believes, because the intrinsic last instant of heating can be the extrinsic beginning limit of the time of cooling.

It should be noted that Burley assumes without proof in this passage of his *Physics* commentary that the alteration is continuous except at the instant of reversal.[13] In fact, the problem of

---

what is *sese* comes after. In addition, whereas "contiguous" applies only to magnitudes in space, *sese* applies to other sorts of magnitudes, such as motion and time. See Burley 1501, ff. 161ra–b, 164va.

12. See appendix B at the end of this volume.

13. Following Averroës, Burley distinguished between the matter of motion and the form of motion, where "matter" refers to what is gained and "form" refers to the transmutation by which it is gained. (Burley 1501, f. 162ra.) Ockham and those who followed him in trying to minimize the number of entities supposed to exist reduced motion to the first of these senses, arguing that in the outside world there was only the movable object and what it successively acquired, with no further transmutation added. In Burley's succession-of-forms theory, however, motion in the first sense was not continuous, so he was forced to use the second sense to preserve continuity of motion. See Burley 1496, ff. 14rb–va. See also Sylla 1973, pp. 237–38; 279–81.

the continuity of alteration rarely occurs in his work in direct form, perhaps because to a faithful Aristotelian it is a foregone conclusion that most motions are continuous. What Burley needs to argue for, on the other hand, are the infinitely numerous mediate indivisible degrees of the succession-of-forms theory; or more exactly, he needs to argue that these are consistent with continuous alteration. If alteration is continuous, then the parts of such alteration must be in immediate succession. But if the parts of motion are immediate, will it not follow that the degrees acquired by these parts of motion are also immediate and not mediate?

Burley examines this problem both in his *Tractatus primus* (a work which arose out of his attempt to explain the physics of the Eucharist in his commentary on the *Sentences*) and in his *Tractatus secundus*. Suppose that a hot body is cooled. As it is changed from being hot to being cold, there will be a first instant, A, at which it is cold. (This is in accordance with the Aristotelian view that every permanent condition or form has a first instant of existence.) Suppose, then, that at precisely that first instant of the body's being cold, something begins to heat it. What can be said about the status of the body immediately after it has begun to be reheated? If it remains cold for a period of time, there will be a degree of cold that is formally the same distance from maximum heat as is some degree of heat—which, Burley claims, implies what he wants to prove: that heat and cold are of the same species of quality. If, however, A is the last instant of the body's being cold, what can be said of the degrees of heat that are induced immediately thereafter? If the body is hot, it must have some degree of heat. Every possible degree of heat is indivisible and has a first instant of existence. If, then, the body has some degree of heat, that degree, whatever it may be, will have a first instant of existence, and the body will therefore have a first instant of being hot. But the body also has a last instant of being cold, namely the instant at which it was first cold and at which the reheating agent was applied; so if there is also a first instant of being hot, instants will be immediate to each other.[14]

14. See appendix C at the end of this volume, ff. 209rb–210ra.

In his *Tractatus primus* Burley accepts this argument as valid but rejects the conclusion as inconsistent with the nature of indivisible degrees, arguing that there must be something wrong with one of the assumptions of the case—namely, that cold constitutes a new permanent form. He concludes that heat and cold are not two species of quality but one, and he postulates a latitude of heat and cold having maximum heat at one end and maximum cold at the other, with a middle degree neither hot nor cold but temperate.[15] Then there will be no minimum degree of cold and no first instant of being cold, and so the case falls apart. In his *Tractatus secundus* Burley solves the problem by referring to the motion (alteration) as well as to the degrees acquired.[16] These are not very good arguments on Burley's part, although perhaps he should be excused for some of their defects. The *Tractatus primus* and *secundus* are very clearly the product of live debate and contain many ad hominem arguments; Burley even bases many of his proofs on parts of his opponents' theories that he himself does not accept.[17]

Of greater interest to me here are contexts in which Burley rejects the conclusion of this sort of argument but finds the fault elsewhere than in the argument's assumptions. In these other contexts Burley uses the tools of medieval logic to block inferences of this sort: If immediately after instant A the body has some degree of heat, and if every such degree has a first instant of existence, then the body will have a first instant of being hot. He does this by arguing that in a proposition such as "Immediately after instant A the body has some degree of heat," the term "some degree of heat" has merely confused supposition because it follows the syncategorematic word "immediately." In such a case one cannot infer that any assignable degree of heat will occur immediately after A, even though there is no interval of time such that it will pass before a degree of heat is acquired.[18] Similar

15. His conclusion is quoted in Sylla 1973, p. 236, n. 36.
16. Sylla 1973, pp. 279–81.
17. A sense of the disputational nature of the *Tractatus primus* may be obtained from the excerpts in appendix C below.
18. Burley does not apply this argument in the case of reheating discussed just above, because there it is assumed that heat (and cold) is a separate species of quality for which, according to Aristotle, there must be a first instant of existence. He does use a similar argument for alteration within a single species of quality—

answers are given by many medieval authors to similar problems. The special advantage of these answers lies in the fact that they preserve the sense of "immediately" by asserting that there is no finite interval such that it will pass before the occurrence of an indivisible, while taking account of the fact that the indivisibles in continua are mediate or dense—i.e., that between any two indivisibles there are infinitely many more.

But even if such an answer provides a good resolution of the problem, it does not, at least at first glance, explain the invalidity of the opponent's inference to the conclusion that there will be a first instant of being hot. Perhaps the specious validity of the opponent's argument can be attributed to a difference between finite and infinite sets. If the conditions of the case remained otherwise the same and there were not infinitely many but, say, only three possible degrees of heat, then one could justifiably infer that (since whichever of the three degrees of heat the body has will have a first instant of existence), the body itself will have a first instant of being hot. The plausibility of the opponent's position depends on thinking in terms of a finite set of degrees. When, however, the set of possible degrees of heat is infinite, as Burley assumes it is, the argument becomes invalid. One cannot infer from the fact that each of the infinitely many degrees of quality has a first instant of existence that the body will have a first instant of being hot. But why not? A further cause of perplexity arises from the fact that the acceptable exposition of the proposition "Immediately after instant A the body will have some degree of heat" seems intuitively weaker than the original proposition. Does the exposition really capture the sense of the original? Is no stronger exposition possible?

Before I try to answer those questions, I want to spell out in greater detail the position that gives rise to them. Burley takes this position also regarding a case involving only instants rather than the degrees of quality gained in alteration: the issues are the same, but the analysis is simpler. Suppose that A is the present instant. What might one say about the instants in the time period immediately after A? An opponent might argue:

---

e.g., for alteration from diminished (remiss) heat to higher degrees of heat. Cf. Sylla 1973, p. 280.

Between the being and the nonbeing of instant *A* there is no intermediate. But the nonbeing of *A* and the being of an instant other than *A* are the same, interchangeably, because this follows logically: *A* is not; therefore an instant other than *A* is, and vice versa. Therefore between the being of *A* and the being of an instant other than *A* there is no intermediate. Therefore after *A* immediately there will be another instant. Therefore in time instants are immediate.[19]

Burley rejects this argument and explains that when one says, "*A* is, and immediately after *A* there will be another instant" the term "immediately" is a syncategorematic word which gives the term "another instant" following it merely confused supposition. In other words, "immediately" is the sort of word that affects the reference of other terms in a proposition, and in this case it makes the term "another instant" refer to many instants in such a way that no one of them can be picked out. In this interpretation, Burley says, the proposition is true and equivalent to "*A* is, and before every completed interval (*medium completum*) another instant will be." One cannot, however, infer from this that "Some other [given] instant will be without an interval," and so the argument does not prove that instants are immediate.[20]

4. An Analysis of Burley's Position

How does this result follow from the character of the reference assigned to "another instant," its merely confused supposition? In general, medieval authors do not make it entirely clear what one can do with terms having merely confused supposition. They say what one *cannot* do, and they deal with special cases. I believe, however, that many if not all cases of terms labeled as having merely confused supposition can be treated in the following way. Terms that have merely confused supposition often appear in propositions not immediately after but at some distance from the syncategorematic word that is described as bringing about their merely confused supposition. Thus, for instance, in the universal affirmative proposition "Every man is an animal," the predicate term "animal" has merely confused supposition, while the

19. See appendix D at the end of this volume, f. 176ra.
20. See appendix D, f. 177ra.

subject term "man" has distributive confused supposition, and
the supposition of these terms is determined by their location
relative to the syncategorematic word "every." One may perform
a logical descent under a term with distributive confused supposition to a conjunction of singular propositions. For example, from
"Every man is an animal" one may descend under its subject term
to the conjunction "This man is an animal, and that man is an
animal, and that other man is an animal . . . ," indicating every
existing man individually.[21] In making this descent we have made
no descent under the predicate term of the original proposition,
but the supposition of "animal" in the new singular proposition is
no longer merely confused but determinate. One can go further,
then, in expounding the proposition by descending to a disjunction of the individuals referred to by the predicate term of each of
the resultant singular propositions: "This man is this animal or
that animal, etc., and that man is this animal or that animal, etc.,
and that other man is this animal or that animal, etc., . . ." and so
on.[22] I suggest, then, that the salient logical characteristic of a
term with merely confused supposition is that no logical descent
can be made under it as it stands but that after a descent has been
made under another (often a previously occurring) term, the supposition of the previously merely confused term is changed and a
descent becomes possible under its occurrences in the propositions resultant from the initial descent.

If I am right in this observation, it can be used to help clarify
such cases as that described by the proposition "Immediately after A there will be another instant." A plausible restatement of
this proposition is "Before any interval after A is completed there
will be another instant." Here "instant" has merely confused supposition, and no logical descent is possible under it unless a descent has previously been made under the term "interval" occurring earlier in the proposition. Descending under "interval," one
has "before the five-minute interval after A is completed there

21. For one exposition of the permissible descents, see Burley 1955, pp. 20–27.
22. The medieval sources do not say that one can descend under a term with
merely confused supposition by a two-step procedure such as the one I have
described. They do, however, explain the first descent under a term with a distributive confused supposition, and there are rules of descent that apply to the
propositions produced in that way. Cf. Burley 1955, p. 20.

will be another instant, . . . before the four-minute interval after A is completed there will be another instant, . . . before the one-second interval after A is completed there will be another instant, . . ." and so on infinitely for every completed interval after A. And on that basis it is possible to descend under the now-determinate occurrences of "instant" in each of the infinitely many resultant propositions: "before the five-minute interval after A is completed there will be . . . the instant four minutes after A, or . . . the instant three minutes after A, etc., . . . and before the four-minute interval after A is completed there will be . . . the instant three minutes after A, or . . . the instant two minutes after A, etc., . . . and before the one-second interval after A is completed there will be . . . the instant one-half second after A, or . . . the instant one-fourth second after A, etc.," and so on infinitely.[23]

It is clear from this two-stage descent that for different sets of intervals chosen in the first descent, correspondingly different sets of instants correspond to the truth of the propositions resulting from the second descent—which helps to show why the second descent could not be made unless the first descent had already been made. If we put it another way, there is no instant after A such that it occurs before the completion of all intervals after A, or there is no instant immediately after instant A. It is clear, further, that in the standard interpretation of merely confused supposition, one is not committed to saying anything about the set of all the instants after A taken collectively but is limited to referring to them individually. In doing so one learns something about the relations of these instants to one another and to the instant A, but nothing about the relation to A of the whole set of instants after A.

Modern mathematics counts infinite sets by putting them into one-to-one correspondence with other infinite sets. Medieval natural philosophers made similar uses of one-to-one correspondences of infinite collections when they supposed, for instance, that if Socrates could count one unit at some instant within each proportional part of an hour (i.e., if he could count one unit in

23. In this descent, obviously, the number of disjuncts within each conjunct as well as the number of conjuncts is infinite; only a selection of each sort of element can be displayed.

243

the first half-hour, a second unit in the next quarter-hour, a third unit in the next eighth, etc.), then by the end of the hour he could have counted an infinite number of units. But despite their ability to put infinite sets into one-to-one correspondence with each other, many medieval philosophers in effect considered all the points of a line or all the instants of a temporal interval or even all the rational numbers as if they were unspecifiable, even when from a modern point of view the set they had in mind was countable—saying, for instance, that there is no such thing as all the instants in a temporal interval or all the integers—one cannot speak of all of them because there is no limit to them.

In trying to construct continuity from indivisibles, especially given Aristotle's definitions, it would be natural to try to define immediacy of sets of indivisibles. If instants can make up continuous time, then it should be possible to show that the set of instants in the first half of an interval is immediate to the set of instants in the second half of the interval. If the first half of an interval is considered as ending at the middle instant of the interval, can it be shown that this middle instant is immediate to the infinite set of instants that comes after it? How could such immediacy be defined, given that no instant in the set of instants after the middle instant is immediate to the middle instant?

I believe that when Burley relies upon the logical concept of merely confused supposition for the solution of the problem of invisibles and continuity, he in effect renounces the possibility of talking collectively about the set of all the indivisibles. Instead of asserting that one can consider all the instants after instant A and show that this set of instants is immediate to A, Burley says merely that if one chooses any completed interval after A, then it is always possible to find an instant that has occurred before the end of that interval. I will call this resolution of the problem a case-by-case or no-infinite-set resolution. Burley's reliance on a no-infinite-set resolution may explain why his exposition of "immediately" appears weak. But a stronger exposition, admitting the possibility of referring to all the instants of an interval otherwise than in merely confused supposition, might have had other, perhaps unacceptable, results, as I will attempt to explain in my discussion of Kilvington below.

5. Burley on Whole Sets of Degrees

It is interesting that in his *Tractatus primus,* where Burley accepted the inference to a first instant of being hot, which he rejected elsewhere, he also attempted to talk about whole sets of degrees at once, whereas his teacher Thomas Wylton used the no-infinite-set approach implicit in Burley's use elsewhere of merely confused supposition. In the first conclusion of the *Tractatus primus,* Burley stated that a quality by its own power could produce a substantial form.[24] According to the usual medieval theory, when fire heats water, eventually turning it into fire, the heat of the fire first induces greater and greater degrees of heat into the water. Water, it is understood, is naturally cold, but it can be heated and qualified by any degree of heat short of the maximum, the degree of fire itself. Therefore, as the heat of the fire acts on the water, it gives it ever-increasing degrees of heat up to but not including the maximum degree. At the end of the action, the maximum degree of heat is introduced, and simultaneously the water must be destroyed and fire generated. According to the usual theory the heat of the fire causes all the heating of the water up to but not including the maximum degree, but it is the substantial form of fire which finally destroys the water, generating fire from it. That this must be so was supported by the basic principle that a cause must be greater than, or as great as, its effect.

What Burley argues, by contrast, is that if the heat of the fire can produce all the heat in the water up to the maximum degree, then it can produce that degree, too. In the usual picture of alteration, at the last instant of alteration the maximum heat and the substantial form of fire first exist. But when they already exist, Burley argues, then there is no need for them still to be, nor can they be, in process of generation. Thus all the work of producing the maximum degree and substantial form must be done in the interval *before* the final instant. But the heat of the fire can do

24. *Tractatus primus,* MS Vat. lat. 817, f. 203ra. "Qualitas in virtute propria potest producere formam substantialem." My references to the *Tractatus primus* will all be to this manuscript.

everything that is done during that interval. Therefore the heat alone can produce what first appears at that final instant, and the help of the substantial form of fire is not required.[25] Obviously, this argument brings in alteration and causality and various other considerations besides the degrees of heat induced into the water. Nevertheless, it seems to arrive at the conclusion that if something can produce all the degrees of heat short of maximum heat, then it can produce the maximum degree also.[26]

Here Burley's teacher Thomas Wylton raised an objection that seems to involve something closely related to the analysis envisaged by Burley for the case of reversed alteration. Wylton argued that the heat of the fire cannot produce anything necessitating the production of the substantial form of fire, because any accidental form or disposition to fire which it produces before the induction of the substantial form of fire is produced at some instant. Since there must be an interval between the instant when that accidental form is induced and the instant when the substantial form is induced, no two instants being immediate, the former cannot necessitate the latter.[27] Thus Wylton argues that when a no-set approach is used, Burley's conclusion does not follow.

25. Ibid., f. 208rb: "Et dixi quod in illo instanti ultimo temporis mensurantis totam transmutationem elementorum adinvicem non requiritur agens pro tunc inducens formam quia pro tunc forma est inducta. Et pro tunc non requiritur inducens. Inductum enim non oportet inducere sicut non oportet agere acta, sed sufficit quod fuit inducens in toto tempore praecedenti . . ."

26. See ibid., f. 203va, ". . . si aliquid possit ⟨esse⟩ in totam alterationem praecedentem et non in terminum, cum Deus possit suspendere actionem cuiuslibet agentis circa illam materiam, tunc, hoc posito (quod Deus suspendat actionem cuiuslibet alterius agentis), sequitur quod terminus alterationis non inducetur in materia, quia non ab alterante nec ab aliquo alio agente, quia actio cuiuslibet alterius agentis circa istam materiam suspenditur, et ita sequeretur quod calor alterans efficeret alterationem infinitam, quia non terminatam, quod est impossibile, tum quia alterationem repugnat infinitas (sexto Phisicorum in fine) tum quia nulla forma materialis potest in motum infinitum."

27. Ibid., f. 203rb, "Huic rationi respondet Reverendus magister noster dominus Cancellarius Londonensis quod calor in virtute propria non potest in aliquam dispositionem necessitatem ad formam substantialem ignis, quia nulla dispositio praecedens dispositionem formae ignis necessitat ad formam ignis, quod patet quia quaecumque dispositio inducitur ante inductionem formae ignis inducitur in aliquo instanti praecedenti instans in quo inducatur forma ignis et inter illa duo instantia est tempus medium in quo tempore medio non est materia sub forma ignis. Et ideo nulla dispositio praecedens necessitat ad formam ignis ex quo illa inducta non statim inducitur forma ignis. Immo per tempus medium est materia sub privatione formae ignis."

Burley replies by conceding that no heat induced before the induction of the fire necessitates the induction of fire. He says, however, that his argument does not require this, but rather only that the heat be able to produce the whole alteration (*totam alterationem*) preceding the induction of the substantial form.[28] This answer is typical of Burley's so-called realist tendencies—of his tendency to treat the motion of alteration as an effect in addition to the degrees of heat produced.[29] It seems to me that Burley's reference to the alteration in this case is not sufficiently justified. Nevertheless, one can see that there are strong reasons for trying to talk in such a case about all of the alteration or collectively about all the degrees of heat induced, not restricting oneself to the individual degrees. Burley's reference to the alteration substitutes, I think, for talk of whole sets of degrees.

In sum, because of his reliance on Aristotle's definitions of continuity, Burley did not think that the infinite mediate indivisible degrees acquired in alteration or the infinite mediate instants in time formed a continuum. He did, however, argue that the motion of alteration by which such indivisible degrees were acquired could be continuous, and he paid particular attention to reversed alterations, arguing that motions of cooling and heating could be immediate to each other. Accepting the immediacy of alterations, Burley had then to show that immediate alterations did not imply immediate indivisible degrees. He accomplished this using the concept of merely confused supposition. I have tried to argue that the use of merely confused supposition has the effect of substituting a case-by-case or no-set approach for talk about whole sets of indivisible degrees. Where talk about whole sets of degrees might otherwise have been required, Burley sometimes brings in an additional reference to the motion of alteration instead.

---

28. Ibid., f. 203rb–va, "Bene tamen verum est et necessarium illud quod dicit magister meus quod non est aliquis calor inductus ante inductionem formae ignis necessitans ad formam ignis nec super hoc fundatur ratio. Sed totum fundamentum istius rationis consistit in hoc quod calor in virtute propria potest in totam alterationem praecedentem formam substantialem ignis."
29. See Sylla 1973, appendix I.

6. Richard Kilvington's *Sophismata*

I based my discussion of Burley's ideas mainly on texts taken from his commentary on Aristotle's *Physics* and from his *Tractatus primus*, a work containing the record of a debate that arose out of Burley's lectures on Peter Lombard's *Sentences*. I want now to turn to a work by Richard Kilvington which comes from yet a third intellectual context, namely from the logical disputations *de sophismatibus* in which undergraduates at Oxford had to participate before they could become bachelors of arts.[30] A medieval sophisma is a puzzling proposition—it may be true but appear false, or be false but appear true, or it may have both a plausible proof and a plausible disproof. The subject matter of such a proposition or the proof or disproof may be taken from many different disciplines. Most of Kilvington's sophismata appear to have physical subjects—for example, bodies becoming whiter or traversing distances—but his techniques of analysis and proof and disproof are those developed in medieval logic.

While Kilvington's major interests in his *Sophismata* might be characterized from many different points of view, it would not be wholly wide of the mark to say that the main lesson of the first large segment of the work concerns the proper use and results of the no-infinite-set approach to dealing with infinite collections. The first four sophismata, for example, involve the comparison of infinite sets of mediate degrees of whiteness starting from zero degree as an extrinsic limit.

The first two sophismata—namely, "Socrates is whiter than Plato begins to be white" (*Socrates est albior quam Plato incipit esse albus*) and "Socrates is infinitely whiter than Plato begins to be white" (*Socrates est in infinitum albior quam Plato incipit esse·albus*)—are both based on a hypothetical case in which Socrates has the maximum degree of whiteness, while Plato is not white at all at the present instant but now begins to be white, acquiring degrees

---

30. See Sylla forthcoming b. I have based my study of Kilvington's *Sophismata* on the text and translation of that work by Norman and Barbara Kretzmann (forthcoming). I am grateful to them for providing me with a copy of their edition.

of whiteness as time goes on.[31] The difficulty involved in these two sophismata is that as Plato begins to be white, he initially takes on degrees of whiteness less than any given degree. Does it not therefore follow that Socrates' whiteness, which is finite in degree, will have an infinite ratio to the whiteness with which Plato first begins to be white? And if Plato is white, while Socrates is infinitely whiter, does it not follow that Socrates is infinitely white? In his solution of these sophismata Kilvington grants both propositions and argues that the proposition "Socrates is infinitely whiter than Plato begins to be white" is equivalent to the conjunction "Socrates is white, and Plato will without interval be white, and there will be no whiteness or degree of whiteness without interval in Plato by means of which the whiteness in Plato will without interval be compared to the whiteness in Socrates." From this conjunction it does not follow that Socrates is infinitely white, and so the difficulty is resolved.

The similarity of this solution to Burley's solution of the problem of reversed alteration should be clear. In each case the key point of the solution is the denial that any given degree of quality is immediately acquired. In Kilvington's comparisons, if one could treat all the acquired degrees of whiteness as a single set, one might then take the lower limit of that set and compare Socrates' whiteness to that limit; but this is precisely what Kilvington does not do.

In subsequent sophismata, Kilvington similarly never treats all of a set of infinitely many degrees at once except by means of a singular term with confused supposition. The fifth sophisma sentence is "Socrates will begin to be as white as he himself will be white," which is referred to a hypothetical case in which the whiteness in Socrates increases throughout all of a long life, a life which, as it is later assumed, is terminated not by a last instant of being but rather by a first instant of nonbeing.[32] In interpreting

31. For a discussion and English translation of the first sophisma, see Kretzmann 1977.
32. "Sophisma 5. Socrates incipiet esse ita albus sicut ipsemet erit albus. Posito quod albedo tota in Socrate intendatur per totam vitam Socratis, et vivat Socrates diu post hoc instans. . . . Et ponatur quod A sit primum instans non esse Socratis."

the sophisma sentence, Kilvington assumes that the expression "as he himself will be white" has confused supposition because of the syncategorematic word "as," which he takes as meaning not only that Socrates must be as white as some degree he will have but, more strongly, that he must be as white as all the degrees he will have.[33] He further interprets "Socrates will be as white as he himself will be white" as equivalent to "At some instant Socrates will be as white as he himself will be white." Then the problem is that at no given instant will Socrates be as white as he will be white because, given any instant of his existence, the whiteness he has at that instant will be less than a whiteness he will have later; for he will live past that instant and become whiter for some time, however short, because there is no intrinsic last instant of his existence but only an extrinsic first instant of his nonexistence. Kilvington's solution of the sophisma, therefore, is to deny that Socrates will begin to be as white as he himself will be white on the grounds that there is no instant at which he will begin to be so. Using the two-step explication of merely confused supposition proposed earlier in this chapter, we may say that since the logical descent to specific degrees of whiteness under the clause "Socrates will begin to be (as) white" is made before the descent to degrees of whiteness under the clause "as he himself will be white," a higher degree of whiteness can always be chosen in the second case.

Thus in these sophismata Kilvington takes the same approach that Burley often takes. He deals with infinitely many degrees of form, but he compares them individually and does not refer to all of a set of infinitely many degrees at once except by a term with merely confused supposition. On the whole I think this tech-

---

33. A way of explaining this with normal supposition theory can be found in Burley 1955. The type of supposition in Burley's theory that fits Kilvington's claims is not merely confused supposition but distributive confused supposition. When a term or expression has distributive confused supposition, according to Burley, descent to any one of the term's supposita is permissible (pp. 24–25). Kilvington himself says that this descent is allowed (in his discussion of sophisma 6). So for Socrates to be as white as he will be white, he would have to be as white as he was in this instant and as white as he was in that instant and as white as he was in a third instant and so on for any instant. Kilvington himself does not use the terms "merely confused supposition" and "distributive confused supposition" but speaks only of supposition being confused. For clarity, I have carried Burley's terminology over to Kilvington's work in my subsequent discussion.

nique provides successful resolutions of the problems Kilvington treats. Kilvington presses the technique farther than Burley does, however, and so reveals more of its consequences. In the remainder of this chapter I want to show that one such consequence is the disclosure of a lack of identity between properties of continua as normally understood and properties of infinitely many mediate indivisibles, when no set of these indivisibles is defined.

7. An Analysis of Kilvington's Sophisma 8

With this in mind, I will consider in some detail Kilvington's sophisma 8, the first in which a comparison of an extrinsically limited series with its limit is made.[34] According to the hypothesis of this sophisma, Plato and Socrates increase equally in whiteness for a period of time A, but Socrates exists at the last instant of the time period, whereas Plato is destroyed. Then Socrates lives on after the last instant of time A and increases further in whiteness. The sophisma sentence is "Socrates will be precisely as white as Plato will be white in any (aliquo) of these [proportional parts of time A]." In the proof of the sophisma sentence, the further increase of whiteness in Socrates is used as the basis of an argument that since Socrates is now less white than Plato will be white in any proportional part of time A, and since he will be whiter than Plato will be white in any proportional part of time A, it follows that he will also be precisely as white as Plato will be white in any proportional part. The instant of his being so will be the instant connecting the interval in which he is less white than Plato to the interval in which he is whiter.

Thus Kilvington interprets the sophisma sentence as meaning simply that there will be at least one instant at which Socrates will be precisely as white as Plato will be white in any proportional part. It does not concern him that Socrates will go on to become whiter, and the further increase in Socrates' whiteness is posited only to assure that Socrates' whiteness will exceed—and so ought also to equal—any whiteness in Plato.

So the question that remains is this: at the last instant of inter-

---

34. See appendix E at the end of this volume.

val A will Socrates be just as white as Plato will be white in any proportional part of A, or will he be whiter? Here, clearly, we have an infinite series of degrees of whiteness acquired by Plato of which there is no intrinsic maximum degree. And we have the degree of whiteness that Socrates has at the last instant of A, where this degree is the degree which Plato's series of degrees approaches as an extrinsic limit. In favor of the view that the degree Socrates has at the end of A is greater than the degree Plato has in any proportional part of A is the consideration that Socrates' whiteness is the extrinsic and not the intrinsic limit of the series of whitenesses Plato has. On the other side, however, is the consideration that there is no determinable amount by which Socrates' whiteness will be greater than Plato's.

Faced with these alternatives, Kilvington concludes that the sophisma sentence is false and that at the instant in question Socrates is not precisely as white as Plato is white in any proportional part of A but rather whiter. He denies that "By something will Socrates be whiter than Plato will be white in any of these" (where the term "something" has determinate supposition), although he concedes that "Socrates will be whiter by something than Plato will be white in any of these" (where the term "something" has merely confused supposition). And so he can go on to claim that "By nothing, however, will Socrates be whiter than Plato will be white in any of these."[35]

By now a set of propositions of this sort should look very familiar. As in the cases discussed earlier, a comparison is made with infinitely many degrees where these degrees are referred to by means of a term with merely confused supposition and so are taken individually rather than treated all together. When Socrates' whiteness is compared with Plato's degrees of whiteness individually, it is never the case that Socrates is precisely as white as Plato is ever white.

35. In paraphrasing the sophisma I have simplified somewhat by assuming that if Socrates is ever precisely as white as Plato in any proportional part of A, it will be at the last instant of A. Kilvington makes no such assumption but leaves it open as to when the instant will be which connects the interval during which Socrates is less white than Plato will be in any proportional part of A and the interval during which Socrates is whiter than Plato will be in any proportional part of A. One might imagine that the instant will be not the last instant of A but rather the last instant of Plato's existence. But Plato's existence is extrinsically limited and so has no last instant.

Kilvington could also argue in this case that the difference between Socrates' whiteness at the end of A and some degree of whiteness acquired by Plato before the end of A is less than any given finite amount. This result appears as his assertion, "By nothing . . . will Socrates be whiter than Plato will be white in any of these." But it is notable that Kilvington nevertheless denies the sophisma sentence. This is a result different from what would be obtained in the case of continua as ordinarily conceived, where two continua that differ by no finite amount are considered equal.

Thus Kilvington's early sophismata are devoted to extrinsically limited dense sets of degrees and the problems these raise—particularly problems of comparison. Repeatedly in the course of his discussions Kilvington uses arguments similar in form to the argument that Socrates' whiteness will be less than Plato's whiteness for a period of time and Socrates' whiteness will be greater than Plato's whiteness for a period of time, and so there must be some instant or period of time when Socrates' whiteness is equal to Plato's. Such an argument ought to be valid if the degrees of whiteness acquired by Socrates form a continuum. (The argument may be construed as an application of the modern intermediate value theorem.) Over and over, however, Kilvington finds reasons why the conclusion of such an argument is to be rejected. In a case like that of sophisma 8 just discussed, Kilvington might argue, for instance, that the last instant of interval A is the first instant at which Socrates is whiter than Plato will be white in any proportional part of A, and so the interval when Socrates is less white than Plato will be white is connected to the interval when Socrates is whiter than Plato will be white, not by an instant at which Socrates is equally white as Plato ever is, but rather by an instant at which Socrates is whiter. There could not also be an instant at which Socrates equaled the whitenesses Plato has had, because if there were such an instant, it would be immediate to the already mentioned instant, which is impossible.[36]

---

36. In a later series of sophismata (33. "Socrates movebitur velocius quam Socrates nunc movetur"; 34. "Plato potest moveri uniformiter per aliquod tempus et aequevelociter sicut nunc movetur Socrates"), Kilvington imagines a situation in which he claims Socrates moves with an instantaneous velocity with which no body could move uniformly: "between a uniform motion by which something can move uniformly slower than Socrates now moves and a uniform motion by which

8. Kilvington's Major Interests in Continuity and Indivisibles

From these examples, I think I can summarize what seem to be Kilvington's major interests concerning continuity and indivisibles. Kilvington is extremely interested in the problems raised by sets that have extrinsic limits, such as the degrees of whiteness associated with Plato's beginning to be white. In analyzing such cases he, like Burley, invariably relies on the standard Aristotelian understanding of the relations of indivisibles to continuity. There is, for instance, absolutely no doubt that a continuum is divided into two by only one indivisible. When he compares an extrinsic limit to the degrees that converge to that limit, Kilvington invariably says that the limit is greater or smaller (as the case may require) than the degrees approaching the limit. Thus, if he imagines a continuum of degrees divided at a degree with that degree belonging to the right-hand side, he says that the degrees approaching the division from the left are less than the minimum degree on the right. So, in sophisma 8, at the last instant of *A* Socrates is whiter than Plato is white in any proportional part of *A*. This seems reasonable. Furthermore, all the commonly accepted medieval distinctions between senses of "begin" and "cease" and between intrinsic and extrinsic limits require that the differences involved here not be blurred; if Kilvington did not maintain a difference here, the medieval theories of first and last instants would be rendered meaningless.[37]

Nevertheless, Kilvington's assertion that the whiteness Socrates has at the last instant of *A* is greater than the whiteness Plato has in any of the proportional parts of *A* leads to some results that may be difficult to accept. Kilvington must claim that Socrates cannot be white at a given instant with a degree of whiteness as white as those with which Plato will be white. By not equating a series of degrees with its limit, Kilvington has, therefore, created

---

something can move uniformly faster than Socrates now moves there is no intermediate uniform motion by which something can move uniformly and precisely as fast as Socrates now moves" (sophisma 34).

37. On first and last instants, see Wilson 1956, pp. 29–56.

intermediate values that appear to break up the continuity of the intervals they occur in. More importantly for the issue that has been my major concern in this chapter, this result is at odds with what would be expected for continua such as lines and so constitutes a reason for denying that the sets of infinitely many degrees imagined by Burley or Kilvington do constitute continua even when Aristotle's requirements for continua are relaxed. This result appears to be at odds with the modern arithmetization of the continuum according to which a line, for instance, can be considered as an infinite set of points.

Nevertheless, there seems to be good reason for denying, with Burley and Kilvington, an equivalence between infinite sets of indivisibles and continua. If indivisibles are admitted, then Kilvington seems justified in concluding that Socrates at the last instant of A has a degree of whiteness that Plato never had in any proportional part of A. In order to arithmetize the continuum, modern mathematics had, among other things, to deny that the addition or subtraction of an indivisible from a set of indivisibles made any difference.[38] In establishing his one-to-one correspondence of numbers and points on a line, Dedekind recognized that there was a difference such as that accepted by Kilvington but then simply erased it by fiat. Dedekind wrote:

> . . . we ascribe to the straight line completeness, absence of gaps, or continuity. In what, then, does this continuity consist? . . . for a long time I pondered over this in vain, but finally I found what I was seeking. This discovery will, perhaps, be differently estimated by different people; the majority may find its substance very commonplace. It consists of the following. In the preceding section attention was called to the fact that every point p of the straight line produces a separation of the same into two portions such that every point of one portion lies to the left of every point of the other. I find the essence of continuity in the converse, i.e. in the following principle: "If all points of the straight line fall into two classes such that every point of the first class lies to the left of every point of the second class, then there exists one and only one point which produces this division of all points into two classes, this severing of the straight line into two portions."
>
> . . . from the last remarks it is sufficiently obvious how the discon-

38. But see Wilson 1956, p. 31.

tinuous domain R of rational numbers may be rendered complete so as to form a continuous domain. . . . If now any separation of the system R into two classes A_1, A_2 is given which possesses only *this* characteristic property that every number a_1 in A_1 is less than every number a_2 in A_2, then for brevity we shall call such a separation a *cut* [*Schnitt*] and designate it by (A_1, A_2). We can then say that every rational number a produces one cut or, strictly speaking, two cuts, which, however, we shall not look upon as essentially different; this cut possesses, *besides,* the property that either among the numbers of the first class there exists a greatest or among the numbers of the second class a least number. . . .[39]

If there are "two cuts, which, however, we shall not look upon as essentially different," there seems to be a lack of correspondence between real numbers (which might be taken as representative of continuous distances) and indivisible points on a line, a lack of correspondence which modern mathematics has agreed to ignore. If one does admit points and lines or indivisible degrees and latitudes of quality, then it does seem to make a difference whether a segment of the continuum is terminated inclusively or exclusively by an indivisible. Yet the length of that segment of the continuum seems to be the same, whether the indivisible is included or not.[40] For all our willingness to relax Aristotle's rather physical conditions for continuity, we seem to have in the work of Burley and Kilvington a persuasive argument that continua and infinite collections of mediate indivisibles have differing properties.

A modern mathematical logician might formalize the views of Burley and Kilvington on this problem and thereby discover, assuming that the formalization was faithful to the original, the source of the differences between their views and modern views on this problem. I have neither space nor competence to do this, but I suggest that the source of the difference very likely lies in

39. Dedekind 1901, pp. 10–13.
40. Burley already, in a sense, suggested this distinction in an attempt to explain what Averroës may have had in mind in distinguishing mathematical and natural contiguity. (Burley 1501, f. 160rb, quoted in note 7 above): "Vel potest dici quod Commentator dicit quod quantum ad distantiam et ad propinquitatem quas considerat mathematicus non differunt continuatio et contiguatio, quia ultima contiguorum sunt simul et ita ultima contiguorum aequaliter distant a quocumque et aeque propinqua sunt cuicumque. Et ideo mathematicus utitur ultimis contiguorum tanquam uno ultimo. . . ." Cf. ibid., f. 172vb.

the no-infinite-set approach taken by the fourteenth-century philosophers. Remaining closer to natural philosophy than to mathematics, medieval logic operated mainly in terms of familiar physical objects. Modern mathematics has come to different conclusions in part by defining infinite sets as individual entities. Although consideration of God's omniscience and omnipotence sometimes led medieval thinkers to go beyond everyday experience, Walter Burley and Richard Kilvington in this case remained instead within the Aristotelian heritage.

Chapter IX

Walter Burley
on Continuity

Calvin G. Normore

1. Aristotelian and Modern Accounts of Continuity

Aristotle's account of continuity differs markedly from the account to be found in Dedekind's work. Whereas for Aristotle two things are continuous only if they have extremes which share the same proper place and are "made one," for Dedekind a set of objects can constitute a continuum only if between any two of the objects there is another.[1] This consideration alone would guarantee that there are no structures which meet both definitions. But Aristotelian and twentieth-century accounts of continuity have a common subject matter. Both are attempts to explain the structure we commonly conceive space, time, and certain kinds of change to have. It is as theories of these structures that these competing accounts must be judged.

2. Fourteenth-Century Reactions to the Aristotelian Account

Aristotle thought that place, time, and at least some changes were infinitely divisible into parts, or intervals, which are bounded by indivisibles. A taste for a simpler ontology might lead one to attempt to eliminate either the intervals or the indivisibles which figure in Aristotle's account. Both these routes were explored in the early fourteenth century. Atomists such as Walter Chatton and Henry of Harclay proposed to construct intervals out

1. See Aristotle, *Physics* V 3 (226b18 ff.), and Dedekind 1901, pp. 7–12.

of indivisibles, while William Ockham, Adam Wodeham, and John Buridan advocated banishing indivisibles altogether. Indeed, early fourteenth-century views on the continuum can themselves be arranged on a spectrum from the finite atomism of Chatton through various intermediate positions to Buridan's pure divisibilism (or continuism).[2]

The success of Dedekind's approach represents a triumph for one form of atomism, but that success is too tenuous to count as a definitive solution to the problems associated with continuity.[3] I am inclined to think that divisibilism after the fashion of Buridan has promise. But what of more nearly Aristotelian views? Is their additional ontological investment repaid by an increase in conceptual clarity? There are many Aristotelian and neo-Aristotelian views on these subjects in the fourteenth century. My concern here is only to lay out and explore part of the view Walter Burley presents in his *Expositio et quaestiones* on Aristotle's *Physics* (Burley 1501). In doing so I will be going over some of the ground covered by Edith Sylla in the preceding chapter but, I hope, from a vantage point far enough removed from hers to provide a different view of Burley's project.

3. Walter Burley on Continuity and Indivisibles

In Aristotle's view, and Burley's, the parts of a continuum usually do not all actually exist. Until a line is divided there is actually only the line and its endpoints; its various segments and their endpoints are only potentially. But there is one perspective from which this difference makes little difference. Burley acknowledges that God sees all the points that are potentially on a line and all the intervals that separate them.[4] This static perspective is

2. Medieval atomism and divisibilism are just beginning to receive the attention they deserve. For recent work see Breidert 1970; Murdoch 1974, pp. 11–32; and, for divisibilism, chapter 9 of Normore 1976.

3. Insofar as it involves operations on sets of more than denumerably many elements, the measure theory which supports modern atomism is unacceptable to intuitionists and constructivists of several persuasions. For a discussion of the problems involved, see Grünbaum 1952 and chapter 3 of Grünbaum 1967.

4. See Burley 1501, f. 176vb: "In response to the second objection, when it is said that God now sees all the points there are in a given line, for instance in line B, I grant it. And I say that God . . . sees some intermediates between all those

especially well suited to investigating problems of the structure of continua.

Why does Burley think that continua "contain" both intervals and indivisibles? His best argument for the existence of indivisibles in space is that a geometrical description of reality requires them. The geometers' definition of the center of a sphere requires that it be a point, and the geometrical description of a sphere rolling on a plane has it touching the plane at only one point. Implicit in such arguments is a kind of scientific realism about mathematical entities—a realism sometimes questioned by Burley's opponents.[5]

For the existence of indivisibles in time Burley has a very powerful argument. Many sentences are about a time in the sense that it is what happens or does not happen at that time which verifies or falsifies the sentence. Contradictories are about the same time and cannot both be true, but if contradictories were about a divisible time, both could be true because one could be true in one part of the time and the other in (or of) another part. Hence the existence of genuine contradictories demands that they be about indivisible times, and so there must be indivisible times for them to be about.[6] This argument did not go unchallenged in the fourteenth century. It relies on a shift between being true at a

points, taking the 'all' collectively." (Ad secundum in contrarium quando dicitur quod Deus modo videt omnia puncta quae sunt in linea data, ut puta in linea B, concedo. Et dico quod Deus . . . videt aliqua media inter omnia illa puncta, accipiendo ly omnia collective.)

5. It is striking that writers such as Albert of Saxony freely refer to entities whose existence they explicitly deny. Albert explains and defends his practice in his *Sophismata*: "just as the astrologers imagine many circles in the heavens which in reality are not there and the geometers imagine indivisible points although there are none such in reality, yet in those sciences it is expedient for such to be imagined for the better and easier treatment of those sciences, so I say no less in the matter under discussion that it is expedient that indivisible instants in time be imagined in order to express definite and precise measures of motions and changes" (sicut et astrologi imaginantur multos circulos in caelo qui in rei veritate ibi non sunt et geometrae imaginantur puncta indivisibilia licet in rei veritate nulla sint talia, tamen in dictis scientiis expedit talia imaginari propter meliorem et faciliorem traditionem dictarum scientiarum, ita non minus dico in propositio quod expedit imaginari instantia indivisibilia in tempore ad exprimendum certas et praecisas mensuras motuum et mutationum—Albert of Saxony 1502, part II, sophisma LXXXXIIII [actually Sophisma 111, not 94]). Albert goes on to explain that the apparent ontological commitments of such language are seen to be merely apparent when it is expounded properly.

6. See Burley 1501, f. 14rb–14va; see also chapters X and XI below.

time and being true at part of a time, and by carefully distinguishing these John Buridan was able to construct a consistent, if rather startling, logical theory in which every sentence is about an interval.[7] The price he pays is that sentences predicating contraries of the same subject can be true at the same time.

Although he thinks there are indivisibles in continua, Burley, following Aristotle, argues that continua cannot be made up of indivisibles as a whole is made up of integral parts because a continuum is extended and an indivisible is not, and the juxtaposition of even infinitely many unextended entities cannot generate an extended entity. Burley's arguments in favor of this last claim depend on our coming to agree that there can be no real difference between juxtaposing indivisibles so that they "touch" and superposing them. Indivisibles cannot touch part to part but must coincide if they touch at all.[8]

It is, I think, important to see just how the force of such arguments has been affected by post-Cantorean work on the continuum. If one takes such arguments as attempts to show the necessary inconsistency of a theory in which, at least in certain cases, elements which have zero length can be combined to yield elements with nonzero length, then it is very likely that they fail. Modern standard measure theory at least seems consistent.[9] But if one takes the arguments to be attacks on the *plausibility* of such a theory, then the only defense I see for the standard modern theory is to point to its role in the elegant edifice of modern mathematics. It is not shown in the standard theory that the union of more than denumerably many sets of measure zero can be a set with nonzero measure; it is *assumed* that this is so.[10]

Although Burley denies that a continuum can be composed of indivisibles, he grants that indivisibles can lie continuously (*continue*) in a continuum; that is, he claims that sentences such as "Continuously there is point after point in a plane" are true. To understand the force of this claim we must understand his use of

7. See Buridan 1966, chap. 7. Buridan's work is discussed in some detail in chapter 9 of Normore 1976.
8. See Burley 1501, f. 175ra.
9. I say "seems" because it is based on set theory and so is not provably consistent.
10. For details see Grünbaum 1952 and chapter 3 of Grünbaum 1967.

CALVIN G. NORMORE

continue. In the context under discussion Burley equates *continue* with *immediate* and goes on to equate *immediate* with *sine medio.*[11] The second of these equations is argued as follows:

> For these, namely *immediate* and *sine medio*, bring in reference to a multitude; for what will be immediately (*immediate*) or without anything intermediate (*sine medio*) will be before every intermediate will be completed. Hence "immediately" or "without anything intermediate" is the same as "before every intermediate" (*ante omne medium*). And therefore I say that this is true: "[Instant] *A* is, and without anything intermediate another instant will be," because before every completed intermediate another instant will be.[12]

11. See Burley 1501, f. 176va: "This, however, is true, namely that continuously there is point after point in a plane, because in that sentence the term 'point' has merely confused supposition by virtue of the distribution imported by 'continuously'; for it is the same to say that continuously in a plane there is point after point and to say that before every divisible complete intermediate there is point after point." (Ista tamen est vera, scilicet quod continue est punctus post punctum in plano, quia in illa ille terminus punctus supponit confuse tantum virtute distributionis (quae) importatur in hoc quod dico continue, quoniam idem est dicere quod continue in plano est punctus post punctum et dicere quod ante omne medium divisibile completum est punctus post punctum.)

12. Burley 1501, f. 177ra: "Ista enim, videlicet immediate et sine medio, importa(n)t multitudinem, quia quod immediate vel sine medio erit ante omne medium completum erit. Unde immediate vel sine medio est idem quod ante omne medium. Et ideo dico quod ista est vera: A est et sine medio aliud instans erit; quia ante omne medium completum aliud instans erit."

The analysis of *continue, immediate,* and *sine medio* which Burley provides refers us to the machinery of supposition theory and in particular to one of its more obscure parts—*suppositio confusa tantum,* merely confused supposition. In her discussion of Burley's views on *immediate* in chapter VIII above, Edith Sylla makes an intriguing suggestion about this type of supposition. Her proposal is that if a term has merely confused supposition, we cannot descend to singulars from it directly, but we can first descend to singulars under the other term in the sentence and then descend from the term we are interested in in each of those singulars. Thus from *B* in

(1) Every *A* is a *B*

we cannot descend directly to

(1') Every *A* is B_1, or every *A* is B_2, or . . .

but from *A* in (1) we can descend to

(2) A_1 is a *B*, and A_2 is a *B*, and . . .

and from *B* in each conjunct of (2) we can descend to

(2') A_i is B_1, or A_i is B_2, or . . .

There are two standard examples of terms with merely confused supposition. One is the predicate term in sentences of the form "Every *A* is a *B*." The other is the subject term in sentences of the form "Only *A*s are *B*s." Sylla's analysis works for both.

But Burley's analysis of merely confused supposition is more general than the examples. In his *De suppositionibus* (see Brown 1972), he claims that "a term has *suppositio confuse tantum* when it supposits for several in such a way that it may be

262

Burley apparently thinks that only an interval can be an intermediate (*medium*) in the required sense. His discussion of the situation in which God sees all the points on a line presupposes this.[13] But if this is his view, he is committed to some rather startling consequences.[14]

4. Consequences of Burley's Account of Continuity and Indivisibles

Preanalytically one might expect the set of sentences describing the way the world is (will be) immediately after a given instant to be a consistent set. But if *medium* refers only to intervals, this expectation will be violated. Consider the following case. It is now time t. At $t + 1$ second a light will be on, at $t + 1/2$ second it will be off, at $t + 1/4$ second it will be on, and so on. If we interpret *medium* as "interval," Burley's account yields the result that

(1) Immediately after t the light will be on
(2) Immediately after t the light will be off

are both true. But this does not refute Burley's view. There is no contradiction in the claim that both (1) and (2) are true, and as Richard Kilvington, a younger contemporary of Burley's, pointed out, one cannot derive contradictions such as "Immediately after t

---

inferred from any one of them and one may descend conjunctively or disjunctively to none." On this account terms which occur *secundo adiacens* may also have merely confused supposition. For example, consider *A* in "There is always an *A*" or "*A*s are everywhere." Sylla's analysis does not extend to these; and while it is not easy to be sure, there seems no good reason to think that Burley thinks sentences involving *semper* and similar expressions should be parsed into sentences to which the analysis is applicable. To favor such parsing would, I think, involve favoring the elimination of tense and modal operators from theoretical discourse.

13. Note also that in his account of *continue* Burley explicitly speaks of a *divisible* intermediate. See n. 11.

14. Almost everything in the discussion which follows is borrowed. From Herzberger 1979 and discussions I had with Herzberger during the summer of 1978 come the framework of the discussion and the idea behind the worm example. In a discussion of the bearing of Herzberger's work on his theory of counterfactuals, David K. Lewis pointed out to me that the considerations Herzberger adduces apply to "immediately." The example of the light switch is borrowed from Thomson 1954–55.

the light will be both on and off" from the theory.[15] Nevertheless, an intuition is violated.

It should be said in Burley's defense that while one can handle this particular example by moving to a "stronger" analysis of *immediate* of the sort discussed by Kilvington,[16] one cannot altogether eliminate the problem in this way. According to the stronger analysis "X immediately after t will be P" is true if and only if there is an instant t' after t such that X is P at t' and X is P at every instant between t and t'. This analysis falsifies (1) and (2), but it remains possible to construct cases in which there is no consistent description of the way the world will be immediately after t. Consider this example. A worm is now one inch long and is growing continuously, so that a month from now it will be two inches long, two weeks from now it will be an inch and a half long, and so on. By the stronger analysis it is true that immediately after now the worm will be more than one and less than two inches long. Every sentence of the form "Immediately after now the worm will *not* be an inch and m $n$ths long" (for every proper fraction m/n) is also true. But the set of all the sentences "The worm is more than one but less than two inches long, the worm is not an inch and m $n$ths long" for every proper fraction m/n is not a consistent set. If the worm is more than one and less than two inches long, then it is an inch and m $n$ths long for some proper fraction m/n.

The stronger analysis discussed by Kilvington and by Norman Kretzmann in chapter X below is the analysis Burley would have been committed to had he meant by *medium* "interval or divisible." So even read this way his theory would countenance the possibility that the sentences telling us how the world will be immediately after now do not form a consistent set. One can brazen this out; it is not as though one's *theory* or analysis of *immediate* were itself inconsistent. But this outcome does, I think, exert pressure in favor of an analysis of *immediate* in the spirit of divisibilism.[17]

15. For relevant Kilvington texts and discussion see chapter X.
16. And by Kretzmann in chapter X.
17. I have in mind an extension of Buridan's view that in a given context "now" picks out a definite stretch of time. The extension would have "immediately after

5. Burley's Account and the Cantor-Dedekind Account

Given Burley's analysis of *continue* we can discuss within his framework most of the problems which arise naturally within atomist frameworks about the structure of the set of indivisibles in a continuum. In particular we can ask whether it satisfies the axioms of the Cantor-Dedekind account. The answer, I think, is yes. Burley's account of first and last instants commits him (whether he is aware of it or not) to a view of the structure of time according to which the set of instants satisfies not only the density postulate but also Dedekind's continuity condition.[18] That Burley thinks the set of instants everywhere dense is evident enough. He argues that any two indivisibles in a continuum are separated by a medium.[19] Since this medium is an interval, it is divisible into intervals which "join" at an indivisible which lies between the two connected by the medium. Dedekind's postulate claims that we cannot divide the indivisibles in a continuum (taken, let us suppose, in their natural order) into two classes S and L such that all the indivisibles in S precede every indivisible in L and such that there is no "last" indivisible in S and no "first" indivisible in L.[20]

Burley regards the truth of a sentence as a thing. To be precise, it is a *res permanens* depending for its existence on whatever it is that makes the sentence true.[21] In keeping with standard medieval

---

X" pick out (in a given context) a stretch of time of a definite length such that there is no time between it and the stretch designated by X. An analysis like this is suggested by some remarks in Albert of Saxony's discussion of *incipit* and *desinit* in his *Sophismata* (Albert of Saxony 1502), part II, sophisma LXXXXIIII (actually sophisma 111).

18. For a discussion of the differences between these conditions see Huntington 1917.

19. See n. 4 above.

20. See Huntington 1917, p. 44.

21. See the *Quaestio de primo et ultimo instanti* appended to Burley's *Physics* commentary in Burley 1501, f. 258ra: "Things which endure through time are of two sorts, one which depends on a process (*res successiva*) for its being and for its being conserved in being, and one which is dependent on a process neither for its being nor for its being conserved. An example of the first sort: the truth of this sentence 'Socrates runs' is a thing (*res permanens*) because from its being the truth

practice, Burley's rules for first and last instants are so designed that if a thing does not have a last instant of existence, it has a first instant of nonexistence, and if it does not have a first instant of nonexistence, it has a last instant of existence.[22] Now if S and L are sets of instants which exhaust the temporal continuum and have no members in common and are such that every member of S precedes every member of L, then there is at least one sentence which is true at every instant in S and false at every instant in L. For example "It is now an instant of S" meets the condition. Suppose S has no last instant. Then the truth of that sentence has no last instant of existence, and so its falsity has a first instant of existence. But it is false just at the instants of L, and so L has a first instant.

I am not claiming that Burley was aware of a condition like Dedekind's, still less that the rules for first and last instants were designed with such a condition in mind. Indeed, in at least one place Burley identifies a sense of "continuous" he seems to think applicable to infinitely divisible magnitudes composed of indivisi-

---

of a sentence, that truth has its being all at once; nor is there one past truth of the sentence and another future [truth]. It follows that the truth of the sentence is a thing (*res permanens*), and such a truth depends essentially for its being and for its being conserved on a process as on a cause; for 'Socrates runs' is true from running being in Socrates." (Res autem quae durat per tempus est duplex: quaedam est dependens a re successiva et per rem successivam in esse et conservari, et quaedam quae nec est in esse dependens a re successiva nec in conservari. Exemplum primi: veritas huius propositionis 'Socrates currit' est res permanens quia ex quo veritas est veritas propositionis et habet esse tota simul, nec est una veritas propositionis praeterita et alia futura. Sequitur quod veritas propositionis est res permanens, et veritas talis dependet essentialiter in esse et conservari a re successiva tamquam a causa; nam ex eo quod Socrati inest cursus haec est vera: 'Socrates currit.')

22. See Burley, *Quaestio de primo et ultimo instanti*, in Burley 1501, f. 258rb: "Therefore I lay down four rules, of which two are about the first instant of a thing's being and the other two about the last instant. The first rule is: in whatever things for which a first instant of the thing's being is to be given there is no last instant of the thing's nonbeing to be given. The second rule is: in whatever things for which a first instant of the thing's being is not to be given, there is a last instant at which the thing has nonbeing, as long as we are speaking of things that are newly acquiring being." (Pono ergo quattuor regulas quarum duae sunt de primo instanti esse rei, aliae duae de ultimo. Prima regula est ista: in quibuscumque rebus est dare primum instans esse rei, in eisdem non est dare ultimum instans non esse rei. Secunda regula est ista: in quibuscumque rebus non est dare primum instans esse rei, in eisdem est dare ultimum instans in quo res habet non esse, loquendo de rebus quae de novo accipiunt esse.)

bles and makes no mention of any further condition.[23] Nonetheless, since it is easy to construct out of rational numbers alone
series which are everywhere dense but would be intuitively regarded as having gaps, it would not be surprising were someone
who attended to the structure of orderings of mediate indivisibles
to notice that density alone would not guarantee the smoothness
of change.

6. Burley's Treatment of Alteration

Although Burley does not to my knowledge assert it, the structure of the set of indivisibles God sees in a continuum appears to
be just that of the indivisible degrees in a latitude of forms in his
theory of such latitudes. Thus some of the problems which arise
for Burley's theory of the intension and remission of forms are
really problems about continuity. Of this sort I think is the problem discussed by Edith Sylla in chapter VIII about whether, when
fire heats water until the water is transmuted into fire, the heat of
the fire suffices for the transmutation or whether the action of the
substantial form of fire is also required. In his *Tractatus primus*
Burley argues that the heat of the fire suffices but that it is not any
particular degree of heat which induces the substantial change
but the production of the whole increase (*alteratio*) which precedes the transmutation.[24]

The problems raised here seem remarkably like those posed in
the much more recent controversy about "supertasks."[25] In the
case Burley discusses, it is agreed that if the heat of the fire can
induce the maximum degree of heat in the water, it can induce
the substantial form of fire; and it is agreed that the heat of the
fire can induce every degree of heat up to the maximum degree.
Asking whether increasing the temperature of the water through

23. See Burley 1501, f. 173va: "It should be understood that the Commentator
here takes 'continuity' for 'divisibility in infinity.'" (Intelligendum quod Commentator hic accipit continuationem pro divisibilitate in infinitum.)
24. For references and discussion, see chapter VIII.
25. For the literature on supertasks see Salmon 1970, especially the contributions
by James Thomson and Paul Benacerraf.

all the half-open latitude of forms [X, max] (where X is some starting point and "max" is the maximum degree) is doing all that is needed to increase it through the closed latitude [X, max] is very much like asking whether if you are traveling on Zeno's racecourse and pass through all its proportional parts (the first half, the next quarter, the next eighth, etc.) you have to do anything else to reach the endpoint. Suppose one heats the water through all the degrees that can be induced by the heat of the fire. In what state will the water be as a result? Logically speaking, it could be in any state. As Paul Benacerraf has emphasized,[26] there is no contradiction in supposing that the water is heated through the degrees up to the maximum and then vanishes or becomes bad coffee. But surely what is required to make the water heat up to (but not attain) the maximum and vanish is different from what is required to make it heat up to the maximum and become bad coffee. What then if we do *only* what is required to heat it up through the interval extrinsically bounded by the maximum degree? What will be its state at the first instant after it is heated if nothing else is done?

Burley apparently thinks that at that instant the water will attain the maximum degree of heat and become fire, presumably because he thinks nothing is required to raise the level of heat by one indivisible and something would be required for the water to go into any other state. This is plausible but not entirely convincing. Perhaps there is no such thing as *only* causing the water to be heated through the series of degrees bounded from without by the maximum. After all, if heating the water through the interval also determines the state of the water at the first instant after the heating, then causing the water to be heated is also causing that state. If causing the water to be heated is *only* that, it must be something else which determines its state the instant after. Nevertheless, if work required is proportional to heat induced, then the additional work required to transmute the water into fire, given that it is being heated up to the maximum, is less than any finite amount. This is not so if the water is merely being heated to some particular degree less than the maximum. In order

26. See Benacerraf 1962, reprinted in Salmon 1970.

for the additional work required to be infinitesimal, the heat of the fire must be inducing *all* the degrees up to the maximum and in a certain order. The induction of an ordered series of degrees is a task different from that of inducing any particular degree and different from the task of inducing all the degrees in some order or other. If it were not so, there would be no difference between the intension of a form from degree x to degree y and its remission from degree y to degree x. It is not easy to characterize this difference in terms of the degrees alone, since it is the same degrees that are involved. I suggest, then, that Burley's invocation of "the whole alteration" as something over and above the degrees involved is an attempt to solve the problem of order—and a respectable attempt.

I began by asking whether views like Burley's repaid their investment in a relatively luxurious ontology. I hope to have shown that the ingredients—intervals, indivisibles, and *alterationes* are none of them idle wheels. Whether Burley's theory is ultimately satisfactory is a more difficult question.

CHAPTER X

Continuity, Contrariety, Contradiction, and Change

NORMAN KRETZMANN

1. The Aristotelian Background

More than one theory of change is employed in fourteenth-century philosophy and theology.[1] In this chapter I assess two of those theories, exploring in some detail a development in the theory I take to be the better of the two. Because both theories purport to be Aristotelian, I begin by briefly surveying the roles of the concepts of continuity, contrariety, and contradiction in Aristotle's own account of change.

Whatever else must be said about change, obviously it involves difference and time. Aristotle's relevant claims regarding those elements may be presented as these two theses:

> I. The difference effected in change is a difference between logical opposites, either contraries or contradictories.
> II. Time is continuous.

Thesis I is developed most systematically in *Physics* V 1 and 2, where Aristotle introduces his fourfold classification of changes, based in part on considering whether the difference effected in the change is between contrary or between contradictory

I am grateful to Barbara Ensign Kretzmann for her help with the Kilvington text, to Paul Spade for his public comments and his private criticisms, and to Eleonore Stump for helping me to improve this paper in several ways with her comments and criticisms.

1. Some of my interest in this topic and almost all of my information about one of the theories I will be discussing stem from a valuable article by Simo Knuuttila and Anja Inkeri Lehtinen: Knuuttila and Lehtinen 1979a. I am particularly grateful to the authors for having sent me a copy of their article in proof.

270

conditions.[2] His general observation regarding the termini of changes, which I have expressed as thesis I, underlies the classification; it may be illustrated in this way. Even if the leaves of a certain plant turn brown whenever and only when they die, we would not describe the leaves as changing from green to dead or from alive to brown.[3] The conditions of being alive and of being brown are logically independent: some living things are brown, but others are not. The recognized termini of change in this case—being green and being brown, or being alive and being dead—are logically opposed to each other: nothing is both green and brown at the same time and in the same respect. (At a single instant the plant may be green in respect of some of its leaves and brown in respect of others; in respect of a single leaf the plant may be green at one time and brown at another.) The form of logical opposition between these two termini of the color change (or between the conditions of being alive and of being dead) is contrariety; the dichotomy between contrary conditions is exclusive but not exhaustive.

There are two ways in which the dichotomy of contraries fails to be exhaustive. A thing may be neither green nor brown either because it is essentially without color, or because it has some third color. The first way need not concern us now, but the second introduces the apparently important notion of conditions intermediate between contrary conditions: the leaves may turn yellow in the course of turning brown. It seems clear, however, that we need not take separate account of intermediate conditions in a philosophical consideration of change between contraries. Since every such intermediary will be a contrary of each of the terminal contraries, any change between contraries via an intermediary can be treated as two successive changes between contraries; we can focus on the change from green to yellow or on the change from yellow to brown in the same way as we focus on the change from green to brown.[4]

2. For a detailed, critical discussion of this material see Morrow 1966. My attention was called to Morrow's article by Knuuttila and Lehtinen 1979a.
3. Aristotle seems to be saying something very much like this in *Physics* I 5, 188a31–b3.
4. Aristotle takes careful account of intermediate conditions in his survey of changes between contraries, but he recognizes, of course, that only contraries (not

Perhaps not only intermediaries are theoretically ignorable in the Aristotelian analysis (as distinct from the Aristotelian classification) of change; for both the change from green to yellow and the change from green to brown can be construed as changes from green to not-green, as changes between contradictory conditions. Nothing is both green and not-green at the same time and in the same respect. That not-both-at-once feature of contrary and contradictory conditions alike may conveniently be designated the *non simul* principle. But contradictory conditions, of course, have this additional feature: given specifications of the time and the respect, everything is either green or not-green. The dichotomy between contradictories is not only exclusive but exhaustive as well.[5]

Although the distinction between contrary and contradictory termini of changes is essential to Aristotle's classification of changes, he seems clearly aware of the possibility of analyzing all changes in terms of contradictories, even those changes— in quantity, in quality, and in location—that are classified as changes between contraries.[6] And so we can, I think, simplify Aristotle's analysis of change without distorting it if for present purposes we take it to consider all changes as changes between contradictories.[7]

The second Aristotelian thesis regarding the elements of

---

contradictories) admit of intermediaries (227a7–10), and he makes the point that a change between contraries via an intermediary can be construed as two changes between contraries (224b30–35).

5. Conceivably it is considerations of this sort that led to the formulation of a conjoint *primum principium complexum*, which Francis of Meyronnes expresses as *De quolibet est affirmatio vel negatio vera et de nullo ambo simul* (quoted in Knuuttila and Lehtinen 1979a, p. 189).

6. E.g., in his notion of *qualified* coming-into-existence and going-out-of-existence. See, e.g., 225a10–20, and 263b9–26, quoted below.

7. Cf. Von Wright 1969, p. 20: "Changes are normally described in terms of states which are contraries rather than contradictories. A change is, e.g. when something grows or shrinks in size, or alters its colour or temperature. A change, generally speaking, is from a state '*p*' to a state '*q*.' But a succession of '*p*' and '*q*' is a *change* only if the two states are mutually exclusive, i.e. if the conjunction of the two is a logical contradiction. A (genuine) change from '*p*' to '*q*' can therefore always be resolved into two elementary changes, as we called them, viz. one from '*p*' to 'not-*p*' . . . and one from 'not-*q*' to '*q*.'"

In this paper I will apply these forms of opposition, contrariety and contradiction, to propositions as well as to conditions (in the traditional if not precisely Aristotelian way). Two conditions, φ and ψ, are mutually contrary if and only if for every individual, *x*, (a) it is not possible both that *x* is φ and that *x* is ψ at the

change—that time is continuous—is even more familiar than the first; its relevance to the analysis of change, particularly in the light of thesis I, may be worth pointing out. If the termini of every change can be viewed as contradictory conditions—ϕ and not-ϕ—then, as we have seen, there can be no time at which x, the individual subject of the change, is in both those conditions at once, and there can be no time at which x is in neither of those conditions. The temporal intervals during which x is ϕ and x is not-ϕ must be exclusive of each other and immediate to each other. Therefore the actual transition from x's being not-ϕ to x's being ϕ must take no time at all; it must be instantaneous. Obviously every change involves a ceasing and a beginning: the ceasing of the one condition and the beginning of its contradictory condition. In the light of the notion of instantaneous transition, just introduced, such ceasings and beginnings take place at instants—instants that serve as limits of the temporal intervals during which the one or the other of the opposed conditions obtains. But since instants cannot be immediate to each other, two intervals immediate to each other must be limited relative to each other by one and the same instant. (Aristotelian instants are mere cuts in the potentially infinitely divisible termporal continuum, and one cut cannot be immediately adjacent to another. Thus any two instants define a temporal interval, no matter how short; and any interval, no matter how short, can be divided by a middle instant into two intervals each of which is only half as long as the original.) Thus the ceasing of one contradictory condition and the beginning of the other must occur at one and the same instant, the instant of transition.[8]

Interpreted in that way, the combination of the two Aristotelian

---

same time and in the same respect, and (b) it is possible that x is neither ϕ nor ψ at the same time and in the same respect. Two propositions, P and Q, are mutually contrary if and only if (a') it is not possible that both P and Q are true at the same time and in the same respect, and (b') it is possible that neither P nor Q is true at the same time and in the same respect. Two conditions, ϕ and ψ, are mutually contradictory if and only if for every individual, x, (a) . . . , and ($-$b) it is not possible that x is neither ϕ nor ψ at the same time and in the same respect. Two propositions, P and Q, are mutually contradictory if and only if (a') . . . , and ($-$b') it is not possible that neither P nor Q is true at the same time and in the same respect.

8. I have discussed some features of Aristotle's theory of time in Kretzmann 1976a. I have sketched its relevance to medieval theories of change in Kretzmann 1976b and Kretzmann 1977.

theses regarding the elements of change may seem to generate a problem. If the ceasing of condition not-ϕ and the beginning of condition ϕ occur at the same instant, then it seems right to say that that ceasing and that beginning are precisely simultaneous. And since condition not-ϕ obtains precisely until it ceases and condition ϕ obtains precisely as soon as it begins, that instant of transition may appear to present a violation of the *non simul* principle. In short, the elements of Aristotle's analysis of change may appear to entail this absurdity: at the instant of transition x is both not-ϕ and ϕ in the same respect.

2. Quasi-Aristotelianism in the Fourteenth Century

One of the two fourteenth-century theories of change I am interested in evidently arose as an attempt to solve that problem within an Aristotelian framework; but because I think that from an orthodox Aristotelian point of view the attempt is misguided and the result unacceptable, I will call this first theory "Quasi-Aristotelianism."[9] Proponents of the other theory, which I will call "Aristotelianism," would be likely to have dismissed the problem as illusory if they became aware of it; some of them, as we shall see, expressly rejected Quasi-Aristotelianism.

Since I will be taking an Aristotelian line, dismissing both the problem regarding the instant of transition and the Quasi-Aristotelian solution, it seems only fair to acknowledge beforehand that there are some genuine problems for the Aristotelian account of the instant of transition. The most important of them may be the difficulty (perhaps the impossibility) of providing a satisfactory Aristotelian account of the instant of transition between such conditions as rest and motion, conditions that can be realized only over a temporal interval.[10] Medieval philosophers,

9. Knuuttila and Lehtinen, who are evidently the first scholars to call attention to the theory I am calling "Quasi-Aristotelianism," left it nameless. Everything I know about the theory I have learned either from Knuuttila and Lehtinen 1979a or from the primary literature they cite there. "Aristotelianism" is the name they use for the position taken by the opponents of that first theory. They also mention, in a single sentence, a third theory of change: "Another type of solution was developed among medieval atomists" (p. 189); and in a footnote attached to that sentence they cite a good deal of literature on the medieval atomists.

10. The most interesting and thorough investigation of this problem known to me is Sorabji 1976. I disagree with the solution Sorabji offers in that article, and as

building on Aristotle, called such conditions "successive," distinguishing them from "permanent" conditions, those that are fully realized at an instant.[11] (In terms of that distinction, my being an American and my being at this particular location are both permanent conditions of mine; but my being *at rest* at this location is a successive condition, as would be my moving through this location on my way between two others.) Thus if the "φ" and the "not-φ" of the problem regarding the instant of transition are each interpreted as a successive condition, this can present real difficulties for Aristotelianism. But the problem in the form in which it gave rise to Quasi-Aristotelianism is, as far as I know, raised in connection with permanent conditions. In such a setting the instant of transition does not present a real difficulty, I believe, whether for Aristotle or for medieval Aristotelianism.

Simo Knuuttila and Anja Inkeri Lehtinen, the scholars who have uncovered the theory I am calling Quasi-Aristotelianism, identify three or perhaps four adherents of it: Henry of Ghent (d. 1293), who might have been surprised to find himself in this company, Hugh of Newcastle (d. after 1322), John Baconthorpe (d. ca. 1348), and Landulf Caraccioli (d. 1351). Their outspoken critics among the Aristotelians are identified by Knuuttila and Lehtinen as Francis of Meyronnes (d. ca. 1328), John of Jandun (d. 1328), Michael of Massa (d. 1337), Francis of Marchia (d. after 1344), and John the Canon (fl. 1340). Although some of the Quasi-Aristotelians were English, all of them, like their critics, had careers that centered around Paris.

Quasi-Aristotelianism was apparently motivated by theological concerns, but it can be presented in a purely philosophical setting. John Baconthorpe puts the problem this way:

> . . . contradictory *termini* that are the *termini* of a single change occur at the same instant—I mean the *ultimum* of the not-being of the form to be generated and the *primum* of its being.[12]

---

was made clear in our public (but unpublished) discussion of the issue at the joint meeting of the Aristotelian Society and the Mind Association in July 1976, he disagrees with my alternate solution.

11. I have discussed the permanent/successive distinction in Kretzmann 1976b and Kretzmann 1977.

12. *Commentary on the "Sentences,"* L. III, d. 3, q. 2, art. 3: ". . . termini contradictorii, qui sunt termini unius mutationis, sunt in eodem instanti, puta ultimum non

And Landulf Caraccioli presents the problem as the conclusion of an argument:

> In instantaneous change both termini occur at the same instant, but in change of that sort the termini are contradictory; therefore contradictories are true at once at the same instant of time.[13]

Such a result cannot be allowed to stand in just that form by any rational being and perhaps particularly by men who, like Baconthorpe and Caraccioli, consider themselves to be true followers of Aristotle. I am calling them *Quasi*-Aristotelians partly because I think they are mistaken in claiming to have found their solution (or support for their solution) in Aristotle, but I want to look at their solution before examining its pedigree.

The essence of the Quasi-Aristotelian theory of change is the concept of the divided instant. In some contexts it is convenient and harmless to think of an indivisible as divided: the line dividing New York from New Jersey is an indivisible (lengthwise), but it is perfectly all right to think of it as both the boundary of New York and the boundary of New Jersey (as long as it is not thought of as a part of either state—since it is no part at all—or as a no-man's-land separating them). Nevertheless, the concept of a divided indivisible is prima facie incoherent, and it must be viewed with alarm, particularly because it is easily conceived. The fact that a horizontal line segment is divided into right and left halves by its midpoint might lead a beginner at geometry to suppose that that point had, in virtue of its office, acquired right and left sides. The Quasi-Aristotelian divided instant is not so unsubtle, though it is, I think, neither coherent nor harmless.

The thin end of the wedge with which the Quasi-Aristotelians split the Aristotelian instant is the idea of the order of nature. Baconthorpe puts it this way:

---

esse formae generandae et primum eius esse . . . ," ed. Saggi 1955, 231.24–26; quoted at greater length in Knuuttila and Lehtinen 1979a, n. 1.

13. *Commentary on the "Sentences,"* L. II, d. 1, q. 1: "In mutatione instantanea uterque terminus est in eodem instanti. Sed in tali mutatione termini sunt contradictorii, ergo contradictoria simul sunt vera in eodem instanti temporis." Quoted at greater length in Knuuttila and Lehtinen 1979a, n. 29.

Continuity, Contrariety, Contradiction, and Change

The termini of a change are separated from each other only as much as the duration of the change that mediates between the termini, but an instantaneous change does not endure except for an instant alone; therefore its termini are separated not in accordance with the parts of a duration, but solely in accordance with the order of nature. . . . the being and the not-being that are the termini of any such change occur at the same instant, although in that same instant there is the order of nature.[14]

In my earlier example of the leaf, the order of nature is this: first green and then not-green; and Baconthorpe is evidently saying that even if those contradictory conditions occur together from the temporal point of view—simultaneously—they are nevertheless not together but strictly sequential in the order of nature. Such a claim seems innocuous enough, left at that; but it is not yet even a putative solution to the apparent problem of simultaneous contradictories, and there are indications of conceptual difficulties regarding instants in his (cautiously expressed) description of a change as *enduring for* an instant and in his locating the order of nature *in* an instant.

The Quasi-Aristotelians come closer to their goal in introducing the Scotistic instants of nature.[15] If there is an order of nature distinguishable from temporal order, it is only convenient to recognize instants of nature, analogous to but definitely not to be confused with temporal instants. And with instants of nature in the picture, a solution to the problem presents itself. For if the

14. *Commentary on the "Sentences,"* L. III, d. 3, q. 2, art. 3: "Termini mutationis non plus distant nisi quantum durat mutatio quae mediat inter terminos; sed mutatio subita non durat nisi per solum instans; igitur termini non distant secundum partes durationis, sed solum secundum ordinem naturae. . . . esse et non esse quae sunt termini alicuius unius mutationis sunt in eodem instanti, licet in eodem instanti sit ordo naturae" (ed. Saggi 1955, 234.24–27; 33–34; quoted at greater length in Knuuttila and Lehtinen 1979a, n. 19). Cf. L. III, d. 3, q. 2, art. 3: "Ergo in subita mutatione vel generatione termini oppositi sunt in eodem instanti, licet secundum diversum ordinem naturae" (ed. Saggi 1955, 235.3–5; quoted at greater length in Knuuttila and Lehtinen 1979a, n. 34). Hugh of Newcastle makes a similar use of the idea of the order of nature in his *Commentary on the "Sentences,"* L. II, d. 1, q. 1, arts. 5 and 6, quoted in Knuuttila and Lehtinen 1979a, n. 21.

15. Knuuttila and Lehtinen do not remark on the association of the concept of instants of nature with Duns Scotus, but it seems likely that the Quasi-Aristotelians derive the notion from him, especially in view of the facts that Hugh of Newcastle and Landulf Caraccioli were both Franciscans (as Scotus had been) at Paris during a period when Scotus's influence among Franciscans was powerful. See also n. 24 below.

temporally simultaneous contradictory conditions of being green and being not-green do not occur at once in the order of nature, then their occurrences in the order of nature may be assigned to distinct instants of nature. Caraccioli presents this view as follows:

> An instant of time measures the indivisibles in changes—viz., instantaneous changes and the acquisitions of changed states as they occur in *motus* [i.e., in changes in quantity, in quality, or in location].
> . . . [But] an instant of nature measures the being and the not-being of things, not insofar as they are or are not acquired under duration or under the permanent and non-permanent things of duration, but just exactly insofar as they are being or not-being. . . . [And so] the indivisible instant for which contradictories are not true at once . . . is an instant of nature. . . . strictly speaking, two . . . instants of nature neither occur at once nor do they succeed each other; indeed, they are two indivisible measures measuring distinct permanent entities.[16]

Thus the simultaneity of contradictories is tolerable in respect of a temporal instant because it can be dispelled in respect of the convenient instants of nature; the compromised indivisibility of the temporal instant can be reinstated in the truly inviolable instants of nature, and the exclusive dichotomy of contradictories can be preserved as long as one remembers that *non simul* means "not at the same instant of *nature."*

Whatever may be said of this theory up to this point, surely it would not occur to anyone to call it Aristotelian, or even Quasi-Aristotelian. The theory's link to Aristotle consists entirely, or almost entirely, in a special interpretation of one difficult passage in *Physics* VIII 8:

16. *Commentary on the "Sentences,"* L. II, d. 2, q. 1: "Instans temporis mensurat indivisibilia in transmutationibus, videlicet instantaneas mutationes et mutata esse ut sunt in motu. . . . Instans naturae mensurat esse et non esse rerum, non ut accipiuntur sub duratione vel non, vel sub permanentia et non permanentia durationis, sed ut praecise esse vel non esse." Quoted at greater length in Knuuttila and Lehtinen 1979a, n. 5. "Secundus articulus est videre pro quo instanti indivisibili non sunt simul vera contradictoria. Et dico, quod illud instans est instans naturae . . . et ideo duo signa vel instantia naturae proprie nec sunt simul nec sibi succedunt, sed sunt duae mensurae indivisibiles mensurantes distincta entia permanentia. . . ." Quoted at greater length in Knuuttila and Lehtinen 1979a, n. 36.

It is also evident that unless one holds that the point (*sēmeion*) that divides the earlier from the later always belongs to the later as regards the thing [i.e., the subject of the change], the same thing will both be and not be at once, and when it has come to be it will not be. The point is, indeed, common to both—the earlier as well as the later—and numerically it is one and the same; but it is not the same in formula (*logō(i)*), being the end of the one and the beginning of the other. As regards the thing, however, it always belongs to the later condition.

Let *ACB* be the time, and let the thing be *D*, and let *D* be white in time *A* and not-white in time *B*. At [instant] *C* it will be both white and not-white; for it is true to say that it is white at any instant of *A* if it was white during all that time, and it is not-white in *B*, and *C* is in both. And so we must not grant that it is white in all [*A*] but must exclude its last instant, *C*, which already belongs to the later time. And if it was becoming not-white and ceasing to be white in all *A*, it became or ceased at *C*. So it is true to say that at *C* the white thing has first become not-white. Otherwise it must be that when it has come to be it is not, and when it has ceased to be it is—either as regards white and not-white, or, generally, being and not-being. [263b9–26]

It is that passage, but especially its first paragraph, to which Baconthorpe appeals in his attempt to show that his own theory of change is Aristotle's, and that the medieval theory of change I am calling Aristotelianism is both unworkable and un-Aristotelian. Baconthorpe claims that in the use other men make of Aristotle in explaining the instant of transition

. . . something false is imposed on the Philosopher. For the Philosopher there does not save the contradiction between being and not-being in that way . . . ; instead, the Philosopher saves the contradiction in this way, that the instant is divided into a beginning and an end in such a way that the instant's first sign, which corresponds to the terminus a quo of an instantaneous change, measures the *ultimum* of the not-being, and its last sign measures the *primum* of the being. . . .[17]

17. *Commentary on the "Sentences,"* L. III, d. 3, q. 2, art. 3: "Respondeo, quod falsum imponitur Philosopho. Non enim salvat Philosophus ibi contradictionem inter esse et non esse per hoc quod non esse mensuratur tempore praecedenti et non sit dare ultimum non esse cui correspondeat instans; sed salvat Philosophus ibi contradictionem per hoc quod dividitur instans in principium et finem, ita quod primo signo instantis, quod correspondet termino a quo subitae mutationis, mensuratur ultimum non esse, et ultimo signo mensuratur primum esse, ut expresse

The peculiar doctrine of the two "signs" of the instant of transition seems to be a consequence of the fact that in the same passage (263b9–26, quoted above) in which Aristotle most clearly suggests a conceptual division of the instant he also uses the word *sēmeion* (*signum* in the Latin translations), one of his words for a point or an instant but more frequently used in the sense of "sign." Aristotle definitely does not talk about "the signs of the instant" (as Baconthorpe says he does),[18] but he does say, "The *sēmeion* is . . . not the same in formula, being the end of the one [interval] and the beginning of the other" (263b12–14), and that was evidently enough to provide the pedigree and perhaps the impetus for Quasi-Aristotelianism.[19] The "signs" of the instant of transition were expressly identified with the instants of nature. Caraccioli, for instance, speaks of "two signs or instants of nature"[20] and uses the concepts interchangeably: "the being and the not-being of one and the same thing that was generated could occur at a single instant of time in respect of distinct signs of nature."[21]

For present purposes, then, Quasi-Aristotelianism may be described as a theory of change that developed in response to the standard medieval Aristotelian account of the instant of transition, an account that struck the Quasi-Aristotelians as entailing the simultaneous occurrence of contradictory conditions. They sought to avoid that outcome by accepting the contradiction in the temporal order and separating the contradictories in the order of nature, accordingly dividing the instant of transition into two

---

patet in textu qui dicit, quod nisi aliquis dividat signum prius et posterius (loquitur de signis instantis), aliquid simul erit et non erit" (ed. Saggi 1955, 233.19–28; quoted at greater length in Knuuttila and Lehtinen 1979a, n. 1).

18. See n. 17 above: "(loquitur de signis instantis)."

19. In his account of the expulsion of original sin from Mary, Henry of Ghent uses the notion of the "signs" of the instant in order to avoid contradiction at the instant of transition and does so in a way that strongly suggests that he is drawing on the passage from *Physics* VIII 8: "peccatum originale in illo instanti simul habuit esse primo et ultimo, sed secundum aliud et aliud signum illius instantis . . . ," quoted at greater length in Knuuttila and Lehtinen 1979a, n. 16. Hugh of Newcastle uses the notion similarly; ibid., n. 21.

20. See n. 16 above: "duo signa vel instantia naturae."

21. Quoted at greater length and without specific location in Knuuttila and Lehtinen 1979a, n. 28: ". . . esse et non esse eiusdem rei quae generabatur pro diversis signis naturae poterant esse in uno instanti temporis."

instants or "signs" of nature, basing their solution primarily on *Physics* VIII 8.

I think it is clear that their interpretation of the crucial passage in Aristotle is unjustified, and I will try to show that they were mistaken in thinking that the medieval theory I am calling Aristotelianism results in contradiction at the instant of transition; but first I want to say something about their use of the concept of the order of nature and about that concept itself.

3. A Critique of Quasi-Aristotelianism

There are just two ways in which conditions can be shown not to occur at once: either they can be shown to occur successively, or it can be pointed out that temporal characterizations such as "at once" and "successively" do not apply at all to the conditions in question (as might be said about the evenness of the number two and the oddness of the number three, for instance). In view of the fact that the problem of the instant of transition is raised regarding such changes as alteration of color, the second of those two ways of showing that the conditions do not occur at once is clearly unavailable; and yet it is the way the Quasi-Aristotelians try to take. For they would divide the single instant of transition into two instants of nature, assigning the one condition to the one instant of nature and its contradictory to the other; and "strictly speaking, two . . . instants of nature *neither* occur at once *nor* do they succeed each other," as we have seen Caraccioli claiming,[22] and it is in *this* way that the apparent violation of the *non simul* principle is supposed to be set aside. But even if we recognize that one of those conditions is naturally prior to the other and distinguish that natural priority from temporal succession, we will simply have made observations that are strictly irrelevant to the worry that the transition between those conditions violates the *non simul* principle; it is only the temporal relationship of those conditions to each other that is at issue in the *non simul* principle. Part of my sense of the inefficacy of the Quasi-Aristotelians' appeal to the order of nature is expressed more

22. See n. 16 above.

than once by John the Canon in explicitly opposing Caraccioli: "to be prior in nature is nothing other than the presupposition of this thing by that thing in respect of a certain otherness of nature" in the things,[23] and presupposition and otherness taken together cannot yield *non simul*.

As for the concept of the instants (or "signs") of nature, it would be hard to ignore Ockham's attack, even though it is directed against Scotus himself rather than against the Quasi-Aristotelians:

> What is that instant of nature at which you say that that which is prior in nature is, and at which it is not posterior? Either it is something outside the soul or it is not. If it is not, then if there were no soul, that thing would not be prior in nature—which is false. . . . Nor can one say that it is outside the soul, for [in that case] it is either substance or accident, and it is inductively evident that it is neither substance nor accident. . . . And so one must hold in complete certainty that there are no instants of nature when one thing is proir to another in nature any more than there are instants of honor or of perfection when one thing is prior to another in honor or in perfection. . . . Thus in general one must hold that there are not any instants of nature or of origin besides the instants of time.[24]

23. *Quaestiones super VIII libros Physicorum Aristotelis*, L. I, q. 4: ". . . esse prius natura non est aliud nisi praesuppositio huius ab hoc in quadam alteritate naturae," quoted at greater length in Knuuttila and Lehtinen 1979a, n. 37; see also L. I, q. 8, quoted ibid., n. 30.

24. Ockham 1978a, 328.86–115: "Tunc enim verum est dicere quod prius fuit in aliquo instanti vel tempore quando posterius non fuit, sed de aliis non est sic dicendum. Sicut quando aliquid est prius natura alio non debet dici quod illud 'prius natura' est in·aliquo instanti naturae in quo non est posterius, vel quod e s t in aliquo priori in quo non est posterius. Cuius ratio est, quia quaero: quid est illud instans naturae in quo dicis illud quod est prius natura esse, et quod in eo non est posterius? Aut est aliquid extra animam aut non. Si non, igitur si non esset anima, non esset illud prius natura, quod est falsum. Similiter inductive patet quod illud instans non potest poni in anima, quia non potest dici actus intelligendi, nec habitus, nec potentia, nec species, secundum potentes species, nec obiectum ipsius animae. Et sic patet inductive quod nihil ipsius animae est tale instans naturae. Nec potest dici quod sit extra animam, quia aut est substantia aut accidens. Et inductive patet quod nec substantia nec accidens. Unde accipiendo Sortem qui est prius natura ista albedine, si Sortes sit in aliquo instanti naturae in quo non est ista albedo, oportet quod illud instans naturae sit Sortes, et tunc Sortes erit in Sorte, vel oportet quod illud instans sit aliqua pars Sortis, et tunc Sortes erit in parte sua, vel oportet quod sit accidens Sorti, et tunc Sortes erit in accidente suo. Et inductive patet quod non est in aliquo accidente suo quod sit illud instans naturae. Nec potest dici quod illud instans naturae sit aliquid extrinsecum Sorti, sicut patet inductive de omnibus extrinsecis Sorti. Et ideo indubitanter est tenendum quod non magis sunt instantia naturae quando aliquid est prius

Continuity, Contrariety, Contradiction, and Change

If Quasi-Aristotelianism could be faulted only because of the uncritical use it makes of some suspect Scotist distinctions or because of its misguided interpretation of a difficult passage in Aristotle, its failure would be unremarkable. But it calls for special criticism because of its claim to be the sole authentic Aristotelian theory of the instant of transition when in fact the "something false" that Baconthorpe accuses other medievals of imposing on the Philosopher is clearly what the Philosopher himself maintained. In setting forth the problem of contradiction at the instant of transition Baconthorpe says:

> . . . if anything were to block it, it would be what almost all the doctors say that the Philosopher says in *Physics* VIII—that one is not to give the *ultimum* of the not-being of the form to be generated, but that the whole preceding time corresponds to that of its not-being and an instant alone corresponds to the *primum* of its being. But that is of course false, because he expressly claims that an instant corresponds to the *ultimum* of the not-being just as to the *primum* of the being. . . . [And so] something false is imposed on the Philosopher. For the Philosopher there does not save the contradiction between the being and the not-being in that way—that the not-being is measured by the preceding time and one is not to give the *ultimum* of the not-being (but rather the *primum* of the being), to which there corresponds an instant; instead, the Philosopher there saves the contradiction in this way, that the instant is divided. . . .[25]

---

alio natura quam sint instantia honoris vel perfectionis quando aliquid est prius alio honore vel perfectione, vel instantia dilectionis quando aliquid est magis dilectum alio, et tamen sicut aliquid est prius natura alio vere, ita vere aliquid est prius perfectione alio. Et ita universaliter tenendum est quod non sunt aliqua instantia naturae vel originis praeter instantia temporis."

Father Gál's note to this passage reads: "Ockham hic arguit contra Ioannem Duns Scotum, qui posuit instantia naturae in divinis, ut ex. gr. in *Ordinatione*, II, d. 1, q. 1, nn. 27–37 (*Opera Omnia* VII, ed. Vaticana, 15–22)." See also Ockham 1978b, q. 3, pp. 532–36; and cf. Adams and Kretzmann 1969, pp. 71–76.

25. *Commentary on the "Sentences,"* L. III, d. 3, q. 2, art. 3: ". . . si aliquid impediret, hoc esset quod quasi omnes doctores dicunt quod Philosophus VIII *Physicorum* dicit quod non est dare ultimum non esse formae generandae, sed ipsi non esse eius correspondet totum tempus praecedens et instans solum correspondet primo esse eius. Sed hoc est falsum, immo, quia expresse ponit quod instans correspondet ultimo non esse sicut et primo esse. . . . falsum imponitur Philosopho. Non enim salvat Philosophus ibi contradictionem inter esse et non esse per hoc quod non esse mensuratur tempore praecedente et non sit dare ultimum non esse cui correspondeat instans; sed salvat Philosophus ibi contradictionem per hoc quod dividitur instans . . ." [Ed. Saggi 1955, 231.34–232.2; 233.19–23] For the continuation see n. 17); quoted at greater length in Knuuttila and Lehtinen 1979a, n. 1.

If Baconthorpe had nothing but the first paragraph (263b9–15) of the passage from *Physics* VIII 8 to work with, he might have a case. But it seems clear to me that the interpretation preferred by "almost all the doctors" is confirmed by Aristotle's development of the example in the second paragraph (263b15–26), where his treatment of the instant of transition as a limit—extrinsic to the interval characterized by not-ϕ and intrinsic to the interval characterized by ϕ—is typical of his treatment of instantaneous change in the *Physics*. And of course, if the instant of transition is conceived of as extrinsically limiting the one interval and intrinsically limiting the other, there is no problem of contradiction at the instant of transition between the permanent conditions not-ϕ and ϕ.[26] At the instant of transition x is ϕ, and during an interval immediately before that instant x was not-ϕ; and "almost all the doctors," those medievals who subscribe to the theory of change I am calling Aristotelianism, would take that conjunction to entail "x begins to be ϕ."[27]

4. Richard Kilvington's Approach to the Problem of Simultaneous Contradictories

One of those genuinely Aristotelian doctors was Richard Kilvington (d. 1361), a member of the older generation of the Oxford Calculators.[28] In his *Sophismata*, written probably around 1325, Kilvington touches in one way or another on most of the issues then current in logic and many of the issues in natural

26. Knuuttila and Lehtinen take a less critical attitude than mine toward the theory put forward by Baconthorpe, Caraccioli, et al., perhaps in part because they do not share my appreciation of the Aristotelian theory of change, as can be seen in these remarks of theirs: "Aristotle's 'solution' to the difficulty [of contradiction at the instant of transition] is to say that the change is instantaneous and the instant belongs to the posterior time with respect to the changing object. . . . in fact the problem as such is left untouched in the Aristotelian doctrine of the instant of change in continuous time" (Knuuttila and Lehtinen 1979a, p. 192). Cf. Sorabji 1976 on this Aristotelian doctrine.

27. For details regarding the analysis of such sentences, see Kretzmann 1976b and 1977. For further discussion of the Quasi-Aristotelians see chapter XI. For another version of the problem of simultaneous contradictories see section 3 of chapter VI.

28. On Kilvington see Bottin 1973a, 1973b, 1974, Kretzmann 1977, and Knuuttila and Lehtinen 1979b. On the Calculators, or Mertonians, see, e.g., Weisheipl 1968 and Sylla 1973.

philosophy.[29] His basic principles and concepts are the same as those of his better known contemporaries at Oxford—e.g., Thomas Bradwardine and the somewhat younger William Heytesbury—but his *Sophismata* differs from the work of the other Calculators in containing nothing that clearly counts as mathematics. Although he was, I think, deeply interested in problems and concepts of the sort that led to the development of the calculus more than three hundred years later, he pursued those interests by means of conceptual analysis rather than calculation. The portion of his work that serves my present purposes best is his sophisma 16, in which he investigates a particularly ingenious version of the problem of simultaneous contradictories.

Because Kilvington is a thoroughgoing Aristotelian regarding the analysis of change, his interest in the possibility of contradiction as a consequence of continuity focuses not on the unproblematic instant of transition itself but on the interval extrinsically limited by that instant. Medieval Aristotelianism is more flexible than Aristotle's own position in *Physics* VIII 8, however, in allowing the instant of transition to be intrinsic to *either* of the intervals of which it is the common boundary,[30] and in Kilvington's version of the problem it is not the earlier but the later interval that is extrinsically limited—i.e., there is a last instant of the earlier condition and therefore no first instant of the later. Put very simply, the question he addresses is this: are there cases of change such that two contradictory propositions are simultaneously true immediately after the instant of transition? He is of course committed to justifying the negative answer to that question—an under-

---

29. The treatise consists of a brief introduction and forty-eight sophismata, a few very short, some very long. Kilvington is also the author of a commentary on the *Sentences* of Peter Lombard (an edition of which is being prepared by John Van Dyk) and of commentaries or questions on Aristotle's *Physics, De generatione et corruptione,* and *Nicomachean Ethics.* The *Physics* commentary has not yet been definitely identified among surviving manuscripts (although Edith Sylla has good reason to think she may have found it), but each of the other works is extant in several manuscripts. The *Sophismata* survives in at least twenty-one manuscripts, several of which do not contain the complete text. With Barbara Ensign Kretzmann I am preparing an edition of the *Sophismata* based on the twenty manuscripts available to us, along with a translation, historical introduction, and philosophical commentary.

30. On the bases supplied by medieval logicians for assigning intrinsic or extrinsic limits see Kretzmann 1976b.

taking that may seem ridiculously easy until one appreciates the cases Kilvington contrives.

In sophismata 12 through 15 Kilvington has been considering problems arising in connection with the traversal of a distance, and particularly with various analyses of the beginning and completion of such a process. In sophisma 15 he rejects as invalid an argument of this form:

> Immediately after instant t it will be the case that p;
> Immediately after instant t it will be the case that not-p;
> ∴ At one and the same time it will be the case that p and not-p.

The ultimate basis of the rejection is the Aristotelian view of time as continuous, which entails the impossibility of there being any instant immediately after another instant, so that "immediately after instant t" can be correctly prefixed to each of two propositions without entailing that there is some single instant at which both propositions are true. One is nevertheless likely to be left with misgivings regarding the rejection of an intuitively valid argument on what seems to be a counterintuitive technicality, and Kilvington concludes sophisma 15 with a promise to make this point clearer in sophisma 16: "For this does not follow: '[Distance] A begins to have been traversed, and A begins to have been not traversed; therefore A at the same time will have been traversed and not traversed,' for a consequence [i.e., inference] analogous to this one is not acceptable, as will be evident in the following sophisma."[31]

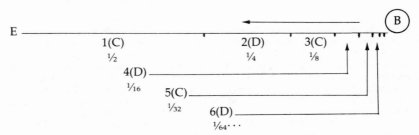

31. "Quia non sequitur 'A incipit esse pertransitum, et A incipit esse non pertransitum; igitur A simul erit pertransitum et non pertransitum,' quia consequentia similis illi non valet, ut patebit in hoc sophismate."

286

Sophisma 16 presents this case (in paragraph b).[32] A plane, E, is divided into proportional parts such that the first proportional part is $1/2$, the second is $1/4$, and the nth is $1/2^n$. Thus the sum of the first two proportional parts is $3/4$ the length of the plane, the sum of the first three is $7/8$, and the sum of the first n proportional parts is $(2^n - 1)/2^n$ the length of the plane. The odd-numbered proportional parts are all designated C and the even-numbered parts D. As shown in the diagram, a sphere, B, is located at the edge of the plane toward which the proportional parts get smaller, and the sphere now begins to move over the plane toward the first (largest) proportional part. Now consider this proposition, A: "B touches a C." The center of the difficulty in sophisma 16, its sophisma sentence, is a claim about that proposition—viz., the claim "A begins to be true." That is, we are to consider whether at the present instant, when the sphere begins to move, it begins to be true that the sphere touches an odd-numbered proportional part. Kilvington proceeds, in standard scholastic fashion, by presenting arguments on both sides of the issue before resolving it.

His argument on the affirmative side (the proof, paragraph c) itself yields an apparently paradoxical result; for in order to prove that the proposition "B touches a C" now *begins* to be true he must show that that proposition, A, now is not true and that A immediately hereafter will be true, and he does so by proving both that B is now at a distance from each C and that there will be no time before B touches a C. His argument can be presented informally in this way. B now is touching a point on a line that extrinsically limits the plane E; it is thus not touching any proportional part of E, although there certainly seems to be *no distance*

---

32. A complete edition and translation of sophisma 16 appears as appendix F at the end of this volume; references to the text will be to the letter-designated paragraphs of the text. Sophismata are typically organized according to an adaptation of the disputational structure characteristic of scholastic literature. Sophisma 16 is organized in this way: (a) sophisma sentence; (b) hypothesis (for the sophisma sentence); (c) proof (of the sophisma sentence, on the hypothesis); (d)–(g) disproof I (of the sophisma sentence, on the hypothesis); (d) first stage; (e) second stage; (f)–(g) third stage; (h) disproof II; (i) reply to the sophisma sentence (affirmative); (j) reply to disproof I; (k) reply to disproof II; (l) objection to reply to disproof II; (m) rejoinder to objection; (n) alternate reply; (o) rejoinder to alternate reply; (p) transition to sophisma 17.

between the location of the sphere and the proportional parts. If *B* were touching a point on the line that extrinsically limits the left-hand side of *E*, it would not be touching any *C*, but neither would it be *at a distance* from each *C*, since the first proportional part, a *C*, is *immediately* to the right of the extrinsically limiting left-hand line. *B*'s present situation, at the right-hand limit of *E*, is different, however, just because there can be no last, smallest proportional part. Between each *C* and the right-hand limit there is a distance—a distance divided into *C*s and *D*s, to be sure, but a distance nevertheless. Once these grounds for claiming that "*B* is at a distance from each *C*" are clear, it becomes particularly important to understand the grounds for claiming as well that there will be no time before *B* will touch a *C*, for surely it takes some time to traverse any distance. But at any instant after the present instant *B* will have traversed some length of *E*, and *every* length of *E* beginning at the right-hand limit of the plane "contains within itself infinitely many *C*s." Thus *before* any designated instant after the present instant *B* will have touched infinitely many *C*s; and since what occurs before *any* instant after the present instant occurs *immediately* after now, immediately after now proposition *A*, "*B* touches a *C*," will be true. And if something will occur immediately after now, there will be no time before it occurs; for if there were any such time, that time would have a middle instant—an instant that would be after now but before the occurrence of what is supposed to occur *before any* instant after now. And so although *B* is now at a distance from each *C*, there will be no time before *B* touches a *C*; in other words, proposition *A* does now begin to be true.

Since Kilvington supports the affirmative side of sophisma 16, we may take him to approve of this proof of the sophisma sentence;[33] by the same token he cannot be held fully accountable for the disproofs even though he may well have devised them. (It is always convenient, and often historically accurate, to think of the arguments opposed to a scholastic author's position as being

33. He evidently approves of it expressly in the unusual additional remark he makes in his affirmative reply to the sophisma sentence: ". . . as the arguments prove." The remark seems especially unusual here because sophisma 16 has only one proof; it does, however, consist of several arguments.

put forward by opponents.) The first of the two arguments for the negative side takes the approach standard for disproofs in Kilvington's *Sophismata*, attempting to reduce the sophisma sentence to an absurdity: If proposition *A* does begin to be true, then contradictory propositions will be true at the same time—*quod est impossibile* (paragraph f). The simultaneous contradictories aimed at in this elaborate disproof (paragraphs d–g) are proposition *A* itself—"*B* touches a *C*"—and its contradictory. For all its detail, disproof I is strategically simple and strong; its development can be presented along these lines.[34] Although proposition *A* happens to be concerned with the sphere's touching an odd-numbered proportional part, the argument Kilvington used in the proof to show that *A* begins to be true can easily be adapted to show that a proposition contrary to *A* also begins now to be true—viz., the proposition that the sphere touches an even-numbered part: "*B* touches a *D*."[35] But if both those propositions—"*B* touches a *C*" and "*B* touches a *D*"—begin now to be true, then both of them will be true immediately hereafter. And since whenever *B* touches a *D* it does not also touch a *C*, it seems likewise to follow that proposition *A* "immediately after this will be true and not true. Consequently contradictories immediately after this will be true" (paragraph e). In the context provided by the discussion in Kilvington's first fifteen sophismata, and especially in the light of his rejection of the inference of sophisma 15, it cannot be taken for granted that the truth of two mutually contradictory propositions immediately after this is tantamount to simultaneous contradiction. For "at the same time" (*simul*) strictly presupposes the possibility of designating a single (shared) instant, and by this point in Kilvington's treatise it is clearly understood that the expression

---

34. My presentation of disproof I here is intended only to bring out its line of argument, not to expound its details, which can be examined in the text provided in appendix F.

35. Disproof I is unquestionably designed to achieve a *reductio ad absurdum* in (the standard) terms of simultaneous contradictories, but the contribution it must make to the development of the sophisma could be made equally well in terms of these contraries. Despite all the explicit references in the disproof to contradictories, the opposed propositions that are most in evidence are not *A* and its contradictory but *A* and its contrary; and if the latter pair had been used throughout the argument, it would have avoided some of the difficulties it encounters. (See n. 37 below.)

"immediately after this" must be taken as designating an interval but not an instant.[36] And so if the argument is really to achieve the *reductio ad absurdum* it seeks, it must somehow show that "Contradictories immediately after this will be true" entails "Contradictories at one and the same instant will be true." Disproof I does undertake to show that entailment, but in a way that is gratuitously troublesome for present purposes.[37] I can bring out everything I need on the negative side of sophisma 16 (and everything the proponent of the negative side is entitled to) by introducing the intuitively acceptable analysis of temporal immediacy that plainly underlies the negative position[38]—viz.,

[S] x immediately after this will be ϕ if and only if there is a future interval extrinsically limited by the present instant such that x will be ϕ at every instant of that interval.

For if we interpret "Contradictories immediately after this will be true" in this (prima facie plausible) sense [S], then, since there can be no interval without infinitely many internal instants, there

36. It may be taken for granted that Kilvington uses these three expressions interchangeably: "Immediately after this p," "Without interval p," "There will be no time before p." (In sophisma 19 he says as much regarding the first two of them.) Certainly all three expressions occur in sophisma 16 with no hint of any distinctions among them, and such distinctions should emerge in the context of this discussion if he has any in mind.

37. The crucial contribution of the second stage is the derivation of "A and F [the contradictory of A] begin to be true," and the derivation is mistaken. The required derivation would be patently unacceptable, and it looks as if we have been presented with a sophistical surrogate. The inference in the third sentence of paragraph e is invalid. (From "Socrates will be white and there will be no time before Socrates will be white" one cannot infer "Socrates *begins* to be white"; one needs "the removing of the present"—"Socrates is not white now"—as well as "the positing of the future.") Either "A and F will be true" must be replaced by "A and F are not true" (its positing of the future is entailed by "there will be no time before A and F will be true"), or "A and F are not true" must be added to the premises. (The MSS provide no help here.) But since A and F are contradictories, one or the other of them must be true now (given the hypothesis, that one is F), and so the only sense in which "A and F are not true" could be accepted is "Not both A and F are true," the "compounded sense." But the sense required for purposes of the disproof as it has been developing is "A is not true, and F is not true," the "divided sense." (See n. 40 below on the compounded and divided senses.) The divided sense is, however, impossible, because A and F are contradictories, although it would have been available if the argument had been developed in terms of contraries instead. (See n. 35 above.)

38. I am grateful to Eric Wefald for his help in clarifying the interpretations of temporal immediacy that play a crucial role in the development of sophisma 16.

will be at least one instant (indeed, infinitely many instants) at which the contradictories A and not-A will both be true.

5. Kilvington's Solution to the Problem

Kilvington's counterattack is two-pronged, employing, first, a distinction between two senses of a proposition crucial to the disproof and, second, a different, weaker analysis of temporal immediacy. His primary target is the fundamental (though not the ultimate) conclusion of the disproof: "A immediately after this will be true and not true" (paragraph d). That conclusion is ambiguous in a way that was taken careful account of by medieval logicians: it may be read either in its "compounded sense" or in its "divided sense"[39]—i.e. (in this case), it may be read as a proposition with a conjoined term, "true-and-not-true," or as a conjunction of two propositions, one affirmative and the other negative.[40] Kilvington begins his reply to the disproof (paragraph j) by granting that conclusion, but only in its divided sense: "A immediately after this will be true, and A immediately after this will be not true." We have the right to assume (and would be right in assuming) that he is tacitly denying the conclusion in its compounded sense. Especially in the context of the discussion that has led from sophisma 15 to sophisma 16, however, it is important to ask whether the divided sense of this proposition *entails* its compounded sense.

Consider these inferences:

[DCP] x is ϕ, and x is ψ,   [DCF] x will be ϕ, and x will be ψ,
$\therefore x$ is ϕ-and-ψ $\therefore x$ will be ϕ-and-ψ

---

39. On the distinction generally, see Maierù 1972, chap. VII, pp. 499–600. For an example of a late medieval treatise devoted to this topic, see Paul of Pergula 1961; see also Maierù 1966.

40. It may be helpful to illustrate the distinction in terms of a different sort of example as well. The proposition "Joan and her husband weigh more than three hundred pounds" is true in the compounded sense—"Joan and her husband *together* weigh more than three hundred pounds"—but false in the divided sense: "Joan and her husband weigh more than three hundred pounds *apiece*," or "Joan weighs more than three hundred pounds, and her husband weighs more than three hundred pounds."

[DCP] presents the inference from the divided sense to the compounded sense in the present tense, and [DCF] presents the same inference in the future tense.[41] [DCP] is valid, but [DCF] is invalid because its premise may be interpreted for different times and its conclusion must be interpreted for only one time. Where ψ is "not-ϕ," [DCP] is trivially valid (because of a self-contradictory premise) and the invalidity of [DCF] is especially flagrant. It might be said on Kilvington's behalf, then, that to derive the compounded sense of "A immediately after this will be true and not true" from its divided sense would be to perpetrate an instance of [DCF] where "ψ" is "not-ϕ." Of course the proponent of the negative side of sophisma 16 would object that "immediately after this" makes a relevant difference, and Kilvington must address that point directly, as he does (beginning in the third sentence of paragraph j).[42]

In terms of inferences from the divided sense to the compounded sense, Kilvington's opponent (real or imagined) may be thought of as claiming that the inclusion of "immediately after this" renders disproof I an instance of the valid inference

[DCFI] x will be ϕ throughout h, and x will be ψ throughout h,
∴ x will be ϕ-and-ψ throughout h

(where h is some interval). [DCFI] obliterates the relevant difference between [DCP] and [DCF]. Kilvington takes up such a claim when he says that it does not follow "that A will be true and not true at the same time."

---

41. Everything said here regarding the inference from the divided sense to the compounded sense in the future tense would apply as well, mutatis mutandis, to such an inference in the past tense (which does not figure in sophisma 16).

42. In the second sentence of paragraph j Kilvington makes a move that is not as clear as it might have been. He rejects "the consequence"—i.e., the inference—leading to the consequent—i.e., the conclusion—"A begins to be true and not true," "understanding the consequent in the compounded sense." If he had made this remark regarding "A immediately after this will be true and not true," it would have been just what is expected here: the express denial of the conclusion of the first stage in its compounded sense. Nowhere in the disproofs is there the consequent "A begins to be true and not true," but I think it is safe to assume that Kilvington is using this proposition here as an alternate version of "A and F begin to be true" (see n. 37 above). If so, he follows his granting of the conclusion of the first stage in its divided sense with his denial of the conclusion of the second stage in its compounded sense. The latter move is a natural extension and reinforcement of the former.

An inference of an "at the same time" conclusion from "immediately after this" premises would ordinarily be rejected (and Kilvington does ordinarily reject it) because of the impossibility of designating an instant to which the *simul* can be attached. But that ordinary basis is not enough for rejecting such an inference in the context of sophisma 16, which provides a situation that seems to generate simultaneous contradictories not only if we (mistakenly) designate an instant "immediately after this," but also if we consider any *interval* immediately after this; and nothing in the concept of temporal immediacy could induce us to believe that we are mistaken in supposing that "immediately after this" designates an interval. The new basis Kilvington provides for his rejection of the inference consists in a weaker (broader, less strict) interpretation of "immediately after this" (and any other of the locutions he treats as interchangeable with that one).[43] It can be appreciated most readily if it is compared at once with the stronger (and intuitively more natural) interpretation introduced earlier:

[S] x immediately after this will be φ if and only if there is a future interval extrinsically limited by the present instant such that x will be φ at every instant of that interval.
[W] x immediately after this will be φ if and only if every future interval extrinsically limited by the present instant is such that there is an instant of that interval at which x will be φ.

Kilvington's rejection of [S] is in the fourth sentence of (j), and his acceptance of [W] is in the fifth. He rejects the stronger interpretation and explains his acceptance of the weaker in terms of the sophisma sentence and hypothesis of sophisma 16, but in a way that suggests what is in any case the truth, that [W] is preferable on general principles. Its preferability rests on the fact that [W] can do everything that [S] can do and more. First, [W], like [S], works perfectly as an interpretation for such paradigms as "Socrates immediately after this will be white" or ". . . will be moving," even though [S] is likely to seem more natural in such cases; and, second, although [S] requires one to reject the sophisma sentence in sophisma 16, [W] enables Kilvington to accept it

43. See n. 36 above.

without having to accept the simultaneous contradictories (or contraries) his opponent points to. For in terms of [W] we can see both that every interval beginning at the present instant is such that there is an instant of that interval at which B will touch a C, and that every interval beginning at the present instant is such that there is an instant of that interval at which B will touch a D (or will not touch a C). In other words, in terms of [W], B immediately after this will touch a C, *and* B immediately after this will touch a D (or will not touch a C). Thus although A immediately after this will be true, "during no continuous time immediate to this instant will A be true," and "in whatever time is taken immediate to this instant A will be infinitely often true and infinitely often false" (paragraph j).

6. Kilvington's Attempted Extension of His Solution

Kilvington's introduction of the weaker interpretation of "immediately after this" marks the philosophical climax of sophisma 16, and although there is a good deal of interesting material in the later portions of the sophisma,[44] the point most pertinent for present purposes can be extracted from the disputational exchange that ends it. There are people, Kilvington reports, who would reply very differently to this sophisma. They use the stronger interpretation of "immediately after this," and as he observes, "if one speaks in that way the sophisma [sentence] is false" (paragraph n). For if A begins to be true, then A immediately after this will be true; and that means, according to interpretation [S], that there is an interval beginning at this instant such that A will be true at every instant of that interval. But there is no such interval; during any interval beginning at this instant A will be true at some of its instants and false at others. As Kilvington puts it in his introduction and adoption of [W], there is "no continuous time immediate to this instant" during which A will be true only; in any interval "immediate to this instant A will be infinitely often true and infinitely often false."

---

44. The objection to Kilvington's reply to disproof II and his rejoinder to that objection (paragraphs l and m), for instance, provide an interesting challenge to and illustration of interpretation [W].

The first sentence of Kilvington's rejoinder to this alternate reply (paragraph o) may imply that his weaker interpretation is the *standard* interpretation, at least among some fourteenth-century logicians, since he describes those other people as "only changing the meaning of the term 'begins'" in their use of the stronger interpretation of "immediately after this."[45] But he charges those who use interpretation [S] with more than debasing the language; he says that they are committed by their interpretation to the absurdity that proposition *A* will be neither true nor false immediately after this.

In making that charge he has gone a step too far, however.[46] Interpretation [S] is less well-suited than [W] to the analysis of propositions involving "begins," but [S] is no more logically absurd than is [W]; in respect of their logical statuses the two interpretations are mirror images of each other. Kilvington's opponent, an adherent of [S], could rebut the charge of absurdity by pointing out that "Immediately after this *A* will be neither true nor false" is true only in the innocuous *divided* sense. That is, although there is no interval beginning at the present instant such that *A* will be *true* at every instant of that interval, and no interval beginning at the present instant such that *A* will be *false* at every instant of that interval, there is an interval beginning at the present instant such that *A* will be *either-true-or-false* at every instant of that interval. If Kilvington's interpretation [W] is characterized as showing us that *contradictories* can both be *true* immediately after this without entailing *the truth of a contradiction*, then, analogously, [S] must be characterized as showing us that *contradictories* can both be *false* immediately after this without entailing *the falsity of a tautology*. Even though Kilvington's charge of logical absurdity in [S] is unjustified, his choice of [W] is justified because [W], unlike [S], provides a basis for taking the affirmative side in sophisma 16, and it is only by taking the affirmative side that one can confront (and dismiss) the possibility that the theory

45. A very useful summary of various medieval analyses of "immediately" is available in the section on *Immediate* excerpted from the *Tractatus exponibilium* of Gaspar Lax (1512) and printed in Guerlac 1979, pp. 199–206. I am grateful to Edith Sylla for calling my attention to the relevance of this material.
46. I am grateful to Paul Spade for calling my attention to this criticism.

of temporal continuity entails the truth of a contradiction in the interval immediately after the instant of transition.

7. Conclusion

I hope that I have shown, in the first place, how the problem of simultaneous contradictories at the instant of transition may appear to arise in Aristotle's account of change and that it does not really arise there; and, in the second place, that the fourteenth-century theory of change put forward by Baconthorpe, Caraccioli, and others addresses a pseudoproblem with a quasi-Aristotelian nonsolution based on a misreading of *Physics* VIII 8; and, in the third place, that at least one orthodox Aristotelian of the fourteenth century, Richard Kilvington, advanced and refined the Aristotelian analysis by devising apparent paradoxes involving simultaneous contradictories in the temporal interval beginning at the instant of transition and adapting the elements of the Aristotelian analysis to the resolution of those paradoxes.

CHAPTER XI

Quasi-Aristotelianism

PAUL VINCENT SPADE

1. The Aristotelian Source of Instants of Nature

In medieval logical texts, the so-called Law of Contradictories was frequently expressed by saying that two contradictories could not be either true or false "together."[1] The word "together" (*simul*) has of course a primary, temporal sense, meaning "at the same time." But Aristotle, in *Categories* 13, distinguished other senses of the word, too, including one sense in which things may be said to be together, or simultaneous, "by nature" (*phusei hama, simul natura*): "Thus we call simultaneous by nature those things which reciprocate as to implication of existence provided that neither is in any way the cause of the other's existence; and also co-ordinate species of the same genus."[2] When two things are not simultaneous by nature, the one may be "prior by nature" (*proteron tē phusei, prius natura*) to the other: "For of things which reciprocate as to implication of existence, that which is in some way the cause of the other's existence might reasonably be called prior by nature."[3] In the *Metaphysics*, Aristotle describes another sense of natural priority, according to which the naturally prior and naturally posterior do not "reciprocate as to implication of existence": "Some things then are called prior and posterior in

---

1. See, e.g., Peter of Spain 1972, I 14, p. 7.25–27: "Lex contradictoriarum talis est quod si una est vera, reliqua est falsa, et econverso; in nulla enim materia possunt simul esse vere vel false." See also William of Sherwood 1937, p. 36.13–14: "Lex contradictoriarum est, quod non possunt simul esse verae neque simul falsae, ut satis patet." Not all authors expressed the law explicitly in these terms; thus, Lambert of Auxerre 1971, p. 19: "Contradictoriarum talis est lex: si una est vera, reliqua est falsa in omni materia et e converso."
2. *Categories* 13, 15a8–11; Ackrill 1963, pp. 40–41.
3. *Categories* 12, 14b11–13; Ackrill 1963, p. 39.

this sense, others . . . in respect of nature and substance, i.e. those which can be without other things, while the others cannot be without *them*—a distinction which Plato used."[4]

2. The Source of Quasi-Aristotelianism

In the fourteenth century, a certain group of authors thought they saw a problem with the Aristotelian analysis of the instant of transition; it appeared to them that at the instant when a thing changes from being φ to being not-φ (or vice versa), it must be *both* φ and not-φ. In order to preserve the Law of Contradictories, therefore, these authors interpreted the word "together" (*simul*) in the common formulation of that law as referring not to temporal simultaneity but to simultaneity by nature. Hence contradictories may be true at the same instant of time, as in the case of instantaneous transition, but they cannot be true at the same "instant of nature."

Simo Knuuttila and Anja Inkeri Lehtinen first called scholars' attention to this curious school of thought,[5] and Norman Kretzmann has given it the name "Quasi-Aristotelianism," on the grounds that its adherents misread the Aristotelian doctrine of instantaneous transition.[6] Quasi-Aristotelianism is the topic of this paper.

I do not propose to argue that Quasi-Aristotelianism is in fact authentically Aristotelian doctrine; I agree with Kretzmann that it is not. And I certainly do not intend to argue that the theory is

4. *Metaphysics* V 11, 1019a1–5 (Oxford translation). See also *Categories* 12, 14a29–35, and *Physics* VIII 7, 260b17–19. In neither of these last two passages, however, is there any explicit reference to nature. Note that, if each of two things can exist without the other and the two are not coordinate species of the same genus, then they are neither naturally simultaneous nor naturally prior and posterior to each other in either of Aristotle's two senses. The relation of "priority" is thus not a linear ordering of nature.

5. Knuuttila and Lehtinen 1979a. Knuuttila and Lehtinen refer to a forthcoming book of theirs on the consideration of change and contradiction in the fourteenth century (ibid., n. 22).

6. See chapter X. It might also be said that these authors missed the Aristotelian doctrine of contradiction. For in at least two places (*Sophistical Refutations* 5, 167a23–27, and 26, 181a1–5) Aristotle makes it clear that to "refute" a claim (and so to show it to be false) is in part to prove that its contradictory is true "at the same time" (not *hama*, but *en tō autō chronō*). Hence the truth of one contradictory is sufficient to establish the falsehood of the other "at the same time."

true. But I will try to argue that the theory is more interesting, and perhaps less bizarre, than it first appears to be. I hope thereby to motivate further research in this still relatively unexplored territory.[7] At the end of the chapter I shall suggest some things one might look for in that research.

Kretzmann argues that Quasi-Aristotelianism fails to recognize that the instant of transition—at least in the case of a transition between so-called permanent conditions—is simply no problem for the Aristotelian theory correctly interpreted.[8] At the end of chapter X above he says that Quasi-Aristotelianism "addresses a pseudoproblem" with a "nonsolution." Whether it is in fact a nonsolution I shall discuss presently; for the moment I want to look more closely at the pseudoproblem.

3. The Problem Addressed by Quasi-Aristotelianism

The standard kinds of examples of instantaneous transition do not bother me—as long as we consider only transitions between "permanent" conditions. I agree with Kretzmann that in those cases what the Quasi-Aristotelians saw was indeed only a pseudoproblem. But Landulf Caraccioli, perhaps the main exponent of Quasi-Aristotelianism,[9] suggests another kind of transition for which the problem may be real. As background for Caraccioli's suggestion it should be remembered that in the Aristotelian analysis every change requires a terminus a quo and a terminus ad quem.[10] In the case of generation, medieval Aristotelianism held that there is a first instant of "being" but no last instant of "nonbeing," that the terminus ad quem is that first instant of being, while the terminus a quo is the entire interval preceding and extrinsically limited by that instant, the interval of "non-

7. The only literature to date on this topic is contained in Knuuttila and Lehtinen 1979a and in this volume.

8. Note that instantaneous transitions between so-called successive conditions present a problem different from the one the Quasi-Aristotelians thought they saw in instantaneous transitions between "permanent" conditions. The latter threatened to violate the Law of Noncontradiction, the former the Law of the Excluded Middle. For a discussion of the problem of instantaneous transition between successive conditions, see Kretzmann 1976b, esp. section VI.

9. Knuuttila and Lehtinen 1979a, p. 190.

10. Aristotle, *Physics* V 1, 224b35–225a2.

being" and, finally, that the generation itself is to be assigned to the first instant of being, the terminus ad quem.[11] Landulf then argues: "When all that which is *per accidens* has been removed, nothing is removed of that which is *per se*. But the whole time preceding the generation is related to it *per accidens*. Therefore, when it has been removed, there will still be the generation in the last instant.[12] But not without its termini. Therefore, in that last instant there will be being and nonbeing, which are the termini of the generation."[13]

As it stands, the argument is perhaps not very compelling, even though Landulf goes on at once to try to prove his minor premise, that the preceding time really is only accidentally related to the generation and so can be removed with impunity.[14] Nevertheless, the kernel of Landulf's argument can perhaps be brought out more forcefully by asking what we are to say about creation, for which there is no preceding temporal interval of nonbeing, since time itself begins with creation (according to the standard medieval account of creation).

Of course creation is not generation or indeed any other kind of Aristotelian change, if only because there is no underlying material or subject.[15] Creation is *ex nihilo*. But perhaps we ought to be less comfortable about denying that creation is a "transition" of some kind or other from nonbeing to being. It is not a temporal transition, to be sure. But if it is not a transition of some sort, if creation makes no "difference," then what has the divine creative

---

11. See, e.g., Kretzmann 1976b, esp. sections IV and V.

12. The designation "the last instant" should pick out an *intrinsic* limit of the preceding time. In keeping with the standard Aristotelian analysis, however, and with his own hypothesis that "the *whole* time preceding . . . has been removed," Landulf presumably intends to refer to the instant that *extrinsically* limits the preceding time.

13. Landulf Caraccioli, *in II Sent.*, d. 1, q. 1: "Remoto omni eo quod est per accidens, nihil removetur de eo quod est per se. Sed totum tempus praecedens generationem per accidens se habet ad eam, ergo eo remoto adhuc erit in instanti ultimo generatio, sed non sine suis terminis. Ergo in illo instanti erit esse et non esse, quae sunt termini generationis." Quoted in Knuuttila and Lehtinen 1979a, n. 33.

14. "Maior patet. Minorem probo, quia ad mutationem instantaneam accidit quaecumque mensuratio successiva. In toto enim tempore praecedenti est alteratio sola, quae accidit generationi propter dispositionem subiecti." Quoted in Knuuttila and Lehtinen 1979a, n. 33.

15. See, e.g., Thomas Aquinas, *Summa theologiae* I 45, 2, obj. 2 and reply.

act accomplished? On the other hand, if it does make a difference, it must make a difference *to something*. To what then? Not to
God, surely. For God remains immutably the same, no matter
what he does and no matter what happens—whether he creates
or not. It must be the creature, therefore, to which creation makes
a difference, since there is no third candidate.[16] But what difference does creation make to a creature? It makes a big difference,
one might say—indeed, the biggest difference of all: it makes the
creature begin to *exist*. But that is not yet a difference; that is only
half a difference. "Difference" is a relational word, and so far we
have only one term of the relation: the existing creature. What is
the other term?

Considerations like these are perhaps not conclusive. But neither are they frivolous to anyone who accepts the doctrine of creation, as both the Quasi-Aristotelians and their opponents certainly did. And if one takes such considerations seriously, one will be
strongly tempted to view creation as a transition between two
contradictory terms or conditions: nonbeing and being. But once
that is done, Landulf has all he really needs: some cases of transition between contradictory conditions are such that the usual
Aristotelian distribution of such conditions over the temporal continuum will simply not work.

Landulf himself may have developed his theory in part at least
on some such basis. For, according to Knuuttila and Lehtinen,
Landulf discussed his view at some length in one of his questions
on the *Sentences*: "Whether the contradictories that are the termini
of creation can pertain to the same thing in the same instant of
time and in the same respect?"[17] Perhaps, then, the Quasi-
Aristotelians were not just addressing a pseudoproblem; perhaps
they had something deeper in mind. I agree that there is no need
for the simultaneous truth of contradictories in the usual or reg-
ulation kind of Aristotelian genesis, and insofar as the Quasi-
Aristotelians focused on such cases they were indeed addressing

16. Cf., e.g., the line of reasoning in Aquinas, *Summa theologiae* I 13, 7, and I 45,
3.

17. "Utrum contradictoria quae sunt termini creationis possunt competere eidem
in eodem instanti temporis secundum idem?" See Knuuttila and Lehtinen 1979a,
n. 22.

a pseudoproblem. But there is another kind of "Genesis" for which there may be a real problem indeed.

4. The Solution Provided by Quasi-Aristotelianism

Kretzmann claims that Quasi-Aristotelianism not only address-es a pseudoproblem but also addresses it with a nonsolution. That is, even if the instant of transition should turn out to be a problem for a correctly understood Aristotelianism—and I have argued that perhaps it does so in the case of creation—still, Quasi-Aristotelianism does not have the resources to solve that problem. On this point Kretzmann is following John the Canon, a critic of Landulf and of Quasi-Aristotelianism in general.[18] John's idea seems to be that the natural priority of one thing over another is quite compatible with their being at the same "instant of nature," so that an appeal to the order of nature is not sufficient to guarantee the natural nonsimultaneity of contradictory condi-tions. That natural nonsimultaneity, however, is the whole basis for the Quasi-Aristotelians' claim to have saved the Law of Con-tradictories from the problem of the instant of transition.

When one looks more closely at John's text, however, it seems he has not made his case:

[For a thing] to be prior by nature is not [for it] to be prior in some instant (*signo*) in which it is not posterior, although Landulf says the opposite. Rather to be prior by nature is nothing else but the presup-position of this thing by that in a certain otherness of nature. For although in theology the Father is presupposed by the Son as the generator is presupposed by the generated, nevertheless because they are both of the same nature, the doctors of theology generally do not posit a priority of nature, but rather one of origin. In this alone do priority of nature and of origin differ, that a priority of nature is a presupposition and dependence of this thing on that in a certain otherness of nature, but [a priority] of origin [is such presup-position and dependence] in an identity of nature. Take careful note of this. But brother Landulf believes the opposite. For he says that whatever things are prior [and posterior] by nature are so related that one is in some instant (*signo*) in which the other one is not. And

18. See section 3 of chapter X.

therefore he says that contradictories can be true together (*simul*) in the same instant (*instanti*) of time, but not of nature.[19]

The text is very interesting, but there is simply no argument in it. There is an illuminating explanation of what it means to be prior by nature—an explanation that seems perhaps to correspond more closely to the Aristotelian notion of natural priority defined in the *Metaphysics*, where there is no "reciprocation as to implication of existence," than to the notion defined in the *Categories*, where there is. (The text is not altogether decisive on this point, but there is certainly no explicit mention of any such reciprocal implication.) There is also a *claim* that natural priority is compatible with natural simultaneity, but there is no real attempt to make that claim good.

In another passage John the Canon refers to the following argument, which he attributes only to a certain "reverend doctor," although the context suggests Landulf:

Every subject is naturally prior to its proper passion. Therefore in that prior condition (*in illo priori*) in which the subject precedes its proper passion, either the passion exists or it does not. If it does exist [in that condition], then the subject does not precede it. If it does not exist [in that condition], it exists in a second instant (*signo*), although these two instants (*signa*) are in the same instant (*instanti*) of time. Otherwise there would be an intervening time in which the subject would exist without its proper passion, which is false. Therefore being and nonbeing, which are contradictories, are verifiable and compossible in the same instant (*instanti*).[20]

19. John the Canon, *Quaestiones super VIII libros Physicorum Aristotelis* I, q. 4: "Ad illam probationem dico de praesenti quod esse prius natura non est esse prius in aliquo signo in quo non est posterius, licet oppositum dicat Landulphus. Sed esse prius natura non est aliud nisi praesuppositio huius ab hoc in quadam alteritate naturae, licet enim pater in divinis praesupponitur a filio sicut generans praesupponitur a genito, quia tamen sunt ambo eiusdem naturae. Ideo communiter a doctoribus in divinis non ponitur prioritas naturae, sed originis. In hoc solum differunt prioritas naturae et originis, quia prioritas naturae est praesuppositio et dependentia huius ab hoc in quadam alteritate naturae, originis vero in identitate naturae. Et hoc nota diligenter. Frater autem Landulphus oppositum huius sentit. Dicit enim quod quaecumque sunt priora natura, sic se habent quod unum est in aliquo signo in quo reliquum non est. Et ideo dicit quod contradictoria esse simul vera in eodem instanti temporis possunt, sed non naturae." [Quoted in Knuuttila and Lehtinen 1979a, n. 37]

20. John the Canon, *super I Physic.*, 8: "Sed contra istam conclusionem arguit unus reverendus doctor qui tenet quod contradictoria possunt de eodem verificari

Notice that this text seems to appeal to a notion of natural priority like that defined in the *Categories*—insofar as a subject and its proper passion "reciprocate as to implication of existence"—and unlike that defined in the *Metaphysics*. John replies to the argument as follows:

> Contradictories are more opposed (*repugnant*) than contraries. . . . But contraries are not compossible in the same instant (*instanti*) of time. Therefore, etc. And therefore I reply and say that in that prior condition (*in illo priori*) in which the subject precedes its proper passion, the passion does not exist. And when you say, "Therefore it is not prior," I deny the consequence. For to be prior by nature is nothing else but the presupposition of this thing by that in an otherness of nature.[21]

Once again, it seems to me, the argument does not succeed. First of all, anyone who is willing to grant simultaneously true contradictories would have little reason to balk at simultaneously true contraries. But even apart from that, John's explanation of natural priority at the end of the passage does not at all justify his denial of the consequence concluding "therefore it is not prior." That is, it in no way explains why John rejects the inference from natural simultaneity to natural nonpriority. Perhaps, in virtue of the different notions of Aristotelian natural priority that seem to be held by John and his anonymous opponent, the point of John's remarks is simply to disagree with his "reverend doctor" over the correct definition of natural priority. But if that is so, it makes for a weak reply. For the inference from natural simul-

---

in eodem instanti temporis, pro diversis tamen signis naturae. Hoc probat sic: Omne subiectum est prius sua passione propria natura. In illo ergo priori in quo subiectum praecedit suam propriam passionem vel passio est vel non est. Si est, ergo subiectum non praecedit ipsam. Si non est et in secundo signo est, cum ista duo signa sint in eodem instanti temporis, aliter tempus esset medium in quo subiectum esse sine propria passione, quod est falsum. Ergo esse et non esse quae sunt contradictoria, sunt verificabilia et compossibilia in eodem instanti." [Quoted in Knuuttila and Lehtinen 1979a, n. 30]

21. "Respondeo et arguo primo contra hanc opinionem, quia magis repugnant contradictoria quam contraria. Ista etiam ab ipsis conceditur et ipsa etiam probabitur consequenter: Sed contraria non sunt compossibilia in eodem instanti temporis, ergo et cetera. Et ideo respondeo et dico, quod in illo priori quo subiectum praecedit propriam passionem, passio est. Et cum dicis, ergo non est prius, nego consequentiam. Nam esse prius natura nihil aliud est quam praesuppositio huius ab hoc in alteritate naturae." [Quoted in Knuuttila and Lehtinen 1979a, n. 30]

taneity to natural nonpriority seems valid using either definition. It is certainly valid in the case of the definitions of natural priority and simultaneity in the *Categories*. In the *Metaphysics*, to be sure (and in the other passages cited in n. 4 above), there is no mention of simultaneity but only of priority. Nevertheless, if we make the minimal assumption that simultaneous entities are prior to exactly the same things, the inference from simultaneity to nonpriority holds there, too. For, on that assumption, if x is naturally both prior to and simultaneous with y, then y is naturally prior to itself. But this violates the asymmetry of natural priority as defined in the *Metaphysics*. In order for John to make his point, therefore, he must deny our minimal assumption. But nothing he says indicates that he would be willing to do this or suggests some other notion of natural simultaneity he could have had in mind. In short, John's reply is not persuasive. And if natural simultaneity is indeed incompatible with natural priority, then it is not at all clear to me that Quasi-Aristotelianism lacks the resources to solve the problem—if it is a problem—that gave rise to it.

5. Problems for Quasi-Aristotelianism

But there is more to the story—and here I simply want to sketch some possibilities and make some suggestions. For instance, to the extent to which the Quasi-Aristotelians thought they saw a problem not just with creation but with instantaneous transitions in general, will not the same problem (or pseudoproblem) arise in the order of nature? If, in the temporal order, the transition from not-ϕ to ϕ can be accomplished only in such a way that contradictory conditions hold in the same instant of time although at different instants of nature, how, in the natural order, is the transition from not-ϕ to ϕ to be accomplished? That is, how is it possible to be not-ϕ at one instant of nature and ϕ at a subsequent instant of nature without being *both* ϕ and not-ϕ in some instant of nature? The same problem (or pseudoproblem) will emerge, and Quasi-Aristotelianism will have gained nothing, if the instants of nature form a continuum, as do the instants of time, or for that matter if the instants of nature are, to use a later terminology, merely densely ordered. Quasi-Aristotelianism must therefore find a way to rule out such a reemergence of the problem, and it is worthwhile investigating the writings of its proponents to discover whether they do in fact have something to say about this.

Although Aristotle had spoken of simultaneity and priority by nature, it was Duns Scotus who seems to have been the immediate source for the Quasi-Aristotelians' talk about "instants of nature." For Scotus this notion appears to be connected with the notion of essentially ordered causes in such a way that x belongs to an "instant of nature" prior to the one to which y belongs if and only if x is prior to y in the order of essential causality.[22] If the Quasi-Aristotelians of the fourteenth century had this sort of thing in mind, then perhaps they regarded the required discontinuity or nondensity of the instants of nature as a simple corollary of the familiar arguments against an infinity of essentially ordered causes. At least some such arguments, whatever we think of their soundness or validity, would indeed have that corollary.[23] Is this connection to be found in the Quasi-Aristotelian literature? That, too, is a point worth investigating.

22. See, e.g., John Duns Scotus, *Opus Oxoniense*, prol., q. 3, a. 8, § 23. For x to be prior to y in the order of essential causality is not necessarily for x to be itself a cause of y. For this complication, which does not affect the main point here, see Scotus's explanation in the passage just cited, and also in his *De primo principio*, chap. 2, conclusions 11–12, in Roche 1949, pp. 28–30. It should perhaps be pointed out that, while Scotus was of course familiar with the Aristotelian texts, his notion of natural priority and posteriority was probably more directly influenced by Avicenna. See, e.g., John Duns Scotus, *Ordinatio* I, dist. 8, pars 2, q. unica, n. 248 (ed. Vaticana, IV, p. 293). Henry of Ghent also cites Avicenna on this notion. See Henry of Ghent, *Quodlibet* VIII, q. 9, *in corp.* (quoted in the notes to Scotus, loc. cit.). Perhaps significantly, both Scotus and Henry are here concerned with the notion of creation, Henry more explicitly than Scotus. Notice, however, that while these passages attribute to Avicenna the notion of a nontemporal priority and posteriority, they do not attribute to him any notion of "instants" of nature.

23. Arguments against an infinite *sequence* of essentially ordered causes, in which each effect has an *immediate* cause, would not automatically rule out a dense ordering in which no effect has an immediate cause. But consider the following argument by Scotus, *Opus Oxoniense* I, d. 2, q. 1, quoted in Wolter 1963, p. 42:5. "Then, too, if an infinite number of essentially ordered causes concurred to produce some effect, it would follow that an infinite number would simultaneously cause this effect, for it follows from the third difference [between essentially and accidentally ordered causes] that essentially ordered causes must exist simultaneously. Now no philosopher assumes this." ("Tum quia si causae infinitae ordinatae essentialiter concurrant ad productionem alicuius effectus; et ex tertia differentia omnes causae essentialiter ordinatae sint simul, sequitur quod infinita sunt simul ad causandum hunc effectum, quod nullus philosophus ponit.")

On the other hand, while some Quasi-Aristotelians, like John Baconthorpe and Hugh of Newcastle, speak freely of the priority and posteriority of instants of nature,[24] Landulf himself does not—at least not in the texts I have seen—John the Canon to the contrary notwithstanding.[25] Landulf says that contradictory conditions that hold in the same instant of time are in *distinct* instants of nature, but I have not found him saying that one of those distinct instants of nature is prior or posterior to the other.[26] Indeed, in one puzzling text Landulf says:

> The third proposition is to see if instants (*instantia*) of nature have a succession or simultaneity with respect to one another. And I say that [they have] neither the one nor the other. Note here that simultaneity and succession do not pertain to indivisible measures, but only to divisible ones; "distinction," on the other hand, pertains to indivisible measures. And therefore two signs or instants (*signa vel instantia*) of nature, properly [speaking], neither are simultaneous nor succeed one another. Instead they are two indivisible measures measuring distinct permanent entities.[27]

I do not know exactly what to make of this. Taken at face value, the text says that we should not think of instants of nature as ordered at all, densely or otherwise. But if that is so, then the alleged Scotistic origin of Landulf's instants of nature becomes rather doubtful. For Scotus's instants of nature certainly are ordered. The question must then be asked why Baconthorpe and Hugh of Newcastle accepted the ordering that Landulf rejected.

There is a great deal more to be learned about the Quasi-Aristotelians. I hope to have established that their doctrine is interesting and not altogether outlandish, one that deserves to be investigated more fully.

24. See, e.g., Knuuttila and Lehtinen 1979a, nn. 1 and 21.
25. See the passage from John quoted in n. 19.
26. See Knuuttila and Lehtinen 1979a, nn. 5, 28–29, 33–36.
27. Landulf Caraccioli, *in II Sent.*, d. 1, q. 1: "Tertia propositio est videre, si instantia naturae habeant adinvicem successionem vel simultatem. Et dico, quod nec hoc nec illud. Ubi nota quod simultas et successio non competunt mensuris indivisibilibus, sed tantum divisibilibus. Sed mensuris indivisibilibus competit distinctio, et ideo duo signa vel instantia naturae proprie nec sunt simul nec sibi succedunt, sed sunt duae mensurae indivisibiles mensurantes distincta entia permanentia . . ." (quoted in Knuuttila and Lehtinen 1979a, n. 36).

Aristotle on the Continuous

1. Continuity in the *Categories* (Translated by J. L. Ackrill)

4b20. Of quantities some are discrete, others continuous. . . .

4b22. Discrete are number and language; continuous are lines, surfaces, bodies, and also, besides these, time and place. For the parts of a number have no common boundary at which they join together. For example, if five is a part of ten the two fives do not join together at any common boundary but are separate; nor do the three and the seven join together at any common boundary. Nor could you ever in the case of number find a common boundary of its parts, but they are always separate. Hence number is one of the discrete quantities. Similarly, language also is one of the discrete quantities (that language is a quantity is evident, since it is measured by long and short syllables; I mean here language that is *spoken*). For its parts do not join together at any common boundary. For there is no common boundary at which the syllables join together, but each is separate in itself. A line, on the other hand, is a continuous quantity. For it is possible to find a common boundary at which its parts join together, a point. And for a surface, a line; for the parts of a plane join together at some common boundary. Similarly in the case of a body one would find a common boundary—a line or a surface—at which the parts of the body join together. Time also and place are of this kind. For present time joins on to both past time and future time. Place again is one of the continuous quantities. For the parts of a body occupy some place, and they join together at a common boundary. So the parts of the place occupied by the various parts of the body, themselves join together at the same boundary at which the parts of the body do. Thus place also is a continuous quantity, since its parts join together at one common boundary.

2. Continuity in the *Physics* (Translated by R. P. Hardie and R. K. Gaye, slightly adapted)

Book V

[The subject of Book V is motion. Since Aristotle claims that continuity is an essential property of every movement, he inserts a chapter—chapter 3—explaining certain terms that he will use when discussing the continuity of motion, immediately following the two introductory chapters, in which he classifies motions into *per se* and *per accidens*, and into changes in respect of quality, quantity, and place.]

226b21. Things are said to be *together* in place when they are in one primary place, and to be *apart* when they are in different places.

Things are said to be *in contact* when their extremities are together.

That which a changing thing, if it changes continuously in a natural manner, naturally reaches before it reaches that to which it changes last, is *between*. Thus between implies the presence of at least three things: for in a process of change it is the contrary that is last: and a thing is moved continuously if it leaves no gap or only the smallest possible gap in the material—not in the time (for a gap in the time does not prevent things having a between, while, on the other hand, there is nothing to prevent the highest note sounding immediately after the lowest) but in the material in which the motion takes place. This is manifestly true not only in local changes but in every other kind as well. [Now every change implies a pair of opposites, and opposites may be either contraries or contradictories; since then contradiction admits of no mean term, it is obvious that between must imply a pair of contraries.][1] That is locally contrary which is most distant in a straight line: for

1. The bracketed sentence has been transferred by the editors, in the interests of sense, from 227a7 TO 226b21.

the shortest line is definitely limited, and that which is definitely limited constitutes a measure.

b34. A thing is *in succession* when it is after the beginning in position or in form or in some other respect in which it is definitely so regarded, and when further there is nothing of the same kind as itself between it and that to which it is in succession, e.g. a line or lines if it is a line, a unit or units if it is a unit, a house if it is a house (there is nothing to prevent something of a different kind being between). For that which is in succession is in succession to a particular thing, and is something posterior: for one is not in succession to two, nor is the first day of the month to the second: in each case the latter is in succession to the former.

227a6. A thing that is in succession and in contact is *contiguous*. [See note 1.]

The *continuous* is just what is contiguous, but I say a thing is continuous when the extremities of each at which they are in contact become one and the same and are (as the name implies) contained in each other. Continuity is impossible if these extremities are two. This definition makes it plain that continuity belongs to things that naturally in virtue of their mutual contact form a unity. And in whatever way that which holds them together is one, so too will the whole be one, e.g. by a rivet or glue or contact or organic union.

Book VI

231a1. Now if the terms "continuous," "in contact," and "in succession" are understood as defined above[2]—things being "continuous" if their extremities are one, "in contact" if their extremities are together, and "in succession" if there is nothing of their own kind intermediate between them—nothing that is continuous can be composed of indivisibles: e.g. a line cannot be composed of points, the line being continuous and the point indivisible. For the extremities of two points can neither be *one* (since of an indivisible there can be no extremity as distinct from some other part) nor *together* (since that which has no parts can have no

2. [*Physics*] v. 3.

extremity, the extremity and the thing of which it is the extremity being distinct).

231b. Moreover, if that which is continuous is composed of points, these points must be either *continuous* or *in contact* with one another: and the same reasoning applies in the case of all indivisibles. Now for the reason given above they cannot be continuous: and one thing can be in contact with another only if whole is in contact with whole or part with part or part with whole. But since indivisibles have no parts, they must be in contact with one another as whole with whole. And if they are in contact with one another as whole with whole, they will not be continuous: for that which is continuous has distinct parts: and these parts into which it is divisible are different in this way, i.e. spatially separate.

Nor, again, can a point be *in succession* to a point or a moment to a moment in such a way that length can be composed of points or time of moments: for things are in succession if there is nothing of their own kind intermediate between them, whereas that which is intermediate between points is always a line and that which is intermediate between moments is always a period of time.

Again, if length and time could thus be composed of indivisibles, they could be divided into indivisibles, since each is divisible into the parts of which it is composed. But, as we saw, no continuous thing is divisible into things without parts. Nor can there be anything of any other kind intermediate between the parts or between the moments: for if there could be any such thing it is clear that it must be either indivisible or divisible, and if it is divisible, it must be divisible either into indivisibles or into divisibles that are infinitely divisible, in which case it is continuous.

Moreover, it is plain that everything continuous is divisible into divisibles that are infinitely divisible: for if it were divisible into indivisibles, we should have an indivisible in contact with an indivisible, since the extremities of things that are continuous with one another are one and are in contact.

232a. The same reasoning applies equally to magnitude, to time, and to motion: either all of these are composed of indivisibles and are divisible into indivisibles, or none. This may be made clear as follows. If a magnitude is composed of indivisibles, the motion over that magnitude must be composed of corresponding indivisible motions: e.g. if the magnitude *ABC* is composed of the indivisibles *A, B, C,* each corresponding part of the motion *DEF* of *Z* over *ABC* is indivisible. Therefore, since where there is motion there must be something that is in motion, and where there is something in motion there must be motion, therefore the being-moved will also be composed of indivisibles. So *Z* traversed *A* when its motion was *D, B* when its motion was *E,* and *C* similarly when its motion was *F.* Now a thing that is in motion from one place to another cannot at the moment when it was in motion both be in motion and at the same time have completed its motion at the place to which it was in motion: e.g. if a man is walking to Thebes, he cannot be walking to Thebes and at the same time have completed his walk to Thebes: and, as we saw, *Z* traverses the partless section *A* in virtue of the presence of the motion *D.* Consequently, if *Z* actually passed through *A after* being in process of passing through, the motion must be divisible: for at the time when *Z* was passing through, it neither was at rest nor had completed its passage but was in an intermediate state: while if it is passing through and has completed its passage *at the same moment,* then that which is walking will at the moment when it is walking have completed its walk and will be in the place to which it is walking; that is to say, it will have completed its motion at the place to which it is in motion.[3] And if a thing is in motion over the whole *ABC* and its motion is the three *D, E,* and *F,* and if it is not in motion at all over the partless section *A* but has completed its motion over it, then the motion will consist not of motions but of starts, and will take place by a thing's having completed a motion without being in motion: for on this assumption it has completed its passage through *A* without passing through it. So it will be possible for a thing to have completed a walk without ever walking: for on this assumption it has completed a walk over a particular distance without walking over that distance. Since, then, everything must be either at rest or in motion, and *Z* is therefore at rest in each of the sections *A, B,* and *C,*

3. Which is *ex hypothesi* impossible (231b28–30)

it follows that a thing can be continuously at rest and at the same time in motion: for, as we saw, Z is in motion over the whole ABC and at rest in any part (and consequently in the whole) of it. Moreover, if the indivisibles composing DEF are motions, it would be possible for a thing in spite of the presence in it of motion to be not in motion but at rest, while if they are not motions, it would be possible for motion to be composed of something other than motions.

And if length and motion are thus indivisible, it is neither more nor less necessary that time also be similarly indivisible, that is to say be composed of indivisible moments: for if the whole distance is divisible and an equal velocity will cause a thing to pass through less of it in less time, the time must also be divisible, and conversely, if the time in which a thing is carried over the section A is divisible, this section A must also be divisible.

232b. And since every magnitude is divisible into magnitudes—for we have shown that it is impossible for anything continuous to be composed of indivisible parts, and every magnitude is continuous—it necessarily follows that the quicker of two things traverses a greater magnitude in an equal time, an equal magnitude in less time, and a greater magnitude in less time, in conformity with the definition sometimes given of "the quicker." Suppose that A is quicker than B. Now since of two things that which changes sooner is quicker, in the time FG, in which A has changed from C to D, B will not yet have arrived at D but will be short of it: so that in an equal time the quicker will pass over a greater magnitude. More than this, it will pass over a greater magnitude in less time: for in the time in which A has arrived at D, B being the slower has arrived, let us say, at E. Then since A has occupied the whole time FG in arriving at D, it will have arrived at H in less time than this, say FJ. Now the magnitude CH that A has passed over is greater than the magnitude CE, and the time FJ is less than the whole time FG: so that the quicker will pass over a greater magnitude in less time. And from this it is also clear that the quicker will pass over an equal magnitude in less time than the slower. For since it passes over the greater magnitude in less time than the slower, and (regarded by itself) passes over KL the greater in more time than KN the lesser, the

time *PQ* in which it passes over *KL* will be more than the time *PR*
in which it passes over *KN*: so that, the time *PQ* being less than
the time *PV* in which the slower passes over *KN*, the time *PR* will
also be less than the time *PV*: for it is less than the time *PQ*, and
that which is less than something else that is less than a thing is
also itself less than that thing. Hence it follows that the quicker
will traverse an equal magnitude in less time than the slower.
Again, since the motion of anything must always occupy either
an equal time or less or more time in comparison with that of
another thing, and since, whereas a thing is slower if its motion
occupies more time and of equal velocity if its motion occupies an
equal time, the quicker is neither of equal velocity nor slower, it
follows that the motion of the quicker can occupy neither an
equal time nor more time. It can only be, then, that it occupies
less time, and thus we get the necessary consequence that the
quicker will pass over an equal magnitude (as well as a greater) in
less time than the slower.

233a. And since every motion is in time and a motion may
occupy any time, and the motion of everything that is in motion
may be either quicker or slower, both quicker motion and slower
motion may occupy any time: and this being so, it necessarily
follows that time also is continuous. By continuous I mean that
which is divisible into divisibles that are infinitely divisible: and if
we take this as the definition of continuous, it follows necessarily
that time is continuous. For since it has been shown that the
quicker will pass over an equal magnitude in less time than the
slower, suppose that *A* is quicker and *B* slower, and that the
slower has traversed the magnitude *CD* in the time *FG*. Now it is
clear that the quicker will traverse the same magnitude in less
time than this: let us say in the time *FH*. Again, since the quicker
has passed over the whole *CD* in the time *FH*, the slower will in
the same time pass over *CJ*, say, which is less than *CD*. And since
B, the slower, has passed over *CJ* in the time *FH*, the quicker will
pass over it in less time: so that the time *FH* will again be divided.
And if this is divided the magnitude *CJ* will also be divided just as
CD was: and again, if the magnitude is divided, the time will also
be divided. And we can carry on this process for ever, taking the
slower after the quicker and the quicker after the slower alternate-

ly, and using what has been demonstrated at each stage as a new point of departure: for the quicker will divide the time and the slower will divide the length. If, then, this alternation always holds good, and at every turn involves a division, it is evident that all time must be continuous. And at the same time it is clear that all magnitude is also continuous; for the divisions of which time and magnitude respectively are susceptible are the same and equal.

Moreover, the current popular arguments make it plain that, if time is continuous, magnitude is continuous also, inasmuch as a thing passes over half a given magnitude in half the time taken to cover the whole: in fact without qualification it passes over a less magnitude in less time; for the divisions of time and of magnitude will be the same. And if either is infinite, so is the other, and the one is so in the same way as the other; i.e. if time is infinite in respect of its extremities, length is also infinite in respect of its extremities: if time is infinite in respect of divisibility, length is also infinite in respect of divisibility: and if time is infinite in both respects, magnitude is also infinite in both respects.

Hence Zeno's argument makes a false assumption in asserting that it is impossible for a thing to pass over or severally to come in contact with infinite things in a finite time. For there are two senses in which length and time and generally anything continuous are called "infinite": they are called so either in respect of divisibility or in respect of their extremities. So while a thing in a finite time cannot come in contact with things quantitatively infinite, it can come in contact with things infinite in respect of divisibility: for in this sense the time itself is also infinite: and so we find that the time occupied by the passage over the infinite is not a finite but an infinite time, and the contact with the infinites is made by means of moments not finite but infinite in number.

233b. The passage over the infinite, then, cannot occupy a finite time, and the passage over the finite cannot occupy an infinite time: if the time is infinite the magnitude must be infinite also, and if the magnitude is infinite, so also is the time. This may be shown as follows. Let *AB* be a finite magnitude, and let us suppose that it is traversed in infinite time *C*, and let a finite period *CD* of the time be taken. Now in this period the thing in motion will pass over a certain segment of the magnitude: let *BE* be the segment that it has thus passed over. (This will be either an exact measure of *AB* or less or greater than an exact measure: it makes no difference which it is.) Then, since a magnitude equal to *BE* will always be passed over in an equal time, and *BE* measures the whole magnitude, the whole time occupied in passing over *AB* will be finite: for it will be divisible into periods equal in number to the segments into which the magnitude is divisible. Moreover, if it is the case that infinite time is not occupied in passing over every magnitude, but it is possible to pass over some magnitude, say *BE,* in a finite time, and if this *BE* measures the whole of which it is a part, and if an equal magnitude is passed over in an equal time, then it follows that the time like the magnitude is finite. That infinite time will not be occupied in passing over *BE* is evident if the time be taken as limited in one direction: for as the part will be passed over in less time than the whole, the time occupied in traversing this part must be finite, the limit in one direction being given. The same reasoning will also show the falsity of the assumption that infinite length can be traversed in a finite time. It is evident, then, from what has been said that neither a line nor a surface nor in fact anything continuous can be indivisible.

This conclusion follows not only from the present argument but from the consideration that the opposite assumption implies the divisibility of the indivisible. For since the distinction of quicker and slower may apply to motions occupying any period of time and in an equal time the quicker passes over a greater length, it may happen that it will pass over a length twice, or one and a half times, as great as that passed over by the slower: for their respective velocities may stand to one another in this proportion. Suppose, then, that the quicker has in the same time been carried over a length one and a half times as great as that traversed by the slower, and that the respective magnitudes are divided, that of the quicker, the magnitude *ABCD,* into three indivisibles, and that of the slower into the two indivisibles *EF, FG.* Then the time may also be divided into three indivisibles, for an equal magnitude will be passed over in an equal time. Suppose then that it is thus divided into *JK, KL, LM.* Again, since in the same time the slower has been carried over *EF, FG,* the time may also be similarly divided into two. Thus the indivisible will be divisible, and that which has no parts will be passed over not in an indivisible but in a greater time.[4] It is evident, therefore, that nothing continuous is without parts.

3. Continuity in *De generatione et corruptione* (Translated by H. H. Joachim)

Book I, Chapter 2

316a. To suppose that a body (i.e. a magnitude) is divisible through and through, and that this division is possible, involves a difficulty. What will there be in the body which escapes the division?

If it is divisible through and through, and if this division is possible, then it might *be,* at one and the same moment, *divided* through and through, even though the dividings had not been effected simultaneously: and the actual occurrence of this result would involve no impossibility. Hence the same principle will apply whenever a body is by nature divisible through and through, whether by bisection,[5] or generally by any method whatever: nothing impossible will have resulted if it has actually been divided—not even if it has been divided into innumerable parts, themselves divided innumerable times. Nothing impossible will have resulted, though perhaps nobody in fact could so divide it.

Since, therefore, the body is divisible through and through, let it have been divided. What, then, will remain? A magnitude? No: that is impossible, since then there will be something not divided, whereas *ex hypothesi* the body was divisible *through and through.* But if it be admitted that neither a body nor a magnitude will remain, and yet division[6] is to take place, the constituents of the body will *either* be points (i.e. without magnitude) *or* absolutely nothing. If its constituents are nothings, then it might both come-

---

4. The slower will traverse *EF* in a greater time than the indivisible time in which the quicker traverses *JK.*

5. I.e. by progressive bisection ad infinitum.

6. I.e. "through and through" division.

to-be out of nothings and exist as a composite of nothings: and thus presumably the whole body will be nothing but an appearance. But if it consists of points, a similar absurdity will result: it will not possess any magnitude. For when the points were in contact and coincided to form a single magnitude, they did not make the whole any bigger (since, when the body was divided into two or more parts, the whole[7] was not a bit smaller or bigger than it was before the division): hence, even if all the points[8] be put together, they will not make any magnitude.

316b. But suppose that, as the body is being divided, a minute section—a piece of sawdust, as it were—is extracted, and that in this sense a body "comes away" from the magnitude, evading the division. Even then the same[9] argument applies. For in what sense is that section divisible? But if what "came away" was not a body but a separable form or quality, and if the magnitude *is* "points or contacts thus qualified": it is paradoxical that a magnitude should consist of elements which are not magnitudes. Moreover, *where* will the points be? And are they motionless or moving? And every contact is always a contact of two somethings, i.e. there is always something besides the contact or the division or the point.

These, then, are the difficulties resulting from the supposition that any and every body, whatever its size, is divisible through and through. There is, besides, this further consideration. If, having divided a piece of wood or anything else, I put it together, it is again equal to what it was, and is one. Clearly this is so, whatever the point at which I cut the wood. The wood, therefore, has been divided *potentially* through and through. What, then, is there in the wood besides the division? For even if we suppose there is some quality, yet how is the wood dissolved into such constituents[10] and how does it come-to-be out of them? Or how are such constituents separated so as to exist apart from one another?

7. I.e. the sum of the now separated parts.
8. I.e. all the points into which the body has been dissolved by the "through and through" division.
9. Cf. above, 316a24–25.
10. I.e. points-of-division and quality.

319

Since, therefore, it is impossible for magnitudes to consist of contacts or points, there must be indivisible bodies and magnitudes. Yet, if we *do* postulate the latter, we are confronted with equally impossible consequences, which we have examined in other works.[11] But we must try to disentangle these perplexities, and must therefore formulate the whole problem over again.

On the one hand, then, it is in no way paradoxical that every perceptible body should be indivisible as well as divisible at any and every point. For the second predicate will attach to it *potentially*, but the first *actually*. On the other hand, it would seem to be impossible for a body to be, even potentially, divisible at all points simultaneously. For if it were possible, then it might actually occur, with the result, not that the body would simultaneously be actually *both* (indivisible and divided), but that it would be simultaneously divided at any and every point. Consequently, nothing will remain and the body will have passed-away into what is incorporeal: and so it might come-to-be again either out of points or absolutely out of nothing. And how is that possible?

But now it is obvious that a body is in fact divided into separable magnitudes which are smaller at each division—into magnitudes which fall apart from one another and are actually separated. Hence (it is urged) the process of dividing a body part by part is not a "breaking up" which could continue *ad infinitum*; nor can a body be simultaneously divided at every point, for that is not possible; but there is a limit, beyond which the "breaking up" cannot proceed. The necessary consequence—especially if coming-to-be and passing-away are to take place by "association" and "dissociation" respectively—is that a body[12] must contain atomic magnitudes which are invisible.

317a. Such is the argument which is believed to establish the necessity of atomic magnitudes: we must now show that it conceals a faulty inference, and exactly where it conceals it.

For, since point is not "immediately-next" to point, magnitudes are "divisible through and through" in one sense, and yet not in another. When, however, it is admitted that a magnitude is "di-

11. Cf. *Physics* 231a21 ff.; *De caelo* 303a3 ff.
12. I.e. every perceptible body: cf. above, 316b21.

visible through and through," it is thought there is a point not only anywhere, but also everywhere, in it: hence it is supposed to follow, from the admission, that the magnitude must be divided away into nothing. For—it is supposed—there is a point every-where within it, so that it consists either of contacts or of points. But it is only *in one sense* that the magnitude is "divisible through and through," viz. in so far as there is one point *anywhere* within it and all its points are *everywhere* within it if you take them singly one by one. But there are not more points than one *anywhere* within it, for the points are not "consecutive": hence it is not simultaneously "divisible through and through." For if it were, then, if it be divisible at its centre, it will be divisible also at a point "immediately-next" to its centre. But it is not so divisible: for position is not "immediately-next" to position, nor point to point—in other words, division is not "immediately-next" to divi-sion, nor composition to composition.

Walter Burley on
Immediate Alterations

Burley 1501, Bk. V, f. 166ra. Sed circa praedicta occurrunt duo dubia. . . . Secundum dubium est an motus diversi secundum speciem vel secundum genus possunt adinvicem continuari. . . . Ad secundum dubium arguo et probo quod motus diversi secundum speciem vel secundum genus possunt adinvicem continuari. . . . Item motus diversi secundum genus vel secundum speciem possunt esse immediata ut motus contrarii possunt esse immediati, quoniam aliquod corpus potest calefieri et in fine calefactionis potest frigidum approximari sibi. Quod quidem frigidum movebit ipsum statim versus frigiditatem. Aliter agens naturale esset approximatum suo contrario per tempus et non ageret in ipsum, quod est inconveniens. Ponatur igitur quod aliquod corpus calefiat et immediate post frigefiat. Illo casu posito illi motus sunt continuati adinvicem et tamen differunt specie. Igitur motus differentes specie possunt adinvicem continuari. Quod autem illi motus continuentur adinvicem, probo quia continua sunt quorum ultima sunt unum. Sed ultima istorum motuum contrariorum sunt unum. Ergo maior patet et probo minorem quia quaero aut illi duo motus habent idem ultimum aut diversa ultima. Si habent idem ultimum, habeo propositum, videlicet quod illi motus sunt continuati adinvicem quia continua sunt illa quorum ultima sunt unum. Si autem detur quod illi duo motus non habent idem ultimum, sed diversa ultima, tunc quaero aut ista duo ultima mensurantur eodem instanti aut alio et alio instanti. Si eodem sequitur quod ultima contrariorum insunt eidem pro eodem instanti quod est impossibile. Si vero detur quod ista duo ultima mensurentur alio et alio instanti cum inter quaelibet duo instantia sit tempus

medium, sequeretur quod inter ultimum prioris motus et principium motus posterioris esset tempus medium. Et ita illi motus
non essent immediati cuius oppositum supponimus. . . .

(166rb) [Reply:] Ad secundum dubium dico quod motus diversi
secundum genus vel secundum speciem non possunt continuari
adinvicem, et hoc ideo quia non possunt habere idem ultimum.
. . . (166va) Ad aliud quando dicitur quod motus contrarii possunt esse habiti ita quod inter illos nihil est medium, concedatur.
Et cum dicitur quod tunc habent idem ultimum, dico quod non est
verum, immo habent diversa ultima. Et quando quaeritur an ista
ultima mensurentur eodem instanti aut alio et alio, dico quod
mensurantur eodem instanti. Et quando dicitur quod tunc ultima
contrariorum inessent eidem simul in eodem instanti, dico quod
ultima contrariorum quorum unum est intrinsecum uni motui et
aliud extrinsecum alteri possunt bene esse simul in eodem subiecto in eodem instanti, tamen ultima contrariorum intrinseca eis
non possunt inesse simul in eodem instanti. Ad cuius intellectum
est sciendum quod nullum ultimum est intrinsecum motui nisi
ultimum motus ex parte post vel aliquod mutatum esse acquisitum per istum motum. Unde nullum initium motus incipientis a
quiete est intrinsecum illi motui. Tamen mutatum esse copulans
partes motus adinvicem est intrinsecum utrique parti. Et tunc
dico quod si terminata calefactione statim incipiat frigefactio, ultimum calefactionis et primum frigefactionis mensuratur eodem instanti. Et hoc est possibile quia ultimum calefactionis est intrinsecum calefactioni et principium frigefactionis est extrinsecum a
frigefactione. Ideo ista possunt inesse eidem in eodem instanti.
Quid autem sit principium motus incipientis a quiete videbitur in
tractatu sequenti.

Walter Burley on Reversed Alteration and the Degrees Acquired

(Texts from his *Tractatus primus:* Vat. Lat. 817, f. 209vb–210rb, 212rb–va, 214va–215rb)

(209vb) Quarta conclusio erat quod formae contrariae, videlicet calor et frigus, albedo et nigredo, sunt eiusdem speciei specialissimae. Istam conclusionem probam per rationes . . . primo logice. . . . Quandocumque aliqua duo aequaliter distant distantia formali a perfectissimo in aliqua specie si unum illorum duorum sit in illa specie reliquum erit in illa specie . . . (210ra) sed est dare aliquam caliditatem et aliquam frigiditatem quae aeque distant distantia formali a summa caliditate. . . . Maior huius rationis est plana et determinata in logica et probo minorem quantum ad utrumque partem. Et suppono duo fundamenta declarata ab Aristotele in scientia naturali. Primum est quod rei permanentis de novo productae in esse per alterationem est dare primum instans in quo habet esse. Et hoc est plana et si Aristoteles non dixisset eam quia in ultimo instanti temporis mensurantis alterationem habet terminus alterationis primo esse, quia aliter aliquod moveretur ad formam quam habet. Secundum fundamentum est quod rei permanentis productae vel corruptae per alterationem non est dare ultimum instans in quo habet esse et hanc scribit Aristoteles et vera esset quamvis Aristoteles eam non scripsisset, quia si esset dare ultimum instans in quo talis res haberet esse illa res corrumpetur in non tempore et ita non per alterationem.

Istis suppositis arguo et suppono quod aliquod transmutetur a calido in frigidum. Tunc per primam suppositionem est dare primum instans in quo est sub frigido et sit istud instans A. Volo tunc quod statim sit approximatum unum agens tantae virtutis in transmutando istud corpus versus summum calidum et in appropinquando ipsum summo calido propinquitate formali quantae virtutis fuit transmutans ipsum (210rb) versus frigidum faciens ipsum formaliter distare a summo calido. Hoc est enim possibile ut satis patet cuilibet intelligenti. Tunc cum non sit dare ultimum instans in quo talis res permanens habet esse, ut patet per secundam suppositionem, sequitur quod adhuc post A erit istud corpus sub frigiditate. Et signetur aliud instans post A in quod istud corpus erit sub frigiditate et sit C. Accipio tunc unum instans ante A in quo istud corpus fuit sub caliditate tantum distans ab A ex parte ante quantum C distat ab A ex parte post, et sit istud instans B. Tunc arguo sic: quantum istud corpus vel forma sub qua erat recessit recessu formali a summo calido in tempore inter A et B tantum accessit accessu formali ad summum calidum in tempore inter A et C et per consequens quantum perdidit de propinquitate formali in tempore inter B et A tantum adquisivit de propinquitate formali in tempore inter A et C. Ergo aeque propinquum formaliter summo calori est in C sicut fuit in B. Sed in C est sub forma frigiditatis et in B fuit sub forma caliditatis. Ergo caliditas quam habet in B et frigiditas quam habet in C sunt vel fuerunt aeque propinqua propinquitate formali summo calori.

(212rb) Quidam reverendus socius et magister credens rationes meas esse sophisticas respondet ad rationes ad quartam conclusionem adductas materia infrascripta, . . . Ad primam rationem meam respondet concedendo casum usque ad istam suppositionem, scilicet quod non contingit dare ultimum instans in quo res permanens producta in esse per alterationem habet esse. Negetur si universaliter accipitur, quia est dare ultimum instans in quo remississimum frigidum habet esse. . . . Si enim calidum approximetur remississimo frigido in primo instanti approximationis manet frigiditas et nunquam postea manebit. . . .

(212va) Licet ista fuit subtiliter dicta tamen videtur quod non sufficit quia dicta in responsione ad primum argumentum repugnant et expresse contradictionem includunt. Probo igitur contra haec dicta 8 conclusiones. Primo quod . . . haec duo, scilicet, quod sit dare ultimum instans in quo res permanens corrumpenda per alterationem habet esse et primum instans in quo res permanens producta per alterationem habet esse claudunt contradictionem. . . . (214va–b) Ad istam rationem dicit dictus socius quod nunquam concessit haec duo, scilicet quod est dare ultimum instans in quo res permanens corrupta per alterationem habet esse et tamen primum instans in quo forma producta per alterationem habet esse, sed dicit quod dixit quod quandoque contingit dare ultimum instans formae permanentis corrumpendae sicut quando fit processus a gradu maximo vel minimo quiescentibus, et ideo ista ratio, ut dicit, non tangit eum. Quod autem sit quandoque dare tale ultimum instans istud dicit se probasse ratione demonstrativa ad quam ego nullum verbum dixi sicut dicit. Dicit etiam quod ipse dixit quod quando est dare ultimum instans formae corrumpendae non est dare primum instans formae producendae.

(214vb–215ra) Contra istam responsionem arguo. . . . Si dicatur quod aliqua forma sequens adquiritur subito ita quod inter ultimum esse frigidi et esse alicuius formae sequentis non est aliquod tempus medium, contra: illa forma tunc adquireretur subito et sic in instanti. Sed cuilibet formae subito inductae est dare primum instans in quo habet esse, ergo esset dare primum instans in quo forma sequens habet esse. . . .

(215rb) Tertio arguo contra dictam responsionem sic: istud quod non est sub specie nisi quia sub aliquo individuo speciei, si sine medio sit sub specie sine medio est sub aliquo individuo speciei. Sed istud mobile transmutatum de frigido in calidum post A instans sine medio erit sub calore quia si esset medium inter ultimum esse frigidi et esse mobilis sub calore in illo medio nec esset sub calido nec sub frigido et sic calidum et frigidum non essent contraria immediata cuius oppositum est suppositum. . . . Istud ergo mobile statim post A sine medio erit sub calore ergo sine medio erit sub aliquo individuo caloris. Sed illius individui caloris sub quo mobile immediate erit est dare primum instans sui esse. Ergo est dare primum formae sequentis.

Walter Burley's Use of Merely Confused Supposition to Reconcile Immediacy of Time with the Mediacy of Instants

(Burley 1501, Bk. VI, 176ra) Deinde arguo in successivis probando quod in successivis indivisibile est immediatum alteri indivisibili. Et hoc sic: In tempore est instans immediatum instanti. Ergo in continuo est indivisibile immediatum indivisibili. Consequentia patet de se et antecedens probo sic. Sit A instans praesens, tunc arguo sic: Inter A esse et A non esse non cadit medium. Sed A non esse et aliud instans ab A esse sunt idem convertibiliter, quia sequitur "A non est; ergo aliud instans ab A est" et econverso. Ergo inter A esse et aliud instans ab A esse non cadit medium. Ergo post A immediate erit aliud instans. Ergo in tempore sunt instantia immediata.

Huic dicitur quod inter A esse et A non esse non cadit medium quia semper alterum istorum est verum et ideo inter veritates harum propositionum non est aliquod medium et eodem modo dicitur quod inter veritates istarum propositionum "A est," "Aliud instans ab A est" non cadit medium, quia quandocumque una istarum non est vera alia istarum est vera, et quamvis inter veritates istarum propositionum non sit aliquod medium, tamen inter A et quodlibet instans aliud ab A est medium.

Contra. Si inter veritates istarum propositionum "A est" et "Aliud instans ab A est" non sit medium, tunc haec "A est" sine medio erit falsa, quia A statim non erit, et sequitur quod illa "Aliud instans ab A est" statim et sine medio erit vera. Sed quandocumque ista erit vera "Aliud instans ab A est" oportet quod aliqua eius singularis erit vera. Sit igitur illa singularis quae erit vera sine medio B, et tunc ista est modo vera "A est" et sine medio erit illa vera "B est" ex quo sequitur quod A et B sunt immediata quia si A et B essent mediata, in medio inter A et B neutra istarum est vera, scilicet nec ista "A est" nec ista "B est."

Item ista est vera "A est, et sine medio tempus erit," sed tempus non est nisi per instans. Ergo sine medio aliud instans erit et per consequens aliud instans ab A erit immediate post A et per consequens in tempore instans est immediatum instanti.

(177ra) [Reply:] Ad rationes vero probantes quod in successivis est indivisibile immediatum indivisibili, dicendum est ad primam cum dicitur quod in tempore est instans immediatum instanti, dicendum quod non est verum. Ad probationem, cum dicitur inter A esse et A non esse non cadit medium et sit A praesens instans concedo quod inter A esse etc. non cadit medium. Et etiam concedo quod inter A esse et aliud instans ab A esse non cadit medium. Et concedo illud aliud quod additur ulterius, scilicet quod A est et immediate post A erit aliud instans.

Ad cuius evidentiam est sciendum quod sincathegoreumata importantia multitudinem habent virtutem confundendi terminum sequentem confuse tantum ut dictum est in logica. Sed hoc quod dico "immediate" est sincathegoreuma importans multitudinem. Similiter hoc quod dico "sine medio" importat multitudinem quia aequipollet uni sincathegoreumatici cum sint praepositio cum suo cathegorali (?cali). Ista enim, videlicet "immediate" et "sine medio" importat multitudinem, quia quod immediate vel sine medio erit, ante omne medium completum erit. Unde immediate vel sine medio est idem quod ante omne medium. Et ideo dico quod ista est vera "A est, et sine medio aliud instans erit," quia ante omne medium completum aliud instans erit. Quia in illa "A est, et sine medio seu immediate aliud instans erit" iste terminus "aliud instans" virtute sincathegoreumatis praecedentis importantis multitudinem supponit confuse tantum. Et ideo non stat determinate pro aliquo uno instanti. Unde non sequitur "Sine medio aliud instans erit; ergo aliud instans erit sine medio" sed est fallacia figurae dictionis, quia procedit a suppositione confusa tantum ad suppositionem determinatam respectu eiusdem multitudinis. Nec etiam valet "Sine medio aliud (*corr. ex* illud) instans erit; ergo sine medio hoc instans erit vel sine medio illud instans erit" sicut non sequitur "Omnis homo est animal; ergo omnis homo est hoc animal vel omnis homo est illud animal." Concedo igitur illam "A est, et sine medio aliud instans erit" et nego illam "A est, et aliud instans erit sine medio." Et ulterius quando arguitur quod si haec indefinita "Aliud instans ab A est" sine medio erit vera, ergo singularis istius "Aliud instans ab A est" sine medio erit vera, dicendum quod non sequitur. Unde haec indefinita sine medio erit vera et tamen nulla eius singularis sine medio erit vera. Et si arguitur contra illam responsionem sic (scilicet illa "'Aliud instans ab A est' sine medio erit vera et tamen nulla singularis erit vera sine medio") tunc haec indefinita erit vera antequam eius aliqua singularis sit vera et per consequens ista "Aliud instans ab A est" aliquando erit vera quando nulla eius singularis erit vera, dicendum concedendo quod illa indefinita "Aliud instans ab A est" sine medio erit vera et tamen nulla singularis eius sine medio erit vera. Nec ex hoc sequitur quod illa indefinita erit vera antequam alia singularis eius erit vera, quia nunquam erit ista indefinita vera antequam aliqua singularis. Ista tamen universalem concedo, quod quaelibet singularis huius erit falsa quando illa erit vera, quia quaelibet singularis huius universalis est vera. Ista tamen est falsa, scilicet "Haec indefinita erit vera cum quaelibet singularis erit falsa," et illa similiter est falsa, scilicet "Haec indefinita erit vera priusquam aliqua eius singularis erit vera," quia in istis tempus consignificatum per verbum supponit determinate cum praecedat dictionem sincathegoreumaticam importantem multitudinem. Et sic denotatur quod in aliqua determinata mensura ut in B vel in C erit ista indefinita vera antequam aliqua singularis eius erit vera, vel quando quaelibet singularis eius erit . . . falsa. Quod falsum est. Nec valet "Ista indefinita erit vera priusquam illa singularis erit vera, et erit vera priusquam illa singularis erit vera, et sic de singulis; igitur prius erit vera quam aliqua eius singularis erit vera," sed sic est fallacia figurae dictionis arguendo a pluribus determinatis ad unum determinatum, quoniam sicut in qualibet parte antecedentis hoc verbum "erit" copulat pro aliquo instanti determinato, ita in conclusione copulat pro aliquo instanti determinato cum dicitur quod haec sit vera (177rb) antequam aliqua singularis huius erit vera.

Ad aliam quando dicitur quod A est et sine medio tempus erit, concedo. Et cum dicitur tempus non instat nisi per instans, concedo. Et propter hoc concedo quod sine medio aliquod instans erit. Nego tamen illam "Aliquod instans erit sine medio," nec sequitur "Tempus erit sine medio; ergo aliquod instans erit sine medio." Bene tamen sequitur "Tempus erit sine medio; igitur sine medio aliquod instans erit."

Richard Kilvington's Sophisma 8

EDITED BY N. AND B. KRETZMANN

SOCRATES ERIT ITA ALBUS PRAECISE SICUT PLATO ERIT ALBUS IN ALIQUO ISTORUM.

Supposito quod Socrates et Plato sint aequaliter albi, et quod per A tempus intendantur eorum albedines aequaliter, et quod in fine A temporis sit Plato corruptus, et tunc vivat Socrates, et, ulterius, per aliquod tempus ultra A intendatur albedo in Socrate. Et sit A tempus quod mensurabit esse Platonis, et demonstrentur per li "istorum" partes proportionales A temporis, ut in proximo sophismate est suppositum.

Tunc probatur sophisma sic. Socrates est minus albus quam erit Plato in aliquo istorum, et Socrates erit magis albus quam erit Plato in aliquo istorum; igitur Socrates erit ita albus praecise sicut Plato erit albus in aliquo istorum. Totum antecedens patet ex casu. Et consequentiam probo, quia capio totum tempus per quod Socrates non erit albior quam Plato erit albus in aliquo istorum et totum tempus per quod Socrates erit albior quam Plato erit albus in aliquo istorum, et sit B primum tempus et C secundum tempus. Tunc B et C tempora continuantur per aliquod instans. Tunc in isto instanti vel erit Socrates ita albus praecise sicut Plato erit albus in aliquo istorum—et habetur propositum—vel erit albior vel minus albus. Si in isto instanti Socrates erit albior quam Plato erit albus in aliquo istorum, igitur per aliquam partem latitudinis albedinis erit Socrates albior in isto instanti quam Plato erit albus in aliquo istorum; et, per consequens, ante illud instans per medietatem alicuius latitudinis albedinis erit Socrates albior quam Plato erit albus in aliquo istorum. Et si hoc, igitur B non est totum tempus per quod Socrates non erit albior quam Plato erit albus in aliquo istorum—quod est contra positum. Si in instanti medio inter B et C Socrates erit minus albus quam Plato erit albus in aliquo istorum, igitur per aliquam partem latitudinis albedinis erit minus albus. Et tunc, sicut prius, post illud instans Socrates erit minus albus quam Plato erit albus in aliquo istorum. Et si hoc, igitur C non erit totum tempus per quod Socrates erit albior quam Plato erit albus in aliquo istorum—quod est contra positum.

Ad oppositum arguitur sic. Si Socrates erit ita albus praecise sicut Plato erit albus in aliquo istorum, vel igitur per tempus erit Socrates ita albus praecise sicut Plato erit albus in aliquo istorum; vel per instans erit Socrates ita albus praecise sicut Plato erit albus in aliquo istorum. Non primo modo, ut patet inductive de quocumque tempore quo Socrates erit albus. Nec in aliquo instanti erit Socrates ita albus, etc., quia in nullo instanti A temporis erit Socrates ita albus praecise sicut Plato erit albus in aliquo istorum; nec in aliquo instanti post A erit Socrates ita albus, etc., quia in quolibet instanti post A erit Socrates albior quam Plato erit albus in aliquo istorum.

Item, si Socrates erit ita albus sicut Plato erit albus in aliquo istorum et Socrates non est ita albus, etc., igitur Socrates incipit vel incipiet esse ita albus sicut Plato erit albus in aliquo istorum— quod est falsum, ut in praecedentibus sophismatibus est argutum.

Ad sophisma dicitur quod est falsum.

Ad probationem dicitur ut prius dicebatur arguendo quod prima consequentia non valet. Et tunc quando arguitur de instanti medio inter B et C, dico quod in isto instanti medio Socrates erit albior quam Plato erit albus in aliquo istorum. Et ultra, negatur consequentia "igitur in isto instanti medio inter B et C per aliquid erit Socrates albior quam Plato erit albus in aliquo istorum." Sed bene sequitur quod in instanti medio Socrates erit albior per aliquid quam Plato erit albus in aliquo istorum. Per nihil tamen erit Socrates albior quam Plato erit albus in aliquo istorum.

Et huic sophismati simile est hoc sophisma.

Richard Kilvington's
Sophisma 16

1. Edition (by N. and B. Kretzmann)

(*a*) A INCIPIT ESSE VERUM.

(*b*) Posito quod A sit ista propositio "B tangit C." Et ulterius ponatur quod B sit unum corpus sphaericum et moveatur super aliquod planum, quod sit E. Et tunc suppono quod "C" sit nomen commune primae parti proportionali in E, et tertiae parti proportionali, et quintae, et septimae, et sic in infinitum. Et sit "D" nomen commune secundae parti, et quartae, et sextae, et octavae, et sic in infinitum de partibus proportionalibus in E. Tunc suppono quod prima medietas E spatii vocetur prima pars proportionalis E spatii, et prima medietas secundae medietatis E vocetur secunda pars proportionalis E spatii, et prima medietas partis relictae vocetur tertia pars proportionalis in E, et sic in infinitum. Et incipiat B moveri in termino E spatii versus primam partem proportionalem E spatii.

(*c*) Tunc probatur sophisma sic. A non est verum, et A erit verum, et nullum tempus erit antequam A erit verum; igitur A incipit esse verum. Consequentia patet per modum communem exponendi hoc verbum "incipit." Quod A non est verum patet, quia B non tangit aliquod C, quia B a quolibet C distat. Et quod nullum tempus erit antequam A erit verum probo; quia si aliquod tempus erit antequam A erit verum, sit igitur quod hora erit antequam A erit verum. Sed probo quod non; quia in aliquo instanti ante finem horae B tanget aliquod C, et quandocumque ita erit, A erit verum. Igitur in aliquo instanti ante finem horae datae A erit verum. Prima pars antecedentis patet; quia sit nunc, gratia exempli, instans medium horae datae. Tunc arguo sic. B pertransivit aliquam partem E spatii, et quaelibet pars E spatii terminata ad punctum a quo incepit B moveri in E spatio continet in se infinita C; igitur B pertransivit infinita C et tetigit infinita C. Et per consequens ante hoc instans fuit A verum. Igitur non labetur tota hora data antequam A erit verum.

(*d*) Ad oppositum sophismatis arguitur sic. A incipit esse verum, et A immediate post hoc erit non verum; igitur A immediate post hoc erit verum et non verum. Et quod A immediate post hoc erit non verum probatur ut sophisma: A erit non verum, et nullum tempus erit antequam A erit non verum; igitur A immediate post hoc erit non verum. Maior patet, quia B tanget D quando non tanget C, et quandocumque ita erit, A erit non verum; igitur A erit non verum. Et secunda pars primi antecedentis patet; quia nullum tempus erit antequam B tanget D in puncto medio, ut probatur per idem argumentum per quod probatur quod nullum tempus erit antequam B tanget C. Et tunc arguitur sic. Quandocumque B tanget D in puncto medio, tunc A erit non verum; sed nullum tempus erit antequam B tanget D in puncto medio; igitur nullum tempus erit antequam A erit non verum.

(*e*) Item, si A immediate post hoc erit verum, igitur eadem ratione et per idem argumentum F immediate post hoc erit verum—sit F contradictorium A. Igitur A et F immediate post hoc erunt vera. Et per consequens contradictoria immediate post hoc erunt vera. Et confirmatur idem argumentum sic. A et F erunt vera, ut probatum est, et nullum tempus erit antequam A et F erunt vera; igitur A et F incipiunt esse vera. Et minor probatur per argumentum primum. Ideo forte conceditur conclusio quod A et F incipiunt esse vera, et quod contradictoria incipiunt esse vera, sicut videtur argumentum probare.

(*f*) Contra, si A et F incipiunt esse vera et neque A neque F est verum, igitur non citius erit A verum quam F. Igitur aeque cito erunt A et F vera. Et, ultra, igitur A et F erunt simul vera—quod est impossibile.

(*g*) Item, arguitur aliter sic. A et F erunt vera; vel igitur A et F erunt simul vera—quod est impossibile, ut prius—vel A et F erunt successive vera, et tunc sequitur quod prius erit A verum quam F vel econtra. Et ita non incipiunt esse vera—quod est falsum, ut prius probatum est.

334

that the first half of the remaining part is called the third proportional part in E, and so on, infinitely. And suppose that B begins to move at the limit of distance E which is opposite to the first proportional part of distance E.

(c) In that case the sophisma is proved in the following way. A is not true, and A will be true, and there will be no time before A will be true; therefore A begins to be true. The consequence is evident on the basis of the ordinary way of expounding the verb "begins." That A is not true is evident, since B is not touching any C, since B is at a distance from each C. And that there will be no time before A will be true I prove; for if there will be any time before A will be true, then suppose that there will be an hour before A will be true. But I prove that that is not the case; for at some instant before the end of the hour B will touch some C, and whenever that will happen, A will be true. Therefore at some instant before the end of the given hour A will be true. The first part of the antecedent is evident; for let now, for example, be the middle instant of the given hour. Then I argue as follows. B has traversed some part of distance E, and each part of distance E limited at the point from which B began to move on distance E contains within itself infinitely many Cs; therefore B has traversed infinitely many Cs and has touched infinitely many Cs. Consequently before this instant A has been true. Therefore the whole of the given hour will not elapse before A will be true.

(d) One argues on the other side of the sophisma in the following way. A begins to be true, and A immediately after this will be not true; therefore A immediately after this will be true and not true. And that A immediately after this will be not true is proved like the sophisma: A will be not true, and there will be no time before A will be not true; therefore A immediately after this will be not true. The major premise is evident, because B will touch a D when it will not touch a C, and whenever that will happen, A will be not true; therefore A will be not true. And the second part of the first antecedent is evident; for there will be no time before B will touch a D at a midpoint, as is proved by means of the same argument by means of which it is proved that there will be no time before B will touch a C. And then one argues as follows. Whenever B will touch a D at a midpoint, at that time A will be not true; but there will be no time before B will touch a D at a midpoint; therefore there will be no time before A will be not true.

(e) Again, if A immediately after this will be true, then for the same reason and by the same argument F immediately after this will be true—let F be the contradictory of A. Therefore A and F immediately after this will be true. Consequently contradictories immediately after this will be true. And this same argument is confirmed as follows. A and F will be true, as has been proved, and there will be no time before A and F will be true; therefore A and F begin to be true. And the minor premise is proved by means of the first argument. And so one might grant the conclusion that A and F begin to be true, and that contradictories begin to be true, as the argument evidently proves.

(f) On the contrary, if A and F begin to be true and neither A nor F is true, then A will be true no more quickly than F. Therefore equally quickly will A and F be true. And further, therefore A and F will be true at the same time—which is impossible.

(g) Again, one argues in another way as follows. A and F will be true; therefore either A and F will be true at the same time—which, as before, is impossible—or A and F will be true successively, and in that case it follows that A will be true before F or vice versa. And so they do not begin to be true—which is false, as was proved earlier.

(h) Again, if A begins to be true, then F ceases to be true—which is false, as I prove. For F without interval after this will be true, as is evident by means of an argument like the first one.

(i) The reply to the sophisma is that it is true, as the arguments prove.

(j) In reply to the argument on the other side one grants in like manner that A immediately after this will be true and that A immediately after this will be not true, on the basis of the same argument. Moreover, the consequence "therefore A begins to be true and not true" is denied, understanding the consequent in the compounded sense. Nor, furthermore, does it follow that A will be true and not true at the same time. And the reason is that from the fact that A begins to be true it does not follow that during some time immediate to this instant and for each instant of that time *A* will be true—which, however, is what would be required if the first consequence were to be acceptable. And it is evident that during no time and for each instant of that time immediate to this instant will *A* be true, for no *C* is exactly adjacent to the limit from which *B* begins to move, and so it will touch no *C* at first; and for the same reason it will touch no *D* at first. And so at no time will the proposition "*B* touches a *C*" or "*B* touches a *D*" be true at first. And so in whatever time is taken immediate to this instant *A* will be infinitely often true and infinitely often false, and *F* likewise will be infinitely often true and infinitely often false. Consequently during no continuous time immediate to this instant will *A* be true. And it must be known that *A* and *F* begin to be true, and that contradictories begin to be true, and yet *A* and *F* do not begin to be true at the same time. And when it is argued "*A* and *F* will be true; therefore either they will be true at the same time—and we have what was proposed—or the one will be true before the other—which was disproved earlier," in reply it must be said that *A* and *F* will be true successively, and neither will be true before the other.

(*k*) In reply to the other form the consequence "*A* begins to be true; therefore *F* ceases to be true" must be granted. And the consequence is granted because *F* now is true and without interval will be not true. Nor are these two incompatible: "*F* without interval will be true" and "*F* without interval will be not true."

(*l*) But this is argued against; and it is proved that from this reply it follows that there is a consequence that is good and absolutely formal, the antecedent of which immediately after this will be true, and the consequent of which immediately after this will be false. I prove this as follows; for this consequence is good and formal: "*B* touches a *C* at the midpoint of that *C*, and *B* does not touch a *C* at the midpoint of the *C* and a *D* at the midpoint of the *D* at once at the same instant; therefore *B* does not touch a *D*." And that antecedent will be true immediately after this, and immediately after this the consequent will be false.

(*m*) And that is to be granted, as the argument proves. And by means of the same argument it is proved that there is a consequence that is good and formal, the antecedent of which begins to be true, and the consequent of which begins to be false. For this consequence is good: "B touches a C or a D, and B does not touch a C; therefore B touches a D." And the whole antecedent begins to be true, and the consequent begins to be false.

(n) Some men, however, say otherwise—that A does not begin to be true, because in the sophisma the term "begins" is expounded in this way: "A is not true, and at each instant of some time immediate to this instant A will be true." And if one speaks in that way the sophisma is false.

(o) But those who say that sort of thing are only changing the meaning of the term "begins." They have to say, in general, that some proposition will be immediately after this, and yet it will be neither true immediately after this nor false—as is the case with A—which is evidently absurd.

(p) One might, however, argue in this way: "If A and F will be true, then, for the same reason—"

Bibliography

Standard editions of ancient or medieval works referred to in the notes to the chapters are included in this list only in cases in which confusion might otherwise result.

Ackrill, J. L. 1963. *Aristotle's "Categories" and "De Interpretatione."* Oxford: Clarendon Press.

Adams, Marilyn McCord, and Kretzmann, Norman. 1969. *William Ockham: Predestination, God's Foreknowledge, and Future Contingents.* New York: Appleton-Century-Crofts.

Albert of Saxony. 1502. *Sophismata.* Paris. Reprint. 1975. Hildesheim and New York: Georg Olms.

Alousi, H. M. E. 1968. *The Problem of Creation in Islamic Thought.* Baghdad: National Printing and Publishing Company.

Al-Sharastānī. 1934. *Kitāb Nihāyatuʾ l-Iqdām fī ʿIlmiʾ l-Kalām.* London: Guillame.

Anonymous. 1929–32. Review of *De sacramento altaris* [Ockham 1930]. *Bulletin de théologie ancienne et médiévale* 1:357–58.

———. 1932. Review of *De sacramento altaris* [Ockham 1930]. *Collectanea Franciscana* 2:273–74.

Ashʿari. 1969–70. *Maqālāt.* n.p.

Averroës. 1954. *Tahāfut al-Tahāfut.* Translated by S. Van den Bergh. London: Luzac.

Badawi, Abdurrahmān. 1968. *La transmission de la philosophie Grecque au monde Arabe.* Paris: Vrin.

Baghdadī. 1910. *Farq.* Edited by Badr. Cairo: n.p.

———. 1920. *Al-Fark Bain al-Firak.* Translated by Kate Chambers Seelye. New York: Columbia University Press.

Barnes, Jonathan. 1975. *Aristotle's "Posterior Analytics."* Oxford: Clarendon Press.

Baron, M. 1969. *Origin of the Infinitesimal Calculus.* Oxford: Clarendon Press.

Baudry, Léon. 1936. "Sur trois manuscrits occamistes." *Archives d'histoire doctrinale et littéraire du moyen âge* 10:129–62.

————. 1958. *Lexique philosophique de Guillaume d'Ockham*. Paris: Lethielleux.

Becker, Oskar. 1932–33a. "Eudoxos-Studien I. Eine voreudoxische Proportionenlehre und ihre Spuren bei Aristoteles und Euklid." *Quellen und Studien zur Geschichte der Mathematik, Astronomie und Physik* 2:311–33.

————. 1932–33b. "Eudoxos-Studien II. Warum haben die Griechen die Existenz der vierten Proportionale angenommen?" *Quellen und Studien zur Geschichte der Mathematik, Astronomie und Physik* 2:369–87.

————. 1934–36a. "Eudoxos-Studien III. Spuren eines Stetigkeitsaxioms in der Art des Dedekind'schen zur Zeit des Eudoxos." *Quellen und Studien zur Geschichte der Mathematik, Astronomie und Physik* 3:236–44.

————. 1934–36b. "Eudoxos-Studien IV. Prinzip des ausgeschlossenen Dritten." *Quellen und Studien zur Geschichte der Mathematik, Astronomie und Physik* 3:370–88.

————. 1934–36c. "Zur Textgestaltung des eudemischen Berichts über die Quadratur der Mondchen durch Hippokrates von Chios." *Quellen und Studien zur Geschichte der Mathematik, Astronomie und Physik* 3:411–19.

————. 1954. *Grundlagen der Mathematik in geschichtlicher Entwicklung*. Freiburg: K. Alber.

————. 1957. *Das mathematische Denken der Antike*. Göttingen: Vandenhoeck und Ruprecht.

Benacerraf, Paul. 1962. "Tasks, Super-Tasks, and the Modern Eleatics." *Journal of Philosophy* 59:765–84.

Bottin, Francesco. 1973a. "Analisi linguistica e fisica Aristotelica nei 'Sophysmata' di Richard Kilmington." In *Filosofia e politica, e altri saggi*, ed. Carlo Giacon. Padua: Antenore.

————. 1973b. "L''Opinio de Insolubilibus' di Richard Kilmington." *Rivista critica di storia della filosofia* 28:568–90.

————. 1974. "Un testo fondamentale nell'ambito della 'Nuova Fisica' di Oxford: I Sophismata di Richard Kilmington." *Miscellanea mediaevalia* 9:201–05.

Bourbaki, Nicolas. 1960. *Eléments d'histoire des mathématiques*. Paris: Hermann.

Boyancé, P. 1974. Review of J. M. Rist's *Epicurus*. *Gnomon* 46:754–55.

Boyer, Carl Benjamin. 1949. *The Concepts of the Calculus; A Critical and Historical Discussion of the Derivative and Integral*. New York: Hafner.

————. 1959. *The History of the Calculus and Its Conceptual Development*. New York: Dover.

Brampton, C. K. 1964. "Guillaume d'Ockham et la date probable de ses opuscules sur l'Eucharistie." *Études Franciscaines* 14:77–79.

Breidart, Wolfgang. 1970. *Das aristotelische Kontinuum in der Scholastik* (*BGPM*, neue folge, I). Münster: Aschendorff.

Brown, M. 1972. "The Idea of Equality in the *Phaedo*." *Archiv für Geschichte der Philosophie* 54:24–36.

Brown, Stephen. 1972. "Walter Burley's Treatise *De Suppositionibus* and Its Influence on William of Ockham." *Franciscan Studies* 32:15–64.

————. Forthcoming. "A Modern Prologue to Ockham's Natural Philosophy."

Brumbaugh, R. S. 1954. *Plato's Mathematical Imagination*. Bloomington: Indiana University Press.

Buescher, G. 1950. *The Eucharistic Teaching of William Ockham*. Washington: Catholic University of America Press.

Buridan, John. 1966. *Sophisms on Meaning and Truth*. Translated and with an introduction by T. K. Scott. New York: Appleton-Century-Crofts.

Burley, Walter, 1496. *Tractatus secundus de intensione et remissione formarum*. Venice.

————. 1501. *In Physicam Aristotelis expositio et quaestiones*. Venice. Reprint. 1972. New York: Georg Olms.

————. 1955. *De puritate artis logicae, Tractatus longior*. Edited by Philotheus Boehner. St. Bonaventure, N.Y.: Franciscan Institute.

Carruccio, Ettore. 1964. *Mathematics and Logic in History and in Contemporary Thought*. Translated by Isabel Quigly. Chicago: Aldine.

Caujoulle-Zaslawsky, Françoise. 1980. "Le temps Epicurien est-il atomique?" *Les Etudes Philosophiques* 35:285–306.

Cohen, I. B. 1958. *Newton's Papers and Letters on Natural Philosophy*. Cambridge, Mass.: Harvard University Press.

Corvino, F. 1958. "Questioni inedite di Occam sul continuo." *Rivista critica di storia della filosofia* 13:191–208.

Dedekind, Richard. 1901. *Essays on the Theory of Numbers*. Chicago: Open Court.

Dicks, D. R. 1959. "Thales." *Classical Quarterly*, n.s. 9:294–309.

Diels, Hermann, and Kranz, Walther. 1968. *Die Fragmente der Vorsokratiker*. 10th ed. Dublin and Zürich: Weidmann.

Dijksterhuis, E. J. 1929. *De Elementen van Euclides*. Vol. I. Groningen: Noordhoff.

Döring, Klaus. 1972. *Die Megariker*. Amsterdam: Grüner.

Eldredge, Laurence. 1979. "Late Medieval Discussions of the Continuum and the Point of the Middle English Patience." *Vivarium* 17:90–115.

Enriques, Federigo, and Mazzioti, Manlio. 1948. *Le dottrine di Democrito d'Abdera*. Bologna: Zanichelli.

Evans, M. G. 1964. *The Physical Philosophy of Aristotle*. Albuquerque: University of New Mexico Press.

Fakhry, Majid. 1958. *Islamic Occasionalism*. London: Allen and Unwin.

Falco, Vittorio de. 1923. *L'epicureo Demetrio Lacone*. Naples: Cimmaruta.

Furley, David. 1967. *Two Studies in the Greek Atomists*. Princeton: Princeton University Press.

————. 1969. "Aristotle and the Atomists on Infinity." *Naturphilosophie bei Aristoteles und Theophrast*. Edited by Ingemar Düring. Heidelberg: Stiehm.

Gale, Richard M., ed. 1967. *The Philosophy of Time: A Collection of Essays*. Garden City, N.Y.: Doubleday.

Grant, Edward. 1978. "The Principle of the Impenetrability of Bodies in the History of Concepts of Separate Space from the Middle Ages to the Seventeenth Century." *Isis* 69:551–71.

Grünbaum, Adolf. 1952. "A Consistent Conception of the Extended Linear Continuum as an Aggregate of Unextended Elements." *Philosophy of Science* 19:288–306.

———. 1967. *Modern Science and Zeno's Paradoxes.* Middletown, Conn.: Wesleyan University Press.

Guerlac, Rita. 1979. *Humanism and Medieval Logic: Juan Luis Vives on the Pseudodialecticians.* Dordrecht: Reidel.

Guthrie, W. K. C. 1969. *A History of Greek Philosophy.* Vol. III. Cambridge: Cambridge University Press.

Hankel, Hermann. 1874. *Zur Geschichte der Mathematik in Alterthum und Mittelalter.* Leipzig: Teubner.

Heath, T. L. 1921. *A History of Greek Mathematics.* Vol. I. Oxford: Clarendon Press.

———. 1926. *The Thirteen Books of Euclid's Elements.* 2d ed. 3 vols. Cambridge: Cambridge University Press.

———. 1949. *Mathematics in Aristotle.* Oxford: Clarendon Press.

Heinze, Richard. 1892. *Xenokrates: Darstellung der Lehre und Sammlung der Fragmente.* Leipzig: Teubner.

Herzberger, Hans G. 1979. "Counterfactuals and Consistency." *Journal of Philosophy* 76:83–88.

Hintikka, Jaakko. 1966. "Aristotelian Infinity." *Philosophical Review* 75:197–218.

Huntington, Edward V. 1917. *The Continuum and Other Types of Serial Order.* Cambridge, Mass.: Harvard University Press.

Ibn Mattawayh. 1975. *Tadhkira.* Edited by S. N. Lutf and F. B. 'Awn. Cairo. n.p.

Joachim, H. H. 1922. *Aristotle on Coming-to-Be and Passing-Away.* Oxford: Clarendon Press. Reprint. 1970. New York: Georg Olms.

Junghaus, Helmar. 1968. *Ockham im Lichte der neueren Forschung.* Berlin: Lutherisches Verlagshaus.

Juwaynī. 1969. *Shāmil.* Edited by Nassār. Alexandria.

Khayyāṭ. 1925. *Intīsār.* Edited by Nyberg. Cairo: n.p.

———. 1957. *Intīsār.* Translated into French by A. N. Nader. Beirut: Editions les lettres orientales.

Kirk, G. S., and Raven, J. E. 1960. *The Presocratic Philosophers.* Cambridge: Cambridge University Press.

Kline, M. 1972. *Mathematical Thought from Ancient to Modern Times.* Oxford: Clarendon Press.

Knorr, Wilbur. 1976. *The Evolution of the Euclidean Elements.* Dordrecht: Reidel.

———. 1978a. "Archimedes and the *Elements*: Proposal for a Revised Chronological Ordering of the Archimedean Corpus." *Archive for History of Exact Sciences* 19:211–90.

————. 1978b. "Archimedes and the Pre-Euclidean Proportion Theory." *Archives internationales d'histoire des sciences* 28:183–244.

————. 1978c. "Archimedes and the Spirals." *Historia mathematica* 5:43–75.

————. Forthcoming. "On the Early History of Axiomatics." In *Proceedings of the Second Conference of the International Union for the History & Philosophy of Science,* edited by J. Hintikka. Dordrecht: Reidel.

Knuuttila, Simo, and Lehtinen, Anja Inkeri. 1979a. "Change and Contradiction: A Fourteenth Century Controversy." *Synthèse* 40:189–207.

————. 1979b. "*Plato in infinitum remisse incipit esse albus*: New Texts on the Late Medieval Discussion on the Concept of Infinity in Sophismata Literature." In *Essays in Honour of Jaakko Hintikka,* edited by E. Saarinen, R. Hilpinen, I. Niiniluato, and M. Provence Hintikka. Dordrecht: Reidel.

Konstan, David. 1979. "Problems in Epicurean Physics." *Isis* 70:394–418.

Krämer, H. J. 1971. *Platonismus und hellenistische Philosophie.* Berlin: De Gruyter.

Kretzmann, Norman. 1976a. "Time Exists—But Hardly, or Obscurely (*Physics* IV, 10; 217b69–218a33)." *The Aristotelian Society.* Supplementary volume 50, pp. 91–114.

————. 1976b. "Incipit/Desinit." In *Motion and Time, Space and Matter,* edited by P. K. Machamer and R. G. Turnbull, pp. 101–36. Columbus: Ohio State University Press.

————. 1977. "Socrates Is Whiter than Plato Begins to Be White." *Noûs* 11:3–15.

————. Forthcoming. "Comments on Murdoch's 'The Analytic Character of Late Medieval Learning: Natural Philosophy Without Nature.'" In *Nature in the Middle Ages,* edited by L. Roberts.

Kretzmann, Norman, and Kretzmann, Barbara Ensign, ed. and tr. Forthcoming. *The Sophismata of Richard Kilvington.* With commentary and historical introduction.

Lambert of Auxerre. 1971. *Logica (Summa Lamberti).* Edited by Franco Alessio. Florence: Nuova Italia.

Lasserre, François, ed. 1966. *Die Fragmente des Eudoxos von Knidos.* Berlin: de Gruyter.

Lasswitz, Kurd. 1890. *Geschichte der Atomistik vom mittelalter bis Newton.* Hamburg and Leipzig: Voss.

Leff, Gordon. 1975. *William of Ockham: The Metamorphosis of Scholastic Discourse.* Manchester: University of Manchester Press.

Loux, Michael. 1974. *Ockham's Theory of Terms: Part 1 of the "Summa logicae."* Notre Dame, Ind.: Notre Dame University Press.

Luria, Salomon Y. 1932–33. "Die Infinitesimaltheorie der antiken Atomisten." *Quellen und Studien zur Geschichte der Mathematik, Astronomie und Physik* 2:106–85.

———. 1945. *Archimedes*. Moscow: Izd-vo Akad. Nauk SSSR. (Russian edition)

———. 1948. *Archimedes*. Translated by Hilde Koplenig. Vienna: Neues Österreich. (German edition)

———. 1970. *Democritea*. Leningrad: Akad. Nauk SSSR.

MacDonald, D. B. 1927. "Continuous Re-creation and Atomic Time in Muslim Scholastic Theology." *Isis* 9:326–44.

Maier, Anneliese. 1949. *Die Vorläufer Galileis im 14. Jahrhundert*. Rome: Edizioni di Storia e Letteratura.

———. 1955. *Metaphysische Hintergründe der spätscholastischen Naturphilosophie*. In *Studien zur Naturphilosophie der Spätscholastik*, vol. 4. Rome: Edizioni di Storia e Letteratura.

———. 1964. *Ausgehendes Mittelalter*. Vol. I. Rome: Edizioni di Storia e Letteratura.

Maierù, Alfonso. 1966. "Il 'Tractatus de sensu composito et diviso' di Guglielmo Heytesbury." *Rivista critica di storia della filosofia* 21:243–63.

———. 1972. *Terminologia logica della tarda scolastica*. Rome: Edizioni dell'Ateneo.

Mau, Jürgen. 1954a. *Zum Problem des Infinitesimalen bei den antiken Atomisten*. Berlin: Deutsche Akademie der Wissenschaften.

———. 1954b. "Raum und Bewegung, zu Epikurs Brief an Herodot 60." *Hermes* 82:13–24.

———. 1955. "Ueber die Zuweisung zweier Epikur-Fragmente." *Philologus* 99:93–111.

Maziarz, E. A., and Greenwood, Thomas. 1968. *Greek Mathematical Philosophy*. New York: Ungar.

Moody, E. A. 1935. *The Logic of William of Ockham*. New York: Sheed and Ward.

Morrison, J. S. 1972. "Antiphon." In *The Older Sophists*, edited by Rosamond Kent Sprague. Columbia, S.C.: University of South Carolina Press.

Morrow, Glenn R. 1966. "Qualitative Change in Aristotle's Physics." In *Naturphilosophie bei Aristoteles*, edited by I. Düring, pp. 154–67. Heidelberg: Carl Winter Universitätsverlag.

Murdoch, John E. 1957. "Geometry and the Continuum in the Fourteenth Century: A Philosophical Analysis of Thomas Bradwardine's *Tractatus de continuo*." Ph.D. dissertation, University of Wisconsin.

———. 1962. "*Rationes mathematice*": *Un aspect du rapport des mathématiques et de la philosophie au moyen âge*. Paris: Université de Paris.

———. 1964. "Superposition, Congruence, and Continuity in the Middle Ages." In *Mélanges Alexandre Koyré*, vol. I, pp. 416–41. Paris: Hermann.

———. 1965. "The 'Equality' of Infinites in the Middle Ages." *Actes du XIe Congrès International d'Histoire des Sciences* 3:171–74.

———. 1969. "*Mathesis in philosophiam scholasticam introducta*: The Rise and Development of the Application of Mathematics in Fourteenth-Century Philosophy and Theology." In *Arts libéraux et philosophie au moyen âge*, Actes du Quatrième Congrès International de Philosophie Médiévale.

———. 1974. "Naissance et développement de l'atomisme au bas moyen âge latin." In *La science de la nature: Théories et pratiques*, Cahiers d'Etudes Médiévales, vol. 2. Montreal: Bellarmin. Paris: Vrin.

———. 1979. "Propositional Analysis in Fourteenth-Century Natural Philosophy: A Case Study." *Synthèse* 40:117–46.

———. Forthcoming a. "Infinity and Continuity." In *The Cambridge History of Later Medieval Philosophy*, edited by N. Kretzmann, A. Kenny, J. Pinborg. Cambridge: Cambridge University Press.

———. Forthcoming b. "The Analytic Character of Late Medieval Learning: Natural Philosophy without Nature." In *Nature in the Middle Ages*, edited by L. Roberts.

———. Forthcoming c. "*Scientia mediantibus vocibus*: Metalinguistic Analysis in Late Medieval Natural Philosophy." *Acts of the Sixth International Congress of Medieval Philosophy*.

Murdoch, John E., and Synan, Edward A. 1966. "Two Questions on the Continuum: Walter Chatton (?), O.F.M., and Adam Wodeham, O.F.M." *Franciscan Studies* 26:212–88.

Nader, A. N. 1956. *Le système philosophique des Mu'tazila*. Beirut: Editions les lettres orientales.

Neuenschwander, E. 1974–75. "Die vier stereometrischen Bücher der *Elemente* Euklids." *Archive for History of Exact Sciences* 14:91–125.

Normore, Calvin G. 1976. "The Logic of Time and Modality in the Later Middle Ages: The Contribution of William of Ockham." Ph.D. dissertation, University of Toronto.

Ockham, William. 1930. *De sacramento altaris*. Edited by T. Bruce Birch. Burlington, Ind.: Lutheran Literary Board.

———. 1944. *The "Tractatus de successivis" Attributed to William Ockham*. Edited by P. Boehner. St. Bonaventure, N.Y.: Franciscan Institute.

———. 1974. *Summa logicae*. Edited by P. Boehner, G. Gál, and S. Brown. In *Guillelmi de Ockham: Opera Philosophica*, vol. I. St. Bonaventure, N.Y.: Franciscan Institute.

———. 1978a. *Expositio in librum praedicamentorum Aristotelis*. Edited by G. Gál. In *Guillelmi de Ockham: Opera Philosophica*, vol. II. St. Bonaventure, N.Y.: St. Bonaventure University.

———. 1978b. *Tractatus de praedestinatione et de praescientia Dei respectu futurorum contingentium*. Edited by Philotheus Boehner and Stephen Brown. In *Guillelmi de Ockham: Opera Philosophica*, vol. II. St. Bonaventure, N.Y.: St. Bonaventure University.

———. 1980. *Quodlibeta septem*. Edited by Joseph C. Wey. In *Guillelmi de Ockham: Opera Theologica*, vol. IX. St. Bonaventure, N.Y.: St. Bonaventure University.

Owen, G. E. L. 1957–58. "Zeno and the Mathematicians." *Proceedings of the Aristotelian Society* 58:199–222.

Paul of Pergula. 1961. *"Logica" and "Tractatus de sensu composito et diviso."*

Edited by M. A. Brown. St. Bonaventure, N.Y.: Franciscan Institute.

Peter of Spain. 1972. *"Tractatus": Called Afterwards "Summule logicales."* Edited by L. M. De Rijk. Assen: Van Gorcum.

Philippson, R. 1929. "Democritea: Demokrit als Mathematiker." *Hermes* 64:175–83.

Pines, S. 1936. *Beiträge zur Islamischen Atomenlehre.* Berlin: Heine.

———. 1961. "A New Fragment of Xenocrates and Its Implications." *Transactions of the American Philosophical Society* 51(2):3–34.

———. 1965. "Thābit ibn Qurra's Conception of Number and Theory of the Mathematical Infinite." *Actes du XIe Congrès International d'Histoire des Sciences* 3:160–66.

Pretzl, Otto. 1931. "Die frühislamische Atomenlehre." *Der Islam* 19:117–30.

Puglia, Enzo. 1980. "Nuove letture nei P. Herc. 1012 e 1786 (*Demetrii Laconis opera incerta*)." *Cronache Ercolanesi* 10:25–53.

Roche, Evan. 1949. *The "De Primo Principio" of John Duns Scotus: A Revised Text and a Translation.* St. Bonaventure, N.Y.: Franciscan Institute.

Ross, W. D. 1923. *Aristotle.* London: Methuen.

———. 1936. *Aristotle's Physics.* Oxford: Clarendon Press.

———. 1949. *Aristotle's Prior and Posterior Analytics.* Oxford: Clarendon Press.

Rudio, Ferdinand. 1907. *Der Bericht des Simplicius über die Quadraturen des Antiphon und des Hippokrates.* Leipzig: Teubner.

Saggi, L. M. 1955. "Commentariola et Textus: Ioannis Baconthorpe textus de Immaculata Conceptione." *Carmelus* 2:216–303.

Salmon, Wesley C., ed. 1970. *Zeno's Paradoxes.* Indianapolis: Bobbs-Merrill.

Sambursky, S. 1956. *The Physical World of the Greeks.* Translated by Merton Dagut. London: Routledge and Kegan Paul.

———. 1959. *Physics of the Stoics.* London: Routledge and Kegan Paul.

———. 1968. "The Concept of Time in Late Neoplatonism." In *Proceedings of the Israel Academy of Sciences and Humanities* 2:153–67.

Sambursky, S., and Pines, S. 1971. *The Concept of Time in Late Neoplatonism.* Texts with translation, introduction, and notes. Jerusalem: Israel Academy of Sciences and Humanities.

Scholz, H. 1928. "Warum haben die Griechen die Irrazionalzahlen nicht aufgebaut?" *Kant Studien* 33:35–72.

Schramm, Matthias. 1962. *Die Bedeutung der Bewegungslehre des Aristoteles für seine beiden Lösungen der zenonischen Paradoxie.* Frankfurt: Klostermann.

Scott, Theodore Kermit. 1966. *John Buridan: Sophisms on Meaning and Truth.* New York: Appleton-Century-Crofts.

Seale, Morris S. 1964. *Muslim Theology.* London: Luzac.

Sedley, David. 1976. "Epicurus and the Mathematicians of Cyzicus." *Cronache Ercolanesi* 6:23–54.

————. 1977. "Diodorus Cronus and Hellenistic Philosophy." *Proceedings of the Cambridge Philological Society*, n.s. 23:74–120.

Shapiro, Herman. 1957. *Motion, Time and Place According to William Ockham*. St. Bonaventure, N.Y.: Franciscan Institute.

Solá, Francisco de P. 1966. "*De Sacramento Altaris*: Dos manuscritos Ockhamistas . . . Introducción, transcripción, y notas." *Pensamiento* 22:279–352.

Sorabji, Richard. 1969. "Aristotle and Oxford Philosophy." *American Philosophical Quarterly* 6:127–35.

————. 1976. "Aristotle on the Instant of Change." *The Aristotelian Society*. Supplementary volume 50, pp. 69–89.

————. 1979. "Aristotle on the Instant of Change." In *Articles on Aristotle*, edited by J. Barnes, M. Schofield, R. Sorabji, vol. III. London: Duckworth. (Expanded version of Sorabji 1976)

————. 1980. *Necessity, Cause and Blame*. London: Duckworth.

Strang, Colin, and Mills, K. W. 1974. "Plato and the Instant." *Proceedings of the Aristotelian Society*. Supplementary volume 48, pp. 63–96.

Stratton, G. M. 1917. *Theophrastus and the Greek Physiological Psychology before Aristotle*. London: Allen and Unwin. New York: Macmillan.

Sylla, Edith. 1973. "Medieval Concepts of the Latitude of Forms: The Oxford Calculators." *Archives d'Histoire doctrinale et littéraire du moyen-âge* 40:223–83.

————. 1975. "Autonomous and Handmaiden Science: St. Thomas Aquinas and William of Ockham on the Physics of the Eucharist." In *The Cultural Context of Medieval Learning*, edited by J. E. Murdoch and E. D. Sylla. Dordrecht: Reidel.

————. Forthcoming a. "Godfrey of Fontaines on Motion with Respect to Quantity of the Eucharist." In *Studi sul XIV secolo in memoria di Anneliese Maier*, edited by A. Maierù and A. Paravicini Bagliani. Rome: Edizioni di Storia e Letteratura.

————. Forthcoming b. "The Oxford Calculators." In *The Cambridge History of Later Medieval Philosophy*, edited by N. Kretzmann, A. Kenny, and J. Pinborg. Cambridge: Cambridge University Press.

Szabó, Arpád. 1969. *Anfänge der griechischen Mathematik*. Munich and Vienna: Oldenbourg.

Tannery, Paul. 1887. *La Géométrie grecque*. Paris: Gauthier-Villars.

————. 1905. "Vermischte historische Notizen." *Bibliotheca Mathematica* (Series 3) 6:111.

Thomson, James. 1954–55. "Tasks and Super-Tasks." *Analysis* 15:1–13.

Toeplitz, O. 1925. "Mathematik und Antike." *Die Antike* 1:175–203.

Van den Bergh, S., tr. 1969. *Averroes: Tahāfut al-Tahāfut*. With commentary. London: Luzac.

Van der Waerden, B. L. 1954. *Science Awakening*. Translated by Arnold Dresen. Groningen: Noordhoff.

Van Ess, J. 1978. *Theology and Science: The Case of Abū Isḥāq an-Naẓẓām*.

Second Annual United Arab Emirates Lecture in Islamic Studies (19 pp.). Ann Arbor: University of Michigan Press.

Vlastos, Gregory. 1953. Review of J. E. Raven's *Pythagoreans and Eleatics*. *Gnomon* 25:29–35.

———. 1959. Review of G. S. Kirk's and J. E. Raven's *The Presocratic Philosophers*. *Philosophical Review* 69:531–35.

———. 1966. "A Note on Zeno's Arrow." *Phronesis* 11:3–18.

Von Wright, G. H. 1969. *Time, Change and Contradiction*. Cambridge: Cambridge University Press.

Waschkies, H. J. 1977. *Von Eudoxos zu Aristoteles*. Amsterdam: Grüner.

Wasserstein, A. 1959. "Some Early Greek Attempts to Square the Circle." *Phronesis* 4:92–100.

Wedberg, Anders. 1955. *Plato's Philosophy of Mathematics*. Stockholm: Almqvist and Wiksell.

Wehrli, R. 1944–59. *Die Schule des Aristoteles*. Basel: Schwabe.

Weisheipl, James A. 1963. "The Concept of Matter in Fourteenth-Century Science." In *The Concept of Matter in Greek and Medieval Philosophy*, edited by E. McMullin. Notre Dame, Ind.: University of Notre Dame Press.

———. 1968. "Ockham and Some Mertonians." *Mediaeval Studies* 30:163–213.

Wheeler, J. A. 1967. "Superspace and the Nature of Quantum Geometrical Dynamics." In *Battelle Rencontres*, edited by C. M. DeWitt and J. A. Wheeler. New York: Benjamin.

———. 1975. "Superspace and the Nature of Quantum Geometrical Dynamics." In *Quantum Gravity*, edited by C. J. Isham, R. Penrose, D. W. Sciama. Oxford: Clarendon Press.

Wieland, Wolfgang. 1962. *Die aristotelische Physik*. Göttingen: Vandenhoeck and Ruprecht.

William of Sherwood. 1937. *Introductiones in logicam*. In *Sitzungsberichte der Bayerischen Akademie der Wissenschaften*. Edited by Martin Grabmann. Philosophisch-historische Abteilung, Heft 10. Munich: Beck.

Williams, Donald C. 1951. "The Myth of Passage." *Journal of Philosophy* 48:457–72.

Wilson, Curtis. 1956. *William Heytesbury and the Rise of Mathematical Physics*. Madison: University of Wisconsin Press.

Wolfson, Harry Austryn. 1976. *The Philosophy of the Kalām*. Cambridge, Mass.: Harvard University Press.

Wolter, Allan B., ed. and tr. 1963. *Duns Scotus: Philosophical Writings*. New York: Nelson.

Zoubov, V. P. 1959. "Walter Catton, Gérard d'Odon et Nicolas Bonet." *Physis* 1:261–78.

———. 1961. "Jean Buridan et les concepts du point au quatorzième siècle." *Mediaeval and Renaissance Studies* 5:43–95.

Index

Infinity and Continuity in
Ancient and Medieval Thought

Designed by Richard E. Rosenbaum.
Composed by Eastern Graphics
in 10 point Linotron 202 Palatino, 3 points leaded
with display lines in Palatino.
Printed offset by Thomson/Shore, Inc. on
Warren's Number 66 Antique Offset, 50 pound basis.
Bound by John H. Dekker & Sons, Inc.
in Holliston book cloth
and stamped in Kurz-Hastings foil.

Library of Congress Cataloging in Publication Data

Main entry under title:

Infinity and continuity in ancient and medieval thought.

Based on papers presented at a conference held at Cornell University, Apr. 20–21, 1979, sponsored by the Society for the Humanities and the Sage School of Philosophy.
  Bibliography: p.
  Includes index.
  1. Infinite—History—Addresses, essays, lectures. 2. Continuity—History—Addresses, essays, lectures. I. Kretzmann, Norman. II. Society for the Humanities. III. Sage School of Philosophy.
BD411.I53   111'.6   81-15209
ISBN 0-8014-1444-X   AACR2